WORLD WAR II
MUSEUMS, MEMORIALS AND HISTORIC DISPLAYS IN THE UNITED STATES
A Tour Guide and Directory

WORLD WAR II
MUSEUMS, MEMORIALS AND HISTORIC DISPLAYS IN THE UNITED STATES
A Tour Guide and Directory

by

Richard E. Osborne

Riebel-Roque Publishing Co.
6027 Castlebar Circle
Indianapolis, IN 46220

ISBN 978-O-9814898-0-3

Date of Publication: 2013
Published and printed in the U S A

Layout and Technical Assistance by
Fayth Dressel

ORDERING ADDITIONAL COPIES OF THIS BOOK
Additional copies of this book may be ordered from:

Riebel-Roque Publishing Co.
6027 Castlebar Circle
Indianapolis, IN 46220
riebel-roque.com
Phone: 317-849-3680

We would like to acknowledge our gratitude to the website WAYMARKING.COM for helping us locate and identify the many WW II memorials in the United States.

TABLE OF CONTENTS

MUSEUMS...
THEY COME, THEY GO, THEY CHANGE...
With time, some Museums close, open, expand, move, merge, change their name, change their hours of operation & change their admission fees.
It is recommended that, if one is interested in seeing a particular Museum, that they phone the Museum or check the Museum's website for the latest visitor information.
Museums also have special exhibits, rotating displays, educational & social events which can affect one's visit.

MEMORIALS...
...consist of anything from a small monument in a park to a multi-storied limestone building.
They seldom change, but the larger ones may change hours of operation and/or admissions fees and have special events that can affect one's visit.
It is recommended that, if one is interested in seeing one of the larger Memorials, that they phone the Memorial or check the Memorial's website prior to a visit.

DISPLAYS...
...consist of anything from a plaque on a wall in a county seat courthouse to a battleship anchored permanently in the harbor. They seldom change, but the larger ones may change hours of operation and/or admissions fees and have special events that can affect one's visit.
Here too, it is best to phone or check the website of the larger Displays prior to a visit.

Please note our **COMPANION** book...

WORLD WAR II **SITES** IN THE UNITED STATES
A Tour Guide and Directory

By Richard E. Osborne

ISBN 0-9628324-9-9

This book identifies and locates the hundreds of military facilities that existed in the United States during WW II – Army camps, airfields, naval bases, prisoner of war camps, ordnance plants, ports of embarkation, military hospitals, buildings and homes related to the war effort or to famous individuals of the wartime era, and much more. At many of these sites, memorials have been erected which are NOT listed in this book because they are so numerous. These memorials can be located by utilizing the above companion book. A good example of such memorials is the one on the site of the former Camp Stoneman in California.

OUR **COMPANION** BOOK

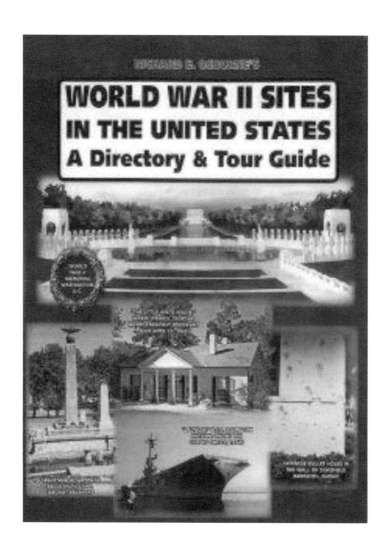

A NATION-WIDE WW II MEMORIAL

THE BLUE STAR MEMORIAL HIGHWAYS

A typical Blue Star Memorial Highway marker

This is a <u>nationwide</u> war memorial that had its beginning soon after the end of World War II to honor those who had fought to defend America's freedoms. It was the inspiration of the National Garden Clubs, Inc. which has a long history of promoting beauty and landscaping along American's highways.

The memorials are generally post-mounted plaques with a blue star at the top and the inscription "A Tribute to the Armed Forces that have Defended the United States of America." Below this tribute is information about the local individuals or organizations that provided that specific marker.

The blue star was taken from the small service flags that families would hang in their windows honoring those members of the family who were then serving in the US Armed Forces. If the individual being so honored perished in WW II, the blue star was changed to gold.

Over the years, the Blue Star Memorial Highways have come to honors men and women who served in all of America's conflicts. Today, there are memorials along some 70,000 miles of US highways and many others are in such places as veterans' hospitals, cemeteries and other locations where it is appropriate to honor American war veterans.

ALABAMA

Alabama was a part of the Old South when WW II started. It had strict racial segregation, areas of severe poverty, lingering popular resentment against Yankees, 43 dry counties out of 67 and a one party political system based on the conservative wing of the Democrat Party. The advent of America's participation in WW II would bring about changes, or the beginning of changes in most of these things.

The state acquired a significant number of new military installations, the expansion of existing military facilities and new war plants. Many Yankees came to the state to be trained in the military services or to work in the defense plant.

Because of its warm climate, Alabama acquired 24 main and branch POW camps which housed some 16,000 Axis POWs.

ALICEVILLE is in the west-central part of state near the Mississippi state line on SR-14 and SR-17.

Aliceville had a prisoner of war (POW) camp nearby - one of the largest in the US.

ALICEVILLE POW MUSEUM AND CULTURAL CENTER: This museum preserves the history and times of the local WW II POW camp which existed near Aliceville during the war. In the Museum are photos, documents, artifacts, paintings, letters and art work - some of which was produced by the German POWs who were housed in the camp.

The Aliceville POW Museum and Cultural Center, Aliceville, AL

The Anniston World War II Memorial in Anniston, AL

There is a 14-minute documentary featuring interviews with former POWs, guards and local citizens. It also shows the POWs at work and play, including the orchestra comprised of POWs. Address: 104 Broad St., Aliceville, Al 35442. Phone and website. 205-373-2363, cityofaliceville.com

ANNISTON is a county seat in east-central Alabama on I-20, US-431 and SR-21.

ANNISTON WORLD WAR II MEMORIAL: This impressive memorial honors those citizens of Calhoun County who gave their lives in WW II. It consists of a stone monument topped with a spread eagle and has a bronze plaque with the names of those individuals so honored. Location: Quintard Av. near downtown Anniston.

ATHENS: Athens is a county seat in north-central Alabama on I-65 and US-72.

ALABAMA VETERANS MUSEUM AND ARCHIVES is located in an old and large railroad freight depot not far from downtown Athens. It was started by the late Kenneth David, veterans' service offices and avid collector of militaria. The Museum is run by local volunteers and honors veterans who served from the Civil War to the present. There is a heavy emphasis on WW II. On display are small arms, flags, medals, field packs, communications equipment, uniforms, photos, a WW II barracks bunk bed and a 1930s household kitchen. The Museum has many social and public gatherings throughout the year and there is a library, an archives and an interesting gift shop. Address: 100 Pryor St., Athens, AL 35612. Phone and website: 256-771-7578; www.alabamaveteransmuseum.com

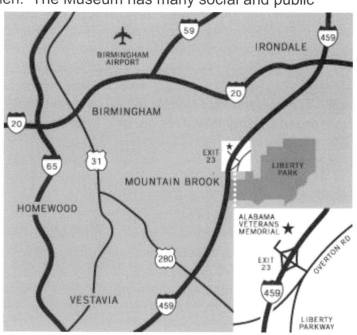

BIRMINGHAM is in the north-central part of state and is Alabama's largest city.

ALABAMA VETERANS MEMORIAL: This is a 21-acre public park just west of Birmingham's Liberty Park with an impressive memorial structure honoring Alabama's veterans from all wars, including a very impressive memorial commemorating WW II. Location: North quadrant of Exit 23 of I-459 and Liberty Park. Phone and website: 205-985-9488 and 800-288-7890; www.alabamaveterans.com

Alabama Veterans Memorial

SOUTHERN MUSEUM OF FLIGHT, just east of the Birmingham Municipal Airport, displays a large number of aircraft and memorabilia from the earliest days of aviation to the present. There is a relatively small collection of WW II airplanes, but there are displays of WW II uniforms, photos, model planes and other artifacts. Address: 4343 73rd Street N., Birmingham, AL 35206, (two blocks east of Birmingham Intl. Airport). Phone and website: 205-833-8226; www.southernmuseumofflight.org

The Tuskegee Airman Exhibit at the Southern Museum of Flight.

DECATURE is a county seat in northern Alabama on I-65, I-565, US-31, US-72 and the Tennessee River.

MORGAN COUNTY WW II MEMORIAL. This memorial is located near the county courthouse in a pleasant park filled with memorials commemorating America's war. The WW II Memorial is attractive and lists the names of those from Morgan County who made the ultimate sacrifice during WW II. Location: 302 Lee St Decatur, AL 35602

The Morgan County WW II Memorial

HUNTSVILLE is a county seat in the north-central part of the state on I-565, US-72 and US-431 and is home of NASA's Redstone Arsenal. Much of America's early postwar space program was developed in Huntsville and the community became known as the birthplace of the American space program.

NASA's space program was headed by Dr. Wernher von Braun who had been in charge of Nazi Germany's rocket program during World War II. In downtown Huntsville is a large civic center is named after Dr. von Braun.

US SPACE & ROCKET CENTER: This is an indoor/outdoor museum adjacent to Redstone Arsenal displaying one of the world's largest collections of rockets and space hardware. Included in the displays are models of the German V-1 "Buzzbomb" rocket and V-2 high-altitude rocket, both of which were used against British and western European cities in the closing months of World War II. Address: One Tranquility Base, Huntsville, AL 35805. Phone and web site: 800-572-7234; www.spacecamp.com/museum/

MOBILE is Alabama's main seaport in the SW part of state on Mobile Bay. Mobile's shipyards built, modified and repaired hundreds of ships during WW II.

The USS Alabama WW II battleship on display in Mobile, AL

***USS ALABAMA* BATTLESHIP MEMORIAL PARK**: This is a 100-acre waterfront open-air park displaying several permanently-anchored warships of WW II and a generous display of aircraft, tanks and other vehicles. The main attraction is the battleship *USS Alabama* which is preserved as it was when in service during WW II. Other displays include the WW II submarine *USS Drum*, the WW II landing ship tank *LST-325*. Also, there is an impressive collection aircraft and other military equipment from WW II. Address: Battleship Parkway, Mobile AL 36601. Phone and website: 251-433-2703; ussalabama.com

The Montgomery County WW II Memorial in Montgomery, AL

MONTGOMERY, the state capitol, is in the south-central part of the state. During World War II, Maxwell Field and Gunter Field, both AAF training fields, were in the area.

MONTGOMERY COUNTY WW II MEMORIAL: Here is one of the earliest WW II Memorials in the country. It was first dedicated in 1946 and refurbished and rededicated in 2010. The Memorial honors those individuals from Montgomery County who died in WW II. The Memorial consists of four pillars, each representing one of the famous Four Freedoms of WW II; Freedom from Want, Freedom of Worship, Freedom from Fear and Freedom of Speech. Location: Lee and Church Sts.

US AIR FORCE ENLISTED HERITAGE HALL: This is a small museum on the grounds of Maxwell AFB, Gunter Annex, which pays tribute to the enlisted men and women of US military aviation. There are displays of enlisted men's uniforms and artifacts, a WW II Sperry Ball Turret and a rare B-32 top turret. Address: Building 1210, Gunter AFB, AL 36114. Phone: 334-416-3202.

The US Air Force Enlisted Heritage Hall in Montgomery, AL

OZARK is a county seat in the SE corner of the state on US-231, SR-27 and SR-249 and is home to Fort Rucker Military Reservation.

US ARMY AVIATION MUSEUM This Museum is on the grounds of Fort Rucker Military Reservation at the corner of Andrews Av. and Novosel St. The Museum traces the history of Army aviation,

especially with regard to light planes and helicopters, from their beginnings to the present. The Museum has one of the largest collections of helicopters in the world including a rare Sikorsky R-4B, the first US military production helicopter which were operational during the last months of WW II. Piper Cub airplanes and other small aircraft are also a main attractions at the Museum. Address: Bldg. 617, PO Box 620610-0610, Ft. Rucker, AL 36330. Phone and website: 888-276-9286 and 334-598-2508; www.armyavnmuseum.org

The Sikorsky R-4B Army helicopter which became operational during the last months of WW II

TUSKEGEE is a county seat 40 miles east of Montgomery off I-85 and on US-29 and US-80. It is the home of Tuskegee Institute long known for offering advanced education for African-Americans. During WW II, the Institute's own airfield and another local airfield were taken over by the US Army Air Forces to train African-Americans as pilots, crew men and service personnel.

TUSKEGEE AIRMEN NATIONAL HISTORIC SITE: This 90-acre site is located at Moton Field Municipal Airport in Tuskegee and is administered by the National Park Service. There is a visitor's center and, as the name implies, the Site honors the Tuskegee Airmen of WW II and traces their backgrounds, training and experiences during WW II. Inside the museum, which was, during the war, the airfield's "Hanger #1," are artifacts, photos and memorabilia related the Airmen along with aircraft components and other displays. The museum has several activities and events during the year. Address: 1616 Chappie James, Av., Tuskegee, AL 36083. Phone and website: 334-724-0922; http://www.nps.gov/tuai

WETUMPKA is a county seat 11 miles NE of Montgomery on US-231, SR-14, SR-170 and the Coosa River.

WORLD WAR II MEMORIAL, WETKUMPKA, AL: This Memorial is dedicated to all of the service personnel of WW II, and to the five Crommelin brothers, local sons who graduated from the US Naval Academy at Annapolis, MD, and served in the US Navy during the war.

The World War II Memorial in Wetumpka, AL

ALASKA

   Alaska was a Territory of the US during WW II but still an important part of the nation. It is 1/5 the size of the lower 48 states and stretches from east to west the same distance that the lower 48 stretches from the Atlantic Ocean to the Pacific Ocean. The Territory's civilian population was recorded to be 72,524 from the 1939 census with a large percentage of them being Native Americans. There was no land connection between Alaska and the lower 48 but this was rectified during the war by the construction of the AlCan Highway through Canada which ran from northern Montana to Delta Junction, AK.

ANCHORAGE is Alaska's largest city and is located at the end of Cook Inlet and on SR-1.

ALASKA AVIATION HERITAGE MUSEUM: This is a large museum with over 40 aircraft on display. About 25% of them are of WW II vintage. The Museum is near Merrill Field, Anchorage's main airport. There is a library, an inviting gift shop, a theater and banquet facilities. Address: 4721 Aviation Dr. Anchorage, AK 99502. Phone and website: 907-248-5325; www.alaskaairmuseum.org

The wing section of a B-24 bomber that crash-landed on Atka Island during the war and is still there. It now serves as a very unique WW II memorial. Note the Reindeer in the distance.

ATKA ISLAND (Aleutian Islands): All of the major Aleutian Islands were involved in WW II in some manner. Atka Island was no exception. It had an operational airfield which supported the battles that took place on Attu and Kiska Islands.

The weather in the Aleutian Islands is often very bad and not conducive to flying, especially in winter. On December 9, 1942, a B-24 Bomber, attempting to land at Atka Airfield, crash landed on the Island – and is still there. The crew survived, but the area is so remote that the plane was abandoned for decades. In 1979, the wreckage was placed on the National Register of Historic Places and left in place where it crashed. The plane remained in relatively good condition thanks, in part, to the cold weather and the absence of vandals and treasure hunters. It now serves as a WW II memorial. Location: Near Bechevin Bay, Atka Island

DENALI STATE PARK: This state park is located on SR-3 midway between Anchorage and Fairbanks at mile marker 147.1.

ALASKA VETERAN'S MEMORIAL is within this park and it honors all of Alaska's veterans from all wars including WW II. It consists of five 20-ft tall concrete panels, one each, representing the Army, Air Force, Navy, Marines and Coast Guard. There is also a visitors' center.

Alaska Veterans Memorial in Denali State Park

DUTCH HARBOR, on Unalaska Island in the Aleutian Island chain, is the largest city in the Aleutian Islands and the only city in the Western Hemisphere to be bombed by the enemy during WW II. The city is located 800 miles west of Anchorage.

ALEUTIAN WORLD WAR II NATIONAL HISTORIC AREA: This 134-acre National Historic Area is operated by the National Park Service and encompasses the footprint of Fort Schatka, a US Army base and coastal defense position that protected Dutch Harbor during WW II. Military structures remaining in the park-like area consist of the Joint Command Post, Officers' Row (homes of high-ranking officers) and the Commandant's House, an aircraft revetment and ammunition magazines, the torpedo assembly building, warehouses, an amphibious aircraft ramp and a small museum.

Near the top of nearby Mount Ballyhoo are the concrete remains of one of Fort Schatka's coastal defense batteries. At 897 feet above sea level, it is the highest defense battery ever built in the US.

There is a visitors' center for the Historic Area at the Unalaska Airport. Contact information by mail; Ounalashka Corp., PO Box 149, Unalaska, AK 99685. Visitor information by phone: in 907-581-1276. Website: http://www.nps.gov/aleu

The propeller of a Japanese ship
that sunk in the Aleutian Islands

FAIRBANKS is one of Alaska's largest cities and is in the center of the state on SR-2, SR-3, SR-6 and SR-11. It was in Fairbanks that US-built Lend Lease aircraft were turned over to Soviet pilots who then flew them into the Soviet Union via Siberia. It was dangerous flying, often in bad weather and over desolate stretches of land and sea.

The Alaska Siberia World War II Memorial
in Fairbanks, AK

ALASKA SIBERIA WORLD WAR II MEMORIAL: This very unique memorial honors both the US and Soviet pilots and air crews who flew the US-built aircraft that were transferred to the Soviet Union under America's Lend Lease Program. There are two bronze statues, one of a Soviet pilot and the other of an American pilot. Not surprisingly, they are wearing cold weather gear. Location: In Griffin Park in downtown Fairbanks.

JUNEAU is the capitol of Alaska, in the Alaskan panhandle's inland waterway and is not accessible by roads.

USS JUNEAU (CL-52) **MEMORIAL** is dedicated to the crew of the cruiser *USS Juneau* which was sunk during the Battle of Guadalcanal in November 1942. All but ten of the crew perished in the attack. Among those who lost their lives were the five Sullivan brothers of Waterloo, IA.

KODIAK ISLAND: This is a large island in the Gulf of Alaska off the southern coast of the Alaska Peninsula and some 300 miles SW of Anchorage. The Island was sparsely settled during the war and its population consisted mainly of native Aleuts. Over the years, two Army coastal defense positions were built on the Island and with the advent of WW II, Kodiak Island's strategic location attracted the US Navy and a Naval Operating Base was built there. Thereafter, the Island became an important part of the defense of Alaska and the North Pacific. Three major military installations existed on the Island during the war, Fort *Abercrombie*, Fort Greely and the US Naval Operating *Base*, Kodiak.

KODIAK MILITARY HISTORY MUSEUM is located on the site of Fort Abercrombie in a restored ammunition bunker which was built in 1943. There are displays of, and information on, Fort Abercrombie and the other wartime installations in the area. Exhibits consist of artillery shells, loaders, bombs, WW II military vehicles, fire control and communications equipment used in the Fort during the war, uniforms, mess gear, flags, photos and more. There is also a library. Location: 1417B Mill Bay Rd., Kodiak, AK. Phone and website: 907-486-7015; http://kodiak.org/museum/museum.html

The memorial in Juneau, AK commemoration the loss of the cruiser USS Juneau during the battle of Guadalcanal, November 1942

The Kodiak Military History Museum of Kodiak Island

ARIZONA

Arizona had been a state for only 29 years when the United States entered World War II. The 1940 census counted 499,261 people in the state of which 57,000 were Native American Indians and 37,000 people of Mexican heritage. With its sparse population, wide open spaces and mild and dry climate, Arizona was a vacuum waiting to be filled and the US Government filled it most generously during the war. Military installations, war plants, internment camps, bombing ranges, airfields, people and money poured into Arizona in a brief span of five years.

BISBEE is a county seat in the SE corner of the state near the Mexican border and on SR-80 and SR-92.

BISBEE WORLD WAR II MEMORIAL: During the war, 76 local men gave their lives in military service and this memorial recognizes them and their sacrifices. The Memorial is of black marble on a

The Bisbee World War II Memorial in Bisbee, AZ

concrete base with a flag pole. The names of the 76 men are etched in the marble. The Memorial pays special tribute to one individual, Art Benko, a highly decorated B-24 Bomber gunner with 16 confirmed kills. Location: On SR-80 just south of town at the Lavender Pit Overlook

PHOENIX/MESA AREA: Phoenix is the capitol of Arizona and Mesa is an eastern suburb. During WW II, the city had 65,000 people and was the largest city in the state. The war would propel its population to over 100,000, a phenomenon typical of many cities in the west.

ARIZONA MILITARY MUSEUM: This museum is east of downtown Phoenix at Papago Park Military Reservation. Exhibits trace the military history of Arizona from the time of the Spanish period to the present, and the roles of Arizona citizens in all of our nation's armed conflicts. There is a large and permanent display on Papago POW Camp, the largest in the US during WW II, and a camp from which a very daring escape occurred. Address: 5636 E. McDowell Rd., Phoenix, AZ 85008. Phone and website: 602-267-2676 or 602-253-2378; www.azdema.gov/museum/index.html

The Arizona Military Museum in Phoenix, AZ

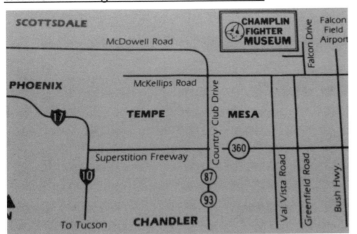

The Champlin Fighter Museum

CHAMPLIN FIGHTER MUSEUM: This museum specializes in collecting, preserving and displaying fighter aircraft of the US and other nations. There are some 40 aircraft in the collection many of which are of WW I and WW II vintage. Also on display are aircraft machine guns, aircraft ground equipment, weapons, photographs and other interesting items. The Museum has facilities for banquets, meetings and reunions and a large and interesting gift shop. Address: 4636 Fighter Aces Dr., Mesa, AZ 85215. Phone and website: 602-830-4540; www.champlinfighter.com

NAVAJO CODE TALKERS MEMORIAL: In the Pacific theater, the US Marine Corps used Navajo Indians as radio personnel. They spoke over the airwaves to each other in their native tongue so that their messages could not be understood by the Japanese. Words that were not in their native tongue would be coded. As an example, a machine gun might be called a buffalo. This memorial honors those men. The Memorial depicts a Navajo Code Talker talking over his radio. Location: Wesley

9

Bolin Memorial Park adjacent to the Arizona State Capitol Building

THE ROYAL AIR FORCE VETERANS MEMORIAL: Before the US entered the war, the British government sent Royal Air Force air cadets to various commercial flying schools in America. One such school was at Falcon Field in Mesa. This memorial honors 23 RAF cadets and one American who died at the field during their training. Location: City of Mesa Cemetery. 1212 N. Center, Mesa, AZ

The Navajo Code Talkers Memorial in Phoenix, AZ

***USS ARIZONA* ANCHOR AND MAST:** The Battleship *USS Arizona* rests on the bottom of Pearl Harbor and is a National Historic Site, but its anchor and mast are here in Phoenix. They were salvaged from the wreck, brought to Phoenix and now serve as a memorial to those who were lost when the ship was sunk during the Japanese attack of December 7, 1941. Location: In Wesley Bolin Plaza in downtown Phoenix on W. Washington St.

WINGSPAN AIR MUSEUM: Military aircraft, vehicles and other military displays are on view at this fine museum but the focus on veterans comes first. There are many veteran displays which include the personal views of veterans, service histories, veterans' events and other related activities of veterans. The Museum is host of many activities through the year and there is a very interesting gift shop. Address: 6555 E. Southern Av, suite 1106 (Superstition Springs, Mall), Mesa, AZ 85206. Phone and website: 480-924-5543; http://wingspanair.org

<u>**QUARTZSITE**</u> is a small community in southwestern Arizona on I-10 and US-95.

The Royal Air Force Veterans Memorial in Mesa, Az

The anchor of the Battleship USS Arizona which was sunk during the attack on Pearl Harbor, December 7, 1941

THE W.A.S.P. MUSEUM: This is part of a larger facility known as the Career and Learning Center in Quartzsite.

As the name of this museum implies, it focuses on the training and activities of the WW II-era "Women's Air force Service Pilots" (WASPs). These were women pilots who volunteered to fly newly-built US aircraft from their place of manufacture to various locations in order to relieve male pilots of military service. Some of the WASPs trained at Quartzsite's local airport and the Museum commemorates the activities and events of that day. There are photos, documents, personal effects, uniforms, training histories, aircraft destinations and other interesting information about this very unique WW II unit. Address: 1555 Dome Rock Rd., Quartsite, AZ 85277. Phone and website: 928-927-5555; www.waspmuseum.com

SACTON is a small community on the Pima Indian Reservation 30 miles SE of Phoenix.

THE MATTHEW B. JUAN, IRA H. HAYES VETERANS MEMORIAL: This unique memorial honors two Pima Indians who fought for their country in both WW I and WW II. The Memorial is named in honor of Matthew B. Juan who was the first of 321 Arizona men to be killed in WW I.

Ira H. Hayes was one of the three Marine survivors of the famous flag raising on Iwo Jima which has been immortalized by the photograph of that historic event. Juan is buried at the Cook Memorial Church yard in Sacaton. Hayes is buried at Arlington, VA.

The Matthew B. Juan, Ira H. Hayes Memorial in Sacaton, AZ

TOMBSTONE, in SE Arizona on SR-82, is an historic city of the Old West and a major tourist attraction. At nearby Fort Huachuca, two all-Negro army divisions, the 92nd and 93rd, were trained during WW II. These divisions then served in both the Pacific and in northern Italy.

FORT HUACHUCA MUSEUM: This museum is one of two museums on the grounds of Fort Huachuca and traces the history of Fort Huachuca from its inception in the 1840s to the present day. Most of the displays relate to the Fort's long history but there is information and displays relating to the WW II period and the histories of the 92nd and 93rd Divisions. There is also a well-stocked and interesting gift shop. Phone and website: 520-533-3638 and 520-533-5736; www.huachuca.army.mil/site/Visitor

US ARMY INTELLIGENCE MUSEUM: This is a second museum on the grounds of Fort Huachuca and features the history of US Army intelligence units and their fascinating activities from the days of the American Revolution to the present. Included in the displays is information related to the US Army intelligence operations during WW II. The Museum also serves as a teaching tool within the Army Intelligence School. Phone: 520-533-1127

TUCSON is Arizona's second largest city and is in SE Arizona on I-10.

11

PIMA AIR & SPACE MUSEUM is just south of Davis-Monthan AFB, and is a multi-building complex with over 300 aircraft and over 125,000 aircraft artifacts. It is one of the largest aircraft museums in the world.

Many of the planes on display are from WW II and from both Allied and Axis nations. The collection includes one or more B-29s, B-26s, B-17s, P-47s, V-1 German "buzz bombs" and more. Some of the planes are one-of-a-kind models. The Museum has its own large and very capable restoration facility which has restored many of the aircraft on display.

The Pima Air & Space has over 300 aircraft on display.

The Arizona Aviation Hall of Fame is also here and pays tribute to famous Arizona citizens associated with aviation. Among those honored is the late Senator Barry Goldwater who was a pilot during the war in the China-Burma-India theater. The Hall of Fame has a sizable research library and there is a large gift shop and a snack bar.

Tours of the nearby Arizona Maintenance and Regeneration Group (AMARG), better known as the "Boneyard," can be arranged at the Museum. AMARG contains thousands of mothballed military aircraft neatly lined up in rows awaiting their destinies. Tours should be reserved at least a week in advance. Address of the Pima Air & Space Museum: 6000 E. Valencia Rd., Tucson, AZ 85706. Phone and website: 502-574-0462 and 502-574-9658; www.Pimaair.org

The 390th Memorial Museum is a museum within a museum. It is inside the Pima Air & Space Museum and commemorates the activities of the 390th Bombardment Squadron of WW II. The main attraction is a beautifully restored B-17G bomber. There is a display on General James Doolittle, a wall of honor, an art exhibit, aircraft models, a library and a research center. The 390th Memorial Museum Address is: 6000 E. Valencia Rd., Tucson, AZ 85706. Phone and website: 520-574-0462 and 520-574-0287; www.390th.org

USS ARIZONA **MEMORIAL:** Located on the campus of the University of Arizona, is this attractive memorial to the battleship *USS Arizona* which was sunk during the Pearl Harbor attack. Hanging from an abstract mast are dog tags bearing the names of the 1177 men who lost their lives aboard the ship.

<u>VALLE</u> is midway between Flagstaff and the south rim of the Grand Canyon on US-180 and SR-64.

PLANES OF FAME MUSEUM is located at the Valle Airport and is a sister museum to the Planes of Fame Museum in Chino, CA. Here, there are displays of aircraft and aircraft-related memorabilia that chronicle the aviation history of the US. Many of the aircraft are in flying condition and are flown regularly and participate in air shows and are used in movies and TV programs. The Museum also has a fine collection of military vehicles. There are many other items on display at the Museum and a nice gift shop. Address: 755 Mustang Way, Valle-Williams, AZ 86046. Phone and website: 928-635-1000; www.planesoffame.org

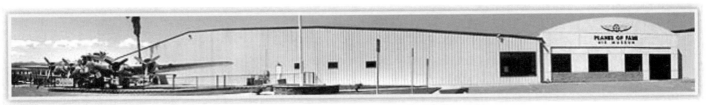

The Planes of Fame Museum in Valle, AZ

YUMA is a county seat in SW Arizona on the Colorado River, I-8 and US-95. It has long been the home of the huge Yuma Proving Ground, a major US Army installation, which is east of the city and extends for many miles across the southern part of the state.

YUMA PROVING GROUND'S HERITAGE CENTER: The Yuma Proving Ground had its beginning during the early years of WW II when it was part of the California-Arizona Maneuver Area which was a training facility for US Army armored units and commanded by General George S. Patton, Jr.
The former headquarters of the Yuma Proving Grounds has been converted into this Heritage

Center which contains a very impressive museum. The Museum traces the history of the Proving Grounds from their beginning during WW II to the present. On display are artillery weapons and munitions, combat gear, uniforms, small arms, photos, a wide variety of military equipment and much more. There is a 20-seat theater in which WW II era films are often shown. Address: In the main administrative area of the Yuma Proving Grounds at 310 C St. Phone and website: 928-328-3394; www.yuma.army.mil/garrison/sites/directorates/

The Yuma Proving Ground's Heritage Center, Yuma, AZ

ARKANSAS

At the beginning of the war Arkansas was a sparsely settled, rural, racially segregated southern state and one of the poorest in the nation. Like other southern states, Arkansas had a virtual one-party political system based on the conservative wing of the Democrat Party. This had resulted in the state's senators and representatives being returned time and again to Washington to gain powerful positions in Congress due to their seniority. In the late 1930s, the state was "discovered" by industry because it had cheap labor, cheap land, a central location and an anti-union atmosphere. By 1939, about 100 new factories had come to the state. The US Army and Navy also discovered the state, and with support from Arkansas's powerful politicians in Washington, new military facilities were built in the state and existing ones expanded.

CONWAY is a county seat 28 miles north of downtown Little Rock on I-40, US-64 and US-65. It is the home of The University of Central Arkansas

UNIVERSITY OF CENTRAL ARKANSAS WORLD WAR II MEMORIAL: Forty six male students that had attended this university perished in WW II. They have been commemorated by this polished stone memorial on the University's campus. Most of those listed were junior grade officers. Location: On Donaghey Av. in Conway, AR

FAYETTEVILLE is a county seat in the NW corner of Arkansas on I-540, US-71, SR-16 and SR-45.

The University of Central Arkansas WW II Memorial in Conway, AR

The construction of the all-wood aircraft hangar during WW II which would later become the home of the Arkansas Air Museum

ARKANSAS AIR MUSEUM is one of two museums located at Fayetteville's Drake Field and is housed in an all-wood WW II hangar. On display are aircraft and artifacts spanning the entire history of aviation in Arkansas. The WW II display is relatively small.

The Museum has a restoration facility which may be viewed by visitors and has a theater. Also located here is the Arkansas Aviation Hall of Fame. Next door is the Ozark Military Museum. Address of the Arkansas Air Museum: 4290 S. School Rd., Fayetteville, AR 72701. Phone and website: 479-521-4947; www.arkairmuseum.org

OZARK MILITARY MUSEUM is located at Drake field and traces the military history of Arkansas. It is housed in a WW II era hangar and has aircraft, vehicles, weapons and other WW II displays. There are also equipment and displays from the Korean and Viet Nam conflicts. Next door is the Arkansas Air Museum. Address of the Ozark Military Museum: 4360 S. School Av., Fayetteville, AR 72701. Phone and website: 479-587-1941; www.ozarkmilitarymuseum.org

FORT SMITH is a county seat in west-central Arkansas on the state line between I-40 and I-540 and on US-64 and US-71.

THE DARBY HOUSE, near downtown Ft. Smith, was the boyhood home of Gen. William O. Darby, the organizer and commander of the Army's 1st Ranger Battalion, better known as "Darby's Rangers." The house is preserved and appears as it did in May 1945 when Darby's parents were informed of

*The Darby House on General Darby St.
in Fort Smith, AR*

their son's death in combat.

On display are memorabilia and artifacts relating to Darby's military career and life in Fort Smith. Darby is buried in the Fort Smith National Cemetery. Address of the Darby House: 311 Gen. Darby St. (N. 8th), Ft. Smith, AR. 72901. Phone: 479-782-3388

FORT SMITH AIR MUSEUM is located in the terminal of the Fort Smith Regional Airport. Its mission is to honor pioneer and military aviators from western Arkansas and eastern Oklahoma. There are over 50 displays honoring local WW II aviators who flew such planes as P-38 fighters, B-17 and B-24 bombers, PBY patrol aircraft and Civil Air Patrol (CAP) air patrols. There is information on the 188th Air National Guard and civilian airline service in the Fort Smith Area. The Museum has no military aircraft. Address: Fort Smith Regional Airport, 6100 McKennon Blvd., Fort Smith, AR 72901. Phone: 479-785-1839

FORT SMITH MUSEUM OF HISTORY, in downtown Fort Smith, preserves the history of the area and the town from its earliest days as an army fort. There are a number of interesting WW II displays including an entire room honoring Gen. William O. Darby, commander of the famous "Darby's Rangers," that saw extensive combat in Europe. The Museum has other exhibits on WW II and on nearby Fort Chaffee. And don't pass up their nice gift shop. Address: 320 Rogers Av., Fort Smith AR 72901. Phone and web: 479-783-7841; www.fortsmithmuseum.com

*The Fort Smith Museum of History
in Fort Smith, AR*

JACKSONVILLE is about 15 miles NE of downtown Little Rock on US-67. The city had a major war plant, the Jacksonville Ordnance Plant, which made munitions.

JACKSONVILLE MUSEUM OF MILITARY HISTORY: When the Jacksonville Ordnance Plant shut down, its administration building was expanded and converted into a 14,500 Sq. ft. military museum with several galleries. Some years later, a veteran's memorial was built adjacent to the Museum. The Museum tells the story of the Ordnance Plant and has other exhibits on WW II. One of the most interesting WW II items in the Museum is a German underwater hedgehog used at Normandy. This is a devise designed to rip the bottom of small landing craft coming ashore. The Museum also has exhibits and information on other US conflicts. There is a library, an educational program and an interesting gift shop. Address: 100 Veterans Circle, Jacksonville, AR 72076. Phone and website:

501-241-1943; www.jaxmilitarymuseum.org (Direction to the Museum: Take US-67 to Jacksonville. Take Exit 9 onto West Main St. and go approximately .4 miles. At the post office, turn left onto Veterans Circle and watch for the Museum).

LITTLE ROCK, located in the center of the state, is the capitol of the state and Arkansas' largest city.

The Jacksonville Museum of Military History,
The former administration building of the Jacksonville Ordnance Plant of WWII

ARKANSAS INLAND MARITIME MUSEUM is located in North Little Rock and emphasizes the naval history of WW II. The Museum has on display two WW II vessels, the submarine *USS Razorback* and the US Navy tug *Hoga*. The *Razorback* completed five missions in the Pacific near the end of the war and was present in Tokyo Bay when the Japanese surrendered. The *Razorback* later served in the Cold War and in Viet Nam, and eventually was used by the Turkish Navy.

The tug *Hoga* was at Pearl Harbor when the Japanese attack came. It was not damaged and succeeded in rescuing sailors, fighting fires, and pulling ships out of harm's way. She later served in the clean-up efforts at Pearl Harbor and continued to serve there throughout the war.

Also at the Museum is a memorial to the submarine *USS Snook* which was lost at sea on May 16, 1945. The *Snook* has become Arkansas's adopted submarine.

The submarine USS Razorback at
the Arkansas Inland Maritime Museum

There are displays at the Museum of artifacts, photos, uniforms and many other items related to WW II. The Museum has a library, theater, an impressive gift shop and is available for private and public events. Address: 120 Riverfront Park Dr., North Little Rock, AR 72114.Phone and web: 501-371-8320; www.aimm.museum/contact.asp

ARKANSAS NATIONAL GUARD MUSEUM: This fine museum is located at Camp Robinson in North Little Rock and, as do most National Guard Museums, traces the history of the state's National Guard. The Arkansas National Guard had four units that saw action in WW II and they, and their WW II history, are exhibited in great detail in the Museum. Most of the units saw action in Italy.

Artifacts and memorabilia related to the units are on display. Address: Camp Robinson, Little Rock, AR. Phone and website: 501-212-5215; www.arngmuseum.com

MacARTHUR MUSEUM OF ARKANSAS MILITARY HISTORY: This is the birthplace of General Douglas MacArthur. It is now a museum which preserves the contributions of Arkansas men and women who served in the US armed forces. Exhibits include information on the MacArthur family, baby Douglas, artifacts, photographs, weapons, documents, uniforms and portray Arkansas's military history at home and abroad.

The Museum building has long been known as the old Tower Building and is the central structure in

MacArthur Park on E. 9th St. in downtown Little Rock. The Park is the site of the former Little Rock Arsenal built in 1836 when Arkansas became a state.

On Jan. 26, 1880, the wife of the Arsenal's commander and civil war hero, Captain Arthur MacArthur, gave birth to their first son, Douglas. Young Douglas was christened at nearby Christ Episcopal Church. The MacArthurs left the Arsenal a few months later and were never posted here again. Through the years, all of the Arsenal's buildings were torn down except for the Tower Building.

There is also a monument in the park dedicated to the 206th Coast Artillery (anti-aircraft) Regiment, a unit comprised mostly of local men that was at Dutch Harbor AK in June 1942 when the Japanese bombed that American city. Museum address: 503 E. 9th St., Little Rock, AR 72202. Phone and website: 501-375-4602; www.arkmilitaryheritage.com

PERRYVILLE is a county seat 38 miles NE of downtown Little Rock on SR-9. SR-10 and SR-60.

PERRY COUNTY WORLD WAR II MEMORIAL: Here is one of the very early WW II memorials, erected in 1947. It commemorates those citizens of Perry County who perished during the war. Etched on the stone memorial is a prayer and the names of those being honored. Location: Perryville County Court House lawn.

ROHWER is a small community in SE Arkansas on SR-1. During the war, one of the several Japanese Relocation Camps was built on the outskirts of the

The Perry County World War II Memorial in Perryville, AR

town which quickly filled up with ethnic Japanese civilians forcefully relocated from the US West Coast.

CAMP ROHWER MEMORIAL: This very interesting memorial is on the grounds of the former Rohwer Japanese Relocation Camp. It consists of a tank body with treads topped by a stone column with an American flag and a star. It honors those young men from the Rohwer Camp who volunteered to serve in the US Army and were killed during the war. Inscribed on the column are their names. All of the names are Japanese and the sculptors of the Memorial were two Japanese Americans. Location: At the site of the former Rohwer Japanese Relocation Camp just north of Rohwer on SR-1

*The Camp Rohwer Memorial
at Rohwer, AR*

SHERIDAN is a county seat 30 mile south of downtown Little Rock on US-167, US-270, SR-35 and SR-46. During the war the local airport was used as an Army Air Forces training field.

17

PLANE CRASH SITE MEMORIAL: On March 12, 1943, a B-17 bomber from Smokey Hill Army Airfield, Salina, KS, crashed near the Sheridan Airfield killing all aboard.

A small stone memorial has been placed at the crash site with the names of the crash victims engraved thereon. Location: Inquire locally.

WALNUT RIDGE is a county seat in NE Arkansas on US-63, US-67, US-412 and SR-34.

WALNUT RIDGE ARMY FLYING SCHOOL MUSEUM: Walnut Ridge's local airfield was taken over by the UA Army Air Forces during the war and used for training purposes. This museum is located on the airfield and traces the field's wartime history. It has a three-fold mission: (1) preserves the airfields rich history, (2) recognize and honor the veterans and civilians who served at the field, (3) educate future generations about the sacrifices made by those who served. In this last category, the

Museum has a list of all of the air cadets who were killed at the field in training. On display are uniforms, documents, photographs and a wide assortment of artifacts and memorabilia related to the field and there is a nice gift shop. Address: 70 S. Beacon Rd., Walnut Ridge, AR 72476. Phone and website: 800-584-5575; www.wingsofhonor.com

The Plane Crash Site Memorial near Sheridan, AR

The Walnut Ridge Army Flying School Museum in Walnut Ridge, AR

CALIFORNIA

California was witness to some of the most traumatic events that happened during WW II in the then 48 United States. When Pearl Harbor was bombed on Dec. 7, 1941 California was racked from north to south with near panic conditions because tens of thousands of its citizens expected similar attacks on California targets, possibly by the same naval force that had attacked Hawaii.

The Panic of December 1941 gradually subsided but never really went away. While Californians were learning to live with war fears, their aircraft and shipbuilding industries exploded with defense work. Unemployment virtually disappeared and everyone was called upon to do their share for the war effort.

New industries of all kinds sprang up all over the state, trainloads of people flocked to California from the east to work in the shipyards and war plants, and Mexicans poured across the border to do the same. During the war, California would receive 11.9% of all US Government war contracts and her plants and workers would produce 17% of all war supplies made in the US. Military bases were built by the dozen, sometimes in little towns that people in the big cities had never heard of. California's deserts became bombing ranges and training centers, her harbors became naval bases, her airports became air bases and training fields. During the course of the war, California would acquire more military installations, by far, than any other state.

As a direct result of the war, millions of Americans "discovered" California for the first time. They liked it and many stayed on after the war. In doing so, they started a trend of strong and steady growth that lasted for many decades. And because of the expansion of the Los Angeles area a new word entered the American vocabulary - smog.

ATWATER is a small community five miles northwest of Merced on SR-99. During WW II, it was home to a large air base, Castle Air Force Base.

CASTLE AIR MUSEUM is a large air museum with more than 70 aircraft on display. Many of the aircraft are WW II models. A large selection of aircraft-related memorabilia and artifacts can also be seen here. The Museum has its own restoration facility, a fine gift shop, a cafe and banquet room and an active events calendar. There is an educational program available as well as group tours. Address: 5050 Santa Fe Dr. Atwater, CA 95301. Phone and website: 209-723-2178; www.castleairmuseum.org

The outdoor aircraft display at the Castle Air Museum in Atwater, CA

BAKERSFIELD is a farming center 100 miles north of Los Angeles. During WW II, there were three local airfields in the area used by the Army Air Forces for training programs.

MINTER FIELD AIR MUSEUM is located on one of the WW II airfields, Minter Field, which is now Shafter Airport, 12 mile NW of Merced on SR-99. The Museum is housed in the AAF's old fire station which was built in 1941. The Museum has a growing number of WW II aircraft, several foreign aircraft and its own restoration facility. In addition, there are WW II vehicles on display, uniforms, radio gear, photos, aircraft models and other artifacts. The Museum has a delightful gift shop and is home to several scheduled air shows. Address: 401 Vultee St., Shafter Airport, Shafter, CA 93263. Phone and website: 661-393-0291; www.minterfieldairmuseum.com

BARSTOW is a desert community 50 miles NE of San Bernardino on I-15, at the end of I-40 and on SR-58. NE of Barstow is Fort Irwin National Training Center.

11TH ARMORED CAVALRY REGIMENTAL MUSEUM: This Museum has two story lines under one roof - the history of military presence since 1844 on what is now Fort Irwin and the history of the 11th Armored Cavalry Division. Inside the Museum are life size dioramas, photos, documents, small arms, uniforms, flags, field equipment and many other artifacts related to the Museums two themes. Outside is a large collection of tanks and other heavy military equipment. The Museum has a library, an educational program and offers group tours. Address: Bldg. #222, First St., Fort Irwin, CA 92310. Phone and website: 760-380-6607; www.museumsusa.org/museums/info/1152778

CARMEL-by-the-SEA: This is a beautiful beach community and popular tourist site just south of Monterrey on SR-1.

WORLD WAR II MEMORIAL: Twenty service men left this beautiful community during WW II and never returned. Their names are engraved on this memorial. Location: In Devendorf Park near the intersection of Mission St. and 6th Av.

The WWII Memorial in Carmel-by-the-sea, CA

DESERT CENTER (Chiriaco Summit): This small community, 47 miles west of Blythe on I-10, was the center of the California-Arizona Maneuver Area, better known as the Desert Training Center. This was the largest army base in the world covering some 18,000 square miles - mostly barren desert. It stretched from the outskirts of Pomona, CA eastward to within 50 miles of Phoenix, AZ, southward to the outskirts of Yuma, AZ and northward into the southern tip of Nevada. It existed primarily to train US forces in desert warfare for the North African campaign General George S. Patton, Jr. commander of the 1st Armored Corps, was responsible for selecting this site in early 1942. As a native Californian, he knew the area well from his youth and from having participated in Army maneuvers here in the 1930s.

The Maneuver Area had several army camps placed at distances from one another so that the troops at any one camp would have their own maneuver training area.

Patton's 1st Armored Corps trained here from April to August 1942 and then departed to take part in the invasion of North Africa in November 1942. Other Army Corps and divisions followed in succession. In all, seven armored divisions and 13 infantry divisions trained here.

The statue of General Patton and his dog at the entrance to the Patton Memorial Museum.

GENERAL PATTON MEMORIAL MUSEUM, located at Desert Center, preserves the history of the Desert Training Center and traces the career of General Patton and his military activities in North Africa and Europe. In the Museum are displays and information on the thousands of servicemen who trained here. There are weapons, uniforms, field gear, books, apparel, living accommodations and more. Outside the Museum are several tanks and military vehicles from WW II and later. At the entrance to the Museum is a large statue of General Patton and his dog Willie. In all, more than one million men trained here. Address: Chiriaco Summit, CA 92201. Phone and website: 760-227-3483; www.generalpattonmuseum.com

<u>FAIRFIELD</u> is 15 miles east of the north end of San Francisco Bay on I-680 and is home to Travis Air Force Base.

TRAVIS AIR FORCE MUSEUM: This fine museum in on the grounds of Travis Air Force Base and has one of the largest collections of military aircraft on the West Coast. Many of the aircraft on display are from WW II both inside and outside the Museum. In addition, the Museum has exhibits on WW II organizations such as the "Flying Tigers," the "Tuskegee Airmen, "The "Hump Pilots" and the "WASPs" (Women's Army Service Pilots). And there is a replica of "Fat Man", the atomic bomb dropped on Nagasaki.

The outdoor display of aircraft at the Travis Air Force in Fairfield, CA

The Museum is also home to the Jimmy Doolittle Air & Space Museum highlighting General Jimmy Doolittle, his crews and planes and his famous raids on Japan of April 1942.

There is a picnic area and an intriguing gift shop with many interesting items for sale. Address: 4400 Brennan Circle, Travis AFB, CA 94535. Phone and website: Museum, 707-424-5605, gift shop 707-424-4450; www.travis.af.mil/units/travisairmuseum.as

<u>FIREBAUGH</u> Is a small community in the San Joaquin Valley on SR-33. During WW II, there was a Army Air Forces training field nearby.

HERITAGE OF EAGLES AIR MUSEUM is an all-volunteer non-profit museum dedicated to the preservation of the Eagle Field Army Air Forces Training Base built here in 1942. The Museum has several WW II era aircraft, military vehicles, uniforms, photographs, information on the Air Base, memorabilia and a complete WW II command radio station. The Museum is located at the local airport. Address: 11100 West Eagle Rd., Firebaugh, CA 93622. Phone and website: 209-392-8264; www.b25.net

The Heritage of Eagles Air Museum in Firebaugh. CA

FRESNO is a county seat in the lower San Joaquin Valley on SR-41, SR-99 and SR-180.

LEGION OF VALOR MUSEUM: This is an impressive building in the city of Fresno that honors the veterans from the Fresno area who served in all of America's wars. There are thousands of items on display including a large collection of military decorations for valor, framed citations, uniforms,

photographs, documents, military equipment and an extensive military art collection. The WW II displays are significant and feature the Doolittle Raid on Tokyo, the Battle of the Bulge, various WW II aircraft, the 442nd all-Japanese Infantry Combat Unit and much more. There is a fine gift shop and the Museum hosts various social events and reunions throughout the year. Address: 2425 Fresno St., Fresno, CA 93721. Phone and website: 559-498-0510; http://legionofvalormuseum.org

The Legion of Valor Museum in Fresno, CA

INDEPENDENCE is a county seat in east-central California east of Sequoia National Park on US-395.

MANZANAR INTEPRETIVE CENTER: This 8,000 Sq. ft. facility is on the site of the Manzanar Relocation Camp which is two miles south of Independence on US-395. This camp was one of 12 such camps in the US where ethnic Japanese from the US West Coast and Latin America were relocated during the war. It has extensive exhibits which focus on the forced relocation of the ethnic Japanese, who they were, where they came from, how they lived and how they were treated. There is a large scale model of the camp, photographs, artifacts, a 22-minute orientation film entitled "Remembering Manzanar," and a one-of-kind bookstore. Address: 5001 US-395, Independence, CA 93526. Phone and website: 760-878-2194 extension 3310 for visitors; www.nps.gov/manz/planyourvisit/interpretive-center.htm

LAKEPORT is a county seat 90 miles north of San Francisco on beautiful Clear Lake, SR-29 and SR-175.

The Pearl Harbor Memorial Mast in Lakeport, CA

PEARL HARBOR MEMORIAL MAST: This interesting WW II Memorial is a nautical mast with a plaque at the base which reads "PEARL HARBOR MEMORIAL MAST. DECEMBER 7,1941- A DATE THAT WILL LIVE IN INFAMY- PRESIDENT FRANKLIN D. ROOSEVELT. THE LAKE COUNTY SURVIORS ASK THAT YOU REMEMBER KINDLY THOSE OF US WHO HAVE PASSED ON AND DEDICATED OUR MEMORIES TO THE FUTURE OF ALL GENERATIONS WHO WILL DEFEND THE FLAG." Location: Liberty Park in Lakeport, CA

LOS ANGELES/LONG BEACH METROPOLITAN AREA:

Los Angeles: During WW II, Los Angeles was the boom town of boom towns. The Los Angeles metropolitan area grew faster than any other major metropolitan area in the US and experienced many social traumas while doing so. By 1943, the population of metropolitan "L.A." was larger than 37 states, and was home to one in every 40 US citizens. By the end of the war, the L.A. area had produced a very large percentage of America's war production.

Japanese American National Museum: This museum is in the Japantown (aka "Little Tokyo") section of Los Angeles. It has numerous displays and artifacts tracing the history of the Japanese people in America. One of the larger permanent displays in the Museum relates the story of the relocation of the ethnic Japanese on the West Coast during World War II.

Adjacent to the Museum is the very impressive memorial known as the "Go For Broke" Monument. That phrase was the unofficial slogan of the Japanese American servicemen of WW II.

The "Go For Broke" Monument at the Japanese American National Museum in Los Angeles, CA

The Monument consists of a large semicircular face of polished black stone, set at an angle facing the sun as it travels across the sky. The Monument's curves back wall lists the names of over 16,000 Japanese American servicemen. Museum address: 369 E. First St., Los Angeles, CA 90012. Phone and website: 213-625-0414; www.janm.org

World War II Russian Veterans Memorial: Yes, we have a memorial in the US dedicated to the

Russian veterans of WW II. In Europe, during WW II, the ground war on the eastern front was several times larger than that on the western front. There were many more Russians fighting the Germans than Americans and Russian casualties were much larger than those of the US or any other Allied nation.

This memorial was dedicated in 2005 and has the inscription "DEDICATED IN HONOR OF AND IN TRIBUTE TO WORLD WAR II VETERANS OF THE FORMER SOVIET UNION." Location: In Plummer Park, 7377 Santa Monica Blvd., West Hollywood, CA 90046

The World War II Russian Veterans Memorial in West Hollywood, CA

The 442nd Infantry World War II Memorial in Los Angeles, CA

442nd Infantry World War II Memorial: The inscription on this impressive memorial says it all. "THIS MEMORIAL IS REVERENTLY PLACED HERE BY THE JAPANESE AMERICAN COMMUNITY, UNDER THE AUSPICES OF THE SOUTHERN CALIFORNIA BURIAL AND MEMORIAL COMMITTEE, IN MEMORY OF THE AMERICAN SOLIDERS OF JAPANESE ANCESTRY WHO FOUGHT, SUFFERED AND DIED IN WORLD WAR II THAT LIBERTY, JUSTICE, AND EQUAL OPPORTUNITY IN THE PURSUIT OF HAPPINESS MIGHT COME TO ALL DEMOCRATIC AND PEACELOVING PEOPLE EVERYWHERE REGARDLESS OF RACE, CREED, COLOR OF NATIONAL ORIGIN, DEDICATED IN MAY 30,1949" Location: Evergreen Cemetery, 204 N. Evergreen Av., Los Angeles, CA

Burbank is one of the larger communities in the Los Angeles area. It is the San Fernando Valley north of Los Angeles and, during the war, was home to one of America's largest aircraft manufacturers – the Lockheed Aircraft Co.

CUT

McCambridge Park World War II Memorial: This Magnificent Park has several memorials dedicated to the WW II era. The memorial pictured is dedicated to those men and women from the Burbank area who died during WW II.

In addition, there is a memorial to the mothers and fathers of those who served in WW II and an interesting memorial to the late actor/comedian, Bob Hope, who entertained troops at home and overseas during the war. Location of the Park: San Fernando and Scott Sts., Burbank, CA

The WWII Memorial at McCambridge Park in Burbank, CA

<u>Chino</u> is one of the many small communities in the Los Angeles area and is about 50 miles east of Los Angeles, and adjacent to, Pomona to the north.

The Planes of Fame Museum in Chino, CA

Planes of Fame Museum: This is one of two very impressive air museums at the Chino Airport. It is a large museum and has an outstanding collection of WW II aircraft. This Museum is a "must see" for WW II buffs.

The Museum has a total of some 150 aircraft, many of which are flyable. There are also many displays of aircraft-related artifacts and memorabilia. The Museum was founded in 1957 making it the first permanent air museum west of the Rocky Mountains.

The Museum hosts a well-attended annual air show and many of its aircraft have appeared in other air shows around the country, in movies and on television. The Museum offers airplane rentals, group tours, has an educational program, a large and fine gift shop and hosts social and public events. Planes of Fame has a sister facility in Valle, AZ where some 40 additional aircraft are on display. Address of the Planes of Fame Museum: 7000 Merrill Ave., #17, Chino, CA 91710. Phone and website: 909-597-3722; www.planesoffame.org

The Yanks Air Museum: This ten acre-150,000 Sq. ft. museum is the second of the two air museums at Chino Airport and is also an outstanding museum. It has a collection of over 160 aircraft, many of them from WW II. The Museum has its own aircraft restoration facility which can be viewed by visitors. Both military and civilian aircraft are in the collection, many of which are flyable. The Museum has many aircraft-related displays and exhibits and a large and interesting gift shop. The Address: 7000 Merrill Ave., Chino, CA 91710. Phone and website: 909-597-1734; www.yanksair.com

Long Beach/SanPedro Area:

The American Merchant San Pedro, CA

The American Merchant Marine Veterans Memorial: This striking memorial, the first national memorial to merchant seamen in the US, honors those merchant mariners who served in all wars and was inspired by the sacrifices of the merchant mariners of WW II. The bronze statue depicts two merchant seamen climbing a Jacob's ladder after making a rescue at sea. Location: South Harbor Blvd. at West 6th St. in San Pedro

The *Lane Victory:* This is a WW II "Victory" Ship permanently berthed in San Pedro, and restored as a memorial to the veterans of the Merchant Marines who served in WW II. A Victory ship is a later version of the more famous "Liberty" ship but with certain modifications to make it faster and more suitable for postwar commercial use. The *Lane Victory* has been restored and is in working condition and cruises are offered. The ship, now a National Historic Landmark, served also during the Korean and Viet Nam Wars and is used frequently in movie and TV productions. Aboard ship is a first rate gift shop, a library and a museum. Address: US Merchant Marines of WW II, Berth 94, PO Box 629, San Pedro Harbor, CA 90733 Phone and website: 310-519-9545; www.lanevictory.org

Los Angeles Maritime Museum: This fine museum, in San Pedro, traces the maritime history of West Coast from the earliest days of sail to the present. There is a respectable amount of material on the WW II era including models of the Victory ship *Lane Victory* and the luxury liner *Queen Mary,* both ships which are in the local area and open to the public.

 The Museum owns a WW II era Army tugboat, the *Angels Gate.* Address: Berth 84; Foot of 6th St., San Pedro, CA 90731. Phone and website; 310-548-7618; www.lamaritimemuseum.org

The SS Lane Victory at its berth in San Pedro, CA

Fort MacArthur Military Museum: This is a small museum in the old WW I era Osgood-Farley battery of Fort MacArthur in Angels Gate Park. The battery was once part of an older fort known as the Fort in San Pedro and was manned and armed during WW II. The Fort's gun positions can be toured and there is an interesting gift shop. Address: 3601 S. Gaffey St., San Pedro, CA 90731. Phone and website: 310-548-2631; www.ftmac.org

Pacific Battleship Center/*USS Iowa*: Here is one of the great relics of WW II, the battleship *Iowa*. She saw action in both the Atlantic and Pacific, during the war, carried President Roosevelt to the Tehran summit meeting in 1943, was Admiral Halsey's flagship, and was present in Tokyo Bay when Japan surrendered, served in the Korean Conflict and served the US Navy for a total of 51 years. She is now open to the public, has a very interesting gift store and is anchored, year-around, in the

Los Angeles Main Channel between the Los Angeles Cruise terminal and the Los Angeles Maritime Museum. Address: 250 Harbor Blvd., San Pedro, CA 90731. Phone and website: 877-446-9261 (ship) and 619-889-6313 (store); www.pacificbattleship.com

The Proud Bird Restaurant in Los Angeles, CA

Proud Bird Restaurant: Here's a very unique WW II historic display - a collection of WW II aircraft at an upscale restaurant. One can dine at this restaurant and peer out of the window and see a P-38, a C-47. a Spitfire and other war birds of WW II in the distance. There are about 20 aircraft in the collection, some of which date back to WW I. You will also see modern jet liners passing overhead because the restaurant is close to Los Angeles International Airport (LAX). Address: 11022 Aviation Blvd., Los Angeles, CA 90045. Phone and website: 310-670-3093; www.theproudbird.com

Hotel *Queen Mary* Seaport: This is a city-owned, history-oriented, hotel and entertainment center located at the Long Beach waterfront with the *Queen Mary* ocean liner as the center's main attraction. The ship was built just before WW II and was, at the time, one of the last great luxury ocean liners of her day.

When the war came, she was converted into a troop transport and carried tens of thousands of GIs to Europe. After the war, she carried tens of thousands home again plus a cargo or two of war brides. She was one of the fastest ships afloat and could outrun any Axis submarine, therefore she usually sailed alone and unescorted. The tactic worked because she was never attacked.

Several years after the war, she was brought to this location and became a floating hotel, convention center and museum with numerous displays on board relating to her WW II service. Guided tours of the ship are available. Aboard the ship is a large shopping area, restaurants, entertainment centers and several gift shops. Package accommodations are available. Address: 1126 Queens Highway, Long Beach, CA 90802. Phone and website: General information 877-342-0738, hotel reservations 877-342-0742; www.queenmary.com

The Queen Mary - now a hotel

Rosie the Riveter Park is a 3.4 acre park located next to what was the huge WW II era Douglas Aircraft Co. plant in Long Beach. During WW II, it was part of the Douglas facility and known as Douglas Park. In the 2000's, a new and larger park was developed on the site of the Douglas Plant and the name, Douglas Park, was transferred to that park. This park was then given its current name. As the name suggests, it honors the thousands of women who worked in the local aircraft industry and shipyard. Billions of rivets were used during the war in both aircraft and ships. This facility is not to be be confused with the Rosie The Riveter National Park in Richmond, CA in the San Francisco Bay area. Location of Rosie the Riveter Park: Clark Av. and Conant St. in Long Beach. Phone: 562-570-1600.

Riverside is one of the larger cities in the Los Angeles area and is 45 miles east of downtown Los Angeles. During the war, and for many years before, it was the host city to a large Army airfield, March Field.

March Field Air Museum: This is a fine museum located at the March Air Reserve Base, the former March Field of WW II. The Museum commemorates the history of, and activities at, March Field

during its long history. The Museum has over 70 aircraft, many of them of WW II vintage. The others range from WW I bi-planes to jets. Many of the planes are flyable. Inside the Museum are displays and exhibits on a variety of related subjects. Adjacent to the Museum is the P-38 Hangar which highlights that aircraft which was one that operated from March Field during the war. The Museum has a library and a very nice gift shop. Address: 22550 Van Buren Blvd., Riverside, CA 92518. Phone and website: 951-902-5949; www.marchfield.org

The March Field Air Museum

San Gabriel is an affluent residential community just east of Los Angeles and was the home town of Gen. George S. Patton, Jr. The church which he and his family attended has a very unique memorial honoring the General.

The Patton Window: This is a stained glass window in The Church of Our Savior (Episcopal) in San Gabriel dedicated to the memory of General George S. Patton, Jr. It depicts St. George, the General's namesake, slaying a dragon whose belly is covered with green swastikas. In the dust clouds rising from the struggle are the names of Patton's victorious battles.
  Also in the church are windows dedicated to the General's mother and father as well as several plaques to him and other members of the Patton family.
  On the church grounds is a life-sized statue of the General in a garden setting. Address: The Church of Our Savior, 535 W. Roses Rd., San Gabriel, CA 91775. Phone and website: 626-282-5147. www.pattonhq.com/church.html. Church personnel are generally willing to receive visitors if the church is not in use. A phone call to the church office is suggested.

"The Patton Window" of The Church of Our Savior, San Gabriel, CA

Santa Ana is a large community 14 miles east of Long Beach.

Lyon Air Museum: This fine museum, located at John Wayne Airport, houses a collection of about half dozen vintage WW II aircraft, all of which have been restored to near new condition. There is also a collection of antique motor vehicles and motorcycles, some of them from the WW II era. The Museum offers group tours and has scheduled social events Address: 19300 Ike Jones Rd., Santa Ana, CA 92707. Phone and website: 714-210-4585; www.lyonairmuseum.org

The Lyon Air Museum in Santa Ana, CA

<u>Santa Monica</u>, directly west of downtown Los Angeles on the Pacific Ocean, was the home of one of the world's leading aircraft manufacturers, The Douglas Aircraft Co. Their C-47 transport plane, and it several versions, were the backbone of Allied air transport systems throughout WW II. The planes were generally known as "gooney birds."

Museum of Flying: This interesting museum was established in 1989 to perpetuate and preserve the aviation history of Santa Monica and was first built on the site of the original Douglas Aircraft Co. factory. The Museum has about 50 aircraft, some of which are flyable. The Museum highlights the Douglas Aircraft Co. and their aircraft. There are also displays of pre-WW II aircraft, postwar jets and NASA vehicles. The Museum has a library, an educational program, an art display, rare artifacts, a nice gift shop and is host to social events. Address: 3100 Airport Av., Santa Monica, CA 90405. Phone and website: 310-392-8822; useumofflying.com

Seal Beach is just east of downtown Long Beach and is home to a long-standing naval facility, US Naval Weapons Station, Seal Beach.

US Submarine Veterans WW II National Memorial West: This is a very impressive memorial at the gate of the US Naval Weapons Station, Seal Beach. It was created by, and dedicated to, USN submariners of WW II. There are 52 monuments with bronze plaques which record the name of all 52 US submarines lost during WW II. The plaques give the date and place each submarine was lost and the names of those aboard. Location: Seal Beach Blvd. and Bolsa Av. in Seal Beach. Phone for the US Naval Weapons Station, Seal Beach: 562-626-7011. Website for the Memorial: www.submarinehistory.com/WWIISubmarineMemorial.html

<u>South El Monte</u> is 15 miles east of downtown Los Angeles.

The US Submarine Veterans National Memorial West in Seal Beach, CA

Military Museum of the American Society of Military Historians:
This interesting museum has over 175 military vehicles on display. Among them are tanks, self-propelled guns, personnel carriers, armored cars, truck, Jeeps, motorcycles and more. Most are of American manufacture, but there are some foreign-made vehicles. Many are of WW II vintage. Some of the vehicles can be rented and the Museum has related artifacts, memorabilia and an education program. Address: The Whittier Narrows Recreation Area, 1918 Rosemead Av., South El Monte, CA 91733. Phone and website: 626-442-1776; http://tankland.com

END OF LOS ANGELES/LONG BEACH METROPOLITAN AREA:

MERCED is a county seat 20 miles NW of Fresno on SR-99 and SR-145.

MERCED COUNTY WORLD WAR II MEMORIAL: Near the top of this handsome stone memorial it reads "MERCED COUNTY CITIZENS WHO MADE THE SUPREME SACFIFICE FOR THEIR COUNTRY." Listed below are their names. This is a farming community with many Hispanic laborers and many of the names on the Memorial are Hispanic. There are several Japanese names also. Location: Merced County Courts House lawn

The Merced County WW II Memorial, Merced, CA

MURRIETA is a small community midway between Los Angeles and San Diego on I-15.

WORLD WAR II MEMORIAL WALL: The people of California were very much aware of what was happening in the Pacific during the war. This memorial depicts the people, places and events that took place in the Pacific theater. Pictures etched on the surface of the wall depict those events. Location: One Town Square, 24601 Jefferson Av., Murrieta, CA 92562

OAKLAND: (See San Francisco and the San Francisco Bay Metropolitan Area)

OROVILLE is a county seat 65 miles north of Sacramento on SR-70 and SR-162.

MILITARY MUSEUM OF BUTTE COUNTY, located in the city of Oroville, preserves the military history, art and memorabilia of Butte County. A large number of the items of display are from WW II. There are military vehicles, motorcycles, bicycles, rocket launchers, antitank weapons, information on carrier pigeons used during WW II and an impressive collection of military posters. Address: 4514 Pacific Heights Rd., Oroville, CA 95965. Phone and website: 530-534-9956; www.surpluscity.com/mmbc/index.html/

PALM SPRINGS is a resort area 90 miles ESE of downtown Los Angeles off I-10. During the war, the community's airport was used as a training field by the US Army Air Forces.

The Palm Springs Air Museum

PALM SPRINGS AIR MUSEUM is a large and beautiful museum at the Palm Springs Airport devoted exclusively to WW II aircraft and the men and women who built them, maintained them and flew them during WW II. There are some 30 WW II era aircraft on display. Many of them are airworthy and are often used in movies, on TV show and airshows.

The Museum has artifacts, artwork, photographs, memorabilia, uniforms, video presentations, a library, a nice gift shop and continuously good flying weather. Guided and educational tours are available and the Museum is available for social events. Address: 745 N. Gene Autry Trail, Palm Springs, CA 92262. Phone and web: 760-778-6262 ext. 222; www.palmspringsairmuseum.org

PASO ROBLES is 30 miles north of San Luis Obispo on US-101 and SR-46. Camp Roberts is nearby and was a major training base during WW II for infantry and artillery units.

CAMP ROBERTS HISTORICAL MUSEUM is on the grounds of Camp Roberts which was built in 1941 and named after a Congressional Medal of Honor recipient, Corporal Harold Roberts. The mission of the Museum is to familiarize visitors with the long legacy of Camp Roberts as a major training site for the American military.

In the Museum are exhibits and displays related to Camp Roberts and its participation in American military history from WW II to the present. There is information about the WACs (Women's Army Corps), civilian workers, visits by celebrities who entertained at the Camp, sports activities, vintage vehicles and more. There is also a library and a well-stocked gift shop. Address: New Mexico Av., Camp Roberts, CA 93451. Phone and website: 805-238-8425 and 805-237-0819; www.militarymuseum.org/camprobertsmuseum.html

PETALUMA is about 35 miles north of San Francisco on US-101.

MILITARY ANTIQUES AND MUSEUM: This is a very unique establishment. It is both a museum and a store selling many kinds of military collectibles including many WW II items. All of the items on display constitute the museum and many are available of sale. There are deactivated arms, swords, bayonets, battlefield relics, home front memorabilia, posters, military books, military toys and a wide variety of WW II items from the US, Britain, Germany, Japan and other foreign countries. They also can offer military motorcycles and vehicles. Address: 300 Petaluma Blvd. N., Petaluma, CA 94952. Phone and website: 707-763-2220; www.militaryantiquesmuseum.com

PORT HUENEME is a deep-water seaport just south of Oxnard off SR-1. During the war, a very specialized naval base was built here for the US Navy's Construction Battalions better known as the "SeaBees."

US NAVY SEABEE MUSEUM is on the grounds of the old Port Hueneme Naval Construction Battalion Center now known as Naval Base Ventura County. The Museum is a lasting memorial to the Seabees and the Navy's Civil Engineer Corps (CEC) who built naval facilities all over the world during WW II and still does so to this day. On display are numerous weapons, uniforms, tools, instruments, underwater equipment, Arctic equipment, vehicles, etc. used by the Engineers and Seabees. There is also a library, an archives and an interesting Museum Store. Museum Address: Naval Base Ventura County, Building 100, Port Hueneme, CA 93043. Phone and website: 805-982-5165; www.history.navy.mil/museums/seabee_museum.htm

RIPON is a small community 14 miles south of Stockton on SR-99.

RIPON WORLD WAR II MEMORIAL: A bronze statue of three WW II servicemen highlights this fine memorial and epitomizes the sacrifice made by small towns throughout the US during the war. The small town aspect is emphasizes because at the base of the statues are the names of 14 Ripon High School graduates from the class of 1940 who gave their lives during the war out of a class of 50 students. Nearby is a memorial wall listing the names of others from Ripon who served in the war. Also nearby is the Ripon Veterans Museum. Location: S. Locust St. at W. First St.

The Ripon World War II Memorial, Ripon, CA

SACRAMENTO is the capitol of California and was a city of 106,000 people at the beginning of the war. Several important military installations were in the area.

CALIFORNIA STATE MILITARY MUSEUM is located in downtown Sacramento in the Old Sacramento State Historic Park. It is dedicated to preserving and honoring the rich legacy of California's military history with special emphasis on the California National Guard.

The Museum has on display over 30,000 military-related documents, papers and memorabilia as well as information on famous Californians such as Gen. George S. Patton, Jr., Jimmy Doolittle, Gen. Henry "Hap" Arnold and others. A significant number of displays are devoted to the WW II era. There is a library and a large archives collection. Address: 1119 2nd St., Sacramento, CA 95814. Phone and website: 916-854-1900; www.militarymuseum.org

SALINAS is a county seat 15 miles east of Monterrey on US-101, SR-68 and SR-183.

1944 BATAAN MEMORIAL: Here is a very unique memorial - a halftrack in a cage. There is a plaque which is inscribed "1944 BATAAN MEMORIAL: THIS

The 1944 Bataan Memorial, Salinas, CA

HALFTRACK, DEDICATED ON APRIL 8, 2006, HONORS THE 105 MEN OF COMPANY 194TH TANK BATTALION FROM THE SALINAS AND PAJAROS CELLEYS. FEW AMERICANS ARE AWARE OF THE HARDSHIPS AND SUFFERING THEY FACED IN THE PHILIPPINES, AND AS PRISONERS OF WAR IN WWII." Location: At the Boranda Historical Center, 333 Boranda Rd.

SAN DIEGO and the SAN DIEGO METROPOLITAN AREA:

San Diego: San Diego had, long before the war, become a "Navy town" because of the many US Navy, Marine and Coast Guard installations in the area. Early in the war, San Diego was chosen as the new headquarters of the Pacific Fleet after the headquarters left Honolulu. It also served as the home base to many of the Navy's Pacific Fleet operations and warships during the war.

Camp Pendleton: This is one of the nation's largest Marine Camps located just north of San Diego. The Camp has three museums. For general information about the Museums contact Commanding Officer, History Museums, HQ SPT BN, Box 555031 Marine Corps Base Camp Pendleton CA 92055.

Marine Corps Mechanized Command Museum is on the grounds of Camp Pendleton and houses working vehicles used by the Marine Corps since 1942. A large part of the collection includes amphibian landing craft of various types used in Marine Corps conflicts. Location: Building 2612 on Vandegrift Blvd.

MCRD (Marine Corps Recruit Depot) Command Museum: This is one of the three Marine museums at Camp Pendleton. It has over 22,000 Sq. ft. of indoor space and has extensive and large and comprehensive display relating the US Marine Corps throughout its long history. Displays on WW II are sizable and informative. There are research archives, an educational program and a fascinating gift shop. Address: Day Hall, building 26, Marine Corps recruit Depot, San Diego, CA 92055. Phone and website: 619-524-6719; www.mcrdmuseumhistoricalsociety.org

WW II/Korea LVT Museum is located at Camp Del Mar, a part of the Camp Pendleton complex, and houses exhibits of amphibious landing vehicles used in WW II and the Korean War. Highlighted in the Museum is the service of the "Alligator" Marines who served during these two conflicts. Location: Building 21561: Phone: 760-725-2195

The WW II/Korea LVT Museum at Camp Pendleton, CA.

San Diego Aerospace Museum in Balboa Park in a large and excellent museum in the Park's multi-building complex. It memorializes the important people and major advances in the field of aviation and aerospace. There are about 90 aircraft in the Museum's collection and the aircraft on display are arranged in galleries. Some of the aircraft were built in San Diego and many of the aircraft are in mint condition.

There is a WW II Gallery as well as a WW I Gallery which highlights planes of those eras. The Museum has a library, a large archives collection, a bountiful gift shop, and an educational program. Guided tours are available. The Museum also has an annex at Gillespie Field, 10 miles. Northeast of downtown San Diego, this serves as a restoration facility, and additional display facility. The Annex is open to the public. Address of the Museum at Balboa Park: 2001 Pan American Plaza, Balboa Park, San Diego, CA 92101. Phone and website: 619-234-8291; www.sandiegoairandspace.org

The San Diego Aerospace Museum

San Diego Aircraft Carrier Museum: This museum floats. It is the retired WW II aircraft carrier *USS Midway* permanently anchored on the San Diego waterfront. This ship was launched during WW II on, March 20, 1945, but was not commissioned until the following September and therefor saw no action in WW II. The ship is of typical WW II design, however, and served the Navy until the 1990s - longer than any other US aircraft carrier.

In 1947, a captured German V-2 rocked was launched from the ship's deck, the first time that that missile had been launched from a moving platform. The *Midway* participated in every American war between WW II and Desert Storm. The ship has about 27 aircraft in its collection but most of them, but not all, are post-war models. There are some 60 exhibits aboard the ship and visitors can enter the crew's sleeping quarters, engine room, officers' quarters, pilots' ready room, post office and jail.

The Museum also has many social and educational events. Address: *USS Midway* Museum, 910 N. Harbor Dr., San Diego, CA 92101.Phone and website: 619-544-9600 www.midway.org

Veterans Museum and Memorial Center: This museum is housed in the chapel building of the former San Diego Naval Hospital at Inspiration Point in Balboa Park. It serves as a host for programs that perpetuate the memories of deceased veterans or members of the US armed forces for all of America's wars. There are rotating displays of military artifacts, uniforms, photographs, memorabilia and art work. The WW II portion of the Museum is well representative. The Museum supports charitable, social and scientific programs, has a educational program and   serves as a meeting place for veteran and other related purposes. Address: 2115 Park

The USS Midway, now a museum at her permanent berth in downtown San Diego, CA

Blvd., San Diego, CA 92101. Phone and website: 619-239-2300; www.veteranmuseum.org

END OF SAN DIEGO and the SAN DIEGO METROPOLITAN AREA:

SAN FRANSICSO and the SAN FRANCISCO BAY METROPOLITAN AREA:

San Francisco: When WW II started, the San Francisco Bay area was one of the most important seaports, commercial and manufacturing centers in the country. With a dozen or so major shipyards, scattered around the Bay, it was #1 in American shipbuilding. In the months just before the war, the area's shipyards were nearing their capacity to build ships. When the US went to war in Dec. 1941 the Bay area's shipyards and other industries suddenly boomed and the Bay area cities quickly became crowded, and then over-crowded, with people. Shortages of many civilian goods and services soon developed and got worse as the war progressed. The Bay area soon acquired a nation-wide reputation as being an area in trouble. Articles were placed in some national publications advising tourists and other would-be visitors <u>not</u> to come to San Francisco because they could not be accommodated.

   In the latter months of the war, living and economic conditions slowly improved, but did not get back to normal until several years after the war.

Lincoln Park: This beautiful park is in the NW corner of the city, and has two interesting WW II memorials. One is a Holocaust memorial, which is located on Legion of Honor Dr. across from the Palace of the Legion of Honor. It commemorates the victims of the Nazi Holocaust. The other is a memorial commemorating the cruiser *USS San Francisco* which saw some of the earliest naval action in the Pacific during the war. The memorial is located near the end of El Camino Del Mar Street and honors the crew and captain of the *San Francisco* which was badly damaged during the Battle of Guadalcanal on the night of Nov. 12-13, 1942. Many of the crew and the ship's captain, Rear Adm. Daniel J. Callaghan, were killed in that battle. Parts of the ship's bridge are incorporated into the monument and still bear the shell holes received during the battle.

Jeremiah O'Brien **Liberty Ship**, a relic of WW II, is permanently moored at Pier 45 at the foot of Taylor St. in the Fisherman's Wharf area of San Francisco. It has been dedicated as the National Liberty Ship Memorial, is a National Historic Landmark and is open to the public. This is an operating ship that has been restored to its wartime condition and takes several cruises each year with fee-paying passengers. Phone and website: 415-544-0100; www.ssjeremiahobrien.org

The USS San Francisco Memorial in Lincoln Park

The West Coast Memorial is a large monument on the west side of the San Francisco Presidio at the junction of Lincoln and Harrison Blvd. on a promontory overlooking the Pacific Ocean. It commemorates the 412 men of the US armed forces who lost their lives in the US waters off the West

Coast during WW II and whose bodies were never recovered. The name, rank and branch of service of all 412 are engraved in the monument.

San Francisco Maritime National Historic Park: This is a very unique national park on the San Francisco water front. It consists of a maritime museum, a library/research facility, a visitor' Center and several historic ships including the WW II submarine *USS Pampanito*. The Museum is located at the foot of Polk St., directly across from Ghirardelli Square, and has many displays on the water transportation of the area since the early 1800s.

The West Coast Memorial in San Francisco

The *Pampanito* is located at Pier 45 at Fisherman's Wharf and is open to the public. During WW II, the submarine made six combat patrols and sank six Japanese ships and damaged four others.

There is an educational program devoted to the *Pampanito* and overnight stays on the submarine are available.

The Visitor's Center is at the corner of Jefferson and Hyde Streets and is a good place to start one's visit. Visitor's Center phone: 415-447-5000. Park website: www.nps.gov/safr

San Francisco War Memorial and Performing Arts Center: This is a complex of several buildings at Van Ness and McAllister Sts. in San Francisco's Civic Center. The complex was begun after WW I and was expanded in the years between the wars. In the Veterans' building a very historical event took place - the birth of the United Nations Organization. It came into being here after WW II. Delegates from the victorious Allied nations met in this building from Apr. 25 to June 26, 1946 to draw up and approve the United Nations Charter. On June 26, 1945, a ceremony was held in the Herbst Theater and representative of 50 nations signed documents creating the United Nations Organization and implementing its Charter. A large mural in the theater depicts that event, and the United Nations Plaza, across from the theater, commemorates the United Nations Organization.

In 1951, the Treaty of San Francisco, which formally ended the war between the United States and Japan, was signed in the Opera House. Address: 401 Van Ness Av., San Francisco, CA 94102. Phone and website: 415-621-6600; http://sfwmpac.org

Alameda is a city on the eastern shore of San Francisco Bay consisting mostly of Alameda Island and was, for many years, home to a huge Navy installation, the US Naval Air Station, Alameda.

Alameda Naval Air Museum: This fine museum is located in the former air terminal building #77 at Alameda Point (the northern part of Alameda Island). It traces the history of the naval air station from WW II up to the time of its closing in 1997.

On display in the Museum are artifacts, photos, aircraft models, stories of wartime workers at the station, old newspapers, documents, uniforms, safety gear and other memorabilia related the the naval air station and its long history. The Museum has archival material and an educational program. Mail address: PO Box 1769, Alameda, CA 94501. Phone and website: 510-522-4262; http://alamedanavalairmuseum.org

***USS Hornet* Museum:** This is one of the most famous aircraft carriers of WW II and is now serving as a floating museum. It is the second *Hornet* of the war. The first *Hornet*, (CV-8), was lost at Midway. This ship (CV-12) was launched just 10 months after that loss and served throughout the remainder of the Pacific war and saw considerable action. The Carrier was reactivated for the Korean War and again for the Vietnam War. It also participated in the recovery of Apollo space capsules at sea during the early days of the US space program. The ship was decommissioned in June 1970 and eventually brought to Alameda Point on the site of the former NAS, Alameda to serve as a floating museum.

There are several vintage aircraft aboard this ship but most are post-war. There is also a gift shop, rental facilities are available and the ship is a National Historic Landmark. Address: 707 W Hornet Av., Alameda CA 94501. Phone and website: 510-521-8448, www.uss-hornet.org

<u>Concord</u> is inland from the San Francisco Bay on the southern shore of the Carquinez Straits and SR-4.

The Port Chicago Naval Magazine National Memorial

Port Chicago Naval Magazine National Memorial: At this site one of the great tragedies of WW II within the United States occurred. Port Chicago Naval Magazine was a storage facility for naval ammunition. On July 17, 1944 two cargo vessels, anchored on either side of a pier, were being loaded with ammunition. Suddenly, one ship, then the other, exploded from an unknown cause killing 320 US Servicemen and wounding many others. Both ships, the pier and a number of surrounding buildings were totally destroyed. The site became a national memorial in 1992 and visitors can still see the remnants of the pier as well as bunkers, revetments and munitions boxcars that were in use at the time of the explosion. Interpretive panels and a large granite monument lists the names of those killed in the blast. Phone and website: 925-228-8860; www.mps.gov/poch/index.htm

The Eagle Park WWII Memorial in Mountain View, CA

Mountain View is NW of San Jose near Moffett Federal Airfield.

Eagle Park WW II Memorial: Here in this beautiful urban park is a memorial honoring those of the local area who served and died in WW II. A memorial plaque lists their names. Location: 650 Franklin, Mountain View, CA.

Novato is a small community in northern Marin County on US-101. During the war, it was home to one of the largest Army Air Forces bases in the area, Hamilton Field.

Hamilton Field Historic Museum is located at the former Hamilton Field air base in the air base's old firehouse. It preserves the history of the base from its beginning in 1935 until it closing in the 1970s.

  Inside the Museum are exhibits pertaining to the importance of the base, the daily lives of those who served here and the base's eventual re-use. There is a research library and an archives collection.
Address: 555 Hangar Av., Novato, CA 94949.
Phone: 415-382-8614

Oakland, the "other" big city in the San Francisco Bay area, is on the eastern shore of the Bay. Before the war, it was a major seaport, manufacturing center and home to several shipyards and military facilities. When WW II began, Oakland became a troubled boom town like some of the other Bay cities. Because of its well-developed port facilities, Oakland became a major embarkation center for both troops and war materials going overs-seas.

The Hamilton Field History Museum in Novato, CA

USS Potomac (Presidential yacht): This was President Franklin Roosevelt's presidential yacht which, in his time, was called "The Floating White House."

  The ship was built in 1934 as the Coast Guard cutter *Electra* but was soon renamed the *USS Potomac* and assigned to serve the President. President Roosevelt had, earlier in his political career, served as the Assistant Secretary of the Navy and had a deep love for the sea and the US Navy. He, his family and associates used the yacht frequently until the US entered the war in December 1941.

The vessel was then handed over to the Navy and used for sonar research. After Roosevelt's death in April 1945, the Yacht was sold and passed through the hands of several owners including Elvis Presley. The vessel's last owners used it for drug smuggling and were eventually caught and the vessel was confiscated by the US government. It was then towed to Treasure Island, sank in an accident, was refloated and sold to the Port of Oakland for $15,000. The vessel is now a National Historic Landmark and permanently berthed at the Oakland waterfront and open to the public. Cruises aboard the yacht are offered to the public, the yacht can be chartered for special events and social activities and available on the yacht including weddings. Address: 540 Water St. (near Jack Square), Oakland, CA 94607.
Phone and website: 510-627-1215;
http://usspotomac.org

The USS Potomac, President Franklin Roosevelt's Presidential yacht, permanently berthed in Oakland, CA

Richmond, on the NE shore of San Francisco Bay was a port city and industrial town of 23,000 people before the war. Then, suddenly, it became one of the Bay area's most explosive boom towns because the port city was selected to be the site of several large shipyards and several other manufacturing entities. Unfortunately, Richmond was to become so overwhelmed by war work and people that it became one of the most troubled communities in America. It is recorded that some war workers had to live in tents, their cars and under bushes.

Rosie The Riveter WW II Home Front National Historic Park and the *Red Oak Victory*: This is a national park devoted entirely to WW II and the people in the Home Front industry who produced the goods of war. Special recognition is given to the American women who made up a large percentage of the wartime work force. The phrase "Rosie the Riveter" became very popular during the war from a war poster showing a muscular woman doing a job usually assigned to men.

There is an interesting memorial in the Park called the "Rosie Memorial" and the centerpiece of the Park is a wartime cargo vessel, the *Red Oak Victory*. This ship was originally built in Richmond, saw many years of service during and after the war, was restored and returned to the Park. It is now open to the public.

This National Park is not to be confused with the city park with the same name, Rosie the Riveter Park, in the Long Beach area of Los Angeles. Address of Rosie the Riveter Home Front National Park: 2566 McDonald Av., Richmond, CA 94804. Phone and website: (park) 510-507-2276, (ship) 510-237-2933; www.rosietheriveter.org

The Rosie the Riveter poster was so popular that it was featured on the cover of The Saturday Evening Post magazine and served as the inspiration for the Rosie the Riveter WW II Home Front National Historic Park.

San Jose is at the southern end of San Francisco Bay.

Japanese American Internment Memorial: This memorial commemorates the ethnic Japanese citizens of California who were forcefully relocated to relocation camps in the interior of the US during the war. The Memorial consists of a large black stone wall with reliefs depicting the forced relocation,

39

the camps and those Japanese young men who volunteered to join the US Army. Location: South 2nd and San Carlos Sts., San Jose, CA

San Leandro is on the eastern shore of San Francisco Bay on I-580 and I-680.

Lost Boats Memorial: This fine memorial commemorates two US submarines that were lost during WW II, the *SS Argonaut* and the *USS Grampus.*
 The centerpiece of the Memorial is a WW II torpedo mounted on two pedestals. Plaques on the Memorial list the names of the sailors lost and the last date of contact with the vessel. At the bottom of

The Japanese internment Memorial in San Jose, CA

each plague is the statement
"MAY THEY REST IN PEACE WHILE ON ETERNAL PATROL." Location: At the San Leandro Marina.

San Rafael is the county seat for Marin County and is on San Pablo Bay, the northern most part of the San Francisco Bay.

The Lost Boats Memorial in San Leandro, CA

World War II Memorial, Avenue of Flags: This is one of a group of war memorials in a park-like setting honoring those who died in America's wars. There is a memorial for WW I, Korea, Viet Nam and a Merchant Marine Memorial.
 The center section of this three section WW II memorial has bronze plaques listing the names of those from Marin County who died during the war. Location: Avenue of the Flags, San Rafael, CA.

The World War II Memorial, Avenue of Flags, in San Rafael, CA

Sunnyvale is eight miles NW of San Jose and was home to a very large naval base, Moffett Field. This facility began in the 1930s as a base for dirigibles.
 During WW II it was used as a base for Navy blimps patrolling the West Coast and for other war-related purposes Moffett Field was closed as a naval facility in 1993.

Moffett Field Historical Society Museum: This is a three-building complex on the grounds of the former Moffett Field and includes the very large and magnificent landmark - dirigible Hangar #1. The Museum traces the history of the Field through its entire existence.
 Exhibits on the WW II era are numerous and informative. There are artifacts, photos, documents, uniforms, flight gear, aircraft models, information on blimps, military manuals, firearms and more. The

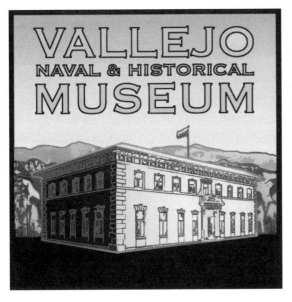

Museum also has an interesting gift shop. Mail Address: PO Box 16, Moffett Field, CA 94035. Phone and website: 650-964-4024; www.moffettfieldmuseum.org

Vallejo, at the NE corner of the San Francisco Bay and the entrance to Carquines Strait, was another Bay area boom town during WW II. The Navy's Mare Island Naval Shipyard, with its huge shipbuilding facilities and other navy operations, was the main employer in the area. Tens of thousands of workers flocked to Vallejo. By 1944, Vallejo's population, which had been 20,000 in 1940, had grown to 100,000.

Vallejo Naval and Historical Museum: This museum, near downtown Vallejo, is the old Vallejo city hall and is on the National Register of Historic Places. The Museum records the history of Vallejo and its close association with the naval base at Mare Island. The Museum has several galleries one of which, the Saginaw Gallery, has permanent exhibits on Mare Island and US Navy history.

   In addition, there is a working periscope from the WW II submarine *Baya* through which one can view the town of Vallejo and Mare Island. The Museum also has a research library and an interesting gift store. Address: 734 Marin St., Vallejo, CA 94590. Phone and website: 707-643-0077; www.vallejomuseum.og

END OF SAN FRANCISCO and the SAN FRANCISCO BAY METROPOLITAN AREA:

<u>SANTA BARBARA</u> is a county seat and a beautiful beach community 95 miles NW of downtown Los Angeles on US-101 and SR-192.

AIRMEM MEMORIAL - SANTA BARBARA: This is a unique WW II memorial in that it honors local men who were aviators during the war and who were killed. Inscribed on the memorial is this tribute, "IN MEMORY OF THE LOCAL AVIATORS WHO PERISHED IN WORLD WAR II." Their names are listed on the memorial. There are 49 of them. Location: East side of the Santa Barbara Airport on Fowler Rd.

<u>VISALIA</u> is a county seat 60 miles north of Bakersfield on SR-63 and SR-193.

The Airmen Memorial – Santa Barbara in Santa Barbara, CA

WORLD WAR II MEMORIAL: Here is a large artistic mural entitled "The Greatest Generation." It is 19 ft. high by 72 ft. long and is the largest such mural on the West Coast. It is lighted at night, handsomely landscaped, and has a flag pole and a fountain.

The pictures on the wall were copied from actual photographs made during WW II. There are pictures of our Presidents, WW II aircraft, ships and ordinary people who served their country. Location: On the southern edge of town at the intersection of S. Mooney Blvd. and W. Caldwell Av.

This is a part of the huge mural that serves as a WW II Memorial for the city of Visalia, CA.

WEED is a small community in northern California in the shadow of Mt. Shasta. It is on I-5 and US-97.

THE GREATEST GENERATION: This interesting memorial is a stylized version of the famous flag rising at Iwo Jima. The sculpture was created by Dennis Smith, an artist, who presented it to his father, a WW II veteran. It is now on public display. Location: Living Memorial Sculpture Garden, 13 miles NE of Weed on US-97

The Greatest Generation Memorial near Weed, CA

COLORADO

Colorado, like most western states, experienced substantial economic and population growth during WW II.

Colorado's manufacturing and agricultural sectors grew at a considerable rate and the Federal Government built several major new installations in Colorado and generously expanded those that already existed. Most of the military bases built or enlarged during the war remained in operation after the war and contributed significantly to Colorado's on-going economy. Colorado also became the home state of the new US Air Force Academy.

ASPEN is a county seat in west central Colorado on SR-82 and is one of the most famous ski resorts in the country. During the war, US Army Ski troops of the 10th Mountain Division were trained nearby.

The 10th Mountain Division Memorial in Aspen, CO

10TH MOUNTAIN DIVISION MEMORIAL: They were the US Army's ski troops and they fought in Alaska and Italy. The Memorial consists of a bronze statue of a ski trooper, on skis, coming down a snowy slope with rifle in hand. On the base of the Memorial is the slogan of the 10th Mountain Division "We Conquer Men and Mountains." Location: 600 E. Dean Ct. at the Aspen Mountain Ski Resort near the Little Dell Gondola

BRECKENRIDGE/LEADVILLE/VAIL AREA: This is ski country. Breckenridge and Leadville are county seats about 65 miles west of downtown Denver and Vail is a world famous ski resort town to the north off I-70. In 1942, the Government built a large training camp, Camp Hale, midway between Breckenridge and Leadville to train US Army mountain troops. Camp Hale was at 9,300 ft. altitude and had abundant snow the year around. The troops training here frequently operated on skis and and in cold weather mountain gear. They later saw considerable action in the Aleutian Islands of Alaska and Italy and suffered numerous casualties. After the war, some of the men who trained here settled here and were instrumental in turning the local area into a skier's paradise. There are two memorials in the area dedicated to the US Army's Mountain Troops.

10TH MOUNTAIN DIVISION MEMORIAL (BRECKENRIDGE): When you enter the Riverfront Park in Breckenridge, CO, you will see a life-sized sculpture of a WW II soldier on skis. This is the 10th Mountain Division Memorial. It pays honor to the 15,000 soldiers who trained at nearby Camp Hale and who later served with great distinction in the Aleutian Island of Alaska and Italy. Location: Riverfront Park, Breckenridge, CO 80424

The 10th Mountain Division Memorial at Breckenridge, CO

The Ski Trooper Memorial at Vail, CO

THE SKI TROOPER MEMORIAL (VAIL): He's seven feet tall carrying skis and dressed in white. This impressive memorial honors the soldiers of the 10th Mountain Division that trained at nearby Camp Hale and later fought in the Aleutian Island of Alaska and Italy. Location: In Vail, near the famous covered pedestrian bridge and the Colorado Ski Museum.

COLORADO SPRINGS is at the foot of Pike's Peak. A new and large Army training camp was built here during the war just south of town - Camp Carson. Infantry and armored divisions trained at Camp Carson as did mountain divisions and WAC (Women's Army Corps) units. Also located here during the war was a large Army airfield, Peterson Field, which was the area's local airport

COLORADO SPRINGS HISTORICAL MILITARY MUSEUM: When you walk into this museum you might encounter the "Dragon Man." That's Mel "Dragon Man" Bernstein. He put this 43,000 Sq. ft. museum together and did a magnificent job of it. There are about 100 military vehicles, some of them foreign-made, lots of other military items and artifacts and some 200 manikins decked out in military gear in the Museum's many displays.

About 85% of the Museum's content is related to the WW II era. One of the most interesting displays is of a sandbag bunker typical of the ones used in WW II. Address: 1220 Dragon Man Dr., Colorado Springs, CO 80929. Phone and website: 719-683-2800 and 719-683-2200; www.dragonmans.com/museum

PETERSON AIR & SPACE MUSEUM: This museum is located on the grounds of the former Peterson Air Force Base and preserves the history of aviation in the Colorado Springs area, the history of Peterson AFB and the history of the North American Aerospace Defense Command (NORAD). There are some 20 aircraft and missiles on display, most of which are post-war. There are many other items on display related to the museum's story and mission. There is a gift shop and the Museum is host to several social events each year. Address: 150 E. Ent Av., Colorado Springs, CO 80914-1303. Phone and website: 719-556-4915; www.petemuseum.org

The Peterson Air & Space Museum near Trinidad, CO

US AIR FORCE ACADEMY: The US Air Force Academy did not exist during WW II. It was built in 1954 after the US Air Force became an independent branch of the armed services. The Academy is 14 miles north of Colorado Springs with access from I-25. There is a Visitors' Center, accessible from I-25 exit 156B, where visitors can arrange tours of the Academy and obtain other basic information. The Center has a gift shop, snack bar and theater. Many of the buildings and other facilities are named after famous individuals of WW II. Visitors may roam the Academy grounds from dawn to dusk and there is a paved nature trail and a picnic area.

In the Academy's cemetery, off Parade Loop Dr., are many veterans of WW II including Air Force Generals, Carl Spaatz, Curtis LeMay, Donavon Smith and George Stratemeyer. There are several memorial walls at the cemetery bearing plaques honoring various air units, many of which are from WW II.

There are restrictions and security measures concerning visitors and it is recommended that visitors phone or contact the Visitors' Center before arriving. Address: US Air Force Academy, USAFA, CO 80840. Phone and website for the Visitors' Center: 719-333-2025; www.usafa.af.mil/information/visitors/index.asp

DENVER is the capitol of Colorado and was another of the west's boom towns during the war. During the war there were an arsenal, fort, military hospital, ordnance plant and three army airfields in the area.

LITTLETON WORLD WAR II MEMORIAL: Littleton is a southern suburb of Denver with an impressive multi-monument memorial honoring those individuals from the local area who served in WW II. It is the center piece of a pleasant city park. Location: In Ketring Park, 6000 S. Gallup St., Littleton, CO

The Littleton World War II Memorial in Littleton, CO

NISEI WAR MEMORIAL: The word"Nisei" means first generation Japanese American – the sons and daughters of the original Japanese immigrants. During WW II, many ethnic Japanese were transferred, by an Executive Order from President Roosevelt, from the US West Coast to relocation camps scattered across the western and central parts of the country. Many of the ethnic Japanese became very angry with the US government for such treatment, but some of the young men of military age, over 30,000 of them, overcame their anger and volunteered for service in the US Army.

They were formed into an Army unit known as the 442nd Regimental Combat Team and served with great distinction in Italy.

This fine memorial honors those men and their loyalty and service to our country. The names of those who gave their lives are engraved in the Monument's stone pillars. Location: In a private cemetery at 430 S. Quebec St., Denver, CO. 80247

The Nisei War Memorial in Denver

USS GRAYLING **(SS-209) MEMORIAL:** The *USS Grayling* was Colorado's submarine and was so acknowledged by the US Navy because many Coloradans served aboard her. Unfortunately, the vessel was sunk in 1943 on her eighth patrol in the Pacific. All hands were lost. The Memorial bears plaques honoring those who served aboard her and is topped with a WW II era torpedo, and has a flag pole at the rear. Location: In a public park at 17th and Sheridan Sts., Denver, CO

The USS Grayling(SS-209) Memorial

GRANADA is a small community in SE Colorado near the Kansas border and on US-50. During the war, one of the Relocation Camps for ethnic Japanese from the US West Coast, Camp Amache, was located nearby

AMACHE REMEMBERED: This memorial is in the old Japanese cemetery at Camp Amache. The inscription on the monument tells the whole story: " DEADICATE TO THE 31 PATRIOTIC JAPANESE AMERICANS WHO VOLUNTEERED FROM AMACHE AND DUTIFULLY GAVE THEIR LIVES IN WORLD WAR II, TO THE APRROXINATELY 7000 PERSONS WHO WERE

45

RELOCATED AT AMACHE, AND TO THE 120 WHO DIES HERE DIRUNG THIS PERIOD OF OPERATION AUGUST 27, 1942- OCTOBER 14, 1945

The Amanche Remembered Memorial near Granada, CO

LEADVILLE (See Breckenridge/Leadville/Vail)

MODEL is a small community in southern Colorado 20 mile NE of Trinidad on SR-350 which is part of the historic Santa Fe Trail.

B-24 BOMBER CRASH SITE MEMORIAL: During the war, two B-24 bombers, on training missions during 1944, collided with each other in midair and the wreckage of both planes crashed on both sides of SR-350 near Model. One man was able to exit his plane and parachute to safety. All of the other crew members of both planes perished. This is a roadside memorial honoring those men and listing their names. Location: At mile marker 15 north of Model on SR-350

PUEBLO was Colorado's second largest city at the time of WW II and had the Pueblo Army Air Base which was the community's local airport. The community was also home to the Pueblo Ordnance Depot.

The B-24 Bomber Crash Site Memorial near Model, CO

B-24 MEMORIAL MUSEUM/FRED E. WIESBROD MUSEUM: This is two museums in one. The Fred E. Wiesbrod Museum is the larger of the two and displays many aircraft from the post-war era. It also preserves the history of the Pueblo Army Air Base of WW II. Inside the Wiesbrod Museum is a smaller museum, the B-24 Memorial Museum, which is dedicated to telling the story of, and preserving the history of, that famous WW II aircraft. While the B-24 Museum does not have a B-24 aircraft, they have a mountain of information about the bomber, its service during WW II, the people who made the aircraft and the crews that flew them. This fine two-in-one museum is located on the grounds of the Pueblo Memorial Airport. There is a nice gift shop and the museum offers other services to visitors. Address: 31001 Magnuson Ave., Pueblo, CO 81001. Phone and website: 719-948-9219; www.pwam.org

The WW II Memorial at Trinidad, CO

TRINIDAD is a county seat on SE Colorado near the New Mexico border on I-25, US-160 and SR-239.

WORLD WAR II MEMORIAL: Trinidad has a very interesting WW II Memorial at the state Welcome Center, south of town. It is one of three memorials. The others commemorate the Korean Conflict and the Viet Nam conflicts. The WW II Memorial lists the names of the men and women from Las Animas County who served in the war. Location: Welcome Center on I-25 south of Trinidad, CO

VALE (See Breckenridge/Leadville/Vale Area)

CONNECTICUT

At the beginning of the war, Connecticut's economy was well diversified into manufacturing, commercial, agricultural and military sectors. The state had 2936 manufacturing establishments, and in 1940 was 3rd in the nation in aircraft production. The state was a leader in the manufacture of submarines, small arms ammunition, machine tools, brass products and the mineral, mica, which was used in the aircraft industry. In 1942 Connecticut was first in the nation in war production per capita.

DANBURY is on the western edge of the state on I-84 and US-7.

MILITARY MUSEUM OF SOUTHERN NEW ENGLAND: This fine museum originated as an effort to maintain the memory of the American tank destroyer units of WW II and has grown to cover the history of all branches of the US military. It concentrates heavily on the military history of the 20th

Century. There are over 10,000 artifacts in the Museum plus dioramas, a magnificent collection of artillery pieces, vehicles and tanks - some of them quite rare. A large percentage of these items are from WW II. There is a gift shop and the museum is active in public events. Tours are available. Address: 125 Park Av., Danbury, CT 06810. Phone and website: 203-790-9277; www.usmilitarymuseum.org

GROTON/NEW LONDON : Groton is on the eastern coast of Connecticut on I-95 and at the mouth of the Thames River. It has long been the home of the US Coast Guard Academy.

US COAST GUARD MUSEUM: This fine museum, on the grounds of the US Coast Guard Academy, preserves the long history of the Coast Guard and its three predecessors, the Revenue-Cutter Service, the Lighthouse Service and the Lifesaving Service.

 On display are uniforms, field equipment, ship, airplane models, photographs, paintings, flags, figureheads and various other artifacts related to the US Coast Guard. The Museum has a library and a nice gift shop. Of special interest to WW II historians is the Academy's training bark *Eagle.* This three-masted sailing ship was a part of the German Navy's training program during WW II and was then known as the *Horst Wessel,* a hero of the Nazi Party. This ship was acquired by the US Coast Guard after the war, renamed *Eagle,* and served as a seagoing classroom for US Coast Guard cadets. Museum address: 15 Mohegan Av., New London, CT 06320. Phone and website: 860-444-8511; www.uscg.mil/hq/cg092/museum/

This is the US Coast Guard training bark Eagle.
During WW II it was a training ship for the
German navy called the Horst Wessel.

US NAVY SUBMARINE FORCE MUSEUM: This is a large memorial museum located on the Thames River in Groton. It is the only submarine museum operated by the US Navy and, as such, has acquired a very large library and document collection on submarine history and has become the primary repository of the records and history of the US Submarine Force.

 In the Museum, are many submarine-oriented artifacts including a working periscope, an authentic submarine control room, two theaters, models of submarines, submarine parts, personal memorabilia, photographs, information on other submersible vehicles, maps, documents and an extensive display wall tracing the development of US submarines from their inception to the present. Along the Front Walk in front of the Museum are four midget submarines, two of which are from WW II. One is Italian and the other Japanese. The Museum has a large library and there is an interesting museum store.

 The Museum is also home to the *USS Nautilus*, the first nuclear-powered submarine. This very historic vessel may be boarded by visitors. Museum address: 1 Crystal Lake Rd., Groton, CT 06340. Phone and website: 860-694-3174 and 800-343-0079; www.ussnautilus.org

HARTFORD/NEW BRITAIN: Hartford is Connecticut's capitol and largest city. During the war its main airport, Brainard Field, was taken over by the US Air Forces and used to train fighter pilots. New Britain is a suburb of Hartford 15 miles to the SW on I-84.

EAST HARTFORD WORLD WAR II MEMORIAL: "LET NONE FORGET THEY GAVE THEIR ALL AND FALTERED NOT WHEN THE CALL CAME." That's one of the inscriptions on this memorial, along with others, that stand as a memorial to all who served and died in WW II from the East Hartford area. Atop the Memorial is a spread eagle and on the back is a very practical drinking fountain. Location: Martin Park, 307 Burnside Av., East Hartford, CT

NATIONAL IWO JIMA MEMORIAL: This is in New Britain and is an impressive 40 foot bronze and granite monument honoring the Americans who fought and died on Iwo Jima in February 1945. It consists of a stature replicating the famous photograph by Joe Rosenthal of the raising of the US flag on Mt. Suribachi. The six Marines that raised the flag are immortalized in the monument and the honored dead are remembered by an eternal flame. Location: SR-9 (Iwo Jima Memorial Expressway) at exit 29 (Ella Grasso Blvd.) in Newington, CT

The East Hartford World War II Memorial

NEW BRITAIN (See Hartford/New Britain)

NEW LONDON: (See Groton/New London)

WALLINGFORD is a small community midway between Hartford and New Haven on I-91, US-5, SR-15 and SR-150.

WW II MEMORIAL: There are three handsome war memorials on the grounds of the city's town hall. The center memorial is dedicated to WW II and in inscribed "1941 HONOR ROLL WORLD WAR II 1945." Listed on the Memorial's seven panels are the names of those from the local community who served in the war. Location: Town Hall lawn, Wallingford, CT

The World War II Memorial in Wallingford, CT

WINDSOR LOCKS is 12 miles north of Hartford on I-91 and SR-20. During the war, The US government built a new airfield west of town to train fighter pilots. It was first named Windsor Locks Air Force Base but was later changed to Bradley International Airport. After the war, it became the area's main commercial airport.

NEW ENGLAND AIR MUSEUM, on the north side of Bradley International Airport, is the largest air museum in New England with a collection of over 80 aircraft. The collection includes aircraft from the days of WW I to post WW II rockets. There is a generous collection of WW II planes plus helicopters, jets and gliders. Inside the museum is an exhibit honoring aviation pioneer Igor Sikorsky, one of the early pioneers in the development of helicopters, and the several firms he was associated with. Also on display are vintage aircraft engines, ballooning exhibits, flight simulators and many other items of interest. The Museum has a large research library, a restoration facility and an impressive gift shop. Address: 36 Perimeter Rd., Bradley International Airport, Windsor Locks, CT 06096. Phone and website: 860-623-3305; www.neam.org

DELAWARE

Although Delaware is one of the smallest states in the Union its 266,000 citizens contributed significantly to America's victory in WW II. Delaware's diversified economy produced many items of war and the state was outstanding in the production of chemicals and related products thanks to the heavy concentration of such industry in the northern part of the state.

DOVER, Delaware's state capitol was a town of only 5500 people during the war. Its local airport was taken over by the US Army Air Forces in 1941 and named Dover Army Air Base. Military aircraft doing anti-submarine patrols along the US East Coast operated from this Base and it also served as a training facility for pilots and air crews.

AIR MOBILITY COMMAND MUSEUM: This museum is on the grounds of Dover AFB - the former Dover Army Air Base of WW II - and has a collection of over 40 aircraft, a few of which are of WW II vintage.

The Museum is located in an old and historic hangar which houses some of the aircraft and has many inside displays. Walking tours are offered and there is a nice gift shop, a conference room, a theater and a canteen. Address: 1301 Heritage Rd. Dover AFB, DE 19902. Phone and website: 302-677-5938; www.amcmuseum.org

LEWES is on Delaware's southern coast on US-1. Just east of the city is the militarily strategic Cape Henlopen at the entrance to Delaware Bay. There, coastal defenses were constructed during the war. Lewes' small airport was used by the military.

FORT MILES ARTILLERY MUSEUM AND TOWERS: Fort Miles, on the coast two miles east of Lewes, was a WW II coastal defense position built on the site of several earlier coastal fortifications. The coastal defenses that remain today were constructed during the early part of WW II and manned by Army Coast Artillery units. The Fort's facilities were eventually incorporated into Cape Henlopen State Park and converted into a museum. Included in the Museum is a WW II coastal watch tower, original WW II barracks buildings, bunkers and guns similar to those used at the Fort during the war. There is also an Orientation Building which has displays and artifacts related to the Fort and its history. Tours of the Fort can be arranged at the Orientation Building. Phone and website: 302-644-5007; www.destateparks.com/fort-miles.asp

DISTRICT OF COLUMBIA

Newspapers, magazines and other publications of the WW II years repeated six words over and over again. They were: Berlin, Tokyo, Rome, London, Moscow and Washington. These were the capitol cites of the six most powerful nations on earth, and it was in these cities that the most powerful men on earth directed the course of the war, the lives and fortunes of millions of people and the future of mankind. Five of the cities paid the high price of war by being heavily bombed and three were captured by the enemy. Only Washington survived the war intact.

When the war started, the District of Columbia was full of museums and monuments dedicated to American's past history. WW II would increase the number of these entities substantially.

As for the US armed forces, their Commander-in-Chief lived at 1600 Pennsylvania Av.- the White House - and scattered throughout the District and spilling into neighboring states of Maryland and Virginia were his generals, admirals and civilian heads of military-related government offices. The generals and admirals would, however, soon move into the new Pentagon building in Virginia.

There was also a generous mix of many and very diversified military installations within the District and the surrounding areas. All of the existing installations were utilized, most of them were expanded and new ones were built.

NOTE: FOR WASHINGTON-AREA SITES <u>OUTSIDE</u> OF THE DISTRICT OF COLUMBIA SEE THE LISTINGS "WASHINGTON, DC AREA" IN MARYLAND AND VIRGINIA.

THE BRITISH EMBASSY, located at 3100 Massachusetts Av. NW, has a larger-than-life statue of Winston Churchill in a garden-like setting for public view. Churchill is standing erect and giving his famous "V for Victory" sign.

FIRST DIVISION MONUMENT: This monument is on the corner of Pennsylvania Av. and 17th St. near the White House grounds. It was originally built to commemorate the men who served and died in this prestigious Army division in WW I. Later, memorials to the veterans of WW II, the Korean Conflict, Viet Nam and Desert Storm were added.

SECOND DIVISON MONUMENT: This monument is in the SW corner of the Ellipse near Constitution Av. and 17th St. Like the First Division Monument, it was constructed to honor the men who served and died in the Division during WW I. Later additions honor those who served in WW II and the Korean Conflict

INTERNATIONAL SPY MUSEUM: This very unique museum introduces the visitor to the little-known world of spying, intelligence, counter-intelligence and other forms of mayhem. Some of the activities of organizations such as the FBI, CIA, NKVD, OSS, and of individuals such as "Wild Bill" Donovan, Julius and Ethel Rosenberg, Cicero, Ian Fleming, Klaus Fuchs, Ted Hall, Mutt & Jeff and other WW II era spies of note are recorded here. Visitors learn how spies lived lives of deceit, and see some of their spy paraphernalia and learn some of the tricks of their trade.

The Museum has a fascinating store with lots of spy gadgetry and information on being a spy. At lunchtime, one can dine at the Spy City Cafe. Address: 800 F St. NW, Washington DC 20004. Phone and website: 202-393-7798; www.spymuseum.org

NATIONAL ARCHIVES: The National Archives is the depository of the official and historical records of the United States. Included within its hundreds of millions of documents are many records from WW II including the personnel records of every individual who served in the US armed forces. There are many WW II documents that were once classified including captured German and Japanese documents. The Archive's film library includes films of the Battle of Midway, the German concentration camps, Nuremberg Trials, Hitler's last will and the personal home movies of Eva Braun, Hitler's mistress. There is a small public display in the Archives building which is

The International Spy Museum in D.C constantly changing and not necessarily devoted to the history of WW II.

The Archives has branches at Suitland, MD and St. Louis, MO. Address in Washington: National Archives and Records Administration, 700 Pennsylvania, Av., Washington, DC 20408. Phone and web: 866-272-6272; www.archives.gov

NATIONAL GUARD MEMORIAL MUSEUM: This 5,600 Sq. ft. museum is located in the National Guard Memorial Building in Washington, DC and relates the history of America's National Guard from Colonial times to the present. The WW II era is well represented.

The National Guard Memorial Museum in D.C

There are artifacts, photos, interactive exhibits and more. And there is a theater, a library and an interesting museum gift shop with a wide selection of interesting items. Address: One Massachusetts Av. NW, Washington, DC 20001. Phone and website: 888-226-4287 and 202-408-5887; www.ngef.org

NATIONAL JAPANESE AMERICAN MEMORIAL TO PATRIOTISM: This is an outdoor memorial to the American citizens of Japanese descent who served honorably and courageously in the American armed forces during WW II. Prominently displayed on the monument are two cranes which are Japanese symbols of longevity and peace. The names of the 800 Japanese American soldiers who died during WW II are inscribed on the memorial. Also inscribed on the memorial are the names, locations and capacities of the WW II relocation camps into which the West Coast ethnic Japanese were interned during the war.

The memorial pays tribute to the loyalty of Japanese Americans at home, while living in the most adverse of circumstances and it acknowledges the failing of American democracy. Nothing is noted, however, of the 10,000 "renunciants" who legally renounced their US citizenship during the war. Location: On a triangular parcel of land bounded by Louisiana Av., New Jersey, Av. and D St. NW.

NATIONAL MUSEUM OF AMERICAN JEWISH MILITARY HISTORY: This museum operates under the auspices of the Jewish War Veterans of the USA and honors Jews who served in the US armed forces in all US wars. Its library and archives serve as a repository for historical documents, objects and memorabilia with regard to the above.

   On display are uniforms, posters, weapons, medals, letters, personal GI equipment and a display of Jewish war veterans who have received the Medal of Honor. Also to be seen, are articles used by Jewish chaplains in the armed forces such as portable arks and altars. Address: 1811 R St. NW, Washington, DC 20009. Phone and web: 202-265-6280; www.nmajmh.org

The Larger of the two memorials in Washington, D.C to Franklin Roosevelt

FRANKLIN D. ROOSEVELT MEMORIAL (West Basin Dr.): This memorial is one of two memorials in the District of Columbia honoring the nation's wartime president, Franklin D. Roosevelt. It is located on the West Basin Dr. and consists of four outdoor galleries, each representing FDR's four terms in office. The memorial shows men standing in a breadline during the Great Depression and FDR in a wheelchair with his faithful dog, Fala, at his feet.

FRANKLIN D. ROOSEVELT MEMORIAL (9th St. and Pennsylvania Av.): This memorial, like the one on West Basin Dr., commemorates the nation's wartime president, Franklin D. Roosevelt. It is much smaller than the one on West Basin Dr. It consists of a simple limestone monument bearing Roosevelt's name and dates of birth and death. This memorial predates the West Basin memorial by some 30 years. FDR personally selected this site while he was still in office saying "If they are to put up any memorial to me, I should like it to be placed in the center of that green plot in front of the Archives Building." Location: Corner of 9th St. and Pennsylvania Av
.

SECOND DIVISION MONUMENT (Listed above with the First Division Monument)

SMITHSONIAN MUSEUM: NATIONAL AIR AND SPACE MUSEUM (DC Location): This museum has the largest aircraft and spacecraft collection in the world. It is so huge, that it is displayed in two locations, one in DC and the other at Dulles Airport, VA. This dazzling array of flying machines and spacecraft includes some of the most famous aircraft in aviation history. There are balloons, rockets, kites, moon rocks, and displays on early flight, flight testing apparatus, air transportation, jet aviation, vertical flight and lunar exploration. This four-story museum in DC has some 20 halls, each with its own aviation theme. In the balloon collection are Japanese bombing balloons recovered from sites in the western United States. In the rocket collection are German V-1 "Buzzbombs" and V-2 rockets. At the Dulles location is the "Enola Gay," the B-29 bomber that dropped the first atomic bomb.

In addition to objects that fly, there is a collection of some 50,000 artifacts, a large research library, a restoration facility, gift shops, theaters, meeting rooms and more. Address of the DC location: 6th and Independence Av. SW Washington, DC 20560. Phone and website: 202-633-1000; www.nasm.si.edu Location: On the Mall between 4th and 7th Sts. on Independence Av.
(For the Dulles facilities see VIRGINIA, WASHINGTON, DC area.)

SMITHSONIAN MUSEUM: NATIONAL MUSEUM OF AMERICAN HISTORY: This large museum is on the Mall and depicts the scientific, cultural and political development of the United States. The Museum contains significant displays on WW II along with all American wars. Some of the finest and rarest artifacts of WW II are displayed here. Tours are available. Address: National Museum of American History, Washington, DC 20560. Phone and website: 202-633-3129; http://americanhistory.si.edu

The National Museum of American History in Washington, DC.

US CAPITOL BUILDING: This is one of America's most recognizable buildings and is the working place of the Legislative Branch of the US Government. It has a long and glorious history paralleling that of the United States and is a "must see" stop for every Washington tourist.

During WW II, it functioned as the meeting place of Congress without interruption and was host to many famous visitors and events. It was here that visiting heads-of-state addressed Congress, that Lend-Lease, conscription, emergency legislation and new taxes were enacted; where America's neutrality laws were made and altered as the nation moved closer to war. It was here, on Dec. 8, 1941, that President Roosevelt gave his "Day of Infamy" speech, which called for the Congress to authorize a declaration war on Japan.

Throughout the war, the building was heavily guarded, sandbagged in some areas and intentionally blacked out at times.

US HOLOCAUST MEMORIAL MUSEUM: This museum, authorized by Congress in 1980 and funded by private means, serves as a living memorial to the six million Jews and millions of other victims of Nazi fanaticism before and during WW II. The Museum's 36,000 Sq. ft. permanent exhibition tells the story of the Jews, Gypsies, Poles, homosexuals, handicapped, Jehovah's Witnesses, political and religious dissident and Soviet prisoners of war who were systematically annihilated in a massive state-sponsored genocide.

At the west entrance to the Museum is the Gen. Dwight D. Eisenhower Memorial Plaza honoring the American commander of the Allied forces in Western Europe and the millions of men who served under him and who put an end to the Nazi tyranny.

The Memorial has an extensive library, archives, theaters, a gift shop and a cafe. Address: 100 Raoul Wallenberg Place SW (formerly 15th St. SW) Washington, DC 20024-2126. Phone and website: 202-488-0400; www.ushmm.org

The bas-reliefs on the walls of the US Navy Memorial depict the history of the US Navy as well as its duties and activities.

US NAVY MEMORIAL is located on Pennsylvania Av. between 7th and 9th Sts. There is a large circular courtyard, the floor of which is a map of the world that powerfully illustrates the size of the earth's ocean areas in relation to the land areas. The statue of the Lone Sailor, stands in the court yard depicting the ordinary US Navyman. A series of bas-reliefs on low walls surrounding the court yard depict various historic naval events. There is a visitor's center, a 242-seat theater and very interesting gift shop. Address: US Navy Memorial Foundation, 701 Pennsylvania Av. NW, Suite 123, Washington, DC 20004-2608. Phone: 202-737-2300

US NAVY MUSEUM: This museum is on the grounds of the Washington Naval Yard and commemorates the Navy's role in all of America's wars and its peacetime contribution and humanitarian service. Events of WW II are well-represented in the Museum and include gun mounts from WW II fighting ships, an F4U Corsair fighter plane, captured enemy equipment, naval mines, coastal-defense artillery, navigational equipment, a complete collection of US Navy decorations and awards, displays on the attack on Pearl Harbor, submarine warfare, a salute to the British Royal Navy, many ship models including several builder's models and a large gift shop. Address: Washington Naval Yard, Building 76, 805 Kidder Breese SE, Washington, DC 20374-5060. Phone and website: 202-433-4882 and 202-737-2300; www.history.navy.mil/NM/USN/

WHITE HOUSE: It's hard to think of a more famous building in America than the White House. This is the residence of the President of the United States and his workplace during his term in office.

During WW II, it was occupied by two presidents and their families, Franklin D. Roosevelt and Harry S Truman. The Roosevelt's lived here from 1933 until 1945 and the Truman's lived here briefly in 1945, and then moved out while it was renovated. They returned in 1953, and stayed until 1957.

During the war years, many important war decisions were made here and when President Roosevelt addressed the nation on radio in is famous "Fireside Chats", he broadcasted from the White House.

Many of the most important and powerful people in the world came as visitors. This too was the meeting place of the Presidents' Cabinets.

On Sunday Dec. 7, 1941, when news came about the attack on Pearl Harbor, the Roosevelt's were here in the White House. Franklin was upstairs in the Presidential Suite with his close friend and adviser, Harry Hopkins, and Mrs. Roosevelt was hosting a luncheon for a ladies' organization downstairs in the Blue Room. Within hours of the attack, the Secret Service and high ranking Army officers descended on the White House to begin preparing it for war. One of the first measures taken was to issue gas masks to everyone. President Roosevelt hung his on the arm of his wheel chair. The Army insisted that anti-aircraft guns be put immediately on the roofs of buildings surrounding the White House. This was done, but some of the guns were wooden dummies because there were not enough guns in the Army's arsenal to meet the need. It was also discovered, a year or so later, that the ammunition hastily placed beside some of the real guns was of the wrong caliber.

Soon after the Pearl Harbor attack, construction began on a bomb shelter beneath the White House. It had 9' thick ceilings, an emergency diesel powered generating system, a ventilating system in case of gas attacks and an escape tunnel that ran to the US Treasury building across the street.

The White House was prepared for, and participated in, trial blackouts along with the rest of Washington.

Parties, receptions and other social activities not related to the war effort were curtailed and the President and Mrs. Roosevelt reduced their participation in outside social activities.

The White House itself was much too small for all of the activities required of the Executive Branch of the Government so many people on the White House staff had to find working and living space elsewhere in Washington because every room in the White House was utilized. Some of the congestion in the White House was relieved with an expansion program that enlarged the east wing, west wing and the basement. The Roosevelt's, nevertheless, remained in the White House throughout the construction.

It was here in the White House, on the afternoon of April 12, 1945, that Vice President Harry S Truman learned from the lips of Eleanor Roosevelt that her husband had died in Georgia and that he was now President of the United States.

When Franklin Roosevelt's body was returned to Washington, it was placed in the East Room where services were held and thousands of mourners paid their respects.

Several months later, at 7 pm Aug. 15, 1945, President Truman, flanked by Cordell Hull, James Byrnes and about a dozen other top governmental officials, announced to reporters gathered in the Oval Office that Japan had surrendered and that WW II had ended.

Tours of the White House are available, and about one million people go through it each year. Address: 1600 Pennsylvania Av. NW, Washington, DC 20500: Visitors' Office phone and website: 202-456-2121; www.whitehouse.gov

All visitors should call the 24-hour Visitors' Office Information line at 202-456-7041 to determine if any last minute changes have been made in the tour schedule.

NATIONAL WORLD WAR II MEMORIAL: This large and impressive memorial is at the eastern end of the Reflecting Pool on the Mall between the Lincoln Memorial and the Washington Monument.

It commemorates the 16 million Americans who served in the US armed forces during the war and the more than 400,000 who gave their lives. The oval-shaped monument consists of memorial walls, commemorative arches, a Flame of Freedom, a cascading waterfall, flags and a large central pool with fountains. There is a Registry of Remembrance containing many names of those who served. The Memorial is operated by the National Park Service and is open to the public 24 hours a day, every day. Phone for general information and website: 800-639-4WW2; www.wwiimemorial.com

The National WW II Memorial in Washington, DC

FLORIDA

When WW II started, the state of Florida was a rural southern agricultural state with a few modest-sized cities and a fairly active winter tourist season. There was lots of empty land, very few modern military establishments and a string of old forts dotting the state's 1146-mile coastline. In early 1940, the state had only eight military installations other than the old forts, but by late 1943, thanks to the war, it would have approximately 170.

The war brought many other changes to the state. Airfields, Army training camps, naval bases, shipbuilding facilities and other manufacturing operations came to Florida during the war bringing a new and important dimension to the state's economy.

Many Allied ships were sunk by German submarines off Florida's coast and four German saboteurs were landed by submarine on her eastern coast near St. Augustine.

Early in the war, both the Army and Navy took great interest in Florida's strategic location and in her good weather for training purposes. At first, the services squabbled over available sites in Florida, but eventually the Army and Navy came to an understanding and divided the state between themselves. The Navy took jurisdiction over the east coast with some exceptions in the Miami and Jacksonville areas, and the Army took over the interior and west coast with the exceptions of the Keys and some areas around Pensacola. The dividing line between their respective spheres of operation, agreed to on Sept. 19, 1942, was known as the Stratemeyer-Towers Line after the general and admiral that worked out the arrangement.

When the Army, Navy and Coast Guard needed housing and training facilities, many of Florida's resort hotels were utilized for that purpose. During the first months of the war, before the training camps were ready, 40% of Florida's tourist space was leased by the military to house the incoming recruits and military personnel. This bought about a sudden disruption in the tourist business for the 1941-42 winter seasons. By the summer of 1942, though, the military began to vacate the hotels and the 1942-43 winter tourist season was much brighter although modest due to the war conditions that made vacations relatively unimportant and, to some extent, unpatriotic. Thereafter, Florida's aggressive tourist industry, seeing its patriotic duty quite clearly and hoping to make the best of a bad situation, proclaimed the state to be a rest and recreational area for weary civilian war-workers.

Florida emerged from the war much different than before. Industry and the military had come to stay and the state's image as a year-around vacationland began to blossom as workers from the north treated themselves to the long and overdue vacations that the Florida advertisements promised.

Homesteaders resumed their trek into the state with war veterans now being given preferential treatment. Increasing numbers of retirees eyed the state's easy climate, recreational opportunities and other comforts. For several years after the war, Florida was the second fastest growing state in the Union after California.

CARRABELLE, 50 miles SW of Tallahassee in the Florida panhandle, was home to the Army's Camp Gordon Johnston, a base that specialized in training soldiers for amphibious landings and assaults.

CAMP GORDON JOHNSTON MUSEUM: This fine 5000 Sq. ft. museum is near downtown Carrabelle and preserves the history and heritage of Camp Gordon Johnston. Inside the Museum are artifacts and memorabilia related to the Camp and its mission as a training facility for Army amphibious operations. There are uniforms, soldiers' personal gear, photos and models of various landing craft. Also, the Museum has an educational and oral history program. Address: 1001 Gray Av., Carrabelle, FL 32322. Phone and website: 850-697-8575; www.campgordonjohnston.com

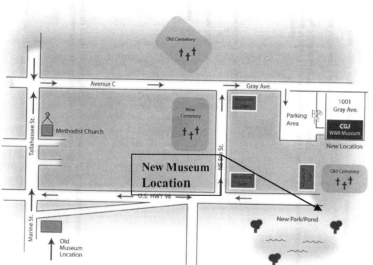

DELAND is a county seat just off I-4 on US-7, US-92 and SR-44 20 miles SE of Daytona Beach. In 1941 the US Navy took over Deland's local airport and converted it into an operational air base for naval aircraft patrolling the Atlantic coast and a training base for naval flight crews.

DELAND NAVAL AIR STATION MUSEUM is on the grounds of Deland's local airport which was the former Naval Air Station, DeLand during WW II. The Museum is in one of the Station's restored WW II buildings, which is on the National Register of Historic Places.

The Museum is filled with military artifacts, uniforms, vintage photos, books, and memorabilia relating to the air station and to the community of Deland. There are several vintage aircraft on display and a room dedicated to WW I. The Museum hosts several social events and air shows during the year. Address: 910 Biscayne Blvd., DeLand, FL 32724. Phone and website: 386-738-4149; www.delandnavalairstation.org

FLEMING ISLAND is an unincorporated area 17 miles SW of Jacksonville on US-17 and the St. Johns River.

WW II MEMORIAL - FLEMING ISLAND: This WW II monument consists of a memorial wall, three flagpoles and is lighted at night. It commemorates all those who lost their lives during WW II. There are also two memorial benches for the use of visitors. Location: In front of a business complex on Town Center Rd.

FORT LAUDERDALE (See Miami/Fort Lauderdale Area

FORT MYERS is a county seat, a popular tourist area and a seaport on I-75 and US-41 and on Florida's west coast.

The WW II Memorial in Fleming Island, FL

*The Iwo Jima Statue
in Ft. Meyers, FL*

IWO JIMA STATUE: This is a 1/3 scale replica of the original Marine Corps War Memorial at Arlington, VA depicting the famous flag raising on Iwo Jima during February 1945. The Statue can easily be seen by motorists crossing the Veterans Memorial Bridge over the Caloosahatchie River. It is maintained by retired Marines. Location: In Eco Park on Colonial Blvd. in the Fort Myers suburb of Cape Coral.

FORT PIERCE is a county seat on the eastern coast of Florida on I-95 and US-1 40 miles north of West Palm Beach. During WW II, the US Naval Amphibious Training Base, Fort Pierce, was located on the coastal beaches opposite the city of Ft. Pierce. As the name implies, it was a training facility for the amphibious forces of the US Navy.

   The US Navy learned from the invasion of Tarawa in the Pacific that they needed teams of men operating underwater to scout intended invasion sites and destroy underwater enemy defense obstacles. This lead to the creation of Naval Combat Demolition Teams (NCDT), later redesigned Underwater Demolition Teams (UDT) or "Frogmen." Some years later, the units were renamed the Sea, Air, Land Teams (SEALS).

NATIONAL NAVY UDT-SEAL MUSEUM: This museum is on North Hutchinson Island off SR-A1A at Pepper Park on one of the beaches used to train the Navy's WWII "Frogmen." On display are boats, submersible vehicles, scuba gear, weapons, demolition apparatus and other related items used then and now. There is considerable information on today's Frogmen - the Navy SEALS.

   The Museum has an educational program and a very interesting gift shop. Address: 3300 North A1A, North Hutchinson Island, Fort Pierce, FL 34949: Phone and website: 772-595-5845 www.navysealmuseum.com. *Photo on page 60*

JACKSONVILLE is one of Florida's larger cities located in NE Florida just south of the Georgia state line.

JACKSONVILL BEACH HEROES OF WW II MEMORIAL: Honored here are the local residents of Jacksonville Beach who gave their lives during WW II. There is a centerpiece flag pole, a plaque bearing the names of those who died, another plaque commemorating American war mothers, a plaque commemorating an American War Mothers Memory Tree and small monuments dedicated to each branch of military service. Location: On the corner of Beach Blvd. and Second Av.

The National Navy UDT-Seal Museum at Ft. Pierce, FL

The World War II – Operation Pastorius – Marker at Ponte Vedra,FL

WORLD WAR II - OPERATION PASTORIUS - MARKER AT PONTE VEDRA: On the night of June 16, 1942, four German spies were landed by submarine on the beach near Ponte Vedra. They buried explosives and other paraphernalia on the beach, then walked to the coastal highway and caught the bus for Jacksonville. They were eventually caught and revealed that they had been landed at this location. This marker is located at the spot where the spies came ashore. Location: In front of the Ponte Vedra Inn and Country Club

KEY WEST AND THE FLORIDA KEYS: These beautiful strings of islands at the southern end of the Florida peninsula was one of the most strategic military locations in the continental US during the war. Around the Florida Keys flowed the great bulk of America's Gulf coast sea traffic and the area was a hunting ground for German submarines. Also from the Keys, American planes and ships patrolled deep into the Caribbean. Needless to say, the area had a strong naval presents. And President Truman liked the place too.

THE LITTLE WHITE HOUSE: In 1946, President Harry S Truman made a visit to the US Naval Base, Key West and was very impressed with the Key West area as a possible presidential retreat. As a result, the former commandant's quarters were remodeled as a winter vacation home and Truman returned several times between 1946 and 1952. He spent a total of 174 days here. His wife, Bess, seldom accompanied him. She referred to Truman's time here as "a man's thing". During the time Truman used the house, it became known as "The Little White House". Truman called the White House in Washington, DC "the great white jail".

In 1948-49, General Eisenhower held a series of meetings here with regards to the creation of the Department of Defense. He returned again as President, in 1956 to recuperate from a heart attack. In later years, Presidents John F. Kennedy and Jimmy Carter used the facility.

The Little White House is a state historic site and is open to the public. It is furnished as it was when Truman resided here. Address: 111 Front St., Key West, FL 33041. Phone and website: 305-294-9911; www.trumanlittlewhitehouse.com

The Little White House in Key West, FL

US COAST GUARD CUTTERS *INGHAM* AND *MOHAWK*: Here are two historic Coast Guard Cutters anchored close to each other and open to the public. Both are National Historic Landmarks and both vessels saw action in WW II.

The *Ingham* was one of the Coasts Guard's largest cutters and was commissioned in 1936. She served as a convoy escort in the North Atlantic and is credited with sinking the German submarine *U-626*. She also served as a patrol craft during the Korean conflict and the Viet Nam war.

The *Mohawk* is a smaller craft, commissioned in 1935 and also served as a convoy escort in the North Atlantic and performed ice patrols. The *Mohawk* was decommissioned in 1948.

There is an interesting gift shop aboard the *Ingham.* Don't pass it up.

Address for both ships: Truman Waterfront (on the west side of the Island), Key West, FL 33041. Phone and website for the *Ingham*: 305-292-5072; www.uscgcingham.org. Phone and website for the *Mohawk*: 305-292-8750; www.uscgcmohawk.org

The US Coast Guard Cutter Ingham at Key West FL

KISSIMMEE (See Orlando/Kissimmee Area)

MADISON is a county seat in northern Florida on I-10, US-90 and ISR-145. It was the home town of one of America's first heroes of WW II, Colin P. Kelly, Jr.

FOUR FREEDOMS MONUMENT: This is a dual-purpose memorial commemorating the famous For Freedoms doctrine of WW II and Madison's home town hero, Colin P. Kelly, Jr. It was one of the earliest WW II memorials erected in the country, first dedicated in 1944.

   The Monument consists of a stone base with four gesturing angels on top and inscriptions on the base remembering Colin P. Kelly, Jr. Location: On the corner of E. Base St. (US-90) and N. Range St., in downtown Madison, FL

MELBOURNE is a county seat on Florida's east coast on I-95 and 30 miles south of John F. Kennedy Space Center.

   During WW II, the US Navy built a new air facility in the area named Naval Air Station, Melbourne. It was used to train Navy and Marine pilots and had an engine and aircraft test facility. After the war, NAS, Melbourne became Melbourne's main airport.

The Four Freedoms Monument in Madison, FL

AVIATION MUSEUM AT MELBOURNE INTERNATIONAL AIRPORT: This is a small museum inside the terminal at the Airport. It relates the history of the airport's construction and use as a naval facility during the war and its use as a commercial airport thereafter. The Museum has artifacts, artwork and other memorabilia from its naval days. There is a Link trainer of the type used to train pilots on the ground prior to flight training. Address: One Air Terminal Parkway, Melbourne, FL 32901. Phone and website: 321-724-1600; www.mlbair.com

MIAMI/FORT LAUDERDALE AREA: When war came to America, Miami was Florida's second largest city with a population of 172,000 people and that many again in the surrounding communities. The war escalated the military's interest in the area ten-fold. Here was one of the most strategic areas of the country with a fine climate which was ideal for training aviators and with easy access to the Atlantic Ocean and the Gulf of Mexico. The Army and Navy also found many large hotels, which they utilized to house new recruits and other military personnel. While in the hotels, recruits were organized into military units and give some rudimentary military training while they awaited transfer to military facilities in Florida and elsewhere which were still under construction.

   Many of the military installations constructed in and around the Miami area remained in operation long after the war.

THE GOLD COAST RAILROAD MUSEUM: This fine railroad museum is built on the floor of an old WW II blimp hangar at the former US Naval Air Station, Richmond (LTA -lighter than air). The parking lot is one of the blimps landing pads.

The Museum has a very interesting relic of WW II - President Franklin D. Roosevelt's bullet-proof Pullman car named the "Ferdinand Magellan." Now a National Historic Landmark, the Pullman car was rebuilt in 1942 from an ordinary Pullman car manufactured in 1928. The railroad car is equipped with 5/8 inch steel armor plate all around and three inch think bulletproof glass. It has two escape hatches, an elevator on the observation deck to lift the President up and down in his wheel chair and the interior was modified for the President's needs and with regards to his handicap. The outer appearance of the car was made to look like and ordinary Pullman car for security purposes. The car

was presented to the President on December 18, 1942 and designated "US Car #1." Roosevelt traveled over 50,000 miles in it and many VIPs of WW II rode with him including Winston Churchill. When Roosevelt died in Warm Springs, GA, the car was part of the train that brought his body back to Washington. Mrs. Roosevelt rode in the car with the body in another car.

After Roosevelt's death, Presidents Truman, Eisenhower and Reagan used US Car #1 in their travels. Museum address: 12450 SW 152nd St. Miami, FL 33177. Phone and website: 305-253-0063 and 888-608-7246; www.gcrm.org

The World War II Memorial in Hallandale Beach, FL

HALLANDALE BEACH WW II MEMORIAL: Hallandale Beach is just south of Hollywood, FL on US-1. At the rear of City Hall, in traffic roundabout stands this memorial. Its center piece is a brown marble obelisk surrounded by six antique cannons. On the top of the obelisk is an eternal (electric) flame. Etched on the obelisk is the following inscription: "DEDICATED TO THE MEMORY OF ALL VETERANS OF HALLANDALE FLORIDA IN GRATITUDE FOR SERVICE TO THEIR COUNTRY. THOSE WHOSE NAMES ARE HERIN INSCRIBED SERVED THEIR COUNTRY DURING WORLD WAR II"

NAVAL AIR STATION, FORT LAUDERDALE AND FLIGHT 19 MEMORIAL: During the war, the US Navy took over Fort Lauderdale's local airport and used it as a training facility for pilots and maintenance personnel on Navy torpedo bombers. Ensign George H. W. Bush, the future President of the US, trained here. The airfield is now Fort Lauderdale International Airport.

The Naval Air Station Memorial in Fort Lauderdale, FL

This memorial consists of a three-bladed propeller similar to those used on the Navy torpedo bombers and is mounted on a rectangular column with plaques. It honors the men and   women who served at the naval station during the war and also commemorates the members of a naval flight of several airplanes, Flight 19, that mysterious disappeared on December 5, 1945 while on a training mission. Their disappearance contributed to the legend of other mysteriously disappearances within the Bermuda Triangle.   Location: At Fort Lauderdale International Airport

ORLANDO/KISSIMMEE AREA, in the center of the Florida peninsula, is one of the best-known areas in Florida and a tourist mecca. It is a transportation hub with Cape Canaveral to the east and the Tampa/St. Petersburg Area to the west.

BATAAN-CORREGIDOR MEMORIAL: This dramatic memorial, located in the southern suburb of

Kissimmee, consists of stone memorials, flag poles and several impressive statues. All depict the Bataan Death March and honor those who were subjected to that cruel event. One statue of interest depicts a Filipino woman offering bread to two soldiers during the Death March. Location: Lakefront Park, at the corner of Lakeshore Dr. and Monument, Av.

One of the several statues at the Bataan-Corregidor Memorial
in Kissimmee, FL

VETERANS OF THE BATTLE OF THE BULGE WW II MEMORIAL: This handsome memorial was dedicated on December 16, 1999, the 55th anniversary of the famous Battle of the Bulge in WW   II. Its focal point is a bronze statue of a proud and victorious GI mounted on a granite base. The monument rests in the center of a 34 ft. concrete and brick star which has lights at the ends of each arm that are continuously illuminated. The insignias of the 41 US infantry and armored divisions that took part in the battle are on display as are the flags of the US, Belgium and Luxembourg. Location: Lake Eola Park on S. Rosalland Av. in Orlando.

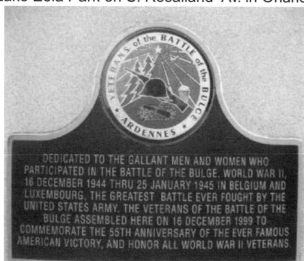

The Veterans of the Battle of the Bulge
WW II Memorial in Orlando, FL

PALATKA is a county seat 50 miles south of Jacksonville on US-17 and SR-16.

USS TANG **MEMORIAL:** The submarine *USS Tang* is credited with sinking 31 enemy ships during her five patrols of WW II. This is a record unexcelled among American submarines. Unfortunately, the *Tang* met an inglorious end when one of her torpedoes malfunctioned, circled about and struck the vessel; all aboard perished. Her commander was awarded a posthumous Congressional Medal of Honor. This Memorial consists of a WW II era torpedo mounted in a stone structure with commemorative plaques.

THE PENSACOLA AREA: This area is at the western end of Florida's panhandle on the Gulf coast. By the time WW II started, there were a number of long-established US Navy installations in the area which would be greatly expanded during the war.

Early in the war, a new Army camp was built nearby in Okaloosa County to train and utilize conscientious objectors. Along the Gulf Coast were a number of old coastal forts which were activated and used during the war in various ways.

The USS Tang Memorial in Palatka, FL

US NATIONAL NAVAL AVIATION MUSEUM: This is a large museum with a seven-story atrium of glass and steel on some 37 acres on the land at US Naval Air Station, Pensacola. It is one of the largest and most beautiful air and space museums in the world and traces the history of US naval aviation from its inception in 1911 to the space age. There are over 150 Navy, Marine and Coast Guard airplanes on display inside and outside of the Museum. The aircraft display is so extensive that a bus tour is offered to view it.

Inside the Museum are many other displays; examples of flight clothing, flight logs, vintage ground equipment, personal momentous, cockpit trainers in which visitors can sit, anti-aircraft guns, a flight simulator and much more. There is a Hall of Fame honoring Navy men who have received the Congressional Medal of Honor, a large IMAX theater, a cafe, a very nice gift shop, a library and archives and a restoration facility. A display in the West Wing highlights Carrier Aviation during WW II and has a replica of the flight deck of the aircraft carrier *USS Cabot*. Address: 1750 Radford Blvd., NAS Pensacola, FL 32508. Phone and website: 850-452-3604 and 850-452-3606; www.navalaviationmuseum.org

PERRY is a county seat in the Florida panhandle on US-19, US-27 and US-98.

WORLD WAR II MONUMENT: You will find this interesting WW II memorial in Perry's Veteran's Memorial Park. A very noticeable part of the granite monument is a large "V" for victory sign. Etched on the front of the monument are depictions of Hiroshima, the fall of Berlin, aircraft, PT-boats, tanks and the D-Day landing. The monument lists the number of deaths, wounded, POWs, MIAs and the total number of casualties.

The WW II Monument in Perry,FL

POLK CITY: This is a small community in central Florida on I-4 and SR-33.

FANTASY OF FLIGHT MUSEUM: This is an excellent air museum and restoration facility in Polk City 12 miles NE of Lakeland. The Museum has over 70 vintage aircraft, many of them from WW II and are flyable. The restoration facility can be viewed by visitors and there is a must-visit gift shop and a very unique restaurant on the premises. The restaurants reflect the atmosphere of the stylish dining establishment associated with the airports of the 1930s and early 1940s. It's interesting menu is served up with an aviation spin. Museum address: 1400 Broadway Blvd. SE, Polk City, FL 33868. Phone and website: 863-984-3500; www.fantasyofflight.com

SAINT PETERSBURG (See Tampa/St. Petersburg Area)

SEBRING is the county seat of Highlands County on US-98 and SR-17 65 miles SE of Tampa. This is one of the state's richest citrus-growing areas.

MILITARY SEA SERVICES MUSEUM: This is the only museum in the US that honors all of the Military Sea Services of the US - the US Coast Guard, US Navy and US Marine Corps. It is dedicated to the memory of the men and women who served in those services and protected our sea shores and the ships that sailed along America's coasts.

On display are artifacts such as rescue equipment, military items, uniforms, posters, flags, photos and more. Also within the Museum, is the *USS Highlands* Room commemorating the WW II attack transport which was named in honor of Highland County. The *USS Highlands* saw action at Iwo Jima, Okinawa and was present in Tokyo Bay when Japan surrendered on September 2, 1945. Museum address: 1402 Roseland Av., Sebring, FL 33879. Phone and website: 863-385-0992; http://milseasvcmuseum.org

USS HIGHLANDS MEMORIAL: On Sebring's courthouse lawn is a large memorial to the WW II attack transport, *USS Highlands, which* was named after Highlands County and saw considerable action in the Pacific during the war. It participated in the invasions of both Iwo Jima and Okinawa.

The Memorial measures 23 x 20 feet and honors those who serve aboard the ship and it heroic activities during the war. Address: 600 S. Commerce Av., Sebring, FL

STARKE is a county seat 35 miles SW of Jacksonville on US-301, SR-16 and SR-100. It is home for Camp Blanding and the Florida National Guard.

CAMP BLANDING MUSEUM AND MEMORIAL PARK: This large museum and park complex is on the grounds of Camp Blanding near the camp's main entrance on SR-16 east of town.

During WW II, nine Army infantry divisions trained here. The Museum contains many items of interest from WW II such as uniforms, weapons, documents, maps, books and other exhibits telling the history of Camp Blanding and the units that trained here. There are displays showing how they worked, trained and lived. There is a restored WW II barracks which was the museum's first home and a 15 foot monument of an infantryman honoring Florida Guardsmen who served in WW II. Also in the Memorial Park are tanks, half-tracks, trucks, jeeps, artillery pieces and memorials, monuments and displays honoring those who served in America's later wars.

The Museum has a large and interesting gift shop and a picnic area. Address: 5629 SR-16 W, Starke, FL 32091. Phone and website: 904-682-3196 campblanding-museum.org

Camp Blanding Museum and Memorial Park is near the main gate of Camp Blanding Military Reservation on SR-16.

<u>TALLAHASSEE</u>, in the north-central part of the state, is Florida's state capitol. During the war, it had a population of only 16,000. Tallahassee's local airport, Dale Mabry Field, three miles west of town, was taken over by the US Army Air Forces and used as an operational base. There are two WW II memorials in the area.

The Florida World War II Memorial in Tallahassee, FL

FLORIDA WORLD WAR II MEMORIAL: This Memorial, on the grounds of the R. A. Gray Building in Tallahassee was dedicated on June 6, 2005, the 61st anniversary of the Normandy Landings. There is a central pillar which is an exact replica of the Florida pillar at the National World War II Memorial in Washington, DC. And there is a walkway lined with 67 plaques, one for each Florida County, honoring those who served from their respective county. Inside the Gray Building is a small, but permanent display dedicated to WW II. Location: 500 S. Bronough St., Tallahassee, FL

LEON COUNTY WORLD WAR II MEMORIAL: On the grounds of the Leon County Courthouse resides this unique and interesting WW II memorial. The centerpiece of the memorial is an aging WW II veteran, with a cane, sitting on a bench in full uniform holding an American flag. Location: 301 S. Monroe St., Tallahassee, FL

TAMPA/SAINT PETERSBURG AREA: These cities, and several smaller ones, are clustered around Tampa Bay on Florida's western coast. Tampa was the state's third largest metropolitan complex during the war and had a relatively well-developed and diversified industrial base, several US Navy installations, two Army airfields and ship building and ship repair facilities. Along the Gulf Coast were several old coastal defense forts that were utilized during the war.

The Leon County WW II Memorial in Tallahassee, FL

ARMED FORCES MILITARY MUSEUM: This large and interesting museum is located in Largo, FL, a suburb of St. Petersburg. It has one of the largest privately-owed military collections in the US. Its founder is John J. Piazza, Jr. and many of the items on display are from the WW II era. In its 50,000 Sq. ft. of floor space, there are tanks, military vehicles, specialized military equipment, small arms, uniforms, posters, an art gallery, memorabilia and much more.

The Armed forces Military Museum in Largo, FL
The Museum has an educational program, a . memorial walk and a very interesting gift shop.
Address: 2050 34th Way North, Largo, FL 33771.
Phone and website: 727-539-8371; www.armedforcesmuseum.com

SS AMERICAN VICTORY **MARINERS MEMORIAL & MUSEUM SHIP:** Here is a WW II museum on a WW II ship. The ship, a Victory-class cargo ship, is moored on the Palm River near the Florida Aquarium in the SE corner of Tampa. It has been restored to its original condition and the ship, as well as its on-board museum, can be explored by visitors. The Museum highlights the history of the of the ship and the US Merchant Marines in general. Touring the ship, visitors will view the ship's three-level cargo hold, its flying bridge, steering stations, galley, hospital, crew's quarters, mess and everything else it took to get its war cargoes overseas to the troops. The ship was also used during the Korean and Viet Nam wars. Address: 705 Channelside Dr., Tampa, FL 33602. Phone and website: 813-228-8766; www.americanvictory.org

The SS American Victory at Tampa, FL

VALPARAISO: Valparaiso, in the Florida panhandle 45 miles east of Pensacola, was a community of less than 300 people and none of the other communities in the area were much larger. But, the area had good flying weather and the

68

degree of isolation the Army Air Corps was seeking for the construction of a facility that was to hold many military secrets. As a result, the US Army Air Force chose this area to build two airfields, Eglin Field, which later became Eglin Air Force Base, and Hurlburt Field.

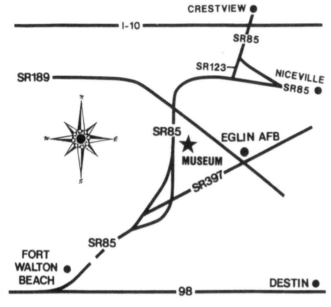

US Air Force Armament Museum
Valparaiso, FL

US AIR FORCE ARMAMENT MUSEUM: This fine government museum is SW of Valparaiso at the junction of SR-85 and SR-189 outside the gate of Eglin Air Force Base. On display is a wide variety of planes, bombs, missiles, vehicles of war and over 5000 Air Force armament items ranging from WW I bombs to the present day modern   weapons. Many items from both enemy and Allied nations are on display along with about half-dozen aircraft from WW II and a German V-1 "Buzzbomb."

There is a theater, education center, art gallery, inviting gift shop and a picnic/playground area. Address: 100 Museum Dr., Eglin AFB, FL 32542. Phone and website: 850-651-1808; www.afarmamentmuseum.com

GEORGIA

Georgia is the largest state east of the Mississippi. During WW II it was very "southern" and rural, and the state's economy was based mainly on agriculture except for a large industrialized area around Atlanta.

Two of the nation's largest military camps, Ft. Benning and Ft. Stewart, were in Georgia and were greatly expanded during the war.

Because of its mild climate and good flying weather, many new military airfields were built in Georgia and many of the state's local airports were taken over by the armed services for the duration of the war. Other military installations were built in Georgia and its industrial base was greatly expanded.

ANDERSONVILLE is a small community 12 miles NE of Americus on SR-49.

ANDERSONVILLE NATIONAL HISTORIC SITE, just south of Andersonville on SR-49, is the site of the infamous Andersonville Prison of the American Civil War. Here, 32,000 Union soldiers, prisoners of war (POW), were crammed into a prison compound built to hold 10,000. Conditions were deplorable and thousands died due to the overcrowding and lack of food and medical attention that the impoverished Confederate Government could not provide.

The Historic Site consists of three entities, the Civil War Prison site, the Andersonville National Cemetery and the National Prisoner of War Museum. Exhibits inside the Museum are dedicated to American POWs of all wars including WW II. The exhibits are not organized by wars, but tell the stories and suffering of US POWs of all wars. The WW II exhibit is extensive and there are displays

that adequately tell the story of American service men held as POWs by the various Axis nation. There is also a display on the American nurses and other American women interned under horrible conditions by the Japanese at the Los Banos and Santo Tomas camps in the Philippines. Another display commemorates the nine American POWs who were killed at Hiroshima by the first atomic bomb blast. The Museum has a theater, numerous artifacts, photos, letters, tools and other items related to the experiences of POWs. Please do not pass up the gift shop. Address: 496 Cemetery Rd., Andersonville, GA 31711. Phone and website: 229-924-0343; www.nps.gov/ande/

This is the entrance to the National Prisoner of War Museum at Andersonville, GA.

ATLANTA AREA: Atlanta, the state capitol, was the largest city in Georgia during the war, the state's largest manufacturing center and the pace-setter for Georgia's economy and political climate. During the war, Atlanta was the largest manufacturing center in the South.

WW II MEMORIAL AT THE GEORGIA WAR VETERANS MEMORIAL COMPLEX: There are a number of memorials in this official state complex commemorating America's wars. And, as would be expected, there is one for WW II. It commemorates all of the citizens of Georgia who perished in WW II and lists their names. Location: Near the Floyd Veteran Memorial Building, 2 Martin Luther King, Jr. Blvd. Atlanta, GA 30334

AUGUSTA is a county seat in east-central Georgia on the South Carolina state line and on I-20, US-1, US-25, US-78, SR-28 and SR-121. During WW II, it was home to several military installations, the Augusta Arsenal, Camp Gordon (US Army Signal Corps), the Army's Oliver

The WW II Memorial at the Georgia War Veterans Memorial Complex in Atlanta, GA

General Hospital and its local airport was used by the US Army Air Forces.

US ARMY SIGNAL CORPS MUSEUM: This museum is on the grounds of Fort Gordon, the home of the US Army's Signal Corps, and focuses on the history of communications within the US Army and tells the story of the Signal Corps since its beginning in 1860. Permanent displays feature early telephones made by Alexander Graham Bell and prototype wireless equipment made by Marconi. Other displays include artifacts, photos, documents and the Museum has an extensive archive collection. Address: ATZH-POM-M, Bldg. 29807, Ft. Gordon, GA 30905. Phone and website: 706-791-2818/3866; www.gordon.army.mil/ocos/museum/

This is the entrance to the Signal Corps Museum in Augusta, Ga.

BRUNSWICK: They built Liberty ships in this community and the citizens are proud of it. Brunswick is a county seat in SE Georgia just east of I-95 and on US-17, SR-17 and the Brunswick River.

BRUNSWICK LIBERTY SHIP WW II MEMORIAL: Here is a large scale model of a WW II Liberty Ship serving as a WW II memorial. It is of the type that was built here in Brunswick during the war. Adjacent to the model ship is a historical marker summarizing Brunswick's Liberty Ship story. Location: Mary Ross Waterfront Park in downtown Brunswick.

The Brunswick Liberty Ship Memorial in Brunswick, GA

COLUMBUS is a county seat in the west-central part of the state on I-185, US-27, US-280 and the Alabama state line. It is the home of Fort Benning, the US Army's principle infantry training facility.

NATIONAL INFANTRY MUSEUM: This excellent museum is on the grounds of Ft. Benning and follows the American foot soldier across more than two centuries of history. His victories, defeats and day-to-day life are interpreted in the artifacts, paintings, sculptures and other items on display. There is an extensive collection of old and modern weapons, military vehicles, documents signed by Franklin Roosevelt, a bust of Adolf Hitler which was "liberated" during WW II, band instruments, and the many other items related to the US Army's infantry.

  The Museum has a gallery of military art, an I-Max theater, a restaurant and a first-rate soldiers' shop. A large part of the Museum's displays are related to WW II. Address: 1775 Legacy Way, Columbus, GA 31903. Phone and website: 706-685-5800 (museum), 706-675-5819 (soldiers; shop); www.nationalinfantrymuseum.com

CORDELE is a county seat 60 miles south of Macon on I-75.

The "Follow Me" statue at Fort Benning, GA

GEORGIA VETERANS MEMORIAL STATE PARK is 13 miles west of Cordele on US-280 and was established as a permanent memorial to all US veterans. It is a typical state park with facilities for camping, hiking, boating, fishing, golfing, picnicking and other outdoor activities. The Park has a small military museum and a outdoor display of military equipment and aircraft. Items from all US wars are on display, but the WW II display is the largest. The Museum is named after Gen. Courtney Hodges, a Georgia native, who commanded the US 1st Army at the Battle of the Bulge. Address: 2459 US-280W, Cordele, GA 31015. Phone and website: 229-276-2371; www.gastateparks.org/GeorgiaVeterans

DOUGLAS: is a county seat in south-central Georgia on US-221, US-441 and SR-32. During the war, there was a privately-owned flight school at the local airport, the Raymond-Richardson Aviation School that was contracted by the US Army Air Forces to train Army aviators and air crews.

WW II FLIGHT TRAINING MUSEUM: This museum, located on the east side of the local airport, is very unique in that it is one of the very few museums in the country that pays tribute to the many privately-owned flight schools that existed around the US during WW II that were contracted by the US Army Air Forces to train pilots and crew members. This Museum is in one of the school's original WW II buildings which is among a cluster of other WW II era buildings.

There are five main areas in the Museum: a library which contains some of the books and manuals used by the trainees, a typical barracks room, an area explaining the training curriculum, an area devoted to the air war of WW II and an area on the US Home Front. Address: 3 Airport Circle, Douglas, GA 31534. Phone and website: 912-383-9111; www.ww2flighttrainingmuseum.org

The WW II Flight Training Museum is located in an original WW II era building at the local airport in Douglas, FL

<u>**ELBERTON**</u> is a county seat in NE Georgia on SR-17, SR-72 and SR-77.

WORLD WAR II STATUE: This is a WW II memorial with a granite statue of a WW II GI at the top in full battle dress. There are inscriptions on the base of the memorial which are dedicated to those who gave their lives during the war. Location: On the lawn of the Elber County Courthouse.

<u>**HINESVILLE**</u> is a county seat 35 miles SW of Savannah on US-84, SR-38 and SR-196. It is home to a huge US Army installation, Fort Stewart Military Reservation, the largest Army installation east of the Mississippi River.

FORT STEWART MUSEUM: This museum is on the grounds of Fort Stewart and has a relatively small WW II display. The Museum, generally, pays tribute to the units that trained here and records the history of Fort Stewart. Special emphasis is given to the 3rd Infantry Division which is currently stationed at Fort Stewart.

Outside is The Museum Park with tanks, anti-aircraft guns, searchlights and other large weapons. The Museum maintains a branch museum at Hunter Army Airfield, another facility at Fort Stewart. Fort Steward Museum Address: 2022 Frank Cochran Dr., Fort Stewart, GA 31314. Phone: 912-767-7885

I-95 WELCOME CENTER: It's an unusual place for a WW II memorial, but lots of people see it. It's near Kingsland Bay, GA just north of the Florida state line.

The World War II Statue in Elberton, GA

MK14 TORPEDO WW II MEMORIAL: It's green and it's real, but it's inert. This WW II era torpedo was donated by the US Submarine Base at Kings Bay, GA which is at the south end of I-95 near St. Mary's GA. It answers the question, "What do you do with surplus WW II torpedoes?" Location: Welcome Center of I-95 near Kingsland, GA

ST. MARYS is a beautiful and historic town in the SE tip of Georgia on I-95 and the Florida state line. For years there was a US Navy Submarine Base in the area.

ST MARYS SUBMARINE MUSEUM: This museum is in downtown St. Mary's on the St.Mary's River. Across the River is Florida. The Museum honors the US Navy's

The WW II era torpedo at the I-95 Welcome Center near Kingsland, GA

Submarine Service and the men and women who served in that very specialized branch of service. There are numerous submarine artifacts and memorabilia included in the Museum and a real periscope that visitors can look through. Exhibits include Civil War submarines, submarine design, submarine controls, torpedoes, the sailors' life aboard a submarine, painting, photos, documents and more. Heavy emphasis is on the WW II era. The Museum has an inviting gift shop, a library, an educational program and museum tours are available. Address: 102 St. Mary's St. West (on the river), St. Mary's, GA 31558. Phone and website: 912-882-2782; stmaryssubmuseum.com

The entrance to the St. Mary's Submarine Museum in ST. Mary's, GA

SANDERSVILLE is a county seat in central Georgia on SR-15, SR-24 and SR-88.

The Washington County WW II Memorial in Sandersville, GA

WASHINGTON COUTY WW II MEMORIAL: As do many county seats in the US, Sandersville has a WW II memorial on the grounds of its courthouse. It is dedicated to the men and women from Washington County that served in WW II. Some 400 names of those who served are etched on the Monument's metal plates. Washington County had one of the highest per capita numbers of citizens serving in WW II. Memorials to other conflicts are nearby.

SAVANNAH, on the northern coast of Georgia at the mouth of the Savannah River, was Georgia's second largest city during WW II. The city had two shipyards that built minesweepers and merchant ships and was home to Hunter Field, a major US Army Air Forces training facility. The Savannah US Army Quartermaster Depot was also here in Savannah.

THE MIGHTY EIGHTH AIR FORCE MUSEUM: On January 24, 1942, just 53 days after the attack on Pearl Harbor, the US Army Air Corps' 8th AF was activated in Savannah at the National Guard Armory on Bull St. The 8th AF became the largest air force in aviation history and it is not surprising

that it has had a prominent place in Savannah history. The 8th AF was America's primary air unit in the European Theatre of Operation,

This two-story, 90,000 Sq. ft. museum in Pooler, a suburb of Savannah, records and traces that history. Through a variety of interesting displays, the Museum features information on the 8th AF, its historic battles, mission experiences, aircraft models, contributions to the war effort and the people who served in the "Mighty Eighth."

There are numerous artifacts and

The Mighty 8th Air Force Museum's B-17 bomber, the "City of Savannah"

memorabilia, a research library, lecture halls, classrooms, a large and interesting gift shop and a large canteen with the atmosphere of a British WW II era pub. Through the year, the Museum is host to many social and educational events. Address: 175 Bourne Av. (US-80), Pooler, GA 31322. Phone and website: 912-748-8888; www.mightyeighth.org

<u>THOMASTON</u> is a county seat in west-central Georgia on US-19, SR-3 and SR-36.

The Upson County WW II Memorial in Thomaston, GA

UPSON COUNTY WW II MEMORIAL: This fine memorial in Thomaston is dedicated to the men from Upson County that gave their lives during WW II. Their names are inscribed on the Memorial. Location: S. Church St. and W. Gordon St. at the old Upson County courthouse.

<u>TOCCOA</u> is a county seat in the NE corner of the state on US-123 and US-441. During the war, a nearby US Army training center, Fort Toccoa, trained thousands of paratroopers and US Army Ordnance Corps maintenance troops.

STEPHENS COUNTY HISTORICAL SOCIETY AND CURRAHEE MILITARY MUSEUM: This 6000 Sq. ft. museum is in Toccoa's renovated railroad depot and commemorates the history of Stephens County with special emphasis on the nearby WW II era Fort Toccoa.

Over 17,000 US Army paratroopers were trained at Ft. Toccoa as were thousands of US Army Ordnance Corps troops. It was at this station that the future soldiers arrived at Toccoa for their training. On display in the Museum are many items related to Fort Toccoa and the men and women who worked and trained at the Fort. There are uniforms, soldiers' gear, posters, photos, artifacts, memorabilia and more. Address: 160 N. Alexander St., Toccoa, GA 30577. Phone and website: 706-282-5055; http://toccoahistory.com

The Stephens County Historical Society and Currahee Military Museum in Toccoa, GA

WORLD WAR II MEMORIAL, TOCCOA, GA: This handsome memorial is dedicated to the men from Stephens's County Ga. who gave their lives during WW II. Their names are listed on the Memorial. Location: On the south lawn of the Stevens County courthouse.

The World War II Memorial, Toccoa, GA

WARM SPRINGS is a very small community in west-central Georgia 25 miles NE of Columbus on U-27, SR-80 and SR-84. It has long been noted for its natural warm springs, the water from which are believed to be medically beneficial. One of the major medical facilities in the area is the Franklin Roosevelt Warm Springs Institute for Rehabilitation.

LITTLE WHITE HOUSE STATE HISTORIC SITE: This is the small cottage built by Franklin Roosevelt in 1932 for his personal use whenever he came to Warm Springs. Roosevelt liked coming here because he felt that the local waters and medical therapy offered were beneficial to his health and strengthened his legs, which had been crippled by polio in 1921. This was the only house that Franklin Roosevelt ever built for himself. FDR personally selected the site, used it first as a private picnic grounds and later built the cottage. During his years as President, many notable people visited the cottage as FDR's guests.

On April 12, 1945, FDR was sitting in the great room of the house writing a speech. Two women were in the room with him. One lady was a portrait painter painting his portrait. The unfinished portrait is still there. The other woman was Lucy Mercer Rutherfurd a long-time and very close friend. Roosevelt suddenly put his hand to his head saying "I have a terrific headache," and then lapsed into unconsciousness. He had suffered a cerebral hemorrhage and died soon afterward.

He was taken to Washington, DC for a state funeral and then buried at his family estate in Hyde Park, NY.

The cottage, the nearby servants quarters and other structures have been preserved as they were when FDR lived here. Two of his automobiles, specially equipped with hand controls, are on display along with many other personal items.

The cottage is open to the public and guides are available to answer questions and offer tours. There is a video on FDR in Georgia, a snack bar, an inviting gift shop and a picnic area. Little White House address: 401 Little White House Rd. (SR-84 Alt.), Warm Springs, GA 31830. Phone and website: 706-655-5870; www.nps.gov/nr/travel/presidents/roosevelts_little_white_house.html

FRANKLIN D. ROOSEVELT STATE PARK, five miles SE of Pine Mountain, is a 10,000-acre park named after Warm Springs' famous resident. Camping, picnicking, hiking, boating, fishing and swimming are available at the park.

WARNER ROBINS: Here is a small community named after the large Air Force base nearby, Warner Robins Air Force Base. The community is on US-23, US-129 and SR-96.

The Little White House at Warm Springs, GA. President Franklin Roosevelt's private residence and the place where he died, April 12, 1945.

MUSEUM OF AVIATION: This is a biggie. This Museum is on the grounds of the Warner Robins Air Force Base and has over 100 aircraft on display. A reasonable number of them are WW II models. Motor tours are provided to cover the large expanse of the displays.

Inside the Museum there are exhibits which highlight the Normandy Invasion, the "Hump" pilots, the Tuskegee Airmen, uniforms and equipment from WW II and an exhibit honoring Congressional Medal of Honor recipients. There is a cafe and a must-visit gift shop. The Museum hosts many events throughout the year, has an educational program and a newsletter. Address: Russell Parkway. Warner Robbins, GA 31088. Phone and website: 478-923-6600; www.museumofaviation.org

The Museum of Aviation at Warner Robins Air Force Base, Warner Robins, GA

HAWAII

Before and during WW II, Hawaii was a territory of the United States and was America's primary military outpost in the Central Pacific Ocean. The Territory consisted of eight large islands and numerous smaller islands strung out in a 1100 mile-long chain from east to west. Most of the islands are of volcanic origin and have a combined land area of 6441 Sq. mi. The 1940 census counted 423,330 people in the Territory of mixed national and racial origin; native Hawaiians, Caucasians, Japanese, Chinese, Filipino and Korean were the larger minorities. Ethnic Japanese made up about ¼ of the total population.

Hawaii's economy was based on two agricultural products, sugar and pineapples and a growing tourist industry. There were many military facilities on the islands which contributed considerably to the Territory's economy.

It was here in Hawaii, on December 7, 1941, that America's involvement in WW II began with the surprise Japanese attack on the US warships anchored in Pearl Harbor and the surrounding military installations.

After the attack, martial law was declared throughout the islands; which meant that, the US Army replaced the territorial government and ruled the Territory by military decree. Under this arrangement, all airfields in Hawaii came under military control and were used for whatever needs the military had.

The Japanese, believing that they would be victorious in the war, intended to eventually occupy the islands, grant them independence as a constitutional monarchy under a cooperative, and yet to be identified, members of the old Hawaiian royal family. The newly-created nation of Hawaii would be open to Japanese settlement and eventually become a member of Japan's huge economic bloc known as "The Greater East-Asia Co-prosperity Sphere." A powerful Japanese naval force would be stationed permanently at Pearl Harbor to insure that American military aspirations stayed on their side of the Pacific Ocean.

SPECIAL NOTE:

For the purpose of listing the WW II sites in Hawaii, the islands are laid out in the geographic order from east to west beginning with the big island of Hawaii and ending with the island of Midway.

HAWAII (the "Big Island"): This is the largest of the Hawaiian Islands and is largely of volcanic origin. All throughout the war, volcanic activity was still in progress near the center of the Island and continues to this day. The Island's population lived primarily around the coasts.

During the war, the US Army Air Forces took over Hilo's airport for military use, built a second airfield, Morse Field, on the southern tip of the island, created a rest and rehabilitation center in Hawaii's Volcano National Park and built a very special US Marine camp, Camp Tarawa.

CAMP TARAWA MEMORIAL: This WW II memorial is near the town of Kamuela in the northern part of the Island on SR-19 and near the entrance to the famous Parker Ranch. It commemorates the many US Marines who came here for rest, recuperation and training after participating in some of the most difficult battles in the Pacific.

Camp Tarawa was created after, and named after, the bloody battle of Tarawa Island. Many of the surviving members of the 2nd Marine Division that invaded and eventually captured the island were sent to the Kamuela area for rest, recuperation and additional training. Some Marine veterans of the Battle of Guadalcanal were also sent here.

Many temporary WW II buildings and other facilities were constructed in the area. With time, the 3rd Marine Division trained here and acquired training in mountain warfare for the coming Battle of Iwo Jima.

The Camp Tarawa Memorial near Kamuela on the big island of Hawaii

The Marines that participated in the famous flag raising at Iwo Jima also trained here. After the war, the Camp was decommissioned and became part of the Parker Ranch.

MAUI: Maui is Hawaii's second largest island and was deeply involved in US military operations in the Pacific during the war. It became an important training and staging area for American service personnel and an important rest and relaxation site. Its beaches were used to train service personnel in amphibious operations which were so critical to America's war in the Pacific. At its peak in 1943-44, there were more than 100,000 soldiers, sailors and Marines on Maui.

Camp Maui Memorial Park, Maui, HI

CAMP MAUI MEMORIAL PARK: This was the site of Camp Maui, a staging area for the 4th US Marine Division. They staged here twice during the war between their military operations in the Pacific. After the war, interested parties established the Memorial Park on the Camp's site to honor those members of the 4th Marine Division who served and were killed during the war. The Park's grounds are immaculate and there are plaques, memorial walls and flags throughout the Park. Location; On Kokomo Rd. just north of Kokomo, Maui

OAHU: Oahu was, and still is, the most populated of all the Hawaiian Island. During the war, it abounded with military installations all around the Island with the gigantic Army, Navy and Marine complex at Pearl Harbor being the largest by far. The military installations on Oahu constituted America's major military bastion in the central Pacific. For this reason, Oahu was the focus of the surprise Japanese attack on December 7, 1941.

SPECIAL NOTE: When visiting the Island of Oahu, there are so many military sites to be seen that it is advisable to consider guided tours. These can save the visitor many hours of trying to find places on their own.

PEARL HARBOR/HONOLULU AND ENVIRONS: When it comes to WW II museums, memorials and historic sites, Pearl Harbor is ground zero. Our involvement in World War II began here with the Japanese attack of December 7, 1941. WW II memorials abound in the Harbor itself, on Ford Island and in the adjoining area. Pearl Harbor is still America's major military installation in the Pacific so some military restrictions apply to visitors.

VISITORS CENTER: It is advisable that visitors start here when visiting Pearl Harbor memorials and sites. Detailed information on the various sites is available and arrangements came be made for visiting all of the sites.

  The Center, itself, is a museum and has facilities such as two digital movie theaters, and educational program, multimedia exhibits, open-air exhibits and a large gift and book shop. Food is also available. The Visitors Center is actually a campus because there are several memorials and monuments on the grounds and next door is the *USS Bowfin* Submarine Museum. Location of the Visitors Center: On the waterfront, just off Kamehameha Dr. and south of the Ford Island Bridge. Phone and website: 808-423-1942 and 808-954-8777; http://pacifichistoricparks.org/pearl-harbor-hawaii.php?page=visitorcenter

The Pearl Harbor Visitors Center is the place to start when visiting Pearl Harbor.

BROTHERS IN VALOR MEMORIAL: During the war, the population of Hawaii was about 25% ethnic Japanese. When the US Army authorized ethnic Japanese men of military age to join the Army, more than half of the number of volunteers came from Hawaii. This Memorial honors those men, specifically the 100th Battalion of the 442 Regimental Combat Team. That Battalion suffered

The Brothers in Valor Memorial in Honolulu

numerous casualties in Italy and became known as the "Purple Heart Battalion." Location: Kalakaua Av. north of Saratoga Rd. in Honolulu.

PACIFIC AVIATION MUSEUM: This excellent museum is on Ford Island which is in the center of Pearl Harbor. At the time of the Japanese attack, there was a US Navy airfield here and most of the American battleships, which were the primary targets of the Japanese attackers, were anchored along the eastern shore of the Island. Two of the naval hangars, #37 and #79, that survived the attack, now constitute the Museum which offers considerable information and detail about the Japanese attack. Most of the Museum's aircraft on display, which consist of WW II models and postwar models, are in hangar #37. In hangar #79 is an aircraft restoration shop that can be viewed by visitors. Hangar #79 still bears some of the bullet holes from the Japanese attack. The Museum has a cafe and an interesting and well-stocked gift shop. Address: 319 Lexington Blvd., Honolulu, HI 96818. Phone and website: 808-441-1000; www.pacificaviationmuseum.org

USS ARIZONA **MEMORIAL:** This is, perhaps, the most famous of all WW II sites in the United States. This important warship was sunk during the Japanese attack on Pearl Harbor, December 7, 1941, with the loss of 1177 lives and has become the undisputed symbol of the Japanese surprise attack. Most of the individuals killed are still aboard the *Arizona* and their names are recorded inside the Memorial on a memorial wall. The ashes of many of those who survived the sinking and have departed are interred under water on the ship's deck.

Leaving for the attack - a display of a Japanese plane about to take off to bomb Pearl Harbor.

The USS Arizona Memorial at Pearl Harbor.

The remains of the ship are clearly visible through the shallow waters of Pearl Harbor. This is a must-see WW II historic site. Visitor access is by boat. Address, phone and website. Same as those shown in the Visitors Center above.

USS BOWFIN **SUBMARINE MUSEUM AND PARK:** This excellent museum is next door to the Pearl Harbor Visitors Center and easily accessible. Its mission is to honor the men and women who served in the US Navy's submarine service during the war. The center piece of the Museum is the WW II submarine, *USS Bowfin,* which is anchored in the water off the Museum's water front. It is accessible to visitors.

The *Bowfin* acquired the nickname the "Pearl Harbor Avenger" because she was so active and so

successful fighting the Japanese Navy. She performed nine war patrols, sank 44 enemy vessels, damaged six more and became one of the most decorated vessels in the US Navy during the war.

Inside the Museum are many artifacts related to the *Bowfin,* her crew and the US Navy's Submarine Service in general. In the Museum is a large-scale 10 ft. long scale model of the *Bowfin* showing her interior in great detail. Address: 11 Arizona Dr., Honolulu, HI 96818. Phone and website: 808-423-1341; www.bowfin.org

The USS Bowfin at the USS Bowfin Submarine Museum and Park.

USS MISSOURI MEMORIAL: America's involvement began with the sinking of the battleship *USS Arizona* and other ships at Pearl Harbor and ended with the Japanese surrender on the deck of the battleship *USS Missouri* in Tokyo Bay. Both of these ships are now within yards of each other in Pearl Harbor.

The *Missouri,* the "Mighty MO," saw action during WW II and served again later during the Korean Conflict. She was decommissioned in the 1950s but recommissioned in the 1960s and saw action in

the Persian Gulf area as late as 1991. She is now a floating museum and open to the public.

Visitors may wander throughout the ship's interior seeing the crews' quarters, officers' quarters, the galleys, command centers and the other working sections of the ship. On the rear of the ship, damage can still be seen where a Kamikaze suicide aircraft hit the ship during the latter days of WW II. Address, phone and website: Same as the Visitors Center Above.

This is the battleship USS Missouri. It was on her deck that the Japanese
surrendered unconditionally in Tokyo Bay on September 2, 1945, thus ending WW II.

USS OKLAHOMA MEMORIAL: This outstanding memorial is on Ford Island within site of the *US*

Missouri. The *Oklahoma,* like the *Arizona,* was sunk during the Japanese attack on Pearl Harbor. But she was raised in 1943, stripped of her guns and other salvageable items and sold for scrap. She met an inglorious end when, in 1947, she accidentally sank while under tow to the mainland where she was to be cut up for scrap.

The Memorial shows the ship etched in stone and there are 429 white marble columns, shaped in the "V for Victory" sign, with the names of the 429 sailors who died aboard her during the attack. Address, phone and website: Same as the Visitors Center above.

The USS Oklahoma Memorial is within sight of the USS Missouri.

USS UTAH **MEMORIAL:** The battleship *USS Utah* was another of the battle ships sunk by the Japanese during their attack on Pearl Harbor. This ship was anchored on the west side of Ford Island and was old - built before WW I - and was being used primarily for training purposes by the US Navy. Fifty eight officers and enlisted men perished in the attack and 461 survived. This Memorial commemorates those who served aboard the *Utah* and the sacrifices they made. The ship remains where she was sunk and part of its superstructure can be seen above water. Location: Western shore of Ford Island

The USS Utah Memorial on Ford Island, Pearl Harbor, the superstructure of the ship can be seen to the left.

END OF THE MUSEUMS AND MEMORIALS AT PEARL HARBOR

HALEIWA WAR MEMORIAL: This memorial is located on Haleiwa Beach on the NW coast of Oahu. It consists of a white obelisk and honors men and women from the local area that died in WW II, Korea and Viet Nam. Their names are carved on the sides of the obelisk. Location: Haleiwa Beach off SR-83

THE NATIONAL MEMORIAL CEMETERY OF THE PACIFIC (THE PUNCHBOWL): Resting in this hollowed spot, an extinct volcanic crater, are many of those who died during the Japanese attack of Pearl Harbor on December 7, 1941. Also interred here are the dead from many of the other WW II battles fought in the Pacific during the war. Dead from the Korean Conflict and Viet Nam are also interred here. The most famous individual in the Cemetery is Ernie Pyle, the famous war correspondent who was killed late in WW II.

The Haleiwa War Memorial

The center piece of the Cemetery is the Memorial Pathway with a variety of memorials from various organizations lining the Pathway on both sides. Additional Memorials can also be seen in other parts of the Cemetery. The gravestones of Congressional Medal of Honor recipients are defined in gold leaf. The Cemetery is now full but is open to the public and is host for many ceremonies and memorial services through the year.

The National Memorial Cemetery of the Pacific (The Punchbowl)

PACIFIC WAR MEMORIAL: On the eastern shore of Oahu on the Mokapu Peninsula is a huge US Marine Base. At the entrance to the Base is an impressive memorial to the Marines who fought and died in the Pacific during the war. Its center piece is a statue of the famous flag raising at Iwo Jima on February 23, 1945. (Photo next page)

THE TROPIC LIGHTENING MUSEUM (SCHOFIELD BARRACKS): When the Japanese attacked Pearl Harbor; the US Army's 25th Infantry Division was in residence at Schofield Barracks, the Army's main facility on Oahu. The Barracks building were strafed by Japanese planes causing some casualties. Japanese bullet holes can still be seen on the concrete walls of the Barracks. Schofield Barracks has remained an Army installation through the years and this Museum is on the

barrack's grounds in Building 361. It commemorates the men of the 25th Division who suffered the attack and later served throughout the Pacific during the rest of the war and in the occupation of Japan. The 25th also served in Korea, Viet Nam and some of America's other conflicts.

In the Museum are uniforms soldiers' gear, small arms, photographs and many artifacts related to the 25th.

Outside the Museum are tanks, anti-aircraft guns and cannons. Address: Waianae Av., Building 361, Schofield Barracks, HI 96857. Phone and website: 808-655-0438; www.25idl.army.mil/

The Pacific War Memorial at the entrance to the US Marine Base of Hawaii

The US Army Museum of Hawaii on Waikiki Beach

US ARMY MUSEUM OF HAWAII: This excellent museum is housed inside Battery Randolph, a coastal artillery battery, at Fort DeRussy – and it is on famous Waikiki Beach. The Museum collection includes some WW II tanks, a collection of small arms, artillery pieces, photographs and a wide range of US Army artifacts from the Korean War, Viet Nam and other conflicts. It also traces the history of Hawaii from before annexation days to the present. Considerable attention is given to WW II. There are exhibits showing and explaining on-going US Army projects in the Pacific and the "Gallery of Heroes" honoring Congressional Medal of Honor recipients. There is a museum store that is well worth your time to visit. Address: 2161 Kalia Rd., Honolulu, HI 96815. Phone and website: 808-955-9552; www.hiarmymuseumsoc.org

MIDWAY ATOLL (MIDWAY ISLAND): The Battle of Midway – June 1942 - was a great American victory during WW II and proved to be the turning point of the war in the Pacific. Many remembrances of WW II remain in the form of old buildings, gun emplacements, remnants of the airfields and other sites. There are several small monuments and a collection of bronze plaques scattered about the atoll. The largest of the memorials is the Midway National Landmark Memorial on Sand Island. It is in a small park with a covered memorial plaque, several WW II era artillery pieces and old anchor.

The Midway National Landmark on Sand Island

IDAHO

For a state with only 534,000 people, Idaho made a meaningful contribution to America's war effort. There were several major military installations in the state, several important manufacturing operations, a relocation camp for ethnic Japanese and about 20 prisoner of war camps.

All eight of the state's major airports were used by the military as well as many smaller airfields.

In the later months of the war, Idaho, like the other western states, was subjected to the Japanese balloon bombing campaign, but it caused virtually no damage in the state.

ATHOL is a small community in Idaho's panhandle 20 miles north of Coeur d'Alene on US-95 and SR-54. Fifteen miles to the east was the US Naval Training Station, Farragut, the second largest naval training facility in the world.

FARRAGUT STATE PARK MUSEUM: Farragut State Park is built on the grounds of the former US Naval Training Station, Farragut and covers some 4000 acres. It has all the amenities of a fine state park plus a small museum which records the history of the site as a WW II naval training facility. The Museum is in the Naval Station's former brig and displays restored vehicles, uniforms, flags, small arms, training equipment, photographs, documents and a large collection of other memorabilia from the training base. Address: 13550 E. Hwy. 54, Athol, ID 83801. Phone and website: 208-683-2425; http://parksandrecreation.idaho.gov/parks/farragut.aspx

BOISE, in the SE corner of the state on I-84, is the capitol of Idaho and, during WW II was the state's largest city.

Boise was home to Boise Barracks, a military camp that was first established in 1863. From 1939, the post was used as an Idaho National Guard encampment and a training center.

Gowen Field, four miles south of downtown Boise, was the city's local airport. In Dec. 1940, the airport was taken over by the Army Air Corps as a training field for pilots and crews of medium bombers.

IDAHO MILITARY HISTORY MUSEUM is located next to the former Gowen Field and relates the history of Gowen Field as well as the history of Idaho in general throughout America's wars from the Philippine Insurrection to the present. There is also information on the WW II Naval Training Center, Farragut, the Idaho National Guard, the cruiser *USS Boise,* which saw considerable action in the Pacific during WW II.

  Also on display are field equipment, medals, photos, US and foreign small arms and equipment, works of art and more. Several military vehicles are displayed outside the Museum. The Museum has a large reference library, publishes a newsletter and has a very nice gift shop. Tours are available. Address: 4748 Lindburgh St. Bldg. 924, Boise, ID 83705 (entrance off of Harvard St). Phone and website: 208-272-4841; http://museum.mil.idaho.gov/contac.html

CL-47 *USS BOISE* MEMORIAL: The US Navy's light cruiser, the *USS Boise*, was in the Pacific when the war with Japan began and she remained there until the war ended. In the interim she took part in many important battles in the Pacific.

  This beautiful memorial commemorates the ship and her crew. In 1978, however, the Japanese got even. She was towed to Japan and sold for scrap. Location: Myrtle St.

WARHAWK AIR MUSEUM: This is a privately-owned 2000 Sq. ft. air museum at Nampa, 15 miles west of Boise on I-84. The Museum is located at the local airport and its mission is to teach and preserve the WW II history from the home front to the war front. Aviation history is given special attention.

  The Museum has a nice collection of aircraft, many of which are from WW II, and there is a restoration facility. Most of the Museum's aircraft are flyable. There are displays of aircraft engines, a Norden bombsite,

The CL-47 USS Boise Memorial In Boise, ID

posters, photographs, uniforms, ration books, personal histories and more.

  The Museum hosts fly-ins and social and other events during the year. Tours are available and there is a gift shop that you should not miss. Address: 201 Municipal Dr., Nampa, ID 83687. Phone and website: 208-465-6446; www.sarhowkairmueum.org

LAVA HOT SPRINGS is a small community in SE Idaho on US-30. During WW II, it suffered a disproportionate number of war casualties compared to other communities its size.

The Warhawk Air Museum, Nampa, ID

WORLD WAR II MEMORIAL: The citizens of this very small Idaho community have erected a handsome stone memorial honoring the citizens of the community who became casualties during WW II.

The World War II Memorial in Lava Hot Springs, ID

REXBURG is a county seat in SE Idaho, 25 miles NE of Idaho Falls on US-20 and SR-33.

LEGACY FLIGHT MUSEUM is located at the Rexburg-Madison Airport in an historic 18,000 Sq. ft. aircraft hangar. It was founded by John Bagley.

On display are about 20 aircraft ranging from pre-WW II to the jet age. Many of the aircraft are flyable. The Museum has a library and is host to several annual air events. Address: Rexburg-Madison Airport, 400 Airport Rd. Rexburg, ID 83440. Phone and website: 208-359-5905; www.legacyflightmuseum.com

The Legacy Flight Museum of Rexburg, ID.

ILLINOIS

When people spoke of America as being the "Arsenal of Democracy" during WW II, they were referring to states like Illinois. This state produced almost every type of weapon used in the war; ships, planes, tanks, trucks, munitions, small arms, steel, diesel and aircraft engines, telephone equipment and thousands of other items of war. Most of these things came from the Chicago metropolitan area which was one of America's great industrial centers.

In 1940, Chicago was the nation's second largest city and had over 9,000 manufacturing plants scattered throughout the four adjoining counties. In those counties, as well as throughout the state, many new manufacturing firms came into being and existing ones expanded to meet the ever-increasing demands of the war. Some plants ran around-the-clock and there was plenty of overtime for the workers. But there was almost always a shortage of workers despite the fact that the state's population grew by about 318,000 during the war years. Illinois became 6th in the nation in war expenditures among the 48 states.

The World War II Memorial in Bath, IL

BATH, on SR-78, is a town on only 300 people but they saw fit to honor their local WW II veterans.

WORLD WAR II MEMORIAL: The inscription on this memorial reads "TO OUR HERO DEAD IN WORLD WAR II, 1941-1945. THE VILLAGE OF BATH PAYS HOMAGE TO THE MEMORY OF THESE VALIANTS WHO GAVE THE LAST FULL MEASURE OF DEVOTION TO THEIR COUNTRY." The names of those who died are etched on the memorial. Location: N. Oak St. (SR-78), in a village park.

BLOOMINGTON is a county seat in central Illinois on I-39, I-55 and I-74.

WORLD WAR II MEMORIAL: As visitors walk into the main entrance of the McLean County Court House, they pass this impressive memorial. It is dedicated to those individuals from McLean County who gave their lives during WW II. Location: At the entrance to the McLean County Court House in downtown Bloomington

BROOKPORT is a small community on the Ohio River opposite Paducah, KY.

The WW II Memorial in Bloomington, IL

Brookport World War II Memorial

BROOKPORT WORLD WAR II MEMORIAL: This memorial consists of a statue of a WW II soldier in combat uniform carrying his M-1 rifle and standing on a pedestal. It is dedicated to the local citizens who served in the war. Their names are listed on the memorial. Location: US-45 and 3rd St.

CHICAGO METROPOLITAN AREA: Chicago was America's second largest city during the war and it and its suburbs contained more than half the citizens of the state of Illinois. The city was a major industrial, commercial and trade center, and the largest railroad hub in the world. A very large variety of war materials were produced in the Chicago area from K-rations to aircraft.

During 1942, several federal agencies, with over 2900 employees, moved to Chicago from Washington, DC to relieve overcrowding there. A year later more federal agencies moved to Chicago and an additional 14,000 people came with them

FIRST DIVISION MUSEUM AT CANTIGNY is located in Wheaton, IL, 25 miles west of downtown Chicago. This was originally the 500-acre estate of the late Col. Robert R. McCormick, editor and publisher of the Chicago Daily Tribune newspaper. Col. McCormick commanded an artillery battalion of the First Infantry Div., "The Big Red One," during WW I and was instrumental in founding the Museum. Cantigny was the first battle in France that the Americans participated in during WW I.

The Museum traces the history of the US Army's First Division and its predecessors from 1776 to the present day and has a significant display of both WW I and WW II artifacts. The WW II collection

The McCormick Mansion at Cantigny Park

has information related to the Division's activities in North Africa, Sicily and Normandy.

The Museum has a Tank Park displaying about 20 tanks from WW I to the present. Also, there is a large collection of military vehicles and weaponry.

The Museum has a large library, a large archives collection, a research facility and produces several publications. Many social and military-related events are held at the Museum throughout the year and the Museum offers facilities rentals for a wide variety of gatherings. Tours are available and there is a gift shop that offers a large and fascinating collection of souvenirs and gifts. Address: One South 151 Winfield Rd., Wheaton, IL 60187. Phone and website: 630-260-8185; www.firstdivisionmuseum.org

GREAT LAKES NAVAL MUSEUM: This is a government-owned museum on the grounds of the Great Lakes Naval Training Station north of Chicago. Its mission is to tell the story of "Boot Camp," the Navy's form of basic training for new recruits.

On display are uniforms, equipment, personal gear of the recruits, photographs, training aids, flags,

Navy periodicals and more. A special section of the Museum is dedicated to the expanding role of women in the US Navy. Address: Building 42, 610 Farragut Av., Great Lakes, IL 60888. Phone and website: 847-688-3154; www.greatlakesnavalmuseum.org

The Great Lakes Naval Museum

KATYN POLISH WAR MEMORIAL: Katyn is a forested area in the western part of Russia and during WW II one of the great atrocities of the war occurred there. During April and May 1940, some 20,000 Polish military officers, political leaders, intelligentsia and others were summarily executed in the Katyn forest and at other locations in the Soviet Union. The act was carried out by the NKVD, the Soviet Secret Police, and was intended to eliminate the leadership of Free Poland, punish the Poles for the great military defeat of Bolshevik forces at the gates of Warsaw in 1920 and set the stage for the Communist takeover of Poland after the war.

The Polish-American community is heart sick over this incident to this day. In the Chicago suburb of Niles, they have erected a magnificent memorial commemorating the memory of those killed. The word "KATYN" and the year "1940" are in large bold letters and feature a statue of the Holy Mother holding a fallen victim. There are also a large cross, flag poles and marble memorials telling of the event. Location: St. Adalbert's Catholic Cemetery, 6800 Milwaukee Av., Niles, IL

The Katyn Polish War Memorial in Niles, IL

MUSEUM OF SCIENCE AND INDUSTRY, in Jackson Park at 57th St. and Lake Shore Dr., is one of the largest and foremost science museums in the world. Among its numerous exhibits are several WW II displays, the most prominent being the German submarine *U-505* which was captured by the US. Navy in June 1944 off the coast of West Africa. Visitors may board the submarine and walk through it.

There is a 20-minute narrative on the dramatic capture of the submarine, plus artifacts from the submarine, such as its log book and personal belongings of the crewmen.

When the submarine was captured, the Americans had every indication to believe that the Germans believed that the submarine had been sunk. Therefore, the Americans did not want the Germans to know that they had captured the submarine along with its crew, secret code books and other important information. Therefore, the submarine's crew had to be imprisoned in such a manner that they were not in contact with other German POWs who, through their personal correspondence back home, might reveal that the submarine was captured and not sunk. Accordingly, the crew was incarcerated for the duration of the war in a secret and closely-guarded POW camp at Camp Ruston, an Army base in Louisiana.

The Museum also has scale models of several WW II ships. In the Museum's airplane collection is a British Spitfire and a German Stuka Dive Bomber. All aircraft are indoors. Address: 57th and Lake Shore Dr., Chicago, IL 60637. Phone and website: 773-684-1414; www.msihicago.org

The forward torpedo room of the German submarine U-505

The "Butch" O'Hare Exhibit at O'Hare International Airport

O'HARE INTERNATIONAL AIRPORT/"BUTCH" O'HARE EXHIBIT: This major airport is named in honor of Lt. Commander Edward H. "Butch" O'Hare who, as a naval aviator in the Pacific, shot down 20 Japanese aircraft and won the Congressional Medal of Honor.

In Terminal Two, there is a memorial to O'Hare which consists of detailed information on him and his military exploits and a restored model of the aircraft he flew, an F4F-3 Wildcat. O'Hare was later killed in action on November 26, 1943. Location: O'Hare International Airport, Terminal Two

UNIVERSITY OF CHICAGO/GEORGE H. JONES LABORATORY, ROOM 405: During the war, almost all major universities in the US made scientific and scholastic contributions to the war effort. One of the war's most significant scientific breakthroughs, however, was made here at the University of Chicago, and stands out above all the others. On Dec. 2, 1942, a group of scientists, working in a make-shift laboratory under the stands of the University's football stadium, created the world's first controlled nuclear chain reaction. This discovery proved that it was feasible to make the fissionable element plutonium out of uranium and thereby produce an extremely powerful bomb using the explosive power generated by the splitting of plutonium atoms. This provided the US with a second type of atomic bomb, the other being a bomb which used enriched uranium.

The experiments were directed by Enrico Fermi, an Italian-born, Nobel Prize winning physicist who had fled Fascist Italy in 1939 because his wife was Jewish. Fermi later became a member of the "Manhattan Project," America's program to create an atomic bomb, and served as the Project's chief consultant for all nuclear physics experiments.

The football stadium is gone, but a bronze marker marks the spot where the famous experiments took place. The marker is on the east side of S. Ellis St. in the middle of the block between 56th and 57th Sts.

Room 405, Jones Laboratory: This room is a National Historic Landmark because in 1942 it was in this room, then a science laboratory, that the man-made element of plutonium was first isolated and weighed. This was another of the important discoveries that lead to the development of the atomic bombs. Jones Laboratory is on the east side of S. Ellis St. several building south of 57th St.

These developments made at the University of Chicago ultimately led to the creation of the Argonne National Laboratory in DuPage County, 25 miles SW of Chicago in 1946. This was a facility built by the Federal Government to pursue further developments in atomic energy and weaponry.

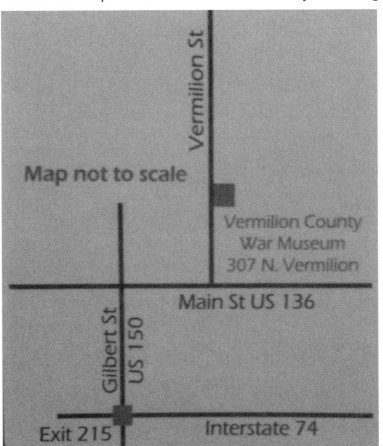

DANVILLE: Danville is a county seat on the eastern border of Illinois near the Indiana state line on I-74, US-136, US-150 and SR-1.

VERMILION COUNTY WAR MUSEUM: Here is a fine 14,000 Sq. ft. county museum that commemorates all of America's wars. It is located in an historic Carnegie Library building and has over 5,000 artifacts with a respectable portion of them being related to WW II. There is a WW II room, a captured Japanese canon, small arms, uniforms, a library, documents and more. The Museum hosts special events during the year including WW II reenactments. Address: 307 N. Vermilion St., Danville, IL 61832. Phone and website: 217-431-0034; www.vcwm.org

The Vermilion County War Museum is near downtown Danville

FLORA is 32 miles south of Effingham on US-45 and US-50.

WORLD WAR II MEMORIAL: This Memorial commemorates those individuals from Clay County who

The World War II Memorial in Flora, IL

gave their lives in WW II. All of their names are listed on the Memorial. It was erected by the citizens of Flora and VFW Post #3999 and the American Legion.

GERMANTOWN is a small community eight miles NE of Peoria on SR-116.

VETERANS MEMORIAL PARK: This is a city park with a beautiful memorial dedicated to those who served in WW II. There is a central monument surrounded by additional monuments with plaques naming those so honored and a cluster of flag poles. Location: Munster St., Germantown, IL 62245

HAVANA is a county seat 35 miles SW of Peoria on US-136, SR-78 and SR-97.

MASON COUNTY SECOND WORLD WAR MEMORIAL: Mason County and local VFW Post #6408 erected this memorial to honor the men and women of Mason County who served in WW II. Listed on the Memorial are the names of those from Mason County who made the final sacrifice. Location: Mason County Courthouse.

The WW II Memorial in the Veterans Memorial Park of Germantown, IL

The Mason County Second War Memorial in Havana, IL

NAPERVILLE is 30 miles west of downtown Chicago just off I-88 on US-34.

VETERANS' VALOR: This unique WW II memorial show five life-sized figures in WW II uniforms and each has a name. They are the likenesses of five young men who attended Naperville High School and served in WW II. All returned home safely. The Memorial also honors the heroism of Naperville's many other veterans who served during the war. Location: Corner of Washington St. and W. Van Buren Av.

94

The Veterans' Valor Memorial in Naperville, IL

PONTIAC is a county seat 25 miles NE of Bloomington on I-55 and SR-116.

LIVINGSTON COUNTY WW II MEMORIAL: This memorial consists of four stone pillars representing the four branches of military service during WW II. They surround a stone monument in the center listing the names of those from Livingston County who died in the war. Location: Pontiac Courthouse lawn.

The Livingston County WW II Memorial

ROCK ISLAND: This is one of the Quad Cities on the Illinois/Iowa border, I-80, I-88 and the Mississippi River. On an island in the River is a military arsenal, Rock Island Arsenal, which is one of the oldest arsenals in the nation and has produced military equipment and arms for the US armed forces from the early days of the republic.

ROCK ISLAND ARSENAL MUSEUM: Here, on the grounds of the Rock Island Arsenal, is a large museum in one of the Arsenal's many old stone buildings.

  The Museum was established in 1905 making it the second oldest military museum in the country after that at West Point. The Museum's mission is, of course, to tell the history of the Arsenal and the many military items that have been manufactured there over the years. The exhibits are very interesting but the WW II exhibit is relatively small. One of the WW II exhibits tells of the M-1 Garand rifle which was the standard infantry weapon of WW II. The Museum has an extensive rifle collection including Garand M-1 rifle serial number two.

  Tours of the Arsenal can be arranged at the Museum and there is a very interesting gift shop. Address: Rock Island Arsenal Museum, Rock Island, IL 61299. Phone and website: 309-782-5021 and 309-782-2979; http://riamwr.com/museum.htm

RUSSELL is in the extreme northeastern corner of the state off I-94 and just one mile south of the Wisconsin state line.

RUSSELL MILITARY MUSEUM is one the larger military museums in the Midwest but the WW II exhibits make up a relatively small portion of the total. In the Museum, and on its eight acres of land, are some 300 military vehicles and aircraft on display including Sherman and Stuart tanks, artillery pieces and half-tracks from WW II. There are additional displays inside the museum including small arms, uniforms, photos and other militaria.

The Museum is host to social and military-related events, has a very interesting gift shop, an educational program and tours are available. Address: 43363 Old Highway 41, Russell, IL 60075. Phone and website: 847-395-7020; www.russellmilitarymuseum.com

SPRINGFIELD, near the geographic center of the state is on I-72 and I-55 and is the state capitol of Illinois.

ILLINOIS STATE MILITARY MUSEUM: This Museum is located at Camp Lincoln, the headquarters of the Illinois National Guard.

The Russell Military Museum

It covers the long history of Illinois' involvement in America's conflicts and honors the many Illinois citizens who served with honor.

The WW II exhibits are a modest portion of the total. Address: 1301 N. MacArthur Blvd., Springfield, IL 62702. Phone and website: 217-761-3910; www.il.ngb.army.mil/museum

WORLD WAR II ILLINOIS VETERANS MEMORIAL: This impressive memorial is located in the Oak Ridge Cemetery in Springfield. It consists of a 22 ton concrete globe, two black granite memorial walls inscribed with details of battles waged in the Pacific

The Illinois State Military Museum

and Europe, a replica of the Iwo Jima flag raising and quotations from both Franklin D. Roosevelt and Harry S Truman. There is a court yard paved with bricks bearing the names of Illinois veterans of the war. Address: Oak Ridge Cemetery, 1499 J. David Jones Pkwy, Springfield, IL.

The WW II Illinois Veterans Memorial

INDIANA

During WW II, Indiana was a major producer of both war materials and food. Virtually all of the state's larger cities had manufacturing plants which turned out things like iron and steel, airplanes, tanks, gasoline and diesel engines, automobiles, trucks, railroad cars, farm machinery, electrical machinery, tires, glass products, pharmaceuticals, landing craft, munitions and the famous Norden bombsite.

ANDERSON is a county seat and one of Indiana's larger cities NE of Indianapolis on I-69.

HISTORICAL MILITARY ARMOR MUSEUM: This is a large privately-owned museum with tons of heavy military equipment. There are tanks, mobile guns, half-tracks, trucks and other pieces of heavy equipment from WW I to the present. Military equipment from the WW II era is plentiful.

Of special interest, is a historical display tracing the evolution of the light tank from WW I to the present.

Many of the displays are "hands on." Tours are available and there are facilities for meetings and other gatherings. Joseph McClain is the museum's Director. Address: 2330 Crystal St., Anderson, IN 46012. Phone: 765-649-8265

ANGOLA: Angola is a county seat in NE Indiana on I-69 and US-20. It is close to both the Michigan and Ohio state lines.

GENERAL LEWIS B. HERSHEY MUSEUM: Angola was the home of General Lewis B. Hershey, head of the Selective Service during WW II. When a young man of military age got a letter from the President of the United States that began with "Greeting," it came from General Hershey's office. The young man had been drafted.

The Museum is on the grounds of Tri-State University and contains personal memorabilia of the General and information on his military career and his service during WW II. There are also exhibits of service memorabilia since the Civil War. Address: One University Av., Angola, IN 46703. Phone: 260-665-4162

ASHLEY is a small community in the NE corner of Indiana on I-69 and SR-4.

ASHLEY WORLD WAR II MEMORIAL: This memorial consists of two WW II artillery pieces and a stone monument that is dedicated to all of those from Ashley who served in the war and lists the names of those who perished.

AUBURN is a county seat 20 miles north of Ft. Wayne on I-69 and is well-known for its outstanding museums of antique cars and

The Ashley, WW II Memorial in Ashley, IN

97

military collections.

THE NATIONAL MILITARY HISTORIC CENTER/WORLD WAR II VICTORY MUSEUM: Here is a biggie - especially when it comes to WW II. This multi-gallery Museum houses one of the most outstanding collections of WW II artifacts in the country and has in its collection some 150 military vehicles. They range from motorcycles to 45 ton tank recovery vehicles. Several of the vehicles are believed to be the last remaining copies in existence.

Some of the vehicles on display actually took part in the Battle of the Bulge and other European battles. Along with this outstanding collection of vehicles, are excellent exhibits of uniforms, weapons, combat gear, documents and interesting personal items of the soldiers such as chow passes, sewing kits and a pocket guide to Germany. The Museum has specialty displays, video presentations, dioramas, an American Veterans Hall of Honor, a library, an ongoing educational program and a don't-miss-seeing gift shop. The Museum's founder is a local Auburn citizen, Dean Kruse. Address: 5634 County Rd. 11A, Auburn, IN 46706. Phone and website: 260-927-9144; www.militaryhistorycenter.org.

The National Military History Center of Auburn, IN

BLOOMINGTON is a county seat 60 miles SW of downtown Indianapolis on SR-37 and SR-46 and is the home of Indiana University.

MONROE COUNTY/BLOOMINGTON WW II MEMORIAL depicts a WW II GI in action advancing towards the enemy. Inscribed on the Memorial is this tribute: "THE SPIRIT OF THE FIGHTING YANK. MEMORIAL TO THE ARMED FORCES OF THE UNITED STATES OF AMERICA WORLD WAR II." Location: The intersection of W. 6th St. and N. Walnut St.

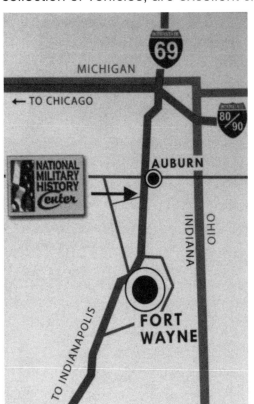
Easy access to the National Military History Center is from exit 126 off I-69. Go west to the second drive on the right

COLUMBUS is a county seat 35 miles south of Indianapolis on I-65, US-31 and SR-46. During the war, it was home to: Atterbury Army Air Base, the military air facility and part of the Camp Atterbury complex which is just to the north at Edinburgh.

ATTERBURY-BAKALAR AIR MUSEUM: This fine museum is on the grounds of the Columbus Municipal Airport (formerly the Atterbury Army Air Base) on the north side of town. Its mission is to preserve the history of Atterbury Army Air Base from its beginning in 1942 during WW II to its present use as a commercial airport.

Many of the displays in the Museum relate to the Air Base's WW II history and its days during the Cold War when it was known as, Bakalar Air Force Base. Personal stories of individuals who served on the base are highlighted and there are displays of, medals, uniforms, documents, photos, scale aircraft models and other items related to the field's military past. There is an extensive exhibit on glider pilots and another on the Tuskegee Airmen.

The Monroe County/Bloomington World War II Memorial in Bloomington, IN

The Museum has an on-going educational program and on the Museum's grounds is the Bartholomew County Memorial for Veterans and the Walk of Honor. Tours are available and the Museum is very active in local affairs. Address: 4742 Ray Boll Blvd., Columbus, IN 47203. Phone and website: 812-372-4356; www.atterburybakalarairmuseum.org

CORYDON, which once was the capitol of Indiana, is a county seat in the southern part of the state on I-64, SR-62 and SR-135.

CORYDON WAR MEMORIAL: This handsome memorial is dedicated in lasting tribute to WW II veterans of Harrison County. It is well landscaped and bears the names of those who served during WW II. Panels have been added to either end of the Memorial commemorating those who served in the Korean Conflict and in Viet Nam. Location: At the intersection of N. Capitol Av. (SR-62) and E. Walnut St.

CRAWFORDSVILLE is a county seat 40 miles NW of Indianapolis on I-74.

THE ROBKEY ARMOR MUSEUM: This is a large 50+ acre museum with dozens of US and foreign military vehicles. Many of them are from

The Corydon War Memorial in Corydon, IN

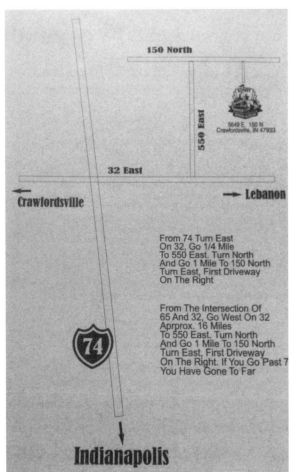

150 North

550 East

5649 E. 150 N.
Crawfordsville, IN 47933

32 East

← Crawfordsville

→ Lebanon

From 74 Turn East
On 32, Go 1/4 Mile
To 550 East. Turn North
And Go 1 Mile To 150 North
Turn East, First Driveway
On The Right

From The Intersection Of
65 And 32, Go West On 32
Aprprox. 16 Miles
To 550 East. Turn North
And Go 1 Mile To 150 North
Turn East, First Driveway
On The Right. If You Go Past 7
You Have Gone To Far

74

↓

Indianapolis

*The Ropkey Armor Museum
in Crawfordsville, IN*

ERNIE PYLE ROADSIDE PARK: This is a pleasant and inviting park named in honor of Dana's most famous resident. There is a stone memorial marker in the park honoring Pyle and facilities that one would expect in such a park. Park facilities include a pavilion, picnic tables, playground, camp sites and an attraction not seen in many parks, a covered bridge. Location: On US-36, 2.2 miles east of SR-71

ERNIE PYLE STATE HISTORIC SITE: This is the birthplace of Ernie Pyle, America's best-known WW II correspondent. The house, originally a farm house, was moved to its present location in Dana after the war.

the WW II era. Vintage aircraft are also on display. The Museum is immaculate, climate-controlled and most of the vehicles are indoors.

There are also displays of memorabilia and artifacts and, as you visit the Museum, you will be entertained by music of the past which is often played over a public address system. Tours are available and the Museum is often the destination of clubs and other groups. Address: 5649 E 150 N, Crawfordsville, IN 47933. Phone and website: 765-794-0238; www.ropkeyarmormuseum.com

CROWN POINT is a county seat in the NW corner on the state on I-65, US-231, SR-5 and SR-55.

WW II TRIANGLE MEMORIAL: Look for the M-4 Sherman Tank. That's the center piece of the WW II Triangle Memorial in Crown Point, IN. Honored by this Memorial are all who served in WW II. The tank is in the northern part of the city and faces north as if it were protecting the city from an attack. Location: At the intersection of N. Main St. and E. Goldsborough St.

DANA is a small community in the west-central part of Indiana near the Illinois state line on US-36 and SR-71. It was the home of the famous war correspondent, Ernie Pyle, who was killed in the Pacific during the last months of the war.

*This WW II M-4 Sherman Tank is the
centerpiece of the WW II Triangle Memorial in Crown Point, IN.*

100

Pyle, a Pulitzer Prize-winning newspaper columnist, wrote from the eyes of the common soldier and gave the folks back home a truthful and realistic account of what was happening in the heads and hearts of their loved ones at the front.

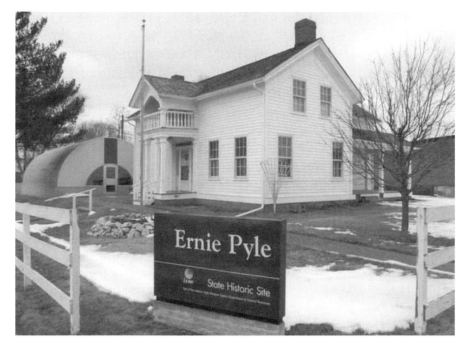

The Ernie Pyle home in Dana, IN

Pyle was killed by a Japanese sniper in 1945 and his death was such a great loss that it was announced personally by President Harry S Truman. Pyle is buried in Hawaii. His home is restored and open to the public and displays many of Pyle's personal belongings. There are two WW II Quonset huts on the property housing many items related to Pyle. And there is a video theater, a research library and a well-stocked and interesting gift shop. Tours are available. Address: 120 W. Briarwood Av., Dana, IN 47847-0338. Phone and website: 765-665-3633 and 765-665-3084; www.erniepyle.org

EDINBURGH is 25 miles south of Indianapolis on I-65 and is home to Camp Atterbury, the headquarters of the Indiana National Guard.

CAMP ATTERBURY MUSEUM AND VETERANS MEMORIAL: Camp Atterbury was a major US Army training facility during WW II and had a large prisoner of war camp.

The Museum, which is on the grounds of the Camp, just inside the main entrance, tells the history of the Camp, the Indiana National Guard and the units that served here during WW II. Artifacts and memorabilia are generously display throughout the Museum. In the adjoining Veterans Memorial Park are tanks, artillery pieces and other army weaponry on display.

One of the main features of the Memorial Park is a limestone wall bearing the crests of the ten major units that utilized the camp during WW II.

Some distance from the Museum is a very unique war relic - a small chapel which was built by Italian prisoners of war who were incarcerated at the Camp during the war. Also, at the entrance to the Camp is a stone with the carving "Camp Atterbury 1942" which was carved by Italian stone cutters who were among prisoners of war. Museum address: Building 427 on Eggleston St., Camp Atterbury, IN. Phone and website 812-526-1744; www.campatterbury.org/museum

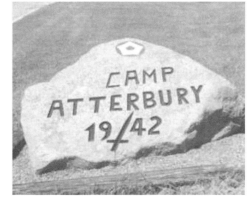

This stone, at the entrance to Camp Atterbury, was carved by Italian stone cutters who were POW's at the camp during WWII.

EVANSVILLE is a county seat and one of Indiana's larger cities. It is in the SW part of the state on I-164 and the Ohio River.

The Four Freedom Bicentennial Monuments in Evansville, IN

FOUR FREEDOMS BICENTENNIAL MONUMENT: This fascinating memorial was dedicated in 1976, the year of America's Bicentennial Celebration. It was inspired by Franklin Roosevelt's speech in 1941 setting as one of America's war aims, the four basic freedoms of mankind, Freedom from Oppression, Freedom of Speech, and Freedom from Want and Freedom of Religion.

The center piece of the Monument consists of four 24-foot tall limestone iconic columns, each bearing one of the Four Freedoms. Surrounding the columns are 50 limestone blocks each bearing the seal of the 50 states. Location: Dress Plaza (along the Riverfront Esplanade) at 411 SE Riverside Dr.

USS LST SHIP MEMORIAL: During the war, Evansville had a ship yard on the river front that built Landing Ships/Tanks (LSTs) and other small vessels for the US Navy. Anchored, now, on the water front is an LST of the type built at the Evansville shipyard. The 330 foot long ship is restored, operative and open to the public. It was acquired by the citizens of Evansville after having served long and well in the US Navy as *325* and then, for many years, in the Greek Navy.

The ship was launched in Philadelphia in Oct. 1942 and participated in several landings in the Mediterranean area as well as the Normandy invasion. LSTs were called the "work horses" of the Navy because they performed so many necessary tasks. They not only landed tanks, trucks, artillery pieces, other heavy items and personnel onto enemy beaches but transported a wide variety of supplies, wounded soldiers and POWs.

Conducted tours of the ship are available and there is a ship's store offering a nice selection of interesting article and souvenirs. Address: The USS LST Ship Memorial, 840 LST Dr., Evansville, IN 47713. Phone and website: 812-435-8678; www.lstmemorial.org

The US Navy's LST 325 which served during WW II. It is now the center piece of the USS LST Ship Memorial in Evansville, IN.

The Vanderburgh County World War II Honor Roll in Evansville, IN

VANDERBURGH COUNTY WORLD WAR II HONOR ROLL: The WW II veterans of Vanderburgh County, Indiana will be forever remembered in this impressive memorial. Their names are inscribed on the memorial. Location: On the Court House lawn in downtown, Evansville, IN

GREENCASTLE is a county seat 47 miles SW of downtown Indianapolis on US-231 and SR-240.

WORLD WAR II "BUZZ BOMB" MEMORIAL: You won't find many WW II memorials like this one. It consists of a genuine V-1 German rocket (Buzz bomb) mounted on a large V-for-Victory stone mount. It took an act of Congress for Greencastle to acquire the Buzz bomb for the Memorial after the war. The project was spearheaded by the local VFW Post #1550.

INDIANAPOLIS, in the geographical center of the state, is the capitol of Indiana and a major transportation hub.

BUTLER UNIVERSITY WW II MEMORIAL: This simple memorial is on the campus of Butler University which is NW of downtown Indianapolis. It commemorates the 92 Butler students who were killed during WW II. Their names are listed on the Memorial. The Memorial also honors all Butler students who served in the war. Nearby is a memorial to those who died in WW I. Location: Butler University is in NW Indianapolis at Sunset Av. and W.46th St.

The WW II "Buzz Bomb" Memorial in Greencastle, IN

103

CLAY TOWNSHIP MILITARY LIBRARY AND MUSEUM is a small library and museum on the north side of Indianapolis. It has a wide selection of WW II artifacts and memorabilia such as small arms, documents, uniforms, photos and more. The Library and Museum is also a gathering place for local social and educational events. Address: 10801 N. College Av., Indianapolis, IN 46280. Phone: 317-846-1257

The WW II Memorial on the campus of Butler University in Indianapolis, IN

CONGRESSIONAL MEDAL OF HONOR MEMORIAL: Located in White River State Park, just west of downtown Indianapolis, is this inspiring memorial. It consists of 27 curved glass walls and pays honor to 3,456 Medal of Honor recipients in 15 different US military conflicts. There is a sound system that plays recorded stories of Medal recipients upon request. Location of White River State Park; just north of W. Washington St. on the western bank of the White River

Watch for the sign for the Clay Township Military Library and Museum on N. College Av.

The Indianapolis Congressional Medal of Honor Memorial near downtown Indianapolis

INDIANA WAR MEMORIAL PLAZA: This is one of the largest war memorials in the USA. It occupies a five-block area in downtown Indianapolis between Meridian, Pennsylvania, New York and Saint Clair Sts. Contained within the Plaza is a multi-story Memorial Building, a park, a cenotaph honoring Indiana's war dead, fountains, a 100 ft. obelisk, military monuments and the National headquarters of the American Legion.

The Indiana War Memorial Plaza In downtown Indianapolis

Indiana War Memorial Building: This is a magnificent multi-story limestone edifice that serves as the main focus of the Plaza. It is at the south end of the Plaza between Vermont and Michigan Sts. In the lower concourse of the building is the Military Museum which focuses on Indiana's military history and has many artifacts from WW I and WW II. There are also displays and information on Korea, Viet Nam and other American conflicts. Tours are available. Address: 431 N. Meridian St., Indianapolis, IN 46204. Phone and website: 317-232-7615; www.in.gov/iwm

***USS INDIANAPOLIS* CRUISER MEMORIAL**, on the Indianapolis Water Company Canal, commemorates the cruiser, *USS Indianapolis*, which was torpedoed and sunk in the Pacific on July, 30 1945 by a Japanese submarine. The ship had just delivered America's first atomic bomb to Tinian Island. This was the atomic bomb that was dropped on Hiroshima, Japan on August 6, 1945.

The ship sank quickly and her brief distress signals were not heard. As a result, most of her crew died in the water due to exhaustion, injury, exposure, thirst and sharks. Only 317 survived out of a crew of 1197.

The names of all 1197 crewmen are inscribed on the monument. Location: The monument is on the east bank of the Indianapolis Water Company Canal at the end of W. Walnut St. which runs west from the 700 block of N. Senate.

LEBANON is the county seat of Boone County and is NW of Indianapolis on I-65, SR-32 and SR-39.

BOONE COUNTY MEMORIAL: This is a 40 acre memorial park on the north side of the city of Lebanon. Its centerpiece is an attractive circular-shaped memorial consisting of ten wausau red marble pillars and a cluster of flag poles with a American flag pole being the tallest and in the center.

In the inner circle of the Memorial are bricks with the names of local men and women who served in the US armed forces and their

The USS Indianapolis Cruiser Memorial near downtown Indianapolis

The Boone County Memorial in Lebanon, IN

service data. Embossed on five of the marble pillars are the Service Emblems of the American military services. The other five pillars commemorate America's five major wars and casualties sustained in each.

The Memorial is maintained jointly by American Legion Post #113 and the VFW Post. #910 and is illuminated at night. Location: 130 E. Ulen Dr. (just off SR-39) in Lebanon

MARION is a county seat midway between Indianapolis and Ft. Wayne on SR-9, SR-15, SR-18 and SR-37.

WORLD WAR II MEMORIAL: "ALL GAVE SOME, SOME GAVE ALL." This inscription is displayed in Marion's WW II Memorial. It is dedicated to all citizens o Grant County who served in WW II and especially to those who "Gave All." Their names are inscribed on the Memorial. Location: On the Grant County Courthouse lawn

PERU is a county seat 60 miles north of Indianapolis on US-24, US-31 and SR-19. It was home to a large US naval air training station during WW II on US-31 ten miles south of Peru. In 1951, the base was taken over by the US Air Force and eventually named Grissom Air Force Base.

GRISSOM AIR MUSEUM: This is a large indoor/outdoor museum on the grounds of the old air base with an interesting display of some 40 aircraft from WW II and later.

Inside the Museum is a generous collection of hands-on display consisting of military memorabilia, artifacts and displays on the history of the airfield. The Museum has a gift shop that is well worth your time to explore and there is an on-going educational program. Tours of the aircraft on display are available. The Museum is in a 16 acre park which has a covered pavilion and other amenities. Address: 1000 W. Hoosier Blvd., (US-31) Grissom AFB, IN 46970. Phone and website: 765-689-8011; www.grissomairmuseum.com (photo next page)

The WW II Memorial in Marion, IN

MAIMI COUNTY WW II WAR MEMORIAL: The city of Peru is in Miami County and those who gave their lives during WW II from Miami County are not forgotten. This tasteful Memorial is located on the Courthouse lawn in downtown Peru and lists their names for all to see for all times.

This B-25 bomber is Grissom Air Museum's "movie star." It appeared in the movie Catch-22 as "Passionate Paulette."

SELLERSBURG is a small community in southern Indiana just north of Louisville, KY on I-65 and US-31.

The World War II Memorial in Sellersburg, IN

WORLD WAR II MEMORIAL: This fine community has seen fit to honor those sons and daughters from the local area who perished in WW II. This is their monument and their names are inscribed thereon. Location: In Sellersburg Memorial Park, at New Albany Av. and Utica St.

TERRE HAUTE is a county seat in western Indiana on I-70, US-40 and US-41/150.

WORLD WAR II WAR MEMORIAL: This fine limestone memorial is a sculptured column with the inscription "WORLD WAR II – KILLED IN ACTION FROM VIGO COUNTY" on the front side. On the back side of the Memorial the names of those so honored are listed. Location: On the Vigo County Courthouse lawn in downtown Terre Haute, IN

VINCENNES is a county seat in SW Indiana on US-41, US-50/150 and the Wabash River. It is a very historic city and was Indiana's first city and served as the state capitol (1813).

INDIANA MILITARY MUSEUM: This magnificent museum is located on a 14 acre site adjacent to the George Rogers Clark National Park. It houses one of the best overall collections of military memorabilia in the entire Midwest with heavy emphasis on WW II. The Museum has well-rounded exhibits of military vehicles, artillery, uniforms, insignias, equipment and related artifacts spanning from the Civil War to the present. The exhibits include tanks and armored vehicles, a WW II Sherman tank and a Japanese type 95 tanks. There are special exhibits pertaining to American General Officers of WW II and other wars, captured war souvenirs, an exhibit on women at war, the US home front, wartime toys, the WW II cruiser *USS Vincennes,* George Army Airfield (across the Wabash River in Illinois), and many other topics.

The outdoor exhibits include numerous vehicles and artillery pieces along with aircraft. Much of it is of WW II vintage. There is a very unique outdoor exhibit - one that you won't find at other museums - a full-scale concrete Normandy gun bunker with an adjacent reenactment grounds complete with battle rubble.

Museum tours are available and there is a must-visit gift shop. Jim Osborne is the man behind it all. Address: 715 S. 6th St., Vincennes, IN 47591. Phone and website: 812-882-1941; ww.indianamilitarymuseum.net. The Museum is easily accessible from US-41 via the Willow St. Exit.

This is a re-creation of a German gun emplacement bunker along the Normandy coastline at the Indiana Military Museum in Vincennes, IN.

IOWA

During the war, Iowa was one of the America's great food-producing states. Iowa is in the heart of the grain belt and produced corn, soybeans, wheat, oats, barley, potatoes, hogs, cattle, sheep, horses and mules. In 1940, Iowa had 210,000 farms, 9,651,000 hogs, 4,688,000 cattle and 2,538,000 people. When the war came, the state had several POW camps and many of the POWs helped to produce Iowa's food. The state also had several manufacturing centers, the largest of which were Burlington, Cedar Rapids and Ankeny.

Near the end of the war, Iowa was subjected to Japanese bombing balloon attacks. These attacks did no serious damage and due the great secrecy surrounding the attacks most Iowa citizens didn't even know they were being attacked.

ALGONA is a county seat in north-central Iowa 40 miles north of Ft. Dodge on US-18 and US-169. During the war, Algona had a large prisoner of war camp holding German POWs.

ALGONA PRISONER OF WAR NATIVITY SCENE: This is half life-size nativity scene build during the war by German prisoners of war at the Alcona Prisoner of War Camp - which is now Algona's airport. The Nativity Scene consists of 60 figures and was built from surplus materials used to build and maintain the Camp. The Scene was first displayed in the Camp along one of the Camp's main

roads and could be seen from the road. It is now on permanent display in its own building at the Kossuth County Fairgrounds which is south of town just off US-169. The scene took more than a year to complete.

In the postwar years, several of the former POWs who worked on the project returned to Algona and were treated by the townspeople as celebrities. Phone and website: 515-295-7519 and 515-295-7241; www.pwcamp.algona.org/nativity.html

The Nativity Scene made by German POWs at Algona POW Camp during the war is preserved and on display at the Kossuth County Fairgrounds in Algona.

CAMP ALGONA POW MUSEUM: As the name implies, this museum commemorates the large prisoner of war camp that existed at Algona during WW II. The citizens of Algona considered their efforts as a major contribution to the war effort. There were more POWs at the camp than there were citizens of Algona.

On display at the Museum are many artifacts from the Camp telling how the POWs lived, who they were and how they were treated. Among the displays are paintings, drawings, poetry and wood carving produced by the POWs. Other displays include uniforms, small arms, photos, documents and more. Address: 114 S. Thorington St., Algona, IA 50511. Phone and website: 515-395-2267 and 515-395-3719; www.pwcampalgona.org

BOONE is a county seat 40 miles NW of Des Moines on US-30.

BATTLE OF THE BULGE MEMORIAL: Here is one of the several monuments in the country that commemorates the Battle of the Bulge, December1944-February 1945, the German's last major offensive in Europe. It caused the Allied forces there great concern and cost 76,890 American dead and wounded.

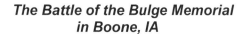

The Memorial is of polished marble and shows images of the various types of military services caught up in the battle; infantry, armor, transportation, artillery, liaison and nurses. It also honors the men and women of Boone County who participated in the Battle. Location: Miles-Lee Park, 5th and Franklin Sts., in Boone, IA

*The Battle of the Bulge Memorial
in Boone, IA*

MAMIE DOUD EISENHOWER BIRTHPLACE: This is the birthplace of Mamie Doud Eisenhower, wife of General Dwight D. Eisenhower, Supreme Allied Commander in Europe and later President of the United States.

This modest Victorian residence has been restored and opened to the public. The first floor of the home is decorated in furnishings of the times when Mamie lived here. Much of the furniture came from members of the Doud family including the bed in the master bedroom in which Mamie was born in 1896. The basement has been converted into a museum and library displaying many of Mamie's personal belongings and items relating to her childhood and adult life. There are also

The birthplace of Mamie Doud Eisenhower in Boone, IA

exhibits on the General. Address: 709 Carroll St. Boone, IA 50036. Phone and website: 515-432-1907; http://mamiesbirthplace.homestead.com

110

CLARINDA is a county seat on southwestern Iowa on US-71 and SR-2.

GLENN MILLER BIRTHPLACE MUSEUM: The "Big Band" leader, Glenn Miller was the best-known popular music-maker in the US before and during WW II. His music defines what we now call the "Big Band Era."
  Miller was born here in Clarinda and his birthplace has been preserved. The city has also created a museum dedicated to his honor which is adjacent to his birthplace. In the Museum are artifacts and memorabilia related to Miller, his music, his life and his service as the leader of the US Army Air Forces Band during WW II. Miller did not survive the war. He died in a mysterious air crash over the English Channel in December 1944. The Museum has a theater, a library and a Glenn Miller-oriented gift shop. This museum is a real string of pearls. Address: 122 W. Clark St., Clarenda, IA 51632. Phone and website: 712-542-2461; www.glennmiller.org

The Glenn Miller Birthplace Museum in Clarinda, IA

DES MOINES is in the south-central part of the state and is Iowa's capitol. During the war, there was an ordnance plant in the area and a large naval air training facility. There were also two old forts that were utilized for the war effort; Fort Des Moines and Camp Dodge.

THE IOWA GOLD STAR MUSEUM: This fine and inspiring museum is on the grounds of Camp Dodge near Johnston, IA, a northern suburb of Des Moines. Camp Dodge is the home of the Iowa National Guard. The Museum, as its name implies, pays tribute to those men and women who perished during the war. The Museum collects preserves and interprets material reflecting Iowa citizens' contributions to the nation's defense. Displays include artifacts, weapons, uniforms, photos, paintings, and large maps showing the areas in which the 34th Infantry Division, which included the

111

Iowa National Guard, fought in WW II. Museum tours are available and there is a Museum store with many interesting souvenirs and gifts. Address: Camp Dodge, 7105 NW 70th Av.,Johnston, IA 50131. Phone and website: 515-252-4531; www.iowanationalguard.com/museum/museum.htm

The Iowa World War II Memorial

THE IOWA WORLD WAR II MEMORIAL PLAZA: This is an impressive memorial just ENE of the Iowa State Capitol Building on E. 13th St. It honors all Iowa citizens who served in WW II. The Memorial's centerpiece is the "Freedom Flame," a 50 foot high stainless steel stylized flame. Leading up to the Flame, is the "Freedom Walk" which is a walkway through the times of WW II beginning with Pearl Harbor. The Plaza floor is a global map showing the major theaters of operation during the war. To the rear of the Plaza is the "Wall of Memories." Location: E. 13th St., Des Moines, IA 50319

WATERLOO is a large city 90 miles NE of Des Moines. One of the community's families, that of Thomas and Alleta Sullivan, was to suffer a terrible loss that was to become one of the tragic - and great - stories of WW II. On the night of Nov. 13, 1942, a Japanese submarine torpedoed the US cruiser *"Juneau"* in the waters off Guadalcanal. The torpedo hit the ship's magazine which exploded causing the ship to sink in 16 seconds. All but 10 members of the crew perished. Among those who died were the five sons of Thomas and Alleta Sullivan. The brothers had enlisted in the Navy together and had requested that they be allowed to serve on the same ship. The deaths of the Sullivans, which so devastated this one family, caused the Navy to revise its regulations and henceforth forbid family members from serving together on the same ship or airplane.

In 1943, the Navy named a newly-built destroyer in their honor, *The USS Sullivan Brothers,* and their mother christened the ship. That destroyer saw action in the latter part of WW II.

In Feb. 1944, Hollywood made a movie of the Sullivan Brothers, called "The Fighting Sullivans," which was shown throughout the country and resulted in a surge of enlistments in the US Navy.

GROUT MUSEUM DISTRICT/SULLIVAN BROTHERS IOWA VETERANS MUSEUM: The Sullivan Brothers are duly honored by this facility, The Sullivan Brothers Iowa Veterans Museum, which is a museum within a larger museum, the Grout Museum. Here, in the Sullivan Brothers Iowa Veterans Museum, visitors can learn all about the famous brothers, their private lives, their family and their service in the US Navy.

The Museum further honors Iowa veterans of America's wars from the Civil war to today's conflicts.

On display are military artifacts relating to Iowa's military past, photos, uniforms, small arms, diaries, letters, oral histories, and more. There is a theater and a museum store that you don't want to miss. Address: Grout Museum District, 503 South St., Waterloo, IA 50701. Phone and website: 319-234-6357; www.groutmuseumdistrict.org/sullivan/contact,cf

The Grout Museum District/Sullivan Brothers Iowa Veterans Museum in Waterloo, IA

KANSAS

Food and airplanes - that's what Kansas produced most of during the war. This large state is in the geographic center of America and in the heart of the Grain Belt. In the Wichita area, a cluster of light aircraft manufacturers had evolved before the war and within a short time this industry was booming. By 1943 the state became the nation's 3rd largest producer of military aircraft after California and New York. And later in the war, B-29 Super fortresses were built here in Kansas.

ABILENE is a county seat 85 miles west of Topeka on I-70.

THE DWIGHT D. EISENHOWER PRESIDENTIAL LIBRARY & MUSEUM: This is a large complex of buildings honoring Abilene's, and Kansas's, favorite son, Dwight D. Eisenhower. "Ike", as he was known throughout most of his life, grew up in Abilene (he was born in Texas). He left Abilene as a young man seeking a career in the Army, attended West Point and rose to be the Supreme Allied Commander in Europe during WW II, and later, President of the United States.

   Ike returned from time-to-time to Abilene during his life time to visit his friends and family, and in the end returned in death. He, his wife Mamie and their first-born son, Doud Dwight Eisenhower, are buried on the grounds of the Center in a chapel known as the Place of Meditation. The other major buildings of the Center are the Eisenhower Family Home, the Museum, Presidential Library and Visitor's Center.

   The Eisenhower home stands on its original site on 4th St. and is furnished with much of the original furnishings and fixtures that were used by the Eisenhower family.

   The Museum is a very large building and consists of five major galleries which contain items

113

associated with Eisenhower, his family and his career.

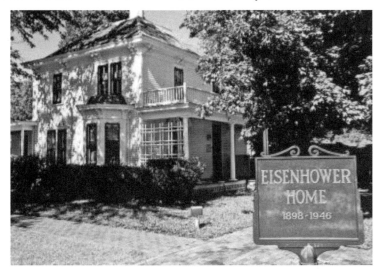

The Library houses the private and official papers accumulated by Eisenhower during his two terms as President. The Visitor's Center orients the visitors, explains the facilities and the various services offered and shows a video on Eisenhower's life. Tours are available including tours of the Eisenhower home. Address: The Dwight D. Eisenhower Presidential Library & Museum, 200 Southeast 4th St., Abilene, KS 67410. Phone and website: 785-263-4751, www.eisenhower.archives.gov/

In this two-story white house, President Eisenhower and his brothers grew to manhood. Their mother lived here until her death in 1946.

AUGUSTA is a small community 20 miles east of Wichita on US-77 and SR-400.

KANSAS MUSEUM OF MILITARY HISTORY: All of America's wars are represented in this fine Museum which has a heavy emphasis on WWII. WW II items on display include vehicles, communications equipment, US Army, Navy and Air Force memorabilia, German and Japanese military artifacts, ammunition, models of aircraft and warships, uniforms, photos, posters, war ration books and many other items. Tours of the Museum are available as is rental space for social and military events. And the Museum has a restoration facility. Address: 135 S. US-77, Augusta, KS 67010. Phone and website: 316-775-1425; www.kmmh.org

Ike stands tall and proud at the Dwight D. Eisenhower at the presidential library museum

GREAT BEND is a county seat in central Kansas 90 miles NW of Wichita on US-56 and US-261.
   When the B-29 bombers became available, they were so big and heavy that new airports with long and thick runways had to be built for them. One such airfield was built just west of Great Bend. After the war, it became Great Bend's municipal airport.

The Kansas Museum of Military History in Augusta, KS

B-29 BOMBER MEMORIAL: To commemorate Great Bend's historical association with the B-29 bomber, this memorial has been built at the airport. It is built on the site of the Army Airfield's WW II headquarters building and consists of a model of the B-29 bomber mounted on a tall stanchion inside a circular arched frame.

<u>GRENOLA</u> is a small community of less than 300 people in SE Kansas on US-160.

FREEDOM PARK WW II MEMORIAL: This small town has a very nice park which is dedicated to the memory of those from the local community who served in WW II. In the park is a memorial which is inscribed with the names of the seven local men who gave their lives in the war. Location: Freedom Park, Railway Av. & Cana St.

The B-29 Bomber Memorial at Great Bend's Municipal Airport

<u>HUTCHINSON</u> is a county seat 40 miles NW of Wichita on US-50, SR-61 and SR-96.

The Freedom Park WW II Memorial in Grenola, KS

KANSAS COSMOSPHERE MUSEUM: Here's a museum that makes the connection between WW II technology and the Space Age. They do so by highlighting the German V-1 and V-2 rockets that appeared during the latter months of WW II. At this Museum, visitors will learn the history of those rockets and their influence on the post-war space race that dominated military thinking for some 50 years and also brought us the many marvelous advances we now enjoy from satellites and space craft.

There are several galleries in the Museum, one of which is known as "The German Gallery." Here, both the German V-1 (Buzzbombs) and V-2 rockets are on display and information is provided on how post-war space engineers built and expanded on the German technology of WW II.

What's more, the Museum has the largest collections of Russian space artifacts outside of Moscow. And, of course, there is heavy emphasis on America's space advances.

The Museum has an educational program, rental space is available for events, museum tours are available and don't miss the "Cargo Store" - the Museum's fine gift shop. Address: 1100 N. Plum, Hutchinson, KS 67501. Phone and website: 800-397-0330; www.cosmo.org

The German Gallery of the Kansas Cosmosphere Museum. Their V-1 (Buzzbomb) is to the left (behind the wall) and their V-2 is to the right.

JUNCTION CITY is a county seat in east-central Kansas 60 miles west of Topeka on I-70. It has long been the home of one of the US Army's main military facilities, Fort Riley.

FIRST INFANTRY MUSEUM: This fine museum is on the grounds of Ft. Riley in the Fort's original hospital building. It chronicles the colorful history of the Fort and that of the American soldier from the Revolutionary War to the present. WW II artifacts make up only a small part of the Museum's displays, but several pieces of WW II-era mechanized equipment are on the grounds outside the Museum.   The Museum has a fabulous gift shop - don't miss it. Address: Building 205, Custer Av., Ft. Riley, Junction City, KS 66442-5000. Phones and website: 785-239-2743; www.uscavalry.org

KANSAS CITY, KS, is the smaller of the two Kansas Cities on the eastern border of the state on the Missouri River. Located here were two aircraft manufacturers, North American Aviation Corp. which made B-25 bombers and Commonwealth Aircraft Co. Inc. which made troop-carrying gliders. Being a river town and transportation hub, Kansas City, KS had several military depots and sub-depots.

Pearl Harbor Park in Mission, KS

PEARL HARBOR PARK: This is a small park in the Kansas City suburb of Mission. Its mission is to keep alive for the local citizens of the area the memory of the heroism and sacrifices made by American service men and women and civilians of Hawaii during the Japanese attack on Pearl Harbor. The centerpiece of the park consists of several marble monuments, a Pearl Harbor relic and a commemorative bench in a patio-like setting. Location: On the corner of Martway and Maple Dr.

LAWRENCE is a county seat midway between Kansas City and Topeka on I-70.

THE WW II MEMORIAL CAMPANILE OF THE UNIVERSITY OF KANSAS. This is a 120 ft. bell tower on the campus of the University of Kansas dedicated to those who fought in WW II. It houses a 53-bell carillon and the bells of the carillon are played on various occasions. On the ground floor is a Memorial Room, engraved on its walls, are the names of the 276 Kansans who gave their lives during the war. The Campanile is located in the heart of the campus opposite Spencer Library on Memorial Drive.

The WW II Memorial Campanile of the University of Kansas

LIBERAL is a county seat in the SE corner of Kansas on US-54, US-83/270 and the Oklahoma state line. During the war, the US Army Air Force built a training field just west of town called Liberal Army Airfield.

MID-AMERICA AIR MUSEUM: This fine museum is on the grounds of Liberal Airport in the former Beech Aircraft Co. factory building. It is the largest air museum in Kansas and one of the largest in the US. It has a collection of over 100 aircraft, mostly single engine. There are about a dozen aircraft of WW II vintage.

The Museum has its own restoration facility, a large and interesting gift shop and a theater.

Throughout the year, the Museum hosts major air shows and other events. Tours of the Museum are available. Address: 2000 W. 2nd St., Liberal, KS 67901. Phone and website: 620-624-5263; www.kansastravel.org /airmuseum.htm

The Mid-American Air Museum of Liberal KS.

LURAY is a very small community in north-central Kansas on US-281 and SR-18.

B-24 BOMBER MEMORIAL: On a stormy night in September 1943, a B-24 bomber crashed near Luray. All 11 members of the crew were killed. In commemoration of that tragic event, the community of Luray has erected a small monument in remembrance of the B-24's crew. Location: Go north of Luray on US-281 approximately five miles, then turn west on a county dirt road to the site which is about four miles from the intersection. Note: The dirt road can be difficult to travel in wet and snowy weather.

The B-24 Bomber Crash Site Memorial near Luray, KS

<u>TOPEKA</u>, in the east-central part of the state, is 50 miles west of Kansas City and is the capitol of Kansas. During the war, the city's local airport was utilized by the Army Air Forces as a training center for the crews of B-24 bombers.

COMBAT AIR MUSEUM: This is one of two museums located at Forbes Field, Topeka's main airport and is one of the larger aviation museums in Kansas. It has a collection of over 30 aircraft, most of which are post-WW II vintage.

The Museum is housed in two hangars, one of which is from WW II. Part of the collection is outdoors.

The Museum has generous displays of aviation artifacts, technical information,

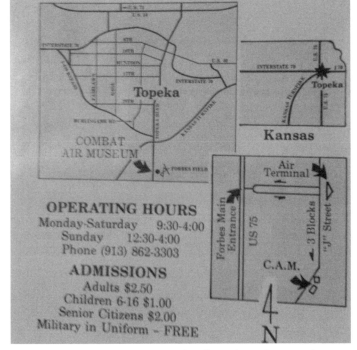

OPERATING HOURS
Monday-Saturday   9:30-4:00
Sunday   12:30-4:00
Phone (913) 862-3303

ADMISSIONS
Adults $2.50
Children 6-16 $1.00
Senior Citizens $2.00
Military in Uniform – FREE

engines, dioramas, art and its own restoration shop. Also on display are missiles, bombs, rockets and scale model aircraft.

During the year, the Museum is host to many aviation and social events. Museum tours are available and there are many items of interest in their fine gift shop. Address: Hangars 602 & 604, "J" St., Forbes Field, Topeka, KS 66619. Phone and website: 785-862-3303; www.combatairmuseum.org

HOLLEY MUSEUM OF MILITARY HISTORY: The Holley Museum of Military history consists of a private collection of military artifacts collected by the Holley family and located in Topeka's Ramada Inn near downtown Topeka. Heavy emphasis is on WW II.

118

There are some 4000 items on display in five galleries. Each gallery is named after a prominent individual: Winston Churchill, Ronald Reagan, Dwight Eisenhower, Franklin Roosevelt and Harry S Truman. There are military artifacts, models, posters, photos, dioramas and more. Address: 420 Southeast 6th St., Topeka, KS 66607. Phone and website: 785-272-6204; www.holleymusem.org

Inside the Holley Military Museum of History

MUSEUM OF THE KANSAS NATIONAL GUARD: This is the second of the two military museums at Forbes Field, Topeka's main airport. The mission of this museum is to tell the story and long history of the Kansas National Guard.

On display are many artifacts and memorabilia items related to the Guard's long history which ranges from the days of the Civil War to the present. WW II displays are well represented.

Inside the Museum is another museum, the 35th Division Museum. During WW II the Kansas National Guard was a part of that Army division. The Museum has a library, an archives collection and an interesting and well-stocked gift shop.

Outside, on the Museum's grounds, are a number of military vehicles, artillery pieces and aircraft utilized by the Guard. Throughout the year, the Museum is host to several military and social activities. Address: 6700 SW Topeka Blvd., Topeka, KS 66619. Phone and website: 785-862-1020; www.kansasguardmuseum.org

The Museum of the Kansas National Guard

WAKEENEY is a county seat in western Kansas on I-70 and US-283.

IWO JIMA MEMORIAL: This memorial is easy to visit because it's right off I-70. It commemorates World War II and specifically the important Battle of Iwo Jima which became so important to the eventual victory in the Pacific. Its statuary replicates the famous flag raising on that island by the US Marines. There is also a 100 ft. flag pole with a 19 ft. x 38 ft. American flag.
Location: Exit 128 from I-70

The Iwo Jima Memorial of Wakeeney, KS

<u>WICHITA</u> is in the south-central part of the state on I-35 and I-135. Of foremost importance to the US military was the cluster of aircraft manufacturers who had established themselves in the Wichita area in the prewar years. The leading companies were Beech, Cessna, Lear, Mooney and Culver Aircraft Companies. These companies specialized in light aircraft and all built military aircraft during the war. The largest aircraft manufacturing operation, however, was a huge new government owned factory built by the Federal Government at Wichita Airport to build B-29 bombers.

KANSAS AVIATION MUSEUM: This museum is in the prewar terminal building of Wichita Airport. The building is on the National Register of Historic Places.

The Museum highlights the importance of Kansas in the history of aviation and displays aircraft and artifacts from the earliest days of aviation. Most of the 40 plus aircraft on display are single engine craft, many of which were built in Wichita. Some of them are military aircraft and relate to WW II.

The Museum has an archives collection, aircraft engines, an educational program, rental facilities, a monthly newsletter and a very nice gift shop. In addition to these amenities, the Museum has a very unique gourmet dining facility - in the old and historic control tower - with an excellent view of the airport. Address: 3350 George Washington Blvd., Wichita, KS 67210. Phone and website: 316-683-9242; www.kansasaviationmuseum .org

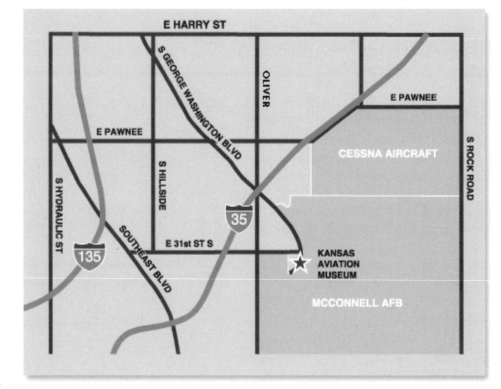

VETERANS MEMORIAL PARK: You have to look far and wide to find a veterans memorial park like this one. It has a large number of military memorials. Here are the major ones:

World War II Memorial
Pearl Harbor Memorial
Purple Heart Memorial
Gold Star Mothers' Memorial
A limestone replica of the cruiser *USS Wichita*
SS Doraldo Submarine Memorial:
The submarine was lost during WW II.
US Submarine Veterans of WW II Memorial
US Marine Corps Veterans Memorial
US Merchant Marine Memorial
USN Hospital Corps Memorial
USN Armed Guard Memorial
Marine Corps League Memorial

In addition to these, there are additional memorials dedicated to the Korean Conflict, Viet Nam, and other American conflicts.

And if that's not enough, there is a multi-story, multi-purpose assembly building, the John S. Stevens Veterans Memorial Building.

The Park is located near downtown Wichita on the Arkansas River. Address: 339 N. Greenway, Wichita, KS 67203. Phone and website: 316-268-4361; www.wichita.gov/cityoffices/park/parks/veterans/veterans.htm

This is one of the many WW II-oriented memorials in Veterans Memorial Park is Wichita.

KENTUCKY

During the Great Depression of the 1930s virtually every segment of Kentucky's economy was depressed. One of the state's counties filed for bankruptcy and others had defaulted badly on their debts. The state's economy rebounded nicely, though, during WW II as demand grew for Kentucky's products of grain, tobacco, potatoes, whiskey, livestock, horses, coal, oil, natural gas, asphalt, and cheap electricity.

Kentucky had a famous politician, Alben W. Barkley, who was a Kentucky senator during the war and Senate Majority Leader. After the war, he became Harry S Truman's Vice President during Truman's second term, 1949-53. Truman also had a Kentuckian in his Cabinet, Frederick M. Vinson, Treasury Secretary.

FORT KNOX is a small community totally within the huge Ft. Knox Military Reservation 35 miles SW

of Louisville on US-31W. It is here that a large part of America's gold reserve is stored.
   During WW II, the Fort was not only America's gold warehouse but was also one of America's foremost training centers for armored units. George S. Patton, Jr. served here in the 1930s and, during WW II, trained much of his armored forces here.

GENERAL GEORGE PATTON MUSEUM: This is an outstanding museum on the grounds of Fort Knox and is one of the largest in the US Army Museum System. The Museum has an outstanding collection of US and foreign tanks, tank recovery vehicles, assault vehicles, trucks, motorized gun

carriages and more. The Museum is dedicated to the preservation of historical materials relating to the US Army's cavalry and armored units, and has several galleries. The Patton Gallery is dedicated exclusively to Gen. George S. Patton, Jr. and displays many of his personal items including his famous ivory-handled pistols, a jeep specially modified by Patton for his personal use and the 1938 Cadillac sedan in which he was riding when he was fatally injured in Dec. 1945. Address: 4554 Fayette Ave., Ft. Knox, KY 40121. Phone and website: 502-624-3812; www.generalpatton.org

The entrance to the Patton Museum at Ft. Knox, KY

FRANKFORT, 20 miles NW of Lexington on I-64, US-60, US-127 and US-421, is the capitol of Kentucky.

KENTUCKY MILITARY HISTORY MUSEUM, near downtown Frankfort, is in the Old State Arsenal building built in 1850 to house the weapons and equipment of the Kentucky State Militia. The Museum emphasizes the military service of Kentucky units from the Revolution to the present.
   WW II displays are well ordered and honor Kentuckians who fought in the various theaters of operation during WW II. A significant amount of WW II artifacts and memorabilia are on display. Address: Capitol Av. and E. Main St. (US-60), Frankfort, KY 40602. Phone and website: 502-564-1792; http://history.ky.gov/sub.php?pageid=83&sectionid=2

HOPKINSVILLE is a county seat in SW Kentucky on US-41 and US-68, 55 miles west of Bowling Green. It is the Kentucky home for one of the US Army's largest military reservations, Fort Campbell, the home of the 101st Airborne Division. The Fort extends across the state border into Tennessee.

DON F. PRATT MUSEUM: This is a fine museum on the grounds of Ft. Campbell and emphasizes the history of the 101st Airborne Div. It is named in honor of Gen. Don F. Pratt, assistant division commander of the 101st Airborne Div. who was killed in a glider crash during the Normandy invasion. The Museum also covers the history of Ft. Campbell and has many WW II items on display including one of the very few gliders remaining in the US that was actually used during WW II.
   There are exhibits on famous airborne generals of WW II - Generals William C. Lee, Maxwell D.

Taylor and William C. Westmoreland. Also on display are personal items belonging to Adolf Hitler, Hermann Goering and Julius Streicher.

  Military vehicles, aircraft and a wide selection of military hardware are on display inside and outside the Museum.

   The Pratt Museum has a library, archives, and educational program and a well-stocked gift shop. Museum tours are available. Address: Building 5702 Tennessee Av., Ft. Campbell, KY 42223. Phone and website: 270-798-3215/4986 (Museum) and 931-431-2003 (gift shop); www.fortcampbell.com/pratt,php

LOUISVILLE, in north-central Kentucky on the Ohio River, was Kentucky's largest city during and after the war. The city's airport, Bowman Field, was taken over by the Army Air Forces and used as a training facility and the city also had a large naval gun factory, an Army hospital and an Army medical depot.

Louisville's World War II Memorial, Metro Hall

WORLD WAR II MEMORIAL, METRO HALL: This impressive Memorial is made of marble and lists the names of local citizens of the armed forces who died during the war. One of the inscriptions on the Memorial reads "MAY THIS MONUMENT BE A CONSTANT REMINDER TO THE LIVING TO CONTINUE THEIR STRUGGLE."
Location: The corner of W. Jefferson and 5th Sts., Louisville, KY

MAYFIELD is a county seat in western Kentucky on the Julian M. Carroll Purchase Pkwy., US-45 and a host of county roads.

MAYFIELD WW II MEMORIAL: This is a large circular memorial with a tall center column. It pays tribute to all branches of the military service that participated in WW II. Location: On the corner of Clements and Gibson Sts.

NEWPORT is one of the cluster of cities opposite Cincinnati, OH.

The Mayfield WW II Memorial in Mayfield, Ky

CAMPBELL COUNTY WORLD WAR II MEMORIAL: This memorial honors those individuals from Campbell Count who served in WW II. Their names are etched on the Memorial. Just down the street is the World Peace Bell. Location: In front of the Campbell County Courthouse, 24 E. 4th St., Newport, KY

123

The Campbell County, KY WWII Memorial

<u>**PADUCAH**</u> is a large city in the western part of Kentucky on the Ohio River.

ALBEN W. BARKLEY MUSEUM is near downtown Paducah. It is an historic Greek Revival House, a famous Kentucky Landmark and listed on the National Register.

The Museum honors Paducah resident Alben W. Barkley who, during WW II, was Kentucky's Senator and the Senate Majority Leader. After the war, Barkley became Harry S Truman's popular Vice President and gained the nickname "The Veep".

The Museum houses papers and a large collection of memorabilia pertaining to Barkley's public and private life. In the living room of the house, which is called the Barkley Room, is Barkley's desk and chair, his Vice-Presidential flag, a picture of Harry S Truman donated by Mrs. Truman, a "Barkley for President" banner and other items of interest. Address: 533 Madison, Paducah, KY 42002. Phone and website: 270-443-0512; www.aboutpacucah.com

The Alben W. Barkley Museum in Paducah, KY

WORLD WAR II MEMORIAL: This interesting memorial consists of a stone monument in the shape of the Roman numeral II - as in WW II. It also has a globe of the world and the seals of each branch of service. It is dedicated to all veterans of WW II. Location: 350 S. 5th St. Paducah, KY

The WW II Memorial in Paducah, KY

124

LOUISIANA

Louisiana was a troubled state before the war. The Great Depression of the 1930s had racked her fragile agrarian economy and the state's political house was in disarray. With the war having begun in Europe, and America beginning to build its defenses, Louisiana's economy began to prosper. In late 1942, POWs began to arrive in the state in large numbers and many were put to work in the sugar cane industry to help ease the nation-wide sugar shortage. By war's end, Louisiana had one of the highest concentrations of POWs of any state in the US.

Louisiana's manufacturing sector also prospered. New metalworking industries evolved in the state especially in the New Orleans area, and for the first time in its history, Louisiana became a major shipbuilding state. The construction of new military bases, and the expansion of existing ones brought still more jobs and more prosperity. The influx of thousands of service personnel and war workers swelled the state's population and caused housing shortages in several areas. New roads, air fields and factories were built, and an all-important road and railroad bridge was rushed to completion across the Mississippi River at Baton Rouge.

During Aug.-Sept.-Oct. 1941, 500,000 US soldiers came to Louisiana to participate in large-scale Army maneuvers that covered most of northern Louisiana and parts of neighboring Texas and Mississippi. In 1942, a second large-scale Army maneuver was held in the state.

By 1945, the state had gained two new industries, the manufacture of synthetic rubber and fish farming. Throughout the late 1940s and into the 1950s, the state remained economically strong, prosperous and politically peaceful.

ALEXANDRIA is in the geographic center of the state on I-49. By the time WW II began, Alexandria had become a substantial military center because of all the military bases in the surrounding area. Most of the military bases were training facilities and during the war some seven million service personnel trained in the Alexandria area.

LOUISIANA MANEUVERS & MILITARY MUSEUM is on the grounds of Camp Beauregard, the home of the Louisiana National Guard, and relates, in considerable details, the military maneuvers that took place in the area before and during the war. It also covers the history of other military events.

The largest maneuvers took place in the summer of 1941 in which two imaginary armies, "Kotmk" (Kansas, Oklahoma, Texas, Missouri and Kentucky – Red Army) did battle with "Almat" (Arkansas, Louisiana, Mississippi, Alabama and Tennessee-Blue Army) over navigation right in the Mississippi River. More than 400,000 troops took part in the Kotmk-Almat conflict and, thanks in a large part to Gen. George Patton's armored forces of Kotmk, the Almat defenders were pushed back, but Kotmk failed to achieve a decisive victory.

Smaller maneuvers were conducted in 1942 and 1943 and a maneuver for 1944 was canceled due to the need for troops for the D-Day invasion. Address: Camp Beauregard, Pineville, LA 71360. Apply at the main gate for admission to the Museum. Phone and website: 318-641-5733; www.la.ngb.army.mi./dmh/immm.htm

BATON ROUGE, the capitol of the state, is located in the SE part of the state on the Mississippi River 70 miles NW of New Orleans. It is an inland seaport able to service ocean-going vessels.

During the war, the city had several large oil refineries which supplied large quantities of petroleum products to the US armed forces and those of the Allies. There was also an Army Air Base and a large prisoner of war compound in the area.

USS KIDD VETERANS MEMORIAL: This is a fully restored historic warship of WW II located in the heart of scenic downtown Baton Rouge. It is named after Admiral Isaac C. Kidd who was killed on the bridge of the battleship *USS Arizona* during the Japanese attack on Pearl Harbor.

The ship saw considerable action in WW II and the Korean War and was awarded eight battle stars. The ship is anchored permanently in the Mississippi River and is not only open to the public but also offers tours, parties and overnights, primarily for school children. The children can sleep on the ship much as the sailors did when the *Kidd* was a fighting ship during WW II.

Another WW II trophy at the Museum is a P-40 fighter plane painted in the colors of the famous Flying Tigers of wartime China. The Flying Tigers were commanded by Gen. Claire Chennault, who grew up in Louisiana. A number of other displays are dedicated to Chennault and the Flying Tigers. Guided tours are available and there is a very interesting gift shop. Address: 305 S. River Rd., Baton Rouge, LA 70802. Phone and website: 504-342-1942; www.usskidd.com

The destroyer USS Kidd at the USS Kidd Veterans Memorial in Baton Rouge, LA

<u>DE RIDDER</u> is a county seat 55 miles SW of Alexandria on US-171 and US-190.

DE RIDDER USO: This is the first building built in the US exclusively for the United Service Organization (USO) a service organization that catered to the needs off-duty military personnel offering a clean and healthy atmosphere. There were thousands of USOs across the nation during WW II and they specialized in providing food, non-alcoholic beverages, light entertainment, dances and other social activities.

The De Ridder USO is located on the corner of SR-26 and 7th Street in downtown De Ridder and is now used as a local civic center. It houses an interesting collection of USO memorabilia and is open to the public. For information contact: Beauregard Tourist Commission, PO Box 1174, De Rider, LA 70634. Phone and website: 337-463-5534; www.library.beau.org/museum/uso.html

The De Ridder USO in De Ridder, LA

126

HOUMA is a unique delta town 45 miles SW of New Orleans in the heart of Cajun country. It was also strategically located for anti-submarine activities in the Gulf and had a large Coast Guard and US Naval air station.

The World War II Memorial in Houma, LA

WORLD WAR II MEMORIAL: The city of Houma has a nice park, the Houma/Terrebonne Veterans Memorial Park. There are several military monuments in the park including this one. It is dedicated to all WW II veterans and describes them in an inscription on the Memorial as the "SOLDIERS OF FREEDOM." Location: Bayou Black Rd. (SR-311), Houma, LA 70360 (in front of the Southdown Plantation

MONROE is a county seat in the north-central part of the state on I-20. During the war, Monroe's local airport was taken over by the US Army Air Forces, renamed Selman Field, and used for the training of air crews and especially navigators.

CHENNAULT AVIATION AND MILITARY MUSEUM: As the name implies, this fine museum highlights the life and career of General Clair Chennault who gained fame as the commander of the famous Flying Tigers that served in China during the early part of WW II. Chennault grew up in the Monroe area.

The Museum is on the grounds of Monroe Regional Airport (Selman Field) and is housed in one of the last remaining WW II buildings at the Airport.

Among the many exhibits in the Museum is a replica of the P-40 fighter plane painted in the colors of the aircraft Chennault's pilots flew and complete with the distinctive Flying Tiger nose art. The Museum has a large collection of artifacts and memorabilia related to Chennault, his career and the Flying Tigers. There is a gift shop that is well worth your time to visit and the Museum has a library. The Director of the Museum is Nell Calloway, Chennault's granddaughter. Address: 701 Kansas Ln., Monroe, LA 71203. Phone and website: 318-362-5540; www.chennaultmuseum.org

NEW ORLEANS is, and always has been, the state's largest city. Like other major cities during the war, it experienced a large influx of war workers and service personnel. The city was the headquarters of the 8th Naval District and the Gulf Sea Frontier Command. Consolidated-Vultee Corp. had an aircraft plant in the city building seaplanes. There were several ship builders including Higgins Industries which built the famous landing craft known as "Higgins Boats."

New Orleans was a major port of embarkation for troops and equipment going overseas, there were two Army camps, Camp Palauche and Jackson Barracks, two naval air stations, an Army Hospital and several prisoner of war camps.

GRETNA WORLD WAR II MEMORIAL: Gretna is a suburb of New Orleans on the west bank of the Mississippi river. Its citizens have honored those individuals from their community who gave their lives during WW II with this handsome granite memorial. Their names are etched into the memorial. Location: In the median of Huey Long Blvd. Between 10th and 11th Sts.

HILTON-NEW ORLEANS RIVERSIDE (hotel): In the front of this hotel is a large-than-life statue of Winston Churchill giving his famous "V-for-victory" sign. Address: 2 Poydras St., New Orleans, LA 70130

The Gretna World War II Memorial in Gretna, LA

JACKSON BARRACKS MILITARY MUSEUM: This museum is on the grounds of Jackson Barracks, the home of the Louisiana National Guard. It is in the post's original powder magazine and relates the history of the Barracks and US military history in general for the past 200 years. There is a generous amount of WW II artifacts, memorabilia and equipment on display.

   The Museum has a 183-seat theater, an air park and various types of military equipment scattered around the grounds. Museum tours are available. During WW II, the powder magazine served as a prisoner of war facility. Address: 6400 St. Claude Av., New Orleans, LA 70146. Phone: 504-952-7819.

THE NATIONAL WW II MUSEUM: This is a large and impressive multi-story museum founded by the late and famous author, Steven Ambrose, who wrote many book on WW II. This is one of several museums in the US that addresses and emphasizes the amphibious invasions of "D-Days" of WW II. The Museum also emphasizes

The Winston Churchill statue in front of the Hilton-New Orleans Riverside Hotel

the importance of the *Higgins Boats* landing craft which was made in New Orleans and was used in both the European and Pacific theaters of operation throughout the war.

   The Museum is divided into several, state-of-the-art, galleries that emphasize amphibious operations in Europe and the Pacific and activities on the American home front. On display are aircraft, tanks, documents, photographs, WW II artifacts and a mockup of the living quarters of the ordinary GI in a barracks.

128

The Museum has two dining facilities. The Stage Door Canteen cafe offers an excellent selection of food and has a weekly series of entertainment. A second dining facility is the Soda Shop which offers breakfast; sandwiches, ice cream, snacks and 1940s type chocolate sodas. Also, there is a large theater that hosts top-of-the-line entrainment and other activities. Don't miss the large and interesting museum store. Guided tours of the Museum are available. Address: The National WW II Museum, 945 Magazine St. New Orleans, LA 70130. Phone and website: 504-527-6012; www.nationalww2museum.org

The entrance to the National World War II Museum in New Orleans, LA

RACELAND is a small community in southern Louisiana 47 miles SW of New Orleans on U-90, SR-1 and SR-182.

FIRST AMERICAN CASUALTY OF WORLD WAR II MEMORIAL: On October 15, 1987, it was written into the Congressional Record that Fredde John Falgout from Raceland, LA was the first American casualty of WW II. Falbout was a sailor on the cruiser *USS Augusta* which, in 1937, was sailing in the China Sea when the ship was hit by a stray shell from a Japanese warship. The shell was intended for a nearby Chinese vessel. Falgout was killed instantly. This is his memorial. Location: Lafourche Visitor Welcome Center, 4484 SR-1 in Raceland

The First American Casualty of World War II Memorial in Raceland, LA

RUSTON is a county seat in north-central Louisiana 30 miles west of Monroe on I-20. During the war, it was home to a large army camp, Camp Ruston that was built in 1942.

LOUISIANA MILITARY MUSEUM is located in Ruston's Memorial Park and covers 150 years of military history in Louisiana. There is a broad selection of fire arms, artillery pieces, uniforms, medals, diaries and more. Only a part of the overall display is devoted to WW II. Address: 201 Memorial Dr. which intersects with E. Georgia St. (SR-80), Ruston, LA 71270. Phone and website: 318-251-5099; www.lamilitarymuseum.com

SHREVEPORT is a large city in the NW corner of the state on I-20 and I-49. During the war, it was home to Barksdale Field, now Barksdale Air Force Base. There was also a WW II ordnance plant in the area.

EIGHTH AIR FORCE MUSEUM: Remember the 8th Air Force of WW II? They tore hell out of Germany's cities, factories and military bases. This Museum honors those who served in the wartime 8th Air Force and displays several of the planes that were utilized by the "Mighty Eighth." Altogether, the Museum's air park has about 30 aircraft.

  Inside the Museum are displays ranging from WW II to the present. Included in the displays is a replica of a WW II briefing room, one of the few such displays in the nation. There is an interesting gift shop which you should not miss. The Museum is on the grounds of Barksdale AFB but is maintained and operated by the 8th Air Force Museum Association which is not part of Barksdale AFB. Address: 88 Shreveport Rd., Barksdale AFB, LA 71110. Phone and website: 318-456-5553 and 318-752-0055; www.8afmuseum.com

The Eight Air Force Museum in Shreveport, LA

MAINE

Of all the states in the nation, Maine is geographically closest to Europe. That made the state an important link in America's connections with her European Allies. Early in the war, before the US became involved, important air routes were established from Maine to Scotland to transport Lend Lease supplies, aircraft, essential materials and personnel to our friends in Europe.

Maine's strategic location was also important to America's defenses. Military forces stationed in Maine were in a position to intercept German submarines approaching the US from Europe, and aircraft and ships from Maine provided vital convoy escort services along sections of the North Atlantic convoy routes.

__BANGOR__ is one of Maine's larger cities and is in south-central Maine on I-95, US-1A SR-9 and the Penobscot River. Just west of town was a large WW II air base, Dow Field, which was one of the air bases in Maine from which aircraft departed for Europe. Dow Field in now Bangor International Airport.

COLE LAND TRANSPORTATION MUSEUM: Did you ever see a bronze Jeep? You can see one here. It's in front of the Cole Land Transportation Museum. And the driver is also in bronze. His likeness is that of Charlie Flanagan killed in WW II and the best friend of Galen Cole, the founder of the Museum.

The jeep and driver is the official State of Maine World War II Memorial, and the Museum has another Memorial, the Purple Heart Memorial. The Museum's founder, Galen Cole, was a Purple Heart recipient from WW II who, while lying wounded, made a pledge to his God and country that he would do his best to leave his community and his fellow man better than he had found them. He kept that promise! The Museum is open daily to the public and is a joy to behold.

Inside the Museum is a large collection of land transportation vehicles including some military vehicles. The Museum is easily accessible off Exit 182A - follow the signs. Address: 405 Perry Rd., Bangor, ME 04401. Phone and website: 207-990-3600; www.colemuseum.org

CAMPOBELLO ISLAND, NEW BRUNSWICK, CANADA: Just across the US border from Lubec, ME is Campobello Island in the Canadian Province of New Brunswick. It has an important WW II site worthy of note.

The Maine State World War II Memorial in front of the Cole Land Transportation Museum in Bangor, ME. The Jeep and driver are made of bronze.

ROOSEVELT CAMPOBELLO INTERNATIONAL PARK, on the western end of the island, was the site of the 34-room summer home of the Franklin D. Roosevelt family. It was here, in Aug. 1921, that Franklin Roosevelt was stricken with polio at the age of 39.

The Roosevelt family used the summer home less and less after Franklin became president and the demands of the job consumed most of his time. The home has been preserved and opened to the public.

The Roosevelt International Bridge connects Lubec, ME with Campobello Island. The Park is administered by a joint US and Canadian Commission and is open daily. Canadian address; 459 Rt-774, Welshpool, New Brunswick E5E 1A4: US address; PO Box 129, Lubec, ME 04652. Phone and website: 506-752-2922 and 877-851-6663; http://rooseveltcampobello.areaparks.com

HOULTON is on the NE edge of the state near the Canadian border about 40 miles south of Presque Isle, ME. Just east of town was a WW II airfield, Houlton Army Airfield.

WORLD WAR II VETERANS MEMORIAL HOULTON HONOR ROLL: This impressive memorial honors 1230 individuals who gave their lives during WW II. It measures 17 ft. across and 11 ft. high and is an impressive structure to behold. At the top of the Memorial is the slogan "ALL GAVE SOME. SOME GAVE ALL." Location: on the grounds of Cary Library, 107 Main St., Houlton, ME 04730

KITTERY is in the SW corner of the state across the Piscataqua River from Portsmouth, NH. It is the home of the Portsmouth Naval Shipyard which is named after, and generally associated with, Portsmouth, NH. The Shipyard, however, is in Maine.

During WW II, the Shipyard specialized in building submarines. In May 1945, after Germany surrendered, four German submarines operating in the North Atlantic came to Kittery to surrender.

SQUALUS/SAILFISH **MEMORIAL**: This memorial, on the grounds of the Portsmouth Naval Yard, consists of the conning tower of submarine SS-192 which began life as the *Squalus*. The *Squalus,* while undergoing test trials, sank off the coast of Maine in 1939 taking the lives of half its crew. The *Squalus* was eventually raised, repaired, renamed *Sailfish* and saw considerable action during WW II.

As *Sailfish*, she won nine battle stars and a Presidential Unit Citation.

OLD ORCHARD BEACH is a beach community 12 miles south of downtown Portland at the end of I-195 and on SR-9 and SR-98.

OLD ORCHARD BEACH WORLD WAR II MEMORIAL: Old Orchard Beach lost about a dozen of its sons during WW II and this memorial exists to honor their memory. In the tall central panel is an ornate sword and the names of the men are inscribed on plaques at the base. Location: In Memorial Park near 1st and Staples Sts.

The conning tower of the WW II era submarine Sailfish in Kittery, ME

PORTLAND, on the SW coast of Maine on the Atlantic Ocean, was Maine's largest city during the war and the state's leading industrial, commercial, trade and cultural center. There are two interesting WW II memorials in the city's Fort Allen Park.

FORT ALLEN PARK ARCTIC CAMPAIGN 1941-45 WW II MEMORIAL: This is a very unique memorial dedicated to the men who served on the many convoys of WW II that sailed the North Atlantic and Arctic Oceans delivering Lend Lease materials from the United States and the United Kingdom to the Soviet Union. These convoys were among the most hazardous missions of the war because of the constant threat of German submarines, aircraft and horrible weather. Scores of ships were lost and some 3000 men and women perished in the process; American, British and Russian. The governments of the United States, the United Kingdom and Russia cooperated in the construction and dedication of the Memorial.

The Fort Allen Park Arctic Campaign 1941-45 WW II Memorial in Portland's Fort Allen Park in Portland, ME

The mast and bell of the WW II cruiser Portland in Fort Allen Park

FORT ALLEN PARK CRUISER *PORTLAND* MEMORIAL is on the beach at Fort Allen Park and overlooks Casco Bay. It honors the men who served on the cruiser *Portland* during WW II. The *Portland* saw considerable action in the Pacific during the war.

The memorial consists of the *Portland's mast* and bell and a monument and plaque list the ship's battle record. Location of both Memorials: Fort Allen Park, Eastern and Promenade, Portland, ME

LIBERTY SHIP MEMORIAL: During the war, many Liberty Ships were built in the Portland area. This memorial stands on the location of one of the largest shipyards in the area and honors the men and women who worked around the clock to build the much-needed ships. The centerpiece of the Memorial is a stylized steel sculpture of the bow of a Liberty Ship. It is 35 Ft. tall and 65 ft. long and is constructed to the actual scale of a Liberty Ship. Location: In Bug Light Park on Cushing Point, off Madison St., in South Portland

USS REUBEN JAMES **MEMORIAL:** The US Navy destroyer, *Reuben James,* was the first US destroyer to be lost in WW II. It was sunk in the North Atlantic on October 31, 1941 by a German submarine and cost the lives of 115 US seamen. At the time, the US was still neutral and the incident created a major diplomatic crisis between the United States and Germany. The sinking of the *Reuben James* was widely

The Liberty Ship Memorial in South in Portland, ME

publicized and portended the bad things that were soon to come.

The city of Portland has chosen to remember the incident and the sailors who perished by this fine memorial. Location: In a water front park off Veranda St. in the community of East Deering

The Reuben James Memorial in Portland, ME

MARYLAND

The state of Maryland had, like many states in the Union, suffered economic hardships throughout the Great Depression. In the late 1930s, however, Maryland's economy was reviving nicely because of a number of factors including, in the late 1930s, the large-scale improvement of Maryland's highways and the construction of many new bridges in this multi-river state.

The city of Baltimore was one of the nation's major seaports and a major industrial center and as the war developed, war plants and other war facilities moved into Maryland in record numbers.

After the war, Maryland continued to prosper and its population continued to increase, especially in the Baltimore-Washington, DC corridor.

ANNAPOLIS in on the eastern shore of Chesapeake Bay 20 miles south of Baltimore and 25 miles ENE of Washington, DC. It is Maryland's capitol and the home of the US Naval Academy.

Maryland's World War II State Memorial in Annapolis, MD

MARYLAND'S WORLD WAR II STATE MEMORIAL: Appropriately, this impressive WW II memorial is located near the Naval Academy. It consists of a four-sided open-air amphitheater surrounded by a 100 ft. diameter ring of 48 pillars that represent the 48 states of the Union at the time of the war.

Etched in the granite are the names of the 6,454 Marylanders who lost their lives during the war. Twenty plaques describe wartime milestones and key events of the war in addition to the contributions made by the 288,000 Marylanders who served in the nation's armed services. Two 14 ft. diameter globes depict the location of the key battle of the war. A seven-sided obelisk, representing Maryland's status as the nation's seventh state is accented by a star which is illuminated at night. Location: The US Naval Academy Bridge, 1920 Ritchie Hwy. (SR-450), Annapolis, MD

US NAVAL ACADEMY MUSEUM: This fine museum is located in Preble Hall on the Academy grounds. It has several galleries which offer exhibits tracing the history of the Academy and demonstrates the role of the Navy in war and peace. On display are ship models, paintings, photographs, ships' instruments, weapons, medals, manuscripts, uniforms, naval artillery pieces, vehicles, aircraft and much more. The WW II era is well represented in the Museum's collection.

The Museum has a large library, and arranges guided tours of the Academy, and be sure to check out the gift shop.

There are several WW II-related memorials on the Academy's campus commemorating the attacks on Hiroshima, the Seabees, the US Marine Corps, the Battle of Midway, the activities of US submarines during the war and the missing in action. Address: US Naval Academy, 118 Maryland Av., Annapolis, MD 21402-5034. Phone and website: 410-293-2108 (Museum) 800-778-4260 (gift shop); www.usna.edu/Museum/

ANNAPOLIS JUNCTION/FORT GEORGE MEADE AREA: This is Fort George Meade country. Annapolis Junction is on SR-32 and SR-295 and just off I-95. It has long been associated with Fort George Meade which is just east of the city.

Rotors
Lampboard
Keyboard
Plugboard

NATIONAL CRYPTOLOGIC MUSEUM: This is the first museum in the US devoted to America's military intelligence services. In its collection are thousands of artifacts related to the making of, and breaking of, military codes - a very important activity in times of both war and peace.

The Museum has several copies of the German's "Enigma" Machine of WW II which were Germany's main encoding/decoding devices used throughout the war. Two of the machines can be operated by visitors.

Also on display is the US Navy's "Bombe" machine used to break the Enigma codes. Other exhibits explain coding devices and methods used as far back as per-Revolutionary times.

There is information on the Navajo Code talkers used by the US Marines in the Pacific and on the USN WAVES and the British Navy's WRENS (female sailors) who frequently operated, and

The WW II German Enigma encoding/decoding machines at the National Cryptologic Museum are available for visitor's use.

became experts at, using the Allied encoding/decoding equipment. Individuals who contributed to advancement in America's intelligence services are identified and honored.

One of the permanent exhibits in the Museum tells the story of America's breaking of the Japanese code prior to the Battle of Midway which was a significant factor in the US Navy's outstanding victory there.

The Museum has a large reference library, and educational program and a one-of-kind gift shop. Address: Colony Seven Rd. (Near the main gate of the NSA campus), Annapolis Junction, MD 20701. Phone and website: 301-688-5849; www.nsa.gov/about/cryptologic_heritage/museum/index.shtml

BALTIMORE is in the north-central part of the state on Chesapeake Bay. By the beginning of the war, it was Maryland's largest city and industrial center, a major shipbuilding center, the nation's 3rd largest seaport in total waterborne commerce and the nation's 7th largest city. The onset of war in Europe brought a welcome surge of prosperity to the city which had suffered considerably during the Great Depression. Baltimore benefited nicely from the Lend Lease Act of 1941 because much of the Lend Lease material sent to Britain went through this port.

In 1942, part of Gen. Patton's forces embarked from Baltimore for the Allied landings in North Africa.

HISTORIC SHIPS IN BALTIMORE (Museum) is located on Baltimore's Inner Harbor on Pier One at the end of Pratt St. The mission of the Museum is to preserve, exhibit and interpret information and artifacts related to the naval history of the Chesapeake Bay area from colonial times to the present.

The Museum has three WW II ships, all of which saw action in WW II and are now open to the public. They are the submarine *Torsk*, the lightship *Chesapeake* and the Coast Guard cutter *Taney*. Seldom does a Museum have such an impressive example of WW II ships as are offered here.

There are many other WW II displays in the Museum which has a library and an educational program. And don't pass up the gift shop. Address: Pier I 301 E. Pratt St., Baltimore, MD 21202. Phone and website: 410-539-1797; www.historicships.org

The WW II submarine USS Torsk at Historic Ships in Baltimore.

MARYLAND MUSEUM OF MILITARY HISTORY: This is Maryland's Army National Guard museum. Like other Army National Guard museums, it tells the long history of that organization and the colonial militia that preceded it. The World War II section is well represented and highlights the activities of the 29th Infantry Division in which the Maryland National Guard served during World War II.

The Museum has many artifacts which include weapons, uniforms, documents, photos, and more. There is a library and an art gallery. Address: Fifth Regiment Armory, 219 29th Division St., Baltimore, MD 21201. Phone and website: 410-576-1496; http://marylandmilitaryhistory.org/aboutmus.php

***SS JOHN W. BROWN* LIBERTY SHIP:** This is a restored WW II Liberty Ship which now serves as a museum and offers cruises to the public entitled "Living History Day Cruises."

The *John W. Brown* named after a labor leader of its day, was built in Baltimore and saw action in Mediterranean and Persian Gulf during WW II and is now on the National Registry of Historic Places.

Conducted tours of the ship are offered when in port and the Ship has a very interesting ship's store that is worth a visit. Location: Clinton Street Pier 1 in Baltimore. Mail address: Project Liberty Ship, PO Box 25846 Highlandtown Station, Baltimore, MD 21224. Phone and website: 410-558-0646; www.liberty-ship.com/html/vtour/index.php

The John W. Brown Liberty ship on public display at Baltimore, MD

CAMBRIDGE is a county seat on the western side of the Delmarva Peninsula on US-50, SR-16 and the Choptank River.

CAMBRIDGE WORLD WAR II MEMORIAL: Inscribed on this impressive memorial are the statements "PEACE TO THE MIGHTY DEAD 1941-1945" and "IN GRATEFUL MEMORY OF OUR VETERANS OF WORLD WAR II." The Memorial consists of a tall column with a carved eternal flame at the top and a low wall bearing inscriptions. Location: Long Wharf Park overlooking the Choptank River

The Cambridge World War II Memorial in Cambridge, MD

FREDERICK is a county seat 45 miles NW of Baltimore on I-70, I-270, US-15 and US-340.

WORLD WAR II MEMORIAL: Honored here are the local area's men and women who served in WW II. Their names are inscribed on the Memorial's long stone wall - there are hundreds of them.

The Park also has memorials to other US military conflicts. Park location: N. Bentz and W. 2nd St., Frederick, MD

The World War II Memorial in Frederick, MD

WORLD WAR II MEMORIAL AT MT. OLIVET CEMETERY: This is a very impressive WW II memorial consisting of two tall pillars, on a semi-circle walkway with a granite marker in the center which has an eternal flame. On top of the pillars are stars and etched into the central pillar are the names of those individuals from Frederick County who gave their lives in the war. Location: Mt. Olivet Cemetery, 515 S. Market St., Frederick, MD

<u>LAUREL</u> is on I-95 midway between Baltimore and Washington, DC and is another city closely associated with the US Army's Fort George Meade which is east of town.

FORT MEADE MUSEUM: This museum is on the grounds of Fort Meade and chronicles the military history of the Fort and the surrounding area from the days of the Revolution to the present. Of particular interest to WW II buffs is a bullet-ridden bust of Adolph Hitler found in the rubble of Berlin. Also on display at the museum, on its beautifully landscaped grounds, are tracked and wheeled vehicles, field artillery, ordnance, communications and medical equipment, small arms, machine guns, uniforms, medals, art works, unit memorials and more. Address: 4674 Griffin Av., Fort George G. Meade, MD 20755-5094. Phone and website: 301-677-6966; www.ftmeade.army.mil/Museum/Index.htm

The World War II Memorial at Mt. Olivet Cemetery in Frederick, MD

<u>OXON HILL</u> is a small community 11 miles south of Washington, DC just off I-95/495 and on SR-210.

OXON HILL MANOR: This was the estate of Sumner Welles, the Undersecretary of State in President Roosevelt's Administration. He was one of Roosevelt's favorite advisers and the President was a frequent visitor to the Manor. It is a 49-room Georgian Style mansion on a beautiful estate.
   The Manor is open to the public, but because it is host to so many events and functions, visitors must have an appointment so as not to conflict with scheduled events. Address: 6901 Oxon Hill Rd., Oxon Hill, MD 20745. Phone: 310-839-7782.

<u>PATUXENT</u>: This area, in the south-central part of the state on Chesapeake Bay and the Patuxent River, has long been a hub of US naval activities. During WW II, it had a naval air station, USN amphibious training base, a mine test station and a torpedo test station.

PATUXENT RIVER NAVAL AIR MUSEUM: This museum in on the grounds of Naval Air Station, Patuxent River and is a one-of-a-kind museum in that it is the only museum in the country offering displays on the testing and evaluation of naval aircraft.
   On display are naval aircraft, engines, models, test pilot gear, photos and a multitude of components and systems evaluated by the personnel of NAS, Patuxent River, some successfully, some not.
   Virtually all of the aircraft on display are post war but one of the exhibits of interest to WW II historians is the Museum's displays on the development of radar which came about during WW II.

There is also a Link Trainer which was produced in large numbers and used extensively during the War. The Museum has a library, an educational program and a well-stocked gift shop. Address: 22156 Three Notch Rd., Lexington Park, MD 20653. Phone and website: 301-863-1900/7418; http://paxmuseum.com. The Museum is immediately outside, and adjacent to, Patuxent River Naval Air Station Gate #1 at the intersection of SR-235 and Pegg Rd.

SUITLAND is nine miles SE of downtown Washington on Suitland Parkway, SR-4 and SR-5.

AIRMEN MEMORIAL MUSEUM is in the town of Suitland, MD. and tells the history of the enlisted US Airman from 1907 to the present. There are several galleries of exhibits which include uniforms, equipment, documents, photographs, diaries, paintings, medals, a WW II Norden bombsite, small arms, captured enemy equipment of WW II and a recreated 1940s orderly room. A large part of the displays and exhibits are devoted to the WW II era.

The Museum was founded by the US Air Force Sergeants Association and tells the history of that important organization. Address: 5211 Auth Rd., Suitland, MD 20746. Phone and website: 301-899-3500; www.afsahq.org

The Airmen Memorial Museum, Suitland, MD

MASSACHUSETTS

When World War II began in Europe in 1939, the state of Massachusetts had the good fortune of finding itself in the right place at the right time. Its growing industrialized economy, its eager work force, geographic location and political stability all contributed to the boom conditions that the state was about to experience. Massachusetts was one of the most industrialized states in the nation. Over 89% of her population lived in cities of 10,000 people or more and a large percentage of those people were associated with manufacturing.

Geographically the state became important to the defense of New England and the US East Coast.

Boston became an assembly point for convoys and other naval operations in the North Atlantic. Before the US entered the war, Massachusetts ports serviced British and Canadian warships and exported Lend Lease goods to Britain and other nations.

AMESBURY is a small community in NE Massachusetts near the intersection of I-95 and I-495.

POLISH-AMERICAN VETERANS WAR MEMORIAL: This unique memorial honors the local veterans of Polish decent who were killed in WW II. It is located on the median of a roadway and has a stone memorial, a flag pole and well-kept

The Polish-American Veterans War Memorial in Amesbury, MA

landscaping. Location: At the intersection of Market St. (Hwy.-150) and South Hampton Rd. (Hwy.-107A)

BOSTON AREA: Boston is the capitol of Massachusetts, its largest city and main economic, industrial and cultural center. At the time of WW II, Boston was the 9th largest city in the country. During the war, Boston was a major ship-building center and one of the principle ports along the East Coast shipping Lend Lease material to the various Allied nations and a major port of embarkation for American service personnel being sent overseas.

  Massachusetts Institute of Technology, in Cambridge, did considerable research on the development of radar, and Harvard University, also in Cambridge, did war-related research on oceanography.

The WW II destroyer Cassin Young on display at the Boston National Historic Park

BOSTON NATIONAL HISTORIC PARK: This is a park consisting of a number of historic sites in the Boston area. They include the Boston Navy Yard (aka Charleston Navy Yard), the Bunker Hill Monument, Dorchester Heights National Historic Site, the Paul Revere House and Faneuil Hall. There are two visitors centers, one at 15 State St. in downtown Boston and the other at the Boston Navy Yard. Most of the sites are connected by a three-mile-long trail that takes the visitor past these and other historic sites.

  Of interest to WW II buffs is the *USS Constitution* display at the Boston Navy Yard where the WW II destroyer *Cassin Young* is on display and open to the public along with the famous 18th century warship, the *USS Constitution*. The *Cassin Young* is named after Capt. Cassin Young who distinguished himself at Pearl Harbor where, as commander of the repair ship *Vestal,* was able to save that ship which was alongside the battleship *Arizona* when it blew up. Later, at the Battle of Guadalcanal, Capt. Young was killed while commanding the cruiser *San Francisco*.

  On display at the Museum are WW II ship models, uniforms, documents, paintings, flags, navigational equipment, medical equipment and small arms. Visitor Center Address (one of two visitors centers): 15 State St., Boston, MA 02109. Phone: 617-242-5642. Visitors Center Address (two of two visitor centers): Boston Navy Yard. Phone: 617-242-5601. Website for the Boston National Historic Park: www.nps.gov/bost

CITY OF SOMERVILLE HONOR ROLL-WORLD WAR II MEMORIAL: Somerville is a suburb of Boston three miles NW of downtown Boston. This impressive memorial, which consists of a large wall and a center flag pole, stands outside Somerville City Hall and, as the name implies, honors those citizens of Somerville who fought in WW II. A small portion of the Memorial is dedicated to President Franklin D. Roosevelt. Location: 93 Highland Av., Somerville, MA 02143

The Somerville Honor Roll-World War II Memorial in Boston, MA

JOHN F. KENNEDY PRESIDENTIAL LIBRARY AND MUSEUM is on Columbia Point, a peninsula that juts out into Boston Harbor just south of South Boston. This Library and Museum honors the memory of John F. Kennedy, the 35th President of the US and a native of Massachusetts. It highlights his life and other members of his Kennedy family.

Included in the numerous displays within the Library is a complete account of John F. Kennedy's WW II service and his brush with death as captain of the ill-fated PT-109 in the Guadalcanal campaign.

The Library and Museum are associated with the University of Massachusetts and the Museum has a cafe. Address: Columbia Point, Boston, MA 02125. Phone and website: 866-JKF-1960 and 617-514-1600; www.jfklibrary.org

The Malden WW II Memorial in Malden, MA

MALDEN WORLD WAR II MEMORIAL: Malden is a northern suburb of Boston on SR-60 and SR-99. The community has an inspiring stone memorial commemorating those from the local area who served in WW II. Their names are listed on bronze plaques and those who died during the war have a star beside their names.

On the bronze plaques listing the names are famous quotations from President Roosevelt, Winston Churchill, Douglas MacArthur and Dwight Eisenhower. Location: In Bell Rock Memorial Park at the corner of Main and Wigglesworth Sts.

WW II MEMORIAL, BACK BAY FENS: In Boston, within Boston's Back Bay Fens, is a grouping of war memorials arranged in a circular pattern. The largest of the three is the WW II Memorial and was the first placed at this location. The most prominent part of the Memorial is a standing bronze angel and behind her a wall with the names of those who served. Location: Back Bay Fens (a parkland and urban wild life center), Boston, MA 02115

FALL RIVER/NEW BEDFORD AREA: These are two old and historic coastal towns in southern Massachusetts just a few miles apart.

BATTLESHIP COVE, MARINE MUSEUM AND FALL RIVER HERITAGE PARK: This is a three-in-one attraction. Battleship Cove is an anchorage for several WW II-related warships, the battleship

The WW II Memorial, Back Bay Fens, Boston

Massachusetts (*Big Mamie*), the cruiser *Fall River,* the submarine *Lionfish*, the destroyer Joseph *P. Kennedy, Jr*, and other WW II crafts. All of the ships saw action in WW II except the *Joseph P. Kennedy, Jr.* which was launched in 1945. This ship was named in honor of the oldest son of Joseph P. Kennedy, Sr. US Ambassador to Britain and brother of President John F. Kennedy. Joseph P. Kennedy, Jr. was killed during WW II, and the destroyer named in his honor saw action in the Korean and Viet Nam Wars.

All of the ships are open to the public. Aboard the *Massachusetts* are the official state WW II, Korean War and Viet Nam War Memorials honoring Massachusetts citizens who gave their lives in those wars. Overnight camping on the *Massachusetts* is permitted.

Aboard the *Joseph P. Kennedy, Jr.* is the Admiral Arleigh Burke National Destroyermen's Museum which tells the history of the ship and has displays on the day-to-day lives of men who served abroad destroyers.

PT boats are on displays which were sister ships to *PT-109*, the craft commanded by young John F. Kennedy in the Pacific. There is also a PT boat library at the site containing one of the largest collections of PT boat archives in the country.

The other two attractions at the park are the Marine Museum which recalls the age of sail and steamship travel from colonial days up to 1937, and the Fall River Heritage State Park, an eight-acre urban park with a visitors center and exhibits on Fall River's textile and nautical history. Address of the complex: Five Water St., Battleship Cove, Fall River, MA 02722-0111. Phone and website: 508-678-1100 and 800-533-3194 (New England only); www.battleshipcove.com

The WW II battleship Massachusetts (Big Mamie), on permanent display at Battleship Cove in Fall River. The ship is open to the public and aboard are the official state memorials dedicated to those who fell in WW II, the Korean Conflict and the Viet Nam War.

FITCHBURG is in north-central Massachusetts on SR-2A, SR-12 and SR-13.

WORLD WAR II MEMORIAL: In 1995, the citizens of Fitchburg erected this attractive stone memorial to those men and women from the city who served in WW II.
Location: Upper Common Park near the center of Fitchburg

The WW II Memorial in Fitchburg, MA

Massachusetts

FRAMINGHAM is 12 miles west of Boston on SR-126 and SR-135. During the war, a large military hospital, Cushing General Hospital, was built in Framingham to care for wounded military personnel.

THE CUSHING CHAPEL: Cushing General Hospital had 95 buildings. One of them was a chapel which has been preserved on its original site as a memorial to the Hospital, its staff and the many patients who were treated here. The Chapel still provides religious services and is available for private activities such as weddings and funerals. Location: In Tercentenial Park on Dudley Rd. Phone and website: 508-680-4815; www.framingham.com/history/hstprsrv/cushingchapel.htm

The interior of The Crushing Chapel in Framingham, MA

GLOUCESTER is a coastal community in the NE part of the state on Cape Ann. It has always had close ties with the sea. Today, it has two memorials dedicated to WW II.

GLOUCESTER WORLD WAR II MEMORIAL: This impressive memorial consists of a stone base with plaques and topped with a globe and a spread eagle. Inscribed on one of the plaques is the statement "GLOUSCESTER REMEMBERS. 1941- WORLD WAR II-1945. THE PEOPLE OF GLOUCESTER PROUDLY DEDICATE THIS MEMORIAL TO OUR CITIZENS WHO SERVED AND SACRAFICED IN THAT MOST DEVASTATING WAR. THEY VALIANTLY FACED THE PERILS OF BATTLR TO RESTORE FREEDOM AROUND THE GLOBE." Location: Intersection of Western Av.(SR-127) and Essex Av.(SR-133)

MERCHANT MARINERS ANCHOR/WW II MEMORIAL: The main feature of this memorial is a large anchor and a stone plaque inscribed "WITH THANKS FROM THE PEOPLE OF GLOUCESTER TO OUR SONS WHO SERVED AS MERCHANT MARINERS 1941-1945." Location: At the north end of Stage Fort Park on Stacy Blvd.

The Merchant Mariners Anchor/WW II Memorial in Gloucester, MA

HOLYOKE is eight miles NW of Springfield on I-91 and US-202. Nearby is a well-known landmark, Mount Tom, and further to the east is Westover Air Reserve Base which, during the war, was Westover Airfield.

The Gloucester World War II Memorial, Gloucester, MA

143

MOUNT TOM B-17 MEMORIAL TRIBUTE: On July 6, 1945, a B-17 bomber, operating out of Westover Airfield, crashed into the side of Mount Tom killing all 25 airmen aboard – an unusually large number of passengers for a B-17. The citizens of the area have erected a polished stone memorial at the crash site listing the names of all aboard and their home states. Location: Mount Tom – ask locally for directions.

LAWRENCE is in NE Massachusetts on I-93, I-493 and the Merrimack River.

The Mount Tom B-17 Memorial Tribute near Lawrence, MA

LAWRENCE WW II MEMORIAL: This is the community of Lawrence's worthy tribute to those individuals from the Lawrence area who gave their lives in WW II. Their names are listed on the Memorial. The Memorial is in a delightful park setting. Location: Campagnone Common on Common and Lawrence Sts. across from City Hall

MILFORD is 30 miles SW of downtown Boston on I-495, SR-109 and SR-163.

MILFORD WORLD WAR II MEMORIAL: This impressive WW II memorial has four statues representing those individuals from New Haven County who served in WW II. They are mounted on a stone base which bears a plaque reading "DEDICATED TO ALL WHO SERVED 1941-1945." Location: Intersection of Broad St. (SR-163) and Armory Lane

The Lawrence WW II Memorial

The World War II Memorial in Milford, MA

NORTH ATTLEBORO: This is a small community in south-central Massachusetts near the Rhode Island border on I-95 and US-1.

WORLD WAR II MEMORIAL SWIMMING POOL: Here's a very unique WW II Memorial - a swimming pool. When you come to see this memorial bring your swim suit. Location: 45 S. Washington St., Attleboro MA

QUINCY is eight miles south of downtown Boston on the Bay and on I-93/US-1/SR-3, SR-3A, SR- and SR-53. The city has two WW II memorials.

The World War II Memorial Pool in North Attleboro, MA

QUINCY WORLD WAR II MEMORIAL: This impressive memorial consists of four bronze statues mounted on a stone base with the inscription "IN MEMORY TO ALL WHO SERVED IN WORLD WAR II 1941-1945." One of the statues is kneeling as if appealing to God. Location: Southern Artery, SR-3A

WORLD WAR II MEMORIAL AT MT. WOLLASTON CEMETERY: Here is Quincy's largest cemetery and it has an impressive WW II memorial dedicated to the veterans of WW II. The Memorial consists of a large circular stone base with a central flag pole and inscriptions commemorating those who served. Location: Mt. Wollaston Cemetery on Sea St., Quincy, MA

SPRINGFIELD, in the SE part of the state near the Connecticut, state line, was a major manufacturing center with a heavy reliance on the manufacture of small arms. One of the main manufacturers of arms in the area was the government-owned Springfield Armory.

The Quincy World War II Memorial Quincy, MA

SPRINGFIELD ARMORY MUSEUM: This fine museum is on the grounds of Springfield Armory in the main arsenal building which dates

back to 1847. It has one of the largest collections of small arms in the world, many of which were designed and manufactured here. There is a major display on the M1 Garand Rifle and its designer, John C. Garand. That rifle was the standard weapon of the US infantry units during WW II.

The Museum has many other interesting displays on WW II small arms and a very nice gift shop with many unique items. Address: One Armory Square, Springfield, MA 01105 (in downtown Springfield just north of State St., US-20). Phone and website: 413-734-8551; www.nps.gov/spar

The WW II memorial in Templeton, MA

145

TEMPLETON is a small community in north central Massachusetts on US-202, SR-2A and SR101.

TEMPLETON WORLD WAR II MEMORIAL: This handsome stone memorial is in the center of town and honors the citizens of the Templeton area who served in WW II. Their names are recorded on the monument's bronze plaque. Location: Town Common, SR-2A

WORCESTER is a county seat near the center of the state on I-190, I-290, SR-9, SR-12 and SR-122.

MASSACHUSETTS NATIONAL GUARD MUSEUM AND ARCHIVES: This interesting museum, housed in an old and ornate armory building, preserves the history and archives of the Massachusetts National Guard from its inception in 1636 as a colonial militia to the present. During WW II, the Massachusetts National Guard was a part of the 26th Infantry Division and saw action in France and Czechoslovakia. Displays in the Museum relate this portion of the National Guard's history. Address: 44 Salisbury St., Worcester, MA 01609. Phone and website: 508-797-0334;http://states.ng.mil/sites/MA/resources/museum

---

MICHIGAN

If Michigan had been an independent country during WW II it could have fielded one of the best equipped armies in the world. Virtually everything a modern army needed was made in Michigan. The huge metropolitan area around Detroit was, and had been for two decades, one of the world's great manufacturing centers, and it had spawned manufacturing operations all over Michigan, into the bordering states and into Canada.

The Corunna World War II Memorial in Corunna, MI

CORUNNA is a county seat 18 miles west of Flint on SR-21 and SR-71.

CORUNNA WORLD WAR II MEMORIAL: Here is one of the earliest WW II memorials in the nation. It was dedicated November 11 (World War I Armistice Day), 1945. Etched on the Memorial is the inscription "ERECTED IN HONOR OF THE MEN AND WOMEN OF CORUNNA AND VICINITY WHO SERVED IN WORLD WAR II." Location: McCurdy Park on the Shiawassee River and Corunna Av. (SR-71)

DETROIT AREA: The area in and around Detroit was one of America's great manufacturing centers, and the heartland of America's automobile industry. In 1940, the census of that year ranked Detroit as America's 4th largest city with 25% of its population foreign born. There were also many military installations in the area.

THE HENRY FORD, at Village Rd. and Oakwood Blvd. is one of the great museums of the world. It contains a multitude of artifacts, inventions and mementos of American social and scientific history. Scattered throughout the Museum are many displays and items related to WW II. Of interest is President Roosevelt's bullet-proof Lincoln known as "The Sunshine Special." There are also limousines used by Presidents Eisenhower, Kennedy and Reagan.

The Henry Ford also has an early VS-300 Sikorsky helicopter made in 1939 and flown personally by Igor Sikorsky to the Museum in 1943 where he landed on the Museum's lawn. This was one of the earliest demonstrations of helicopters that would come into use for military purposes during the last months of the war. Address: 20900 Oakwood Blvd. Dearborn, MI 48124. Phone and website: 313-271-2455 and 800-835-5237; www.thehenryford.org

President Franklin Roosevelt's "Sunshine Special" limousine at The Henry Ford.

The WW II Memorial in the Purple Heart Memorial Gardens, Wyandotte, MI

PURPLE HEART MEMORIAL GARDENS: This cemetery is the final resting place of many war veterans and has a very appropriate name and a thought-provoking memorial dedicated to the WW II veterans buried here. Mounted on a stone pedestal is a bronze sculpture of a GI aiding a wounded companion. Location: Purple Heart Memorial Gardens, Wyandotte, MI

TUSKEGEE AIRMEN NATIONAL MUSEUM: During WW II, the US Air Forces enlisted black men, for the first time in US history, to train and serve as pilots of single engine fighter planes and multi-engine bombers. This was a ground-breaking event in American's racial history. The men came from all over the country and were trained in Alabama. Some 450 served in combat overseas creating an admirable military record.

This museum honors those men and relates their military service and their experiences in serving in a formerly all-white air force. Address: 6325 W. Jefferson Av., Detroit, MI 48209. Phone and website: 313-843-8849; www.tuskegeeairmennationalmuseum.org

The Tuskegee Airmen National Museum in Detroit

FRANKENMUTH is 16 miles south of Bay City on I-75 and SR-83.

MICHIGAN'S OWN MILITARY AND SPACE MUSEUM: Michigan's veterans of all branches of service are honored here in this fine museum. The Museum has a number of interesting displays related to WW II and an outstanding collection of over 600 military uniforms of which some 120 are on display at all times. Many of them are WW II era and there are uniforms from some 17 Congressional Medal of Honor recipients from various wars.

   Michigan's astronauts are also honored in the Museum. Address: 1250 Weiss St., Frankenmuth, MI 48734. Phone and website: 989-652-8005; www.michigansownmilitarymuseum.com

GRAND HAVEN is on Lake Michigan 25 miles WNW of Grand Rapids.

U.S COAST GUARD MEMORIAL PARK is on the shore of the Grand River in front of the present-day Coast Guard Headquarters. It commemorates the Coastguardsmen who have served at Grand Haven and the memory of the Coast Guard cutter *Escanaba* which had long been stationed at Grand Haven but was called away for overseas duty in 1942. The *Escanaba* was eventually sunk by a German submarine.

   Another Coast Guard cutter, *Acacia,* is also honored here. It was sunk by a German submarine in the Caribbean in Mar. 1942. The Tri-Cities Historical Museum in downtown Grand Haven has displays on the *Escanaba* and other activities in the Grand Haven area during WW II.

GRAND RAPIDS is a county seat in western Michigan 60 miles WNW of Lansing on I-96 and I-196.

GERALD R. FORD LIBRARY & MUSEUM is in two locations near downtown Grand Rapids and honors the 38th President of the United States who was a resident of Grand Rapids.

   The Museum traces the private and public lives of President Ford including his military service during WW II. Included in the many displays are details on his career as an officer in the US Navy. Ford rose from Ensign to Lt. Commander and served aboard the carrier *Monterey* as gunnery officer, assistant navigator and athletic director. Address of the Museum: 303 Pearl St. NW, Grand Rapids, MI 49504. Phone for the Museum: 616-254-0400. Address of the Library: 1000 Beal St. Grand

148

Rapids, MI 48109. Phone for the Library: 734-205-0555. Website for both the Museum and Library: www.ford.utexas.edu

The Grand Rapids World War II Memorial

GRAND RAPIDS WORLD WAR II MEMORIAL: This fine memorial consists of two stone columns, several inscribed tablets, a spread eagle and reflecting pool. It is in a park-like setting and honors those citizens of Grand Rapids who served in WW II. Location: Creston Library grounds, 1563 Plainfield Av. NE

KALAMAZOO is a county seat in SW Michigan on I-94 and US-131.

KALAMAZOO AIR MUSEUM AND THE GUADALCANAL MEMORIAL MUSEUM: This is two museums in one and is located near the Kalamazoo-Battle Creek International Airport. The principle museum, often referred to as the "Air Zoo," is a very large air museum with a large collection of aircraft, many of which are of WW II vintage and much of the aircraft collection is indoors.

The Museum is also a unique amusement park with many interactive displays, amusement rides, flight simulators, a theater, character actors, and other things not normally found in museums.

Large murals and many artifacts and aircraft-related memorabilia are on display.

The Guadalcanal Memorial Museum occupies a large area within the air museum and describes in detail the various phases of the Battle of Guadalcanal, America's first major offensive of WW II. The Guadalcanal Museum contains many artifacts from the actual battle and outside of the museum is a bronze statue of a GI scratching the name of a fallen buddy on a makeshift cross. This statue is intended to honor the more than 6000 US servicemen who died on the island.

The Museum also has a cafe and a gift shop with many interesting items. Address for both museums: 6151 Portage Rd., Kalamazoo, MI 49002. Phone and website: 269-382-6555 and 866-524-7966; www. Airzoo.org

MUSKEGON is a county seat in west-central Michigan on Lake Michigan and I-96 and US-31.

GREAT LAKES NAVAL MEMORIAL AND MUSEUM: The centerpiece of this interesting museum is the WW II submarine *Silversides* which is anchored on the south side of the Muskegon Channel. The submarine was launched just a few days after the attack on Pearl Harbor and served in the Pacific throughout the war. The *Silversides* had 14 war patrols and its crew sank 23 enemy ships and damaged 17 more. This was the third highest sinking record of all US submarines and the *Silversides* is the sole survivor of the top three ranking submarines. After the war, it served for many years as a training vessel.

The complete story of the *Silversides* is told in the Museum and many related artifacts are on display.

Another veteran ship of WW II at this museum is the US Coast Guard Cutter *McLane.* During the war, the *McLane* was operating out of Ketchikan, Alaska. While on patrol during July 1942, she picked up sonar reading on a Japanese submarine off the coast of Alaska. She gave chase,

dropped numerous depth charges and succeeded in sinking the Japanese submarine *RO-32.*

At the Museum, there is a large theater and nice restaurant and a fascinating gift shop. The Museum hosts many activities during the year and has an overnight program. Address: 1346 Bluff St., Muskegon, MI 49441: Phone and website: 231-755-1230; www.silversidesmusem.org

PORT HURON: This is a county seat on the eastern boundary of the state on the St. Claire River, the Canadian border, I-69 and I-94.

The Great Lakes Naval Memorial and Museum and the USS Silversides in Muskegow, MI

SPIRIT OF THE FIGHTING YANK MEMORIAL: The center piece of this realistic memorial is a bronze statue of a GI in full battle gear approaching the enemy. Inscribed on the pedestal is the notation "WE DEDICATE THIS MEMORIAL, NOT TO REMEMBER WAR, BUT TO REMIND US FOREVER OF THE PRIVILEGES OF PEACE AND FREEDOM." Location: Veterans Cemetery near the intersection of Gratiot Av. and Krafft Rd.

ROSCOMMON is a county seat in north-central Michigan 13 miles SE of Grayling on I-75 and SR-18.

CIVILIAN CONSERVATION CORPS (CCC) MUSEUM: This museum and camp site, located at North Higgins Lake State Park, is not a true WW II site. Rather, it is a preserved pre-war

The Spirit of the Fighting Yank Memorial in Port Huron, MI

Depression-era Civilian Conservation Corps (CCC) camp, a make-work project of the Great Depression era. It is significant to the history of WW II, however, in that the buildings seen here are the predecessors to hundreds of thousands of temporary wooden buildings built by the US Government at military installations all over the world. In 1940, the US Government made the decision not to build many permanent buildings at military bases, but instead to build large numbers of temporary buildings based on pre-war CCC building designs. Also, thousands of existing CCC buildings, like those seen here were pressed into military service during the early part of the war.

As the ranks of the CCC declined, camp after camp was abandoned and many of the buildings were torn down in sections and moved to military locations and re-assembled.

During the summer of 1942, the Federal Government declared all CCC camps in America surplus and turned them over to the War Dept. Some CCC camps were used in their original condition as small unit training camps, secret training camps, POW camps and for other purposes. One CCC camp in Maryland became President Roosevelt's famous mountain retreat known as "Shangri-La" (later "Camp David"). Address: 11747 N Higgins Lake Dr. Roscommon, MI 48653. Phone and website: 989-348-6178; www.michigan.gov/cccmuseum

SAGINAW is a county seat in east-central Michigan on I-75 and SR-46.

WW II MEMORIAL/VETERANS MEMORIAL PLAZA: The city of Saginaw has a large and beautiful Veterans Memorial Park in which there are several memorials dedicated to America's various conflicts. The WW II memorial consisted of tall limestone columns with lower wings. On the wings are engraved the names of those individuals from the local area that gave their lives in WW II. Location: Veterans Memorial. Park

This is a typical barracks building used at CCC camps all over the country during the Depression. Many of them were used during WW II and the building's design and construction became the fundamental design for hundreds of thousands of temporary wooden buildings built by the government at military installations all over the world.

TROY is 25 miles north of downtown Detroit on I-75 and SR-59.

The WWII Memorial/Veterans Memorial Plaza in Saginaw, MI

WORLD WAR II FOUR FREEDOMS MEMORIAL: Early in the war, President Roosevelt and Prime Minister Churchill met in Newfoundland and announced to the world that one of their aims of WW II was to insure the Four Freedoms to mankind. Those Four Freedoms are Freedom of Speech and Expression, Freedom of Worship, Freedom from Want and Freedom from Fear.

This memorial commemorates that event and the Four Freedoms doctrine. It consists of a tall marble column generously carved showing WW II servicemen and a globe of the world. Location: White Chapel Memorial Park Cemetery, 621 W. Long Lake Rd. at Crooks Rd., Troy, MI

The World War II Four Freedoms Memorial in Troy, MI

MINNESOTA

Minnesota contributed in many ways to the war effort. The state had major manufacturing enterprises in the Minneapolis-St. Paul area and rich farms that produced grain, dairy products and meat. Perhaps the state's most outstanding contribution, though, was iron ore, a very important commodity for any nation at war. Minnesota's iron ore mines are in the northern part of the state and were America's main source of this very necessary commodity. Needless to say, the mines were worked feverishly during the war, often around-the-clock.

ANOKA is a county seat 28 miles NW of downtown Minneapolis on US-10, US-169 and the Mississippi River.

ANOKA VETERANS MEMORIAL: A bronze statue of Congressional Medal of Honor recipient, Richard K. Sorenson, in full battle dress is the center piece of this fine memorial. The Memorial goes on to honor all Minnesota veterans of WW II. Location: John War Park on US-10 near Main St.

The Anoka Veterans Memorial of Anoka, MN

AUSTIN is on the SE edge of the state on I-90 near the Iowa state line. Just before the war, the town's major meat packing company, the Geo. Hormel Co. developed a ham-like meat product called "Spam" packed in small meal-size cans. During the war, Spam proved to be an ideal way to provide a tasty and nutritious meat product to servicemen all over the world and to our food-short Allies. Therefore, tons of Spam were produced and shipped to nearly every corner of the globe. Almost every GI, airman and sailor ate Spam at one time or another during the war.

SPAM MUSEUM: This 16,500 Sq. ft. museum in downtown Austin tells the story of Spam as well as that of the Hormel Meat Co. which produces Spam. Many of the displays relate to Spam's important role in WW II and many WW II veterans and history buffs visit the museum each year. It is the biggest attraction in town and Austin is, at times, referred to a "Spam Town USA." Along with many of the WW II artifacts in the Museum related to Spam are photos of "Slammin' Spammy," the WW II bomb-throwing pig and patriotic mascot.

There is a cafe at the museum which serves Spam and other foods and Spam tasting is available. There is a Spam Store and guest what's for sale there. The Museum also has Spam festivals. Address: 1937 Spam Blvd., Austin, MN, 55912-3690 - watch for road signs leading visitors to the Museum. Phone and website: 507-437-5100 and 507-437-5641; www.Spam.com

BRAINERD Is a county seat near the center of the state on SR-21 and SR-371.

BATAAN DEATH MARCH MEMORIAL: The 34th Tank Battalion of the Minnesota National Guard was in the infamous Death March after the fall of the Bataan Peninsula in the Philippines - and the people of Brainerd will never forget. This Memorial commemorates the men of that brave unit.

Nearby are two WW II era tanks used by this unit. Location: In front of the National Guard Armory on Wright Rd. just west of SE 13th St. in Brainerd

LITTLE FALLS is a county seat near the geographic center of the state 90 miles NW of Minneapolis/St. Paul on US-10, SR-27 and SR-371. Just to the north of the city is the large Army military reservation, Camp Ripley, home of the Minnesota Army National Guard.

The Bataan Death March Memorial in Brainerd, MN

MINNESOTA MILITARY MUSEUM: This is the official museum of the Minnesota National Guard and is located on the grounds of Camp Ripley. The Museum's mission is to preserve the artifacts and history of Minnesota's militia and National Guard, and interpret military history as experienced by citizens of the state. Displays from America's conflicts, including WW II, include military vehicles, aircraft, amphibious landing craft, artillery pieces, small arms, field equipment, uniforms, medals, insignias, ordnance and captured enemy equipment. There is a special display on the Jeep which was first tested at the Camp. The Museum also has a library, archives and a very nice gift shop - check it out. Address: 15000 Highway 115, Little Falls, MN 56345. Phone and website: 320-616-6050; www.mnmilitarymuseum.org

LONG PRAIRIE is a county seat in central Minnesota on US-71 and SR-27.

LONG PRAIRIE WORLD WAR II MEMORIAL: This is a stunning five story memorial wall which commemorates the American victory at Iwo Jima during WW II. The wall depicts the rugged terrain of the island and has graphic murals of the US Marines that took the island. At the top of the wall is statuary commemorating the famous flag rising on Mt. Surabachi.

Nearby is another mural showing the American Cemetery at Omaha Beach in France. There are a number of black granite panels with inscriptions, a memorial to women who served in WW II and a WW II Sherman tank.

Location: Veterans Memorial Park, on the corner of Central Av. and First St. near downtown Long Prairie

The five-story Iwo Jima Memorial in Veterans Park in Long Prairie, MN

MINNEAPOLIS/ST. PAUL AREA: These twin cities comprise the political, economic, industrial and cultural heart of Minnesota. The area became an important air link with Alaska and Canada and a transit center for Lend Lease supplies going to the Soviet Union.

MINNESOTA STATE CAPITOL BUILDING AND THE MINNESOTA WORLD WAR II MEMORIAL:
Many state capitol buildings and county seats around the country have relics of WW II sitting on their lawns, but the relic on the lawn of Minnesota's State Capitol Building is quite unique. It is the gun that fired America's opening shots of WW II. The gun is a 4" naval gun removed from the destroyer *Ward* during the ship's later conversion to a fast transport.

On the morning of Dec. 7, 1941, before the Japanese air attack began on Pearl Harbor, the *Ward* was patrolling the entrance to the Harbor. Suddenly, crewmen spotted a small suspicious vessel trying to enter Pearl Harbor and sank it with rounds fired from this gun. The suspicious vessel turned

out to be a Japanese midget submarine that was positioning itself in order to take part in the coming attack. Location: At the State Capitol Building on Aurora and Constitution Avenues in downtown St. Paul

On the mall adjacent to the Capitol Building in the very impressive Minnesota World War II Memorial. This consists of a large rectangular area with 12 black granite panels honoring the 326,000 Minnesotans who served in WW II and the 6,000 who gave their lives. At the center of the rectangular space is a map of Minnesota surrounded by bronze stars honoring the state's heroes.

The 4" gun from the destroyer Ward used to sink a Japanese midget submarine at Pearl Harbor on the morning of Dec. 7, 1941 in St. Paul, MN

MINNESOTA AIR NATIONAL GUARD MUSEUM, located at Minneapolis-St. Paul International Airport, has about 15 vintage aircraft on display, several of which are of the WW II era. The Museum highlights the activities of the Minnesota Air National Guard in war and peace and has many displays related to the history of the Minnesota Air National Guard. Many aircraft engines are also on display. There is also a nice gift shop and museum tours are available. Address: 670 General Miller Dr., St. Paul, MN 55111. Phone and website: 612-713-2523; www.mnangmuseum.org

***USS SWORDFISH* SUBMARINE MEMORIAL:** The *USS Swordfish* was lost at sea near Okinawa in January 1945 with all hands on board. This memorial commemorates that submarine and those sailors who were lost. It consists of a WW II torpedo mounted on a stone base with plaques. The plaques bear the names of those lost. Location: In Como Park near the Lakeside Pavilion near 1360 Lexington Parkway N. in St. Paul, MN

The USS Swordfish Memorial in St. Paul

MISSISSIPPI

Mississippi, in America's "Deep South", was one of the "Sun Belt" states that the War Department turned to when the need arose to train hundreds of thousands of new soldiers and airmen. And later, when the need arose to house tens of thousands of prisoners of war the War Department looked again to Mississippi. Here was cheap land, a warm climate, uncongested skies, hard-working people and cooperative state and local governments.

In the fall of 1941, the state became a part of a three-state Army maneuver area1 in which some 400,000 soldiers tested their new skills and training.

CENTREVILLE is in SW Mississippi near the Louisiana state line on SR-33 and SR-24. During the war, the federal government built a major training camp in the area for Army infantry divisions. The facility was known as Camp Van Dorn.

CAMP VAN DORN WORLD WAR II MUSEUM: This fine museum is in downtown Centreville and relates the history and mission of this important WW II training camp. In the Museum are artifacts, photos, documents, uniforms, captured war trophies, weapons, newspapers, information on the battles in which the divisions trained at Camp Van Dorn took part, and many training and every-day items the soldier at Van Dorn used. There is also information on the WACs (Women's' Army Corps) which had units training here.

The Museum has an educational program, a library and a very nice gift shop. Also the Museum hosts social activities throughout the year. Address: 138 E. Main St., Centreville, MS 39631. Phone and website: 601-645-9000; www.vandornmusuem.org

GREENVILLE is a county seat on the western edge of the state on the Mississippi River and US-82 and SR-1.

GREENVILLE WW II MEMORIAL: "IN MEMORY OF THOSE WHO SERVED IN WORLD WAR TWO." That's what is inscribed on this handsome mosaic memorial. There is also a 48-star American flag inscribed on the Memorial and a flag pole. Location: End of Washington St. on the Mississippi River, Greenville, MS

The Greenville WW II Memorial.

GULFPORT is a county seat on Mississippi's coast, US-49 and US-90. Nearby, during the war, was a major US Navy installation which trained Sea Bees (USN Construction Battalions of the Navy's Civil Engineer Corps).

SEABEE MUSEUM, GULFPORT BRANCH: This is a very interesting museum near downtown Gulfport which honors the history of the US Navy's Seabees. The Seabees came into existence during WW II (1942) and have been an important part of the US Navy ever since. During WW II, the

Seabees built port facilities, airfields, roads, warehouses, shore encampments and just about everything the navy needed ashore. Information on what the SeaBees built and where they built it are well documented in the Museum in the form of artifacts, photos, construction equipment, documents and exhibits.

The Museum is host to reunions and other social events and there is an inviting museum store. Address: 324 3rd St., Gulfport, MS 39502 Phone and website: 228-871-3619 and 228-865-9480; www.seabeehf.org/museum/

HATTIESBURG is a county seat in SE Mississippi 60 miles north of the coast on I-59, US-11, US-49, and US-89. Twelve miles south of town on US-49 was Camp Shelby a large Army training base for infantry divisions.

The Seabee Museum in Gulfport, MS

AFRICAN AMERICAN MILITARY HISTORY MUSEUM: During the war, the US Army was officially segregated, and separate USO (United Service Organization) facilities were built for African Americans serving in the armed forces. This museum resides in the last of those USO buildings in the US. It was built in 1942 for the African American soldiers training at Camp Shelby and is now on the National Registry of Historic Places.

As a museum, it traces the history of African Americans in US military service from the days of the US Army's "Buffalo Soldiers" of the 1800s to the present. The WW II period is well-represented. There are hundreds of artifacts; uniforms, medals, photos, documents, personal affects, documents, maps and more. Also honored

The African American Military History Museum in Hattiesburg, MS

in the Museum are the 500 African American nurses who served during WW II. There is an exhibit called the Hattiesburg Hall of Honor, honoring the local African American residents of the Hattiesburg area that served in the US military. Address: 305 E. 6th St., Hattiesburg, MS 39401. Phone and website: 601-450-1942; www.hattiesburguso.com

MISSISSIPPI ARMED FORCES MUSEUM: This is a fine state museum on the grounds of Camp Shelby which is 12 mile south of Hattiesburg on US-49. The Museum features the military activities in Mississippi since 1812 to the present. There is a large collection of artifacts and memorabilia related to WW II. The WW II collection is laid out in chronological order and records the activation and expansion of Camp Shelby during the war, events at Pearl Harbor, the fall of the Philippines and the prisoner of war camps in Mississippi. There is also a sizable display on women in the military.

Missouri

Museum tours are available and the Museum has a gift shop that you might do well to explore. Address: Building 850, Camp Shelby, MS 39407. Phone and website: 601-558-2757; www.armedforcesmuseum.u.

The Mississippi Armed Forces Museum
Camp Shelby, MS

Laurel, MS 39440. Phone and website: 601- 428-4008; www.veteransmemorialmuseum.org

LAUREL is a county seat 32 miles NE of Hattiesburg on I-59. At the beginning of the war, the city's local airport was taken over by the US Army Air Forces and used as a training facility.

VETERANS MEMORIAL MUSEUM:
There's lots of WW II stuff here as well as artifacts and memorabilia from other US wars. In front of the Museum is a WW II M-60 tank.

The Museum covers 6,000 Sq. ft. and has displays of field equipment; US, German and Japanese small arms; artillery shells; uniforms; military medals; photos and a WW II torpedo. There is also a library and a *at* inviting gift shop. Address: 920-Hillcrest Dr.,

The Veterans Memorial Museum in Laurel, MS

MISSOURI

Missouri was the home of one of America's two WW II Presidents, Harry S Truman (Independence, MO) and one of the war's more famous generals, Omar Bradley (Clark, MO).

In April 1944, Missouri's senator Bennet Champ Clark introduced a piece of legislation in the US Senate that would affect virtually every service man and women that served in WW II and in the post war years, the "GI Bill of Rights".

During the war, POW camps were plentiful in Missouri and helped the state's farmers plant and harvest the crops.

After the war, Missouri went through an adjustment period like most other states, but recovered rapidly and went on to prosper in the postwar years.

BRANSON is in SW Missouri near the Arkansas state line on US-65 and SR-165. It is well-known as an entertainment and music center.

THE STAGE DOOR CANTEEN AT THE WELK RESORT: Fans of bandleader Lawrence Welk are well aware that his band stemmed from the 1940s and survived into the 1990s and frequently played music from the WW II era.

   During the war, various theatrical groups around the country established Stage Door Canteens where service personnel were welcomed and entertained by people in the entertainment business. Lawrence Welk and his band participated in this undertaking. In later year, Welk built an upscale resort complex at Branson and gave the resort's restaurant the name "Stage Door Canteen." The restaurant serves breakfast, lunch and dinner, has live entertainment and is decorated in the manner of the WW II stage door canteens. Address of the Welk Resort: 1984 State Rd. 165, Branson, MO 65616. Phone and website: 417-336-3575; www.branson.com/branson/welk/welk.htm

VETERANS MEMORIAL MUSEUM: This popular 18,000 Sq. ft. museum pays tribute to the American men and women who served in America's wars of the 20th Century in all branches of the armed services. In the Museum are ten great halls covering the wars and conflicts including halls devoted to WW I, WW II, Korea, Vietnam, Desert Storm. On display are artifacts, weapons, uniforms, flags, personal histories, medals, murals, art work and more.

   Outstanding in the WW II hall is a massive bronze sculpture of American soldiers in action created by Fred Hoppe, an internationally renowned bronze sculptor. This sculpture is the world's largest bronze war memorial, weighing over 15 tons and 70 ft. long. It depicts a line of 50 life-sized WW II

soldiers storming a beach. Each soldier represents one of the 50 states. Surrounding the sculpture are the names of the over 400,000 Americans killed in WW II. In addition, there are other bronze sculptures throughout the Museum. This is a museum well worth your time, and don't pass up the gift shop. They have some unique and fabulous items. Address: Veterans Memorial Museum, 1250 W. 76 County Music Blvd., Branson, MO 65616. Phone and website: 417-336-2300; www.veteransmemorialbranson.com

The world's largest war memorial bronze sculpture
depicting 50 WW II soldiers storming a beach.
Each represents one of the 50 US states. In Branson, MO

FULTON, 20 miles SE of Columbia, is a college town which had a population of about 8,300 people during the war. Soon after the war ended, Britain's wartime Prime Minister, Winston Churchill, was invited to speak at Fulton's Westminster College. In the speech, Churchill coined the phrase, " the Iron Curtain," that aptly defined the newly established political and geographical division in Europe between the Communist World and the Free World.

   This dividing line existed for another 43 years throughout the Cold War and was constantly referred to as the Iron Curtain.

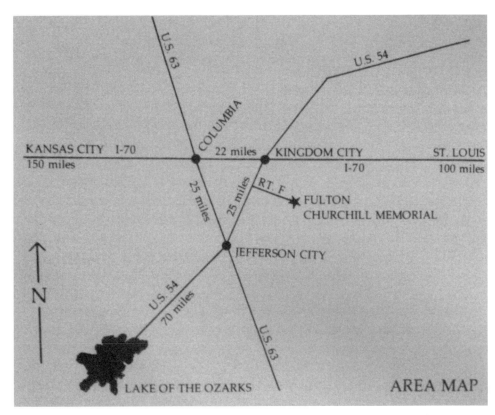

AREA MAP

WINSTON CHURCHILL MEMORIAL & LIBRARY is on the grounds of Westminster College and commemorates Churchill's famous "Iron Curtain" speech of Mar. 5, 1946. The Memorial pays special tribute to the wartime British leader and subjects related to the Cold War. The Memorial and Library are located in an 800-year-old church built built in England by Christopher Wren and known as St. Mary the Virgin, Aldermanbury. The church was severely damaged in the London blitz of 1940 and was left unrestored after the war. In the mid-1960s, it was dismantled and brought to Fulton in segments and restored to house the Winston Churchill Memorial and Library. The sanctuary is used regularly for church services and the lower level of the church comprises the Memorial and Library. There are numerous displays on Churchill's six decades of public service and his blueprint for world peace.

In Nov. 1990, President Ronald Reagan added another touch to the Memorial when he dedicated a transplanted section of the Berlin Wall that had been an actual part of the Iron Curtain. In the Memorial & Library is a nice gift shop with lots of unique items relating to Churchill, his speech and his life. Address: Westminster College, 501 Westminster Av., Fulton, MO, 65251. Phone and website: 573-592-5369; www.churchillmemorial.org

INDEPENDENCE (See Kansas City/Independence area)

JEFFERSON CITY is the capitol of Missouri. It is in the central part of the state on the Missouri River, US-50, US-54 and US-63.

MUSEUM OF MISSOURI MILITARY HISTORY: This is Missouri's National Guard museum. It traces the history of the Guard from its inception to the present. The World War II era is well represented and relates the history of the Missouri Guardsmen who fought in

The Museum of Missouri Military History at Jefferson City, MO

the Philippians and were forced to take part in the infamous Bataan Death March.

In the Museum are many military artifacts related to the National Guard and their participation in America's conflicts. Address: Missouri National Guard, 2302 Militia Dr., Jefferson City, MO 65101. Phone and website: 888-526-6664; www.moguard.com/moguard-museum-of-missouri-military-history.html

KANSAS CITY/INDEPENDENCE AREA: Kansas City and Independence are twin cities in the west-central part of the state on the Missouri River. Across the river is Kansas City, KS.

Harry S Truman, Missouri's senator up until 1945, lived most of his life in Independence. In 1942, Truman's reputation and notoriety soared when he headed a Senate committee that conducted a highly publicized investigation into waste and corruption in the construction of military camps and bases around the US. Truman's investigation, which was squeaky-clean, brought forth disclosures of wrong-doing that caused a national uproar and brought about needed reforms. Truman's prestige rose to the point where, in 1944, President Franklin Roosevelt selected him to be his Vice Presidential running mate for the coming national elections. Roosevelt was re-elected for his fourth term and Truman became Vice President. On Apr. 12, 1945, President Roosevelt died suddenly in Georgia and Truman acceded to the Presidency. He was the first Missourian to hold that office.

The National World War I Museum in Kansas City, MO

NATIONAL WORLD WAR I MUSEUM: Without question, World War II was a continuation of World War I which was known at the time as "The Great War."

This 80,000 Sq. ft. museum is part of a larger WW I memorial complex known as Liberty Memorial. Inside the Museum are artifacts and displays that trace the history of WW I and makes its connection with WW II clear in many ways. The mission of the Museum is to make the experiences of the World War I era meaningful and relevant for present and future generations.

In 2004, the Museum was designated by the US Congress as the nation's official World War I Museum.

Inside the Museum, are World War I era artillery pieces, small arms, uniforms, posters, photographs, documents and much more. The Museum has a library, a cafe - The "Over There Cafe" - and a museum store where one will find ample information and memorabilia on World War I. Address: 100 W. 26th St., Kansas City, MO 64108. Phone and website: 816-784-1918; www.the worldwar.org

TRUMAN FARM HOME: For a brief period in his life, Harry S Truman was a farmer. This is his farm home which is located on Blue Ridge Blvd. in the southern suburb of Grandview. The farm house was built in 1894 and between 1906 and 1917 young Harry S Truman lived here with his family and helped his father farm the surrounding land. The farm land has long been developed but the house remains and has been restored and opened to the public. It is furnished with items from the early 1900s including some things that belonged to the Truman family. Address: 12301 Blue Ridge Blvd., Grandview, MO 64030. Phone and website: 816-254-2720; www.nps.gov/hstr/historyculture/truman

HARRY S TRUMAN HISTORIC DISTRICT: This is an area near-downtown Independence that was Harry Truman's neighborhood when he moved to the city. He knew every inch of it because he spent most of his life here and walked through the area frequently on his daily morning walks.

   To tour the district, it is recommended that the visitor obtain a local map or take a conducted tour. Maps, tickets and tour information are available at the Ticket & Information Center located at the corner of Truman Rd. and Main St. 223 N. Main St. Independence, MO 64050. Phone: 816-254-2720

HISTORIC INDEPENDENCE SQUARE & INDEPENDENCE SQUARE COURTHOUSE: Here, in this old courthouse, lawyer Harry Truman began his political career as a County judge. His courtroom and office are restored to the period when he presided, and an audio-visual presentation traces his life before he became President. Address: Truman Office & Courthouse, 112 W. Lexington, Independence, MO 64050. Phone: 816-881-3000

TRUMAN HOME (219 N. Delaware): Harry & Bess Truman lived in this house from the time of their marriage in 1919 until their deaths. During Truman's Presidency, this 14-room Victorian house became known as the "Summer White House" because he returned to it frequently - to escape the terrible summer heat in Washington, DC.

   Upon her death in 1982, Mrs. Truman donated the house and grounds to the United States. It is now a National Historic Site and open to the public. It is decorated in period furnishings and in the garage is the Truman's last personal car, a 1972 Chrysler Newport sedan. Harry Truman purchased the automobile new and Bess Truman used it until her death in 1982 at which time the odometer read 18,000 miles.

   Across the street, at 216 N. Delaware, is the former home of Harry Truman's aunt, Margaret Noland. It was here that young Harry Truman and a high school classmate, Bess Wallace, would meet to study Latin. Bess Wallace eventually became Mrs. Truman.

   To visit the Truman Home, obtain tickets at the Ticket & Information Center, 223 N Main St., Independence, MO 64050. Phone of the Ticket & Information Center: 816-254-2720

The Home of President Harry S and Bess Truman in Independence, MO

TRUMAN LIBRARY & MUSEUM: This magnificent museum and library is at the northern end of the Truman Historic District on US-24 and N. Delaware St. It contains Truman's official and personal papers, memorabilia, artifacts and family belongings. President and Mrs. Truman are buried side-by-side in the court yard.

   Of special interest in the Museum is a reproduction of the Oval Office of the white House circa 1948 when Truman was President. On the desk is a sign with a motto that is closely associated with Truman, "The Buck Stops Here," The Museum has exhibits of Truman's boyhood, his military career in WW I, his life as a civilian soon afterwards, then as a local politician, a senator, Vice President, President and ex-President.

Other exhibits offer extensive information on the critical closing months of WW II which were Truman's first months as President. There are also displays on the historic post-war Potsdam Conference and the Korean War which erupted during Truman's last term in office. Other displays include the table upon which the United Nations Charter was signed, a piano Truman played at the White House, china and paintings form the White House, memorabilia form the battleship *Missouri*, a presidential limousine, several of Truman's personal cars and several audio-visual presentations. There is also a fascinating museum store which has ample information on the Truman family and reproductions of the "The Buck Stops Here" sign which you can put on your own desk. Address: 500 W. US-24, Independence, MO 64050. Phone and website: 816-268-8200 or 800-833-1225; www.trumanlibrary.org

LACLEDE is a small community in north-central Missouri on US-36, SR-5 and SE-139. Nearby is the General John L Pershing Boyhood Home State Historical Site.

WORLD WAR II MEMORIAL IN LACLEDE: The Army Mothers of Post 15 erected this stone memorial in 1951 to commemorate those men from Linn County who gave their lives during WW II. Engraved on this handsome stone memorial are the names of the men and the dates they died. Location: The corner of Grove St. (SR-5) and Cole St.

The World War II Memorial in Lacrede, MO

LAMAR is in the SW corner of the state 25 miles NNE of Joplin on US-60 and US-71. In 1884, Harry S Truman was born in Lamar.

HARRY S TRUMAN STATE HISTORIC SITE consists primarily of the modest 1 1/2-story frame house in which Harry S Truman was born on May 8, 1884. His father, John A. Truman, was a farmer and dealer in livestock. The family lived in this house only 11 months after Harry was born. They then moved to Belton, MO, then to Grandview, MO and finally settled in Independence, MO in 1890. The house measures 20 x 28 feet and has four rooms downstairs and two room upstairs. There is an outdoor smokehouse and a hand-dug well. Address: 1009 Truman Av. Lamar, MO 64759. Phone and website: 417-682-2279; www.mostateparks.com/park/harry-s-truman-birthplace-state-historic-site

MALDEN is in the SE corner of the state on US-62 and SR-25. In 1942, the US Government built a Army Air Forces training field three miles NW of town for use by the Troop Carrier Command. After the war, the site became an industrial center and a regional airport.

MALDEN ARMY AIRFIELD PRESERVATION SOCIETY MUSEUM: This is a small museum that keeps alive the memory of Malden Army Airfield. The Museum displays momentous, photographs, uniforms documents, posters and other item related to the Army Airfield as well as the other US military services. There is a Veterans Memorial Wall which pays tribute to the men and women who have served their country. Address of the Malden Industrial Park Office: 3077 Mitchell Dr., Malden, MO 63863. Phone and website: 573-276-2279; www.maaps.net

MEMPHIS is a county seat in the NE corner of the state on US-135 and SR-15.

SCOTLAND COUNTY WORLD WAR II MEMORIAL: Here is a very unique WW II memorial. It is beneath a four-column covered WW I memorial. This is very fitting because WW II was, in many ways, a continuation of WW I. The WW II Memorial is of red granite and is inscribed with the names of those men from Scotland County who gave their lives in WW II. Location: On the grounds of the Scotland County Courthouse, 117 S. Market St.

The Scotland County World War I and World War II Memorial in Memphis, MO

MEXICO is a county seat in northeastern Missouri on US-4, SR-15 and SR-22.

THE MISSOURI EXERCISE TIGER ARMY AND NAVY MEMORIAL: "Exercise Tiger" was a large-scale Allied amphibious training exercise carried out in late April 1944 at Slapton Sands, England on the English Channel. The American soldiers and sailors participating in the Exercise were preparing for the Normandy invasion which took place on June, 6, 1944. While the Exercise was in progress,

German torpedo boats attacked the lightly defended Allied landing craft and sank eight US Navy LSTs (Landing Ship Tanks) killing 749 US Army and Navy personnel. Aboard one of the LSTs was Missouri's 3206th US Army's 3206th US Army Quartermasters Corps. This memorial, which consists of an LST anchor in an enclosed setting and a memorial plaque commemorates those men from Missouri that died in the attack. Location: On the corner of N. Washington St. and E. Monroe St. at the Audrain County Courthouse

The Missouri Exercise Tiger Army and Navy Memorial in Mexico, MO

RICHMOND is a county seat 33 miles NE of downtown Kansas City on SR-10 and SR-13.

RAY COUNTY WORLD WAR II MEMORIAL: Both WW II and Korean war veterans are honored by this three-panel stone memorial. Their names are inscribed in the Memorial. Facing the panels are two commemorative stone benches. Also inscribed in the Memorial are the dates "WORLD WAR II DECEMBER 1941-AUGUST 1945" and "KOREAN WAR 25 JUNE 1950 27 AUGUST 1953." Location: On the lawn of the Ray County Courthouse, N. Thornton St., Richmond, MO

The Ray County World War II Memorial in Richmond, MO

163

SAINT JOSEPH is 35 miles north of Kansas City on the Missouri River. The town had a large Army Quartermaster Depot during the war which was a sub-depot of the Kansas City Quartermaster Depot, and the city's local airport was taken over by the US Army Air Forces and used for training by the Air Transport Command.

NATIONAL MILITARY HERITAGE MUSEUM is in downtown St. Joseph in an old and very ornate building which is one of four buildings in the Museum complex. The Museum's main building served as a US Marine Corps reserve Training Center for a time after WW II. Now, as a museum, it preserves the military heritage of all branches of the US military both during wars and between wars. The Museum has some 20,000 artifacts which include vehicles, uniforms, medals, equipment, models, dioramas, weapons and more. There are also displays on the home fronts of the various

wars. The Museum has an outstanding collection of over 10,000 books, videos and magazine articles relating the US military heritage. WW II history is well represented in the Museum. The Museum has an educational program and participates in civic activities. And there is an impressive gift shop - don't pass it up. Address: 701 Messanie St., St. Joseph, MO 64501. Phone and website: 816-233-4321; www.nationalmilitaryheritage museum.org

The main building of the National Military Heritage Museum in St. Joseph, MO

SAINT LOUIS: In 1939, when WW II began in Europe, St. Louis was already a city on the move. It was experiencing a building boom, up 30% over 1938, and the city was well on its way to eliminating industrial smoke pollution that plagued many other large US cities at the time. There was also an exciting and bold plan underway to build a national park in downtown St. Louis. Forty square blocks of slums and blighted area on the city's waterfront were to be demolished and turned into the national park honoring Thomas Jefferson and commemorating the great western migration.

The metropolitan St. Louis area had long been a major industrial center and as America's war needs increased so did the fortunes of the area's manufacturers. In late 1941, the Federal Government transferred the Rural Electrification Administration and the Farm Security Administration to St. Louis to relieve overcrowding in Washington, DC.

During WW II, the city had an old Army garrison post,, Jefferson Barracks, an Army airfield, a medical depot, a US Naval air station and two ordnance plants.

JEFFERSON BARRACKS COUNTY PARK/BATTLE OF THE BULGE MEMORIAL: These are the ground of the Historic Jefferson Barracks which was a US Army post from 1857 to 1946. It was very active during WW II. The 1,702 acre Park has several historical buildings and many of the amenities associated with a public park.

The Battle of the Bulge Memorial in Jefferson Barracks County Park in St, Louis, MO

In 1997, the Battle of the Bulge Memorial was dedicated to commemorate that critical battle of WW II. The Memorial consists of a stone monument and four flag poles. The flags flying from the poles are those of the United State, the United Kingdom and the countries of Belgium and Luxembourg in which the Battle took place. Location: Jefferson Barracks County Park, at the end of S. Broadway St. where it turns into Kingston Rd.

The Soldiers' Memorial Military Museum in St. Louis, MO

SOLDIERS' MEMORIAL MILITARY MUSEUM is located in downtown St. Louis and serves a memorial to all US veterans. It was dedicated by President Franklin Roosevelt in 1936 to commemorate St. Louis citizens who died in WW I.

The area around the Memorial was later developed into a park named Memorial Plaza honoring St. Louis men and women who died in both WW I and WW II. Across the street from the Soldiers' Memorial Military Museum are memorials honoring those who died in WW II, and other US conflicts. The Museum honors all St. Louis citizens who have died in military service since 1800 and has displays of uniforms, small arms, artillery pieces, ordnance, medical equipment, ship and vehicle models, medals, flags, photographs and paintings. Address: 1315 Chestnut St., St. Louis, MO 63103. Phone and website: 314-622-4550; http://stlsoldiersmemorial.org

WORLD WAR II MEMORIAL COURT OF HONOR: This WW II memorial is near downtown St. Louis and has, as its center piece, a 40 ft. limestone monument in the shape of a broken blade. Carved into the monument are bas relief figures showing soldiers in battle. Location: N. 13th St. and Market St

The World War II Memorial Court of Honor near downtown, St. Louis, MO

SAINT ROBERT is on I-44 70 miles NE of Springfield. It is the home of Fort Leonard Wood, a huge military complex which was built for the US Army in 1941-42 and still serves the Army to this day.

MUSEUM COMPLEX: This is a very unique complex of three military museums in one large building on the grounds of Ft. Leonard Wood. Each museum operates separately, has its own staff, provides its own exhibits and has separate gift shops.

There is a fourth museum on the grounds at a different location, the Fort Leonard Wood, MO Temp Museum, which tells the story of Ft. Leonard Wood with emphasis on the WW II era.

US Army Chemical Corps Museum: This museum in the Museum Complex traces the history of the Army's chemical corps from its inception to the present. The Museum is divided into several galleries with one being the WW II Gallery. The other galleries are devoted to other conflicts and subjects.

There are thousands of items on display in the Museum including gas masks, gas canisters, gas-firing weapons, biological and radiological weapons, historic documents, photographs and more. There is also a library and the Museum has an educational program.

US Army Engineer Museum: This museum in the Museum Complex highlights the history of the Army's Engineer Corps as well as that part of Ft. Leonard Wood's history associated with the US Army Engineers.

On display are many pieces of equipment used by the Engineers including bulldozers and floating bridges. Also to be seen are weapons, surveying and mapping equipment, mine detectors and other specialized equipment used by the US Army Engineers.

US Army Military Police Corps Museum: This museum in the Museum Complex tells the story of the Army's MPs, how they began, how they function now and in years past.

On display are law enforcement devices, uniforms, photos, documents, weapons. The Museum emphasizes the MP's roll in both peacetime and wartime.

The Fort Leonard Wood, MO Temp Museum: This is the fourth museum at Ft. Leonard Wood which is at a different location from the Museum Complex above. It is a collection of several WW II-era buildings, preserved and restored to their original condition, on a large wooded site. There are WW II barracks buildings, a mess hall, day rooms, orderly rooms and a regimental command quarter. The interiors of each of the buildings are restored to their WW II-era conditions. In the barracks, the bunks are made up GI style, there are clothes hanging on the racks, rifles are stacked and the foot lockers are ready for inspection. In the mess hall, the tables are lined up awaiting the hungry GIs, there's a coal-burning stove, food preparation tables and oak ice boxes in the kitchen. The day room, orderly room and regimental command quarter are similarly furnished with authentic WW II artifacts and furnishings.

In other buildings, are exhibits devoted to the history of Ft. Leonard Wood, General Leonard Wood, information on the prisoners of war held at Ft. Leonard Wood during WW II and other historic relics and artifacts.

The message here at The Fort Leonard Wood Museum is that the buildings built by the US Army Engineers during WW II were damn good buildings and built by men who trained at Ft. Leonard Wood.

Address for the Museum Complex: 495 South Dakota Av, Ft. Leonard Wood, MO 65473. Phone for the Chemical Museum 573-596-4944, phone for the Engineer Museum 573-596-0780, phone for the Military Police Museum, 573-596-0604. Website for the Museum Complex: www.wood.army.mil/wood_cms/usaes/2900.shtml

The so-called temporary (Temp) WW II buildings built at Ft. Leonard Wood during WW II by US Army engineers who trained at Fort Leonard Wood

MONTANA

The people of Montana call their beautiful state "Big Sky Country." During WW II, the Army Air Forces heartily agreed and put thousands of war planes into Montana's Big Sky for training purposes and as Lend Lease planes which carried vital military supplies to our wartime ally, the Soviet Union. In the process, the military services used 26 of the state's 106 airfields.

In 1942, Montana became the new gateway to Alaska. In that year, the Alaskan Highway (AlCan Highway) was completed from northern Alberta, Canada to Fairbanks, AK and a series of air fields, called the "Northwest Staging Route," were built and paralleled the highway. These routes were along the eastern slope of the Canadian Rocky Mountains where the land was flat and the routes relatively safe from enemy attacks. Most trucks and aircraft going to Alaska from the "lower 48" now passed through Montana making the state a huge staging area for Alaska-bound traffic.

GREAT FALLS is a county seat and one of the state's larger cities in the east-central part of the state. It is on the Missouri River, I-15 and US-87. During the war, there were two large military airfields in the area.

MALMSTROM AIR FORCE BASE MUSEUM & AIR PARK: This museum and air park is located on the grounds of Malmstrom AFB and record the history of the base from its beginning to the present. Included are displays on the various units stationed here, a reconstructed WW II barracks room, small arms, uniforms, ordnance items, maps, photographs, paintings, a Lend-Lease diorama and more. Also on display is one of the largest collections of military model airplanes in the Northwest.

Tours of the Museum are available and the Museum has a gift shop which offers many interesting

The Malstrom Air Force Base Museum and Air Park in Great Falls, MT

items.

In the air park, are vintage aircraft and missiles. Address: 21 77th St. North, Great Falls, MT 59402. Phone and website: 406-731-2705; www.malstrom.af.mil/museum

HELENA is in the west-central part of the state on I-15 and I-90. It is the capitol city of Montana and had, during the war, two important army facilities in the area, Fort William H. Harrison, a decades old Army post, and Camp Rimini that specialized in training sled dogs for use in northern climes.

MONTANA MILITARY MUSEUM: This museum is located at Fort William Henry Harrison, the home of Montana's National Guard. It relates the history of the Guard from its inception in 1866 to the present with ample information on the Guard's participation in World War II.

Among the WW II exhibits, there is information about the US Army's Special Forces which had a large training facility in Montana during the war. Also there is information on Camp Rimini where war dogs and sled dogs were trained. Other exhibits highlight the famous Lewis and Clark Expedition that passed through Montana on its way to the Pacific Ocean.

Outside the Museum are tanks, artillery pieces and other heavy weapons and don't pass up the gift shop. Address: Fort William Henry Harrison, MT 59636. Phone: 406-324-3550.

USS HELENA (CA-75) **MEMORIAL:** There were two *USS Helena* cruisers during WW II. The first (CL-50), was damaged at Pearl Harbor during the Japanese attack. She was repaired and saw lots of action in the Pacific but was lost in enemy action in 1943. The second *USS Helena (CA-75),* was purchased by the citizens of Helena, MT through war bonds and also saw action in the Pacific and the Atlantic. She then served the US Navy until 1972.

The citizens of Helena salvaged the ship's propeller and bell and constructed this memorial. There is a low wall at the Memorial with plaques honoring those who serve aboard her. Location: In Heritage Pioneer Park at Wong and Chance Gulch Sts.

The USS Helena Memorial in Helena, MT

MISSOULA is an old and historic western town near the west-central edge of the state on I-90, US-12 and US-93. Fort Missoula, built in 1876-77, was the city's primary military installation and was utilized to full capacity during WW II. The city now has two military museums within walking distance of each other.

HISTORICAL MUSEUM AT FORT MISSOULA: This museum is in the Fort's old Quartermaster's Warehouse which was built in 1911. It traces the long history of the Fort and also preserves much of the history of Missoula County and western Montana. The Museum's exhibits rotate, and there is a respectable WW II collection. The Museum has a library, an educational program, a very nice gift shop and is available for public and social events. Address: Bldg. 322, Fort Missoula, Missoula, MT 59804. Phone and website: 406-728-3476; www.fortmissoulamuseum.org

This map will lead you to both the Historical Museum of Ft. Missoula and the Rocky Mountain Museum of Military History in Missoula, MT

ROCKY MOUNTAIN MUSEUM OF MILITARY HISTORY: Spend a little more time at Fort William H. Harrison and visit this interesting museum which is within walking distance of the Historical Museum of Fort Missoula. The RMMMH, as it is often called, is housed in the former 1910 quarters of the Fort's commanding officer and records the history of the US military from the Frontier period to the present. Special attention is given to the men and women who served in the US military. As for WW II, there are displays on various aspects of the war, on the 4th Infantry Division and on WW II internment.

The Museum also holds various events throughout the year and has a newsletter. Address: Fort William H. Harrison, Missoula, MT 59807. Phone and website: 406-549-5346; www.fortmissuola.org

MISSOULA MEMORIAL ROSE GARDEN/WORLD WAR II MEMORIAL: The city of Missoula has a beautiful rose garden dedicated to the Memory of WW II. In the Garden is a small oblisk bearing the names of those individuals from the Missoula area who served in the war. The Garden is easily accessible via US-12, Montana Av. and Brooks St.

There are also memorials in the Garden commemorating other US conflicts. Location: Missoula Memorial Rose Garden in Missoula, MT

POLSON is a county seat 50 miles north of Missoula on US-93 and SR-35 and at the southern end of Flathead Lake.

The WW II Memorial in Missoula's Memorial Rose Garden

MIRACLE OF AMERICA MUSEUM, in Polson, has a large and interesting collection of western, pioneer, patriotic and military artifacts including a considerable collection of WW II items. This is more than a collection, it is a tribute to the men and women who made and used the many antique, and very useful, things on display.

Among the WW II artifacts are small arms, ordnance, posters, captured enemy equipment, uniforms, sheet music, post cards, wartime ads, GI's letters from home, a WW I and WW II kitchen, and several military vehicles. One vehicle of note is a WW II era amphibious DUKW (Duck) which was used after the war in the logging industry for many years. It was used to push logs around in Montana's rivers and lakes.

The Museum has three WW II era GAMA GOATS, a 6-wheel drive heavy-duty amphibious vehicle with articulated steering. There is an ambulance version and a cargo version of this vehicle. Also to

be seen here are gas masks including a gas protection device for a baby which has the appearance of an incubator. And too, there is a rare airborne Cushman motor scooter dropped by parachute and used by US paratroopers. Many of the Museum's vehicles are operable and used in parades. On occasion, visitors are offered rides. And don't pass up the gift shop. It has a fascinating collection of souvenirs and momentous. Address: 36094 Memory Lane (US-93), Polson, MT 59860. Phone and website: 406-883-6804; www.miracleofamericamuseum.org

This is some of the military hardware to be seen at the Miracle of America Museum in Polson, MT

NEBRASKA

During WW II, Nebraska was a sparsely populated state with an economy based almost totally on agricultural. WW II brought significant changes to Nebraska especially in the field of manufacturing and new military installations. During 1942, there was a great surge of industrial activity in the state with the building of many new war plants in her larger cities and many new military installations at various location in the state.

ASHLAND is a small community midway between Omaha and Lincoln on I-80, US-6 and SR-63.

STRATEGIC AIR AND SPACE MUSEUM: This is a very large air and space museum with a collection of over 30 aircraft and missiles. Many of the aircraft are from the WW II era and many are inside the Museum.

The Museum has a heavy emphasis on the post war era and the activities of the Strategic Air Command (SAC) which was created by the US Air Force in 1946 based on the air war experiences of WW II. There are a considerable amount of exhibits, artifacts and informative displays related to WW II. Some of the WW II exhibits highlight the life and career of WW II General Curtis LeMay, the "Father" of SAC; the air war in Europe and the Pacific, atomic weapons, airborne units, the Tuskegee

The Strategic Air and Space Museum at Ashland, NE

Airmen, the Doolittle raid on Tokyo, the manufacturing of bombers and more.

The Museum offers tours, overnight stays and has an educational program. There is a snack bar and a must-see museum shop. Address: 28210 West Park Highway, Ashland, NE 68003 (easily accessible from I-80 at Exit 426). Phone and website: 402-944-3100; www.sacmuseum.org

CRAWFORD is in the NW corner of the Nebraska panhandle on US-20 and SR-71. Just to the west of town, on US-20, is old Fort Robinson, a fort dating back to the pioneer days. Fort Robinson is now a state park.

FORT ROBINSON MUSEUM: When you reach Crawford, NE, you are in the old Wild West. Fort Robinson was built in the days of Red Cloud Indian wars and was utilized by the US Army until after WW II. During WW II it housed German Prisoners of war and information on that period is in the Museum. Also during WW II, the Army trained war dogs here for the K-9 Corps and that, too, is recorded in the Museum's displays. The Museum has in its collection the only known war dog kennel from WW II. Address: Fort Robinson State Park, US-20, Crawford, NE. Phone and website: 308-665-2919; www.nebraskahistory.org/sites/fortrob/

HOLDREGE is a county seat in south-central Nebraska on US-6/34 and US-183. During WW II there was a prisoner of war camp in the area.

NEBRASKA PRAIRIE MUSEUM: You will see lots of Nebraska history in this museum including the history of the nearby WW II prisoner of war camp which held German POWs. One room in the Museum, the German POW exhibit room, tells the story. Also, built on the Museum's grounds is a replica of one of the POW guard towers that existed at the camp. Address: US-183 North, Holdrege, NE 68949. Phone and website: 308-995-5015; www.nebraskaprairie.org

LEXINGTON is a county seat in south-central Nebraska on I-80.

HEARTLAND MUSEUM OF MILITARY VEHICLES: This is a large museum just south of Lexington with some 100 military vehicles on display. Most are of WW II vintage. There are tanks, halftracks, trucks, Willys and Ford Jeeps, ambulances and some foreign-made equipment including captured German equipment. Of special interest, is an Allis Chalmers halftrack snow tractor used to rescue downed airmen in snowbound areas.

Also on display are weapons, uniforms, engines, photographs, documents and everyday necessities used by soldiers in the field. The Museum has an interesting gift shop and is accessible from I-80 exit 237. Address: 606 Heartland Rd., Lexington, NE 68850. Phone and website: 308-324-6329, www.heartlandmuseum.com

LINCOLN is the capitol of Nebraska in the east-central part of the state on I-80 and US-77. The city has a large central park, Antelope Park, which contains a sunken garden, a rose garden, a Children's Zoo, a golf course, swimming pool, tennis courts and other amenities one would find in a large city park.

ANTELOPE PARK: In addition to the many amenities in this park, there are some 15 memorials, most of which relate to WW II. There are memorials dedicated specifically to World War II in general, Pearl Harbor, Airborne, Air Force, Coast Guard, Prisoners of War, K-9 Corps, China/Burma/India (CBI) Theater, Military Medical Corps, women in the military, Special Forces, Merchant Marines, Seabees, Naval Armed Guards and Recipients of the Purple Heart. When you come to this park, plan to spend some time here. Location: SE of downtown Lincoln along the south side of Capitol Parkway/Normal Blvd.

The Seabee Memorial in Antelope Park, Lincoln, NE

NORFOLK is in NE Nebraska on US-81 and US-275.

NORFOLK WORLD WAR II MEMORIAL: This handsome WW II memorial stands behind a replica of the Statue of Liberty and commemorates the citizens of the local area who served in WW II. The Memorial is well landscaped, has benches and flag poles.
Location: Norfolk's Central Park, 705 S. 8th St.

The Norfolk World War II Memorial in Norfolk, NE

OMAHA, in eastern Nebraska on the Missouri River, was Nebraska's largest city during the war. During WW II, it was home to a large US Army Air Forces training facility which consisted of Fort George Crook and Offutt Field.

The minesweeper Hazard on permanent display at Freedom Park, Omaha, NE

FREEDOM PARK is one mile south of Omaha's Epply Field Memorial-Omaha Municipal Airport on the west bank of the Missouri River and accessible via SR-165.
On display here are two ships, the WW II-era minesweeper *USS Hazard* and the postwar training submarine *USS Marlin*. *Hazard* is a steel-hulled minesweeper of the Admirable class and the only one of 106 built still in existence. *Hazard* was built in 1944 and served as a minesweeper, a patrol ship, a convoy escort, a radar picket ship and did anti-submarine duties. She served at Okinawa and in several other naval actions in the Pacific. Retired in 1971, the ship was brought here, put on permanent display, and has been designated a National Historic Landmark.

The *Marlin* was built in 1953 and served until 1974.

Also on display in the park is the anchor and anchor chain of the WW II aircraft carrier *Wasp*, a huge ship's propeller and minesweeping equipment. Tours of the ships and the park are available. Address: 2497 Freedom Park Rd., Omaha, NE 68110. Phone and website: 402-444-5900; www.cityofomaha.org/parks/contact-us

VICTORY '95 - 50th ANNIVERSARY WW II MEMORIAL: Dedicated in 1995, the 50th anniversary of the end of WW II, this memorial pays tribute to all aspects of the war. Soldiers, parents, women factory workers and children. All are depicted in this Memorial in individual sculptures along with three flag poles. Inscribed in the Memorial is the tribute "IN HONOR OF THOSE WHO SERVED ON THE BATTLE FRONT AND THE HOME FRONT."

Location: Heartland of American Park in downtown Omaha at 8th and Douglas Sts.

WAHOO is a county seat in eastern Nebraska 35 miles west of downtown Omaha and has a WW II torpedo on the courthouse lawn.

TORPEDO MEMORIAL: A WW II torpedo, mounted on a concrete pedestal on the lawn of the Saunders County Court House, serves as Wahoo's memorial to those from the local community who served in WW II. One might ask, "Why a torpedo in landlocked Nebraska?" The answer is that the city has a very active chapter of the WW

Victory '95 - 50th Anniversary WW II Memorial in Omaha, NE

II Submarine Veterans Association who were responsible for the creation of the Memorial. Location: Saunders County Court House lawn

The Torpedo Memorial in Wahoo, NE

NEVADA

Nevada is one of the larger states in the country but during WW II it was the least populated of all the states. On Jan. 1, 1940, the cumulative head count in the state was estimated to be 110,000 people, 390,000 cattle and 845,000 sheep. Much of the state was desert waste land and mountains which were of little value in peacetime, but not necessarily in wartime. When the military services needed wide open spaces to use as maneuver areas and bombing and gunnery ranges, Nevada's assets fit the bill.

The boom times for Nevada began in 1940 and never really ended, and the Federal Government played a big role in starting the boom. Nevada was one of several states in the US southwest where the Federal Government spent huge sums of money on war-related projects and, in Nevada; it spent more money per capita than in any other state in the country.

By 1946, it was estimated that the state's population had increased by about 50% from 1940 to 156,000 people. And, another new industry was beginning to emerge - casino gambling.

HENDERSON, 10 miles SE of Las Vegas on I-515 and US-95, did not exist before the war. It was built by the Federal Government during the war to house workers at a huge new plant built nearby, Basic Magnesium, and Inc. This plant refined magnesium ore from nearby mines. The Government planned to abandon Henderson and the plant after the war, but the plant survived and so did Henderson. The town was eventually incorporated by Las Vegas in 1953 with a population of over 40,000 people.

CLARK COUNTY MUSEUM, in Henderson, traces the history of Henderson from its WW II beginning as well as the history of Clark County. The Museum has considerable material on WW II because that era was so important in the development of the local area.

On the grounds of the Museum is one of the original houses built by the Federal Government to house the families of the workers at Basic Magnesium, Inc. The house is painted and furnish as it was when it was new in 1941. It is open to the public and has WW II displays and memorabilia. Museum address: 1830 S. Boulder Hwy. (US-93/95), Henderson, NV 89002. Phone and website: 702-455-7955; www.accessclarkcounty.com

WEST WENDOVER is on the Nevada/Utah border on I-80, US-93 and SR-58. Across the state line is Wendover, Utah. During the war, Wendover Army Airfield, just south of Wendover, Utah was where the US Army Air Forces crews practiced in their B-29 bombers for the coming atomic bomb attacks on Japan. The air unit that delivered the bombs was known as the 509th Composite Group.

509TH COMPOSITE GROUP/WW II MEMORIAL: It was the development of the B-29 bomber that made the Atomic bomb attacks on Japan possible. These huge planes had the capacity to carry the 10,000 lb. bombs from the remote Pacific island of Tinian to the Japanese mainland and return. The missions were carried out by the US Air Forces 509th Composite Group.

The 509th Composite Group/WW II Memorial in West Wendover, NV

This memorial commemorates that air group and their training here at nearby Wendover Army Airfield.

The 509th dropped two atomic bombs on Japan which resulted in the sudden and victorious ending of WW II.

The Memorial consists of a stone column with a model of the B-29 at the top and inscriptive plaques. Location: West Wendover Blvd. (SR-58) near the post office, in West Wendover, NV

NEW HAMPSHIRE

New Hampshire is one of our smaller states, but yet, it contributed significantly to the war effort. The large Portsmouth Naval Ship Yard was one of the major shipbuilding yards in the country. The yard is actually in Maine, but most of the people who worked there were from New Hampshire.

The state also contributed in many other ways toward the war effort.

COLEBROOK is a small community in northern New Hampshire on US-3, SR-26 and SR-145.

ROLL OF HONOR WW II MEMORIAL: With this memorial, the community of Colebrook honors those individuals from the local area who served in WW II. The Memorial consists of a stone monument with a plaque that gives the names of those people so honored. Location: In the Town Square near downtown Colebrook at the corner of US-3 and Bridge St.

The Roll of Honor WW II Memorial in Colebrook, NH

MANCHESTER is one on the state's larger cities and is in southern New Hampshire on I-93, I293, US-3, SR-101 and SR-104.

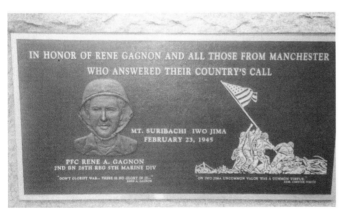

IWO JIMA MEMORIAL: This is a modest, but handsome memorial honoring a home town boy, Marine PFC Rene Gagnon. He was one of the five Marine who raised the flag on Mt. Suribachi on Iwo Jima and is in the famous photograph immortalized by photographer Joe Rosenthal. Beneath his bas-relief image on the Memorial is a quotation by him, "Don't glorify war...there is no glory in it." Location: City Park near downtown Manchester

Marine PFC Rene Gagnon is honored on Manchester's Iwo Jima Memorial in downtown Manchester, NH

NASHUA is a county seat in southern New Hampshire on I-293, US-3 and SR-111.

The WW II Memorial in Nashua, NH

NASHUA WW II MEMORIAL: This beautiful memorial is in Deschenes Park which is named in honor of a WW I veteran. The Memorial, the largest in the Park, consists of a large wall with 12 large bronze plaques and honors the men and women from the local area who served in WW II. In front of the wall are smaller stone pedestals with bronze plaques commemorating other American wars. There is also an attractive Purple Heart Memorial in the Park. Location: Deschenes Park in downtown Nashua, NH

PITTSBURG: This is ski country. Pittsburg is in northern New Hampshire on US-3 and SR-145.

WORLD WAR II HONOR ROLL-PITTSBURG: In Pittsburg's Town Park are several memorials including this one honoring the local residents of the area who served in WW II. Inscribed on that Memorial are over 100 names and the words "DEDICATED TO MEMBERS OF THE ARMED FORCES WHO SERVED IN WORLD WAR II." Location: Pittsburg Town Park on Main St.

The World War II Honor Roll-Pittsburg Memorial in Pittsburg, NH

One of the Wright Museum's tanks tried to bust out of the Museum but they stopped it just in time.

WOLFEBORO is in east-central New Hampshire on beautiful Lake Winipesaukee and SR-109/28.

WRIGHT MUSEUM: This fine, privately-owned, museum has a magnificent collection was WW II vehicles, artifacts and memorabilia. There are tanks, including a rare 42-ton Pershing tank, halftracks, Jeeps, an ambulance, motorcycles and more. A very unique feature of the Museum is the "Time Tunnel." Visitors walk through the years 1939 to 1945 viewing displays of WW II events for each year.

There is an archives collection, a library, an educational program, a 1940s soda fountain and a tank charging right through the museum's wall. Twice a year, the Museum has an event called "Family Day" which is a BBQ cookout and other festivities, and rides are offered in some of the military vehicles. The Museum also had a theater, publishes a newsletter and has a fine gift shop that you don't want to miss. Address: 77 Center St. (SR-28/109), Wolfeboro, NH 03894. Phone and website: 603-569-1212; www.wrightmuseum.org

NEW JERSEY

The state of New Jersey was a very important cog in the American War Machine. The state's strategic location, strong agricultural base and industrial economy were all-important assets during World War II.

The northeastern corner of the state is part of the dynamic New York City metropolitan area and the northern shore of New Jersey forms the western shore of the lower Hudson River and the western edge of New York Bay. For some 25 miles in this area the New Jersey shore was lined with piers, docks, warehouses, manufacturing plants and other industrial facilities. Railroads from all over the nation terminated on New Jersey's waterfront making New Jersey one of America's great centers of both rail and water transportation.

Inland, from this waterfront area, sprawled a huge industrial area that stretched half way across the state and down to New Brunswick.

At the end of the war, New Jersey ranked 9th in the nation in the value of its manufactured goods.

DIVEABLE WW II SHIP WRECKS IN NEW JERSEY COASTAL WATERS: Several American and Allied ships were sunk by German submarines in New Jersey's coastal waters and some are diveable. Local inquiries should be made by interested divers. One German submarine was sunk off the New Jersey coast and is also accessible to divers.

U-869 **DIVE SITE:** Sixty miles off New Jersey's shore lies the German Submarine U-869 in some 230 ft. of water. This submarine was thought to have been lost off the coast of Morocco, but in 1997, professional divers visited the submarine and discovered its true identity. It is believed that the submarine was sunk February 11, 1945 in an attack by the US destroyer escorts *Howard D. Crow* and *Koiner*. The submarine is accessible only to professional and experience sports divers. Some artifacts have been retrieved from the submarine.

ATLANTIC CITY is on the southern coast of New Jersey at the end of the Atlantic City Parkway. It is a very popular tourist center and its waterfront Boardwalk is famous.

ATLANTIC CITY WORLD WAR II MEMORIAL: This unique WW II Memorial is on the Atlantic City Boardwalk. It is wall mounted and depicts several GIs charging forward into action. It is a tribute to fallen war heroes and bears many of their names. Location: On the Atlantic City Boardwalk near the Information Center.

The Atlantic City World War II Memorial in Atlantic City, NJ

BELMAR is a small coastal community about midway down New Jersey's coast and on SR-35, SR-71 and SR-136.

BELMAR WORLD WAR II MEMORIAL: Inscribed on this stone memorial is the inscription "FOR GOD AND COUNTRY. THIS TABLET IS ERECTED IN HONOR OF THE MEN AND WOMEN OF BELMAR WHO ANSWERED THEIR COUNTRY'S CALL IN WORLD WAR II." The names of those who paid the supreme price are listed on the memorial. Location: Near Main and 13th Sts. In Belmar, NJ

The Belmar World War II Memorial in Belmar, NJ

BLACKWOOD is a small community ten miles south of Camden on SR-42 and SR-168.

BLACKWOOD WORLD WAR II MEMORIAL/GLOUCESTER TWP: This memorial is in the old historic district of the community of Blackwood. It consists of a large stone tablet with a recessed bronze plaque and is located in its own landscaped area. Honored on the plaque are those individuals for the local area who served in WW II. Location: On the corner of Black Horse Pike (SR-168) and Church St. (County Rd. 534) in Blackwood, NJ

CAMDEN is a county seat on the east bank of the Delaware River, opposite Philadelphia, and is one of New Jersey's larger cities. It is a major road, rail and water transportation hub.

The Blackwood World War II Memorial/ Gloucester Twp. Memorial in Blackwood, NJ

In the eastern suburb of Cherry Hill, the city park, Cooper River Park on Park Blvd., has a number of military memorials three of which relate to WW II. And what's more, the city has an unusually large number of WW II memorials and displays.

COOPER RIVER PARK:

Bataan Death March Memorial: This inspiring memorial in Cherry Hill's Cooper River Park honors those Americans and Filipinos who were forced to make the terrible Bataan Death March in early 1942. The Memorial consists of a five foot high memorial and flag pole sitting in a circular bed of pebbles and surrounded by a circular wall. In the memorial is a very detailed plaque telling the story of the Death March in detail and the number of Americans and Filipinos involved.

The Bataan Death March Memorial in Cooper River Park, Camden, NJ

Holocaust Memorial/Memorial Grove: This is the second WW II memorial in Cooper River Park. It honors the millions of European Jews murdered by the Nazis during WW II. The Memorial consists of a symbolically constructed eternal flame stretching toward the sky. It sits on a polygon base which has the names of the various concentration camps in which the Jews were imprisoned and murdered.

The Holocaust Memorial/Memorial Grove In Cooper River Park Camden, NJ

Polish American Congress WW II Memorial: This is the third WW II memorial in Cooper River Park. It honors the members of St. Joseph Roman Catholic Church, a predominately Polish congregation, who gave their lives in WW II. Their names are listed on the Memorial. The Memorial consists of highly polished black stone and there are two patios and four ornamental benches adjoining the Memorial.

BATTLESHIP *NEW JERSEY* MUSEUM: Here is one of the great relics of WW II. The battleship *New Jersey,* now anchored at Camden's waterfront, saw action in the Pacific at Kwajalein, Eniwetok, New Guinea, Truk, Saipan, the Philippines, Iwo Jima, Okinawa and participated in the sinking of the giant Japanese battleship, *Yamato.*

At various times, the *New Jersey* was the flagship of Admirals Halsey and Spruance.

The ship also has to its credit the fact that it did not lose a single crewman in combat throughout WW II. In the post war years, the *New Jersey* served in Korea, Vietnam and the Middle East.

The *New Jersey (BB-62)* was launched at the nearby Philadelphia Navy Yard on December 7, 1942, exactly one year after the attack on Pearl Harbor. Throughout her long history, the ship was modified and updated several times; much of the equipment aboard is post-WW II. But the big 16 inch guns of WW II are still there. For visitors interested in the guns, the Museum offers a two-hour Firepower

The WW II Battleship New Jersey on display at the Camden, NJ waterfront.

Tour in which the specifications and operations of the guns are explained in great detail. Visitors can also visit the bridge, the brig, crews' quarters, stay overnight and sleep in a crewman's bed and have lunch in the ship's mess. The ship is available for a wide variety of social and special events including marriages.

The *New Jersey* was decommissioned in 1991 and by that time had become the most decorated ship in US Navy history. Address: 62 Battleship Place, Camden, NJ 08103. Phone and website: 866-877-6262 or 856-966-1652; www.battleshipnewjersey.org

8TH WARD WW II WAR MEMORIAL: This memorial, located in Camden's 8th Ward, honors the citizens of the Camden area who fought in WW II. The main column is about eight feet tall with wings that list the names of 24 citizens of the Camden area who died in the war. Also listed are the names of over 900 others who served in the various military branches. Location: Broadway and Jefferson Sts., Camden, NJ

The 8th Ward WW II War Memorial in Camden, NJ

HONORING WORLD WAR II VETERANS MEMORIAL (Collingswood): This handsome memorial honors those individuals from the Collingswood area, an eastern suburb of Camden who gave their lives in WW II. The names of 50 men and 1 woman are inscribed in the Memorial. Location: Knights Park, Browning Rd. and Collings Av., Collingswood, NJ

The Honoring World War II Veterans Memorial in Collingswood, NJ

CAPE MAY/WILDWOOD: Cape May is a peninsula at the southern end of the state and at the end of the Garden State Parkway. It guards the entrance to Delaware Bay and the US Navy had two major facilities there during the war, Naval Air Station, Cape May, which was a permanent naval installation, and Naval Air Station, Wildwood which was built in 1943 and, after the war, became a commercial airport.

NAVAL AIR STATION WILDWOOD AVIATION MUSEUM: During the war, many airfield hangars were built of wood to save steel. This museum is in such a hangar, Hangar #1, and it's huge - 92,000 Sq. ft. (the size of two football fields) - and it's made of wood. Hangar #1 is on the National Register of Historic Places. Special tribute in the Museum is paid to the sailors and naval airmen who gave their lives during WW II.

The Museum has about 20 aircraft on display but most of them are post war. However, the Museum has one of the most interesting flying objects of WW II, a German V-2 rocket. Also, there are many artifacts from WW II including a collection of WW II posters and numerous photos from 1943-45. The Museum has a library, an interesting gift shop, an educational program and is available for social and other events. Address: Naval Air Station, Wildwood, 500 Forrestal Rd., Cape May Airport, NJ 08242. Phone and website: 609-886-8787; http://usnasw.org

The Naval Air Station Wildwood Aviation Museum - in a WW II era all-wood hangar

FORT MONMOUTH is an old US Army Signal Corps facility in northeastern NJ on SR-35, south of Sandy Hook and near the Ocean.

The Army Signal Corps World War II Memorial at Fort Monmouth, NJ

U.S ARMY SIGNAL CORPS WORLD WAR II MEMORIAL: This impressive memorial is on the grounds of Fort Monmouth and honors the many members of the Army Signal Corps who gave their lives during WW II. It is located on the Fort's main drill field. Permission is required to visit the Memorial. Location: Fort Monmouth on Sherrill Av. near Wallington Av.

HAMMONTON is a small community in south-central New Jersey on US-206 between the Atlantic City Expressway and US-30.

One of two WW II memorials on the grounds of the Hammonton Historical Society building in Hammonton, NJ

VETERANS PARK MEMORIAL: Here is a very unique double feature - two WW II memorials side by side. They are on the lawn of the Hammonton Historical Society Building along with other memorials. Both memorials honor those who served in WW II and those who died. Location: Belleview Av. and Vine St., Hammonton, NJ 08037

JERSEY CITY (See Newark/Jersey City Area)

MILLVILLE is a southern suburb of Vineland which is in the south-central part of the state on SR-49 and SR-47. During the war, the US Air Forces took over Millville's local airport and converted it into a training facility for fighter pilots.

The Millville Army Air Field Museum in Millville, NJ

MILLVILLE ARMY AIR FIELD MUSEUM is located at the Millville Airport in the original WW II headquarters building and records the history of the airfield during and after WW II. Highlighted in the Museum are the famous P-40 and P-47 fighter planes and the men who trained in them here at Millville Army Air Field. On display are uniforms, memorabilia, artifacts related to the WW II history of the Airfield. The Museum has a newsletter and offers tours. Address: 1 Leddon St., Millville Airport, Millville, NJ 08332. Phone and website: 856-327-2347, http://p47millville.org

NATIONAL PARK is a small community on the Delaware River across from Philadelphia just off I-295.

NATIONAL PARK WW II MEMORIAL: This stone memorial with wings pays honor to those individuals from the local area who gave their lives in WW II. Their names are inscribed on the Memorial. Location: In a small park on the corner of Hessian Av. and Grove Rd.

NEPTUNE TOWNSHIP is in east-central New Jersey near the ocean. It stretches eastward from the Garden State Parkway to the ocean. State roads 18, 33, 35, 66 and 71 pass through the township.

WORLD WAR II MEMORIAL, NEPTUNE TOWNSHIP: Honored here in this handsome four-column memorial are the men and women from Neptune Township who served in WW II. There are inscriptions on the Memorial and a flag pole. Location SR-71 at the entrance to Ocean Grove, NJ

The National Park WW II Memorial in National Park, NJ

NEW BRUNSWICK is 25 miles SW of Newark on US-1 and US-130.

RUTGERS UNIVERSITY WORLD WAR II MEMORIAL: Like every university in the country, Rutgers had many students and former students who served in the military during WW II. Rutgers has erected a handsome memorial to commemorate their own. It consists of two stone columns surrounded by plagues that list the names of those who served. Location: On Rutgers University College Av. Campus

The World War II Memorial, Neptune Township, NJ

THE NEWARK/JERSEY CITY AREA: This was the largest urbanized area of the state of New Jersey and a part of the metropolitan area of New York City. Newark was the largest of several cities on the New Jersey side of the Hudson River and New York Bay and had many military installations during the war.

KATYN MASSACRE 1940 MEMORIAL: This is one of the most dramatic WW II memorials in the United States. It commemorates the massacre of some 5,000 Polish Army officers by the Soviet Union's secret police, the infamous NKVD, in Katyn Forest in the Soviet Union in 1940. The victims were prisoners of war captured by the Soviets during their invasion of Poland in 1939. This act was a brutal attempt by the Soviets to eliminate the pro-western leadership corps of the Polish Army and set the stage for an eventual Soviet takeover of Poland.

The Rutgers University World War II Memorial, New Brunswick, NJ

The statue atop the large stone base shows a Polish Army officer with his hands tied behind his back being stabbed to death by the bayonet of a rifle. Location: Exchange Place, at the base of Montgomery St. on the Jersey City Waterfront Walkway

The very dramatic Katyn 1940 Memorial in Jersey City, NJ

LIBERTY STATE PARK - WORLD WAR II MEMORIAL: From this state park, one can see the Statue of Liberty and in the foreground there is a dramatic WW II Memorial. It is a 15 ft. bronze statue called "Liberation" that depicts an American soldier carrying an emaciated survivor out of a German concentration camp. The Memorial is dedicated to America's role of preserving freedom and rescuing the oppressed. Location: I-78 at exit 148.

This 15' bronze sculpture is in Liberty State Park in Jersey City, NJ

NEW JERSEY NAVAL MUSEUM/USS LING is located in downtown Hackensack on the waterfront The WW II-era submarine, *Ling,* is the main attraction and serves as a memorial to those who served aboard American submarines during WW II.

The submarine was commissioned June 8, 1945 and served only during the last months of the war. In 1960, she was converted to a training submarine and in 1971 was decommissioned and brought to this location in 1973.

Other displays at the Museum include a Kaiten type two-man Japanese suicide submarine, a two-man German Seahund type submarine (not suicide) used for coastal patrols. Also to be seen, are artillery pieces, military vehicles, scale models, photographs, ordnance and more.

The Museum is operated by the Submarine Memorial Association and offers tours, facilities for social events and has an educational program. Address: 78 River St., Hackensack, NJ 07601. Phone and website: 201-342-3268; www.njnm.com

The World War II era submarine Ling at the New Jersey Naval Museum in Hackensack, NJ

WORLD WAR II MEMORIAL - WEST ORANGE: The bronze plaque on this memorial reads "1941 1945 WE HOLD IN REVERENCE THE MEMORY OF THE WEST ORANGE MEN WHO GAVE THEIR LIVES IN WORLD WAR II. MAY THEIR SACRIFICE BRING PEACE TO MANKIND." The Memorial was sponsored by the Gold Star mothers of West Orange and lists the names for the 124 men from West Orange who were killed in the war. Location: 66 Main St. West Orange, NJ (a western suburb of Newark)

RARITAN is a small community in north central New Jersey near the intersection of US-202 and US-206.

JOHN BASILONE MEMORIAL: Raritan was the home of John Basilone, a US Marine, who was awarded the Congressional Medal of Honor on Guadalcanal during the battle for Henderson Field. He is credited with killing 38 or more Japanese

The World War II Memorial in West Orange, NJ

soldiers during that battle.

   This impressive memorial has a statue of Baselone in action holding a Browning machine gun. Location: At the intersection of Canal St. and Old York Rd./Somerset St. in Raritan, NJ

SEA GIRT is a beach community on the central coast of the state, and SR-71.

NATIONAL GUARD MILITIA MUSEUM OF NEW JERSEY: This museum is located at the New Jersey National Guard Training Center in Sea Girt and traces the history of New Jersey's National Guard which is one of the oldest in the nation.

The John Basilone Memorial in Raritan, NJ

   Included in the Museum is information on New Jersey's Air National Guard and the New Jersey Naval Militia. The Museum has some 4000 artifacts, many of these related to WW II. There are numerous WW II photos and a static display of military vehicles and aircraft. The Museum is also home to the Center for US War Veterans Oral History Project. Address: Sea Girt Av. and Washington Av., Sea Girt, NJ 08750. Phone and website: 732-974-5966; www.state.nj.us/military/museum

TRENTON, in the west-central part of the state on the Delaware River, is the capitol of New Jersey.

NEW JERSEY WORLD WAR II MEMORIAL: This is the official WW II memorial of the state of New Jersey and it is magnificent. It honors the more than 500,000 New Jersey citizens who served in the military during WW II. Inside a granite pillared dome stands "Lady Victory," a 12 foot bronze figure holding a sword in one hand and the wreath of peace in the other. Under her left foot she crushes the flags of Nazi Germany and Imperial Japan. Behind Lady Victory stands another sculpture, the Lone Soldier, a life-size bronze figure designated to represent any Soldier, Sailor or Airman. The Lone Soldier hold an M-1 rifle at the ready.

Encircling Lady Victory are markers recognizing the five armed forces and the Merchant Marines. At

The official and magnificent WW II Memorial of New Jersey, Trenton, NJ

the entrance to the Memorial are the five flags of the armed forces and the Merchant Marine. Two 12 foot high, 40 foot long curved walls surround the Memorial. One describes the war in Europe and the other the war in the Pacific.

In the year 2045, the 100th anniversary of the ending of WW II, two time capsules will be buried in the Memorial for future generations to ponder. Location: 125 W. State St. (across from the Capitol Building) Trenton, NJ

WRIGHTSTOWN is 15 miles SE of Trenton on SR-545 and SR-528 and has long been associated with Fort Dix, one of the US Army's oldest and largest military installations.

FORT DIX MUSEUM: This museum, located at Ft. Dix, tells the history of the Fort from its beginning in 1917 to the present. There are displays on the Fort's construction, its use as a Civilian Conservation Corps Camp (CCC) during the Depression, its activities before and during WW II, unit histories and the role of women at Fort Dix. Also to be seen are military vehicles both inside and outside the museum, uniforms, posters, small arms, machine guns and more. Address: 6501 Pennsylvania Av. Fort Dix, NJ 08640. Phone: 609-562-2334/6501

NEW MEXICO

In the 1940s, New Mexico was called the Sunshine State. That name was very appropriate because sunshine is an important asset in wartime and it was one of the reasons the US military was attracted to New Mexico. Sunshine and a moderate climate are important in the training of aviators and ground troops, the housing of POWs and enemy aliens and in the conducting of outdoor technical research. Another big asset New Mexico had to offer was its wide open spaces which are ideal for proving grounds and bombing and gunnery ranges. And it had an ideal location for testing an atomic bomb.

During the war years, the state had 17 POW camps and two large enemy alien internment camps giving it a relatively high per capita population of POWs and interned aliens. Most of those individuals incarcerated worked for the military or in agriculture.

Today, as you travel across New Mexico on I-10, you will note that this stretch of highway is designated "The Pearl Harbor Memorial Highway."

SPECIAL NOTE; THE NEW MEXICO/BATAAN DEATH MARCH – A BITTER CONNECTION: The infamous Bataan Death March of early 1942 has a special place in the history of the state of New Mexico. In January 1941, the New Mexico National Guard was mobilized and sent to the Philippine Island because many of the guardsmen spoke Spanish and that language was still spoken in the Islands.

When the Japanese attacked the Philippine Islands in December 1941, the New Mexicans fought well but eventually retreated to the Bataan Peninsula and the Island of Corregidor with the rest of the US and Filipino forces. They eventually surrendered and were forced to take part in the infamous Bataan Death March. They were then incarcerated in Japanese prisoner of war camps for the rest of the war under terrible conditions.

By the time they were liberated by advancing American forces in 1945, nearly half of their original number of 1800 men had perished and many of the survivors were injured or sick. When the citizens of New Mexico learned of the fate of their national guardsmen, they were outraged. Being a sparsely-settled state, the tragedy touched many New Mexican families. The citizens of the state then became very bitter against anything Japanese. For many years after the war, ethnic Japanese were not welcome in some parts of the state.

Through the decades that followed, many memorials have been erected in New Mexico commemorating the victims of the Death March. Also, US-70 between Las Cruces and Alamagordo is named the "Bataan Veterans Memorial Highway." In several cities in New Mexico, there are schools, streets and other public places named after Bataan.

ALAMAGORDO is a county seat in the south-central part of the state on US-54 and US-70 80 miles NNE of El Paso, TX. To the north and west of the town is one of the largest desert wildernesses in the nation consisting of thousands of square miles of desolate mountains and dry valleys. Dominating this desolate landscape was a hundred-mile-long natural outcropping of gypsum which, over the eons, had been ground by natural forces into a fine white sand. This phenomenon of nature gave the general area its popular name, The White Sands Area of New Mexico. When, late in the war, the Federal Government had need of a place to test its most secret of secret weapons, the atomic bomb, it chose the White Sands area for the test site, and Alamagordo became the major staging and supply point for the test.

On July 16, 1945 that test, the detonation of the world's first atomic bomb, took place at a desert location called "Trinity," 55 miles NNW of Alamagordo. The blast could be seen and felt by everyone in the town and in many small towns around. No one at the time knew what it was because of wartime secrecy, but when the war ended abruptly a month later, the people of Alamagordo were told about that mysterious blast in the desert and that they had witnessed, with their own eyes and ears, the dawning of the atomic age.

ALBUQUERQUE is the state's largest city and is near the geographic center of the state at the junction of I-40 and I-25. During WW II, this was one of the cities of the Great Southwest that was discovered by both the military and industry. Sizable new military bases and factories came to Albuquerque and, with them, many people. Albuquerque's central location in the Great Southwest and its mild climate were contributing factor to its wartime growth. By 1950, the city's population had more than doubled from before the war.

ANDERSON/ABRUZZO INTERNATIONAL BALLOON MUSEUM: This unique museum traces the history of ballooning and has many interesting exhibits on that very specialized subject. Of interest to WW II buffs in the Museum's collection is an intact Japanese bombing balloon complete with envelope (gas bag), some ropes and its bomb and ballast ring. Attached to the ring are several incendiary bombs that were intended to start forest fires in the US West.

Some 10, 000 of these balloons were released in Japan to attack North American in 1944/45 and were carried across the Pacific by the upper jet streams. This balloon came down near Tremonton, Utah. Very few such exhibits now exist in the US.

The people at the Museum are very knowledgeable on the Japanese bombing balloons and the Museum has a permanent display entitled "Balloons at War." There is also a cafe, a theater and a very nice gift shop. Address: 9201 Balloon Museum Dr. NE, Albuquerque, NM 87113. Phone and website: 505-768-6020; www.balloonmuseum.com

BATAAN MEMORIAL PARK is one of the several fine parks in the city of Albuquerque and serves as a living memorial to those citizens of New Mexico that served in the Philippines during the war. Location: 748 Tulane Dr. NE, Albuquerque, NM

NATIONAL MUSEUM OF NUCLEAR SCIENCE & HISTORY: This fine 30,000 Sq. ft. museum is in Albuquerque's museum district near downtown Albuquerque. It traces the history of atomic energy from its inception to the present day and explains important events that took place in New Mexico with regard to atomic science. Prominently featured in the Museum is the history of the wartime "Manhattan Project" that developed, produced and tested the first atomic bomb.

On display are replicas of "Little Boy," the enriched uranium atomic bomb which was dropped on Hiroshima, and "Fat Man," the plutonium atomic bomb which was first tested in New Mexico and later dropped on Nagasaki.

The Museum also has replicas of the hydrogen bomb, modern-day atomic bombs, the first British-made atomic bomb, an example of the WW II Norden bombsight which was used to drop the bombs on Japan and artifacts from every-day life at Los Alamos when it was the center for the entire Manhattan Project during the war.

Another unique exhibit is a Lego model of the Chicago Pile-1 where Enrico Fermi and his associates first demonstrated that atomic reactions could be controlled.

The Museum has a library, classrooms, a conference room, an art display, and educational program, a theater, and numerous displays on the current use of atomic energy.

The National Museum of Nuclear Science and History
In Albuquerque, NM

Displayed outdoors is a WW II B-29 bomber, similar to the ones that dropped the atomic bombs on Japan. Several postwar aircraft are also on display. The Museum Store has many fascinating souvenirs and items that you won't find elsewhere. Address: 601 Eubank at Southeast Blvd. (one mile south of I-40), Albuquerque, NM 87116. Phone and website: 505-245-2137; www.nuclearmuseum.org

ERNIE PYLE PUBLIC LIBRARY: This library was the former home of the famous WW II correspondent and Pulitzer Prize winner Ernie Pyle. Pyle lived for several years in Albuquerque. Pyle and his wife built the house in the 1930s from plans drawn up by Ernie himself. They lived here until 1940. Inside the library is a bust of Pyle and a small display commemorating his life. Pyle wrote about this Albuquerque house from time-to-time in his columns. Pyle was killed on the island of Ie Shima on April 18, 1945 by a Japanese sniper. Address: 900 Girard SE, Albuquerque, NM 87106. Phone and website: 505-256-2065; www.cabq.gov/library/branches.html

VETERANS MEMORIAL PARK: This beautiful city park has all the amenities of a fine city park and there are several memorials in the Park, one of which relates to WW II.

US Submarine Veterans WW II Memorial: A portion of the inscription on the Memorial reads "TO REMEMBER AND SHOW APPRECIATION TO ALL U.S SUBMARINERS AND SUPPORT PERSONNEL DURING WORLD WAR II." The inscription goes on to detail the exploits ad successes of the US Submarine Service during the war. Location: 1100 Louisiana Blvd. SE, Albuquerque, NM near the Gibson Gate to Kirkland Air Force Base.

The US Submarine Veterans WW II Memorial in Veterans Memorial Park, Albuquerque, NM

CARLSBAD is a county seat in the SE corner of the state on US-65, US-180 and US-285 near the Texas state line. The city has two memorials commemorating the Bataan Death March; the Bataan Memorial Bridge on Greene St. over the Pecos River, and the Bataan Recreational area on the Pecos river between the Upper and Lower Tansil Dam.

DEMING is a county seat in the SW corner of the state on I-10.

LUNA MIMBRES MUSEUM, near downtown Deming, is the city's main museum and has extensive displays on Deming's history and that of the surrounding areas.
   Just south of the Museum is Veterans Memorial Park dedicated to the memory of those who served in New Mexico's National Guard and were forced to participate in the infamous Bataan Death March. There is a memorial in the Park commemorating those individuals and another memorial commemorating the attack on Pearl Harbor.
   Inside the Museum is a very fine museum shop with a wide variety of gifts and souvenirs. Address: 301 S. Silver St., Deming, NM 88030. Phone and website: 505-546-2382; www.deminglunamimbresmuseum.com

The Bataan Death March Memorial in the Luna Mimbres Museum's Veteran Memorial Park, Deming NM

GALLUP is a county seat in the NW part of the state on I-40. Just to the north of the city is a large Navajo Indian Reservation.

NAVAJO CODE TALKERS WW II MEMORIAL: It is fitting that this memorial be located in Gallup because many of Gallup's neighbors to the north - who are Navajo Indians - served in the US Marine Corps in the Pacific during the war. They were utilizes as radio operators conversing with each other in the Navajo language which was unintelligible to the Japanese. This memorial honors those Navajos Marines who served. Location: At the entrance to the Civic Center Plaza on old route US-66

HANOVER is a very small community in SW New Mexico on SR-356 near the southern end of Gila National Forest. Grant County and the Cobre Consolidated School District have designated a part of the school district's property as the "Bataan Memorial Outdoor Classroom." This is an undisturbed natural area used to familiarize students with the natural landscape and fauna of New Mexico.

The Navajo Code Talkers Memorial in Gallup, NM

JARALES is a small community 35 miles south of Albuquerque on I-25 and SR-314.

WAR HEROES MEMORIAL: This very small town lost eight of its sons during the Bataan Death March fiasco and this memorial was erected in their honor. All eight had Hispanic names and are inscribed on the Memorial. The Memorial was dedicated on Memorial Day May 26, 1986 by Lt. General Leo Marquez, USAF. Location: On SR-314

The War Heroes Memorial in Jarales, NM

LAS CRUCES is a county seat in south-central New Mexico on I-10, I-25, US-70 and the Rio Grande River.

VETERAN'S PARK: This large city park has a thought-provoking life size statue of two US soldiers on the Bataan Death March and another soldier. The Memorial is illuminated at night.
  Also in the Park is a large circular Veterans Wall and an adjoining memorial which commemorates the US campaign in the Philippine Islands during WW II. Location: Roadrunner Parkway, Las Cruces, NM

WHITE SANDS MISSILE RANGE MUSEUM is 20 miles east of Las Cruces and three miles south of US-70 at its own location. This museum has one of the largest collection of missiles in the country displayed in a park adjacent to the Museum. There are displays tracing the history of the White Sands facility as a missile site from its beginning in 1945 to the present.
  The Museum has information on early nuclear weapons, rockets,

The Bataan Death March Memorial in Veteran's Park, Las Cruces, NM

189

rocket launchers and other related weapons of war and peace. Included in the displays are German V-2 rockets similar to those tested at White Sands at the end of the war and an American-built version of the German V-1 "Buzzbomb" called the "Loon."

Most of the other missiles are of postwar vintage. Inside the Museum there is information on Werhner von Braun, the WW II German scientist who directed Germany's missile program and later, after the war, made a significant contribution to America's emerging missile program.

And don't pass up the very interesting gift shop. It has items from local artists and a variety of goods featuring the missile range logo and other aspects of White Sands. Address: White Sands Missile Range Museum, Las Cruces, NM 88002. Phone and website: 505-647-1116; www.wssmr-history.org

LOS ALAMOS, 25 miles NW of Santa Fe, was not a town before the war. It was the site of the Los Alamos Ranch School for Boys, an exclusive boys' school in a forest on top of a huge mesa. The boys' school was purchased by the US government early in the war and, by war's end, had become the city of Los Alamos - and it became world-famous.

In 1942, this beautiful and isolated spot was chosen personally by Maj. Gen. Leslie Groves and Dr. J. Robert Oppenheimer, the top men of America's super-secret "Manhattan (Atomic Bomb) Project," to be the site of a new science city. The Manhattan Project's best scientists soon gathered in this secret isolation and attempted to produce an ultra-powerful explosive device that the latest theories and research in atomic science indicated was possible.

The school had 790 acres of land with lots of empty adjacent land for further expansion. The school's existing buildings were vacant and could house some 500 people immediately. The owner was anxious to sell so the deal was made. The buildings of the school were utilized by the arriving scientists while dozens of new structures were built to house their sophisticated equipment and their associates who would follow. Los Alamos thus became the "wizard's workshop" of the Manhattan Project. It was also known as "the hill."

Atomic research was going on at dozens of labs around the country, but the Los Alamos lab was the only one focusing exclusively on bombs.

On August 6, 1945, the first of the bombs, "Little Boy," which was produced at Los Alamos, was dropped on the Japanese city of Hiroshima. On August 9, a second bomb, "Fat Man," also made at Los Alamos, was dropped on Nagasaki. Their destructive power was so awesome that the Japanese leaders realized they had no defense against such weapons and within days sued for peace bringing about the sudden and unexpected end to WW II. And soon afterwards, the world learned of Los Alamos, New Mexico.

The Bradbury Science Museum in Los Alamos, NM

BRADBURY SCIENCE MUSEUM, in Los Alamos, is part of the Los Alamos National Laboratory and relates the early history of the development of the atomic bombs and the part played in their development by the people at Los Alamos. Some of the first hardware used in the development of the atomic bombs is displayed along with replicas of the two WW Atom bombs, "Little Boy" and "Fat Man." Other displays include a statue of Dr. Robert Oppenheimer, Director of the Manhattan Project; documents; photos; information on the people involved and life style in Los Alamos during WW II. Other displays explain the various uses for atomic energy, both military and commercial. There are exhibits on modern day uses for atomic energy and ongoing nuclear research. The Museum has a theater, an auditorium and a well-stocked and very interesting gift shop. Address: 1350 Central Av., Los Alamos, NM 87544. Phone and website: 505-667-4444; www.lanl.gov/museum

LOS ALAMOS COUNTY HISTORICAL MUSEUM is housed in the Guest Cottage of the former Los Alamos Ranch School. General Leslie Groves resided in this house when he visited "the hill." The Museum records the history of Los Alamos County from prehistoric times through the development of the atomic bomb. Displays related to the WW II era include photographs of the development and testing of the first atomic devices, newspaper articles of the time, military uniforms and other related artifacts. There is also an archives collection and a very nice gift shop. Address: 1050 Bathtub Row, Los Alamos, NM 87544. Phone and website: 505-662-4493/6272; www.losalamoshistory.orgMuseum.htm

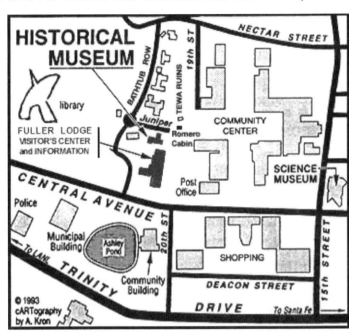

RATON is a county seat near the northern border of the state on I-25, US-64/87 and SR-72.

RIPLEY PARK: near the center of Raton, has a touching WW II memorial consisting of a statue depicting a man going off to war and his wife and child saying goodbye to him. Also in the Park is a memorial entitled "Remember Pearl Harbor." Park location: N. Second St and Savage Av., Raton, NM

SANTA FE: the state's capitol, is in north-central New Mexico on I-25 and US-285. One of the public buildings in the city is named the "Bataan Memorial Building," located at 407 Galisteo St. Within the Memorial Building is an eternal flame commemorating those New Mexicans who suffered through the Bataan Death March.

The WW II Memorial in Ripley Park Raton, NM

BATAAN MEMORIAL MUSEUM: This fine museum is maintained by the New Mexico National Guard and covers the military history of New Mexico from its earliest days to the present.
  On display in the Museum are exhibits on the Bataan Death March as well as uniforms, artwork, photos, maps, sculptures, weapons, etc. Address: 1050 Old Pecos Trail, Santa Fe, NM 87505. Phone and website: 505-474-1670; www.bataanmuseum.com

NEW MEXICO'S ETERNAL FLAME

MEMORIAL: Here is yet another memorial to the victims of the Bataan Death March who were members of the US Army's 200th Coast Artillery Regiment. This tall and impressive memorial is topped by a spread eagle with the eternal flame in front of it. The inscription on the Memorial reads at its ending "...TO PERPETUATE THIS SACRED MEMORY AND HONOR THE HEROIC DEAD OF THE 200TH BOTH LIVING AND DEAD, PEOPLE OF NEW MEXICO THIS MONUMENT." Location: On the State Capitol grounds, Santa Fe, NM

New Mexico's Eternal Flame Memorial in Santa Fe, NM

SANTA TERESA is on the southern border of the state and is a western suburb of El Paso,TX.

WAR EAGLE AIR MUSEUM: Located at the Dona Ana County Airport, this large museum is dedicated to collecting, restoring and displaying historic aircraft. Many of the 30-some planes in their collection are from the WW II and the Korean Conflict. Most of the aircraft are in flying condition.

There is a large collection of antique automobiles, military vehicles and aircraft and military-related items. The Museum has rental facilities for events, an educational program and a gift shop that offers many interesting items.

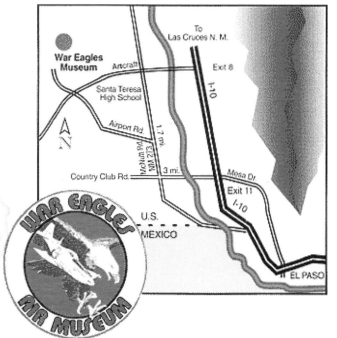

The War Eagles Museum in Santa Teresa, NM

Address: 8012 Airport Rd., Santa Teresa, NM 88008. Phone and website: 575-589-2000; www.war-eagles-museum.com

TAOS is a county seat in north-central New Mexico on US-64, SR-68 and SR-522. In the downtown central district of the city is a large civic and convention center with several large meeting halls. One of the halls is named the "Bataan Hall." There is also a Bataan Memorial in nearby Taos Plaza. Address of the civic and convention center: 120 Civic Plaza Dr., Taos, NM

WHITE SANDS: (See Alamagordo)

NEW YORK

The state of New York was America's most populous state during WW II. It had a population of 13,479,000 with more than half of that population living in the New York City Metropolitan area. Just before WW II, New York State experienced very hard economic times because of the Great Depression which had begun in New York City with the stock market crash of 1929. During those terrible years, however, the state had a young and energetic Governor, Franklin D. Roosevelt, who began at once to take aggressive and, at times, controversial measures to combat the problems created by the Great Depression. Roosevelt's measures seemed to help, and he soon caught the nation's attention as a man of action. In 1932, he was nominated by his party for the presidency of the United States and won by a landslide vote. Roosevelt and his supporters considered this as a mandate from the American people to take his New York-tested Depression-fighting policies to Washington and implement them on a national scale. These policies became the nucleus of Roosevelt's famous "New Deal" program which was designed to put people back to work with government assistance.

The coming of WW II brought new problems to New York. First, there was the great fear that New York might be attacked. These fears were not unfounded because all three major Axis nations, Germany, Italy and Japan, had plans to attack New York if the opportunities came about. Also German submarines became very active in New York waters early in the war and German saboteurs landed (and were eventually caught) on Long Island less than seven months after the US entered the war. Furthermore, New York City had tens of thousands of Axis aliens and ethnic nationals whose presence fostered fears of subversion and sabotage. The 1940 national census showed that there were 2,853,000 foreign-born people in the state including 316,800 Germans and 584,000 Italians. Soon after America went to war, there was talk of relocating these people away from the New York area to camps in the interior as was to be the fate of the ethnic Japanese on the US West Coast. The relocation of so many people, however, would have been a logistical nightmare, so the Government took a wait-and-see attitude and the relocation never came about.

ALBANY AREA: This area is 130 miles north of New York City near the juncture of the Hudson and Mohawk Rivers. Albany is the state's capitol.

The WW II destroyer escort USS Slater, on public display in Albany, NY.

DESTROYER ESCORT HISTORICAL MUSEUM - *USS SLATER*: Here, on Albany's water front, is one of only three surviving US Navy WW II destroyer escorts, the *USS Slater*. During the war, 563 of these vessels were built. Their primary mission was that of convoy escort and the *Slater* saw action in both the Atlantic and Pacific.

After the war, she was sold to the Greek Navy and saw many more years of service in the Mediterranean Sea. It is now a floating museum and is open to the public. Tours of the ship are provided and overnight camping is a popular activity aboard the ship. Address: The Snow Dock, 141 Broadway, Albany NY 12202 at the foot of Madison St. adjacent to Dunn Memorial Bridge. Phone and website: 518-431-1943; www.ussslater.org

NEW YORK STATE WORLD WAR II MEMORIAL: Like most states, New York has a state WW II memorial. This state memorial is near the state Capitol Building in downtown Albany and is in a beautifully landscaped setting with pools and a memorial centerpiece topped with a spread eagle. It is dedicated to all those citizens of New York who served and died during the war. Location: Empire State Plaza, Albany NY

The New York State World War II Memorial in Albany, NY

WATERVLIET ARSENAL MUSEUM: This fine 30,000 Sq. Ft. museum, about ten miles north of Albany, is on the grounds of Watervliet Arsenal in an historic 1859 Arsenal storehouse which is made almost entirely of cast iron sections. Watervliet Arsenal is America's oldest continually active arsenal. The Museum relates the history of the Arsenal and the guns which were made here - including the big 16" guns used on American battleships of WW II. Many other WW II-era guns were made here and are prominent in the Museum's displays.

Some of the Arsenal's manufacturing methods are shown and there is information on how the guns were used. There is also an archives and research facility. Address: 800 3rd Av., Watervliet, NY 12189. Phone and website: 518-266-5805; www.wva.army.mil/museum.ph

AUBURN is a county seat in upstate New York in the Finger Lakes area on US-20, SR-5, SR-34 and SR-38.

WORLD WAR II MEMORIAL: Auburn, NY, like many county seats across the US, has a handsome memorial dedicated to WW II. This memorial commemorates the citizens of Auburn who gave their lives in WW II. Their names are inscribed on the memorial. Location: Downtown Auburn in a small city park on Genesee St.

The WW II Memorial in Auburn, NY

BUFFALO/NIAGARA FALLS AREA: This was a highly industrialized and strategically located area at the western terminus of the Erie Canal. It is also a popular tourist area.

BUFFALO WORLD WAR II MEMORIAL: Located in the Kaisertown section of Buffalo, this impressive memorial honors the local citizens who served in WW II. An inscription on the Memorial reads "TO HONOR THE MEN AND WOMEN WHO SERVED OUR COUNTRY IN THE SECOND WORLD WAR, 1941-1945." Location: Houghton-Stachowski Park on Clinton St.

The Buffalo World War II Memorial in Buffalo, NY

The ships at Buffalo Naval and Servicemen's Park, Buffalo, NY

BUFFALO NAVAL AND SERVICEMEN'S PARK is located on Buffalo's waterfront at the foot of Pearl and Main Streets. It has as its main attraction, three warships from the WW II era. They are the cruiser USS *Little Rock*, built in 1944 but too late to see action in the war and later converted to a guided-missile warship; the destroyer USS *Sullivans*, built in 1943 and named after the five Sullivan brothers of Waterloo, IA; and the submarine USS *Croaker*, which, during WW II, sank the Japanese cruiser *Nagaro* and several enemy merchant vessels. All of the vessels are open to the public. Also on display at the Park is memorabilia and information concerning the US Marines, POWs, and women is the US military, Polish armed forces and more. Address: One Naval Park Cove, Buffalo, NY 14202. Phone and website: 716-847-1773; www.buffalonavalpark.org.

SEABEE MEMORIAL at FISHERMAN'S PARK: This is a beautiful park located in North Tonawanda along the east side of the Niagara River and several miles upstream from the fall. Its centerpiece is a large diesel-powered tractor with blade – the type the Seabees used. There is a large memorial wall several flagpoles and it is all set in a garden-like plot. Location: Fisherman's Park on Seaway Trail (SR-265/384)

FARMINGDALE is a small community on Long Island east of, and adjacent to, Bethpage.

AMERICAN AIR POWER MUSEUM is located at the Republic Airport in Farmingdale and has a collection of some 20 aircraft, most of which are from WW II. The Museum's exhibits highlight the aircraft of WW II, their uses and the personnel who flew them. There are several military vehicles, aircraft-related artifacts, memorabilia, photos and more. The Museum has an educational program, hosts air shows and offers rides in some of its aircraft. Address: 1230 New Highway, Farmingdale, NY 11735. Phone and website: 212-843-8010 and 631-293-6398; www.americanairpowermuseum.com

The Seabee Memorial in Fisherman's Park in North Tonawanda, NY

GENESCO is a county seat in western New York on I-390, US-20A, SR-39 and SR-63.

1941 HISTORICAL AIRCRAFT GROUP (Museum): This interesting air museum was founded in 1994 and is dedicated to the restoration, preservation, display and flight of aircraft of the WW II and Korean War eras as well as the recognition of all US Military personnel for their service and sacrifice. It is located at the Genesco Airport and has about 20 aircraft, many of them of WW II vintage. The Museum has air shows, restoration projects and there are several military vehicles on display. Inside the Museum are artifacts, aircraft models, memorabilia and a fine gift shop. Address: 3489 Big Tree Ln., Genesco, NY 14454. Phone and website: 585-243-2100; www.1941hag.org

GLOVERSVILLE is a small community in east central NY and is one of the southern entrances to the Adirondack Mountains. It is just north of the Johnstown on SR-29A.

FULTON COUNTY WW II VETERANS K.I.A. (KILLED IN ACTION) MEMORIAL: This handsome memorial consists of a large central limestone monument, six black polished granite smaller monuments and seven flag poles. On the center monument is a plaque which reads "IN HONOR AND IN MEMORY OF THE MEN AND WOMEN FROM FULTON CONTY WHO SERVED IN THE ARMED FORCES OF THE UNITED STATES-WWII-1941-1945." The granite monuments are dedicated to each branch of military service. Location: In a small park on Kingsboro Av. between E. State St. and Gregory St.

HAMMONDSPORT is a small community in western New York just north of Bath on the southern end of Lake Keuka and SR-54A.

The Fulton County WW II Veterans K.I.A.
Memorial in Gloversville, NY

THE GLENN H. CURTISS MUSEUM: Hammondsport was the home of one of America's greatest aircraft designers, Glenn H. Curtiss. Curtiss' career began before WW I and extended well into WW II. In his pre-WW I years he built bicycles, motorcycles and primitive aircraft and became involved in motorcycle and aircraft racing. He gained many honors and national fame in these sports.

He soon got involved in early military aircraft and, at the time of WW I, successfully flew an airplane to and from a specially built flight deck on the battleship *Pennsylvania.*

During WW I, he built the famous "Jenny" airplane which was used as a military trainer and, after the war, became a favorite of the daring-do "Barnstormers."

During WW II, he developed the famous P-40 fighter plane – the plane of "Flying Tiger" fame. He also was instrumental in the development and production of other WW II aircraft.

The Museum provides great detail on Curtiss' life and career, has models of his aircraft and motorcycles and many related artifacts. There is ample information on his activities during WW II, a library, an educational program and a gift shop with many interesting items. Address: 8419 State Rd. 54 (Hammondsport Airport), Hammondsport, NY 14840. Phone and website: 607-569-2160; www.glenncurtissmuseum.org

HAUPPAUGE is one of the many small communities in central Long Island. It is on I-495, SR-347 and SR-454.

SUFFOLK COUNTY WORLD WAR II MEMORIAL: This interesting WW II memorial is a circular monument, 30 ft. in diameter and 3 1/2 ft. high. On the outer rim, around the circumference, are several plaques. Each plaque gives dates and limited detail about a significant battle or campaign Of the war. The interior of the monument is white cement engraved with two maps. One shows the European Theater of Operations and the other the Pacific Theater. Location: In front of the H. Lee Dennison building 100 Veterans Hwy. (SR-454), Hauppauge, NY

The Suffolk County WW II Memorial in Hauppauge, NY

HORSEHEADS is a small community five miles north of Elmira on SR-14 and SR-17.

WINGS OF EAGLES DISCOVERY CENTER: Here is a fine museum located at the Elmire-Corning Airport just west of Horseheads. The Museum has some 40 aircraft, some of which are WW II vintage and some in flying condition. Also in the Museum's collection are flight simulators, aircraft artifacts and memorabilia. The Museum offers tours, has an educational program, hosts social events and has a very interesting gift shop. Address: 343 Daniel Zenker Dr. Suite 101, Horseheads, NY 14845. Phone and website: 607-358-4247; www.wingsofeagles.com

HYDE PARK is seven miles north of Poughkeepsie on the east bank of the Hudson River. During the war, it was a community of less than 1000 people but was known world-wide as the home of President Franklin D. Roosevelt. Today, there are three very important historic sites in the area, all related to the Roosevelt family.

FRANKLIN D. ROOSEVELT NATIONAL HISTORIC SITE is two miles south of Hyde Park on SR-9 and is administered by the National Park Service. This 200-acre estate was built in 1826 and was the home of the Roosevelt family. Franklin's father purchased the estate and additional land in 1867 and remodeled the main house around 1915. The estate appears today almost exactly as it did during the last years of Franklin Roosevelt's life. Included on the grounds are the original stables, an icehouse, a walking trail and the Rose Garden which contains the graves of Franklin and his wife, Eleanor. Also buried on the estate are John Roosevelt, their son, and Fala, their dog.

Visitors begin their tours of the estate at the Henry A. Wallace Visitors Center. Wallace was FDR's Vice-President during most of WW II. Tickets can be purchased here for tours of the Historic Site and the Franklin D. Roosevelt Presidential Library and Museum. There is a film presentation acquainting visitors with the Historic Site.

Also a part of the Historic Site is the Top Cottage which Franklin had built for himself as a retreat and a facility designed to accommodate his wheel chair-bound life style.

The Visitors' Center has a bookstore, a cafe and provides a shuttle bus to The Eleanor Roosevelt National Historic Site (See below). Guided tours of the historic sites and education programs are also

197

available. Address: 4079 Albany Post Rd., Hyde Park, NY 12538. Phone and website: 800-FDR-VISIT (800-337-8474); www.nps.gov/hofr

FRANKLIN D. ROOSEVELT LIBRARY AND MUSEUM: This facility is adjacent to the Home of Franklin D. Roosevelt National Historic Site and was America's first presidential library. It was built and dedicated in 1941 while Franklin was still alive. The land was donated by the President and the library contains thousands of volumes of manuscripts pertaining to Roosevelt's four terms as President. The Museum displays personal and public artifacts of the President and his family and there is a research room and a very large archives collection. On display are numerous photographs, official documents, personal letters, works of art, gifts from heads of state and family memorabilia.

   Other exhibits trace the lifetime careers of both Franklin and Eleanor. The Museum offers an educational program, participates in public events and has a fascinating gift shop. Don't pass it up. Address (same as the FDR National Historic Site): 4079 Albany Post Rd., Hyde Park, NY 12538. Phone (same of the FDR National Historic Site): 800-FDR VISIT (800-337-8474). Website: www.fdrlibrary.marist.edu

ELEANOR ROOSEVELT NATIONAL HISTORIC SITE: This site is located on SR-9G a few miles from the Franklin D. Roosevelt National Historic Site. It consists of a not-so-modest cottage called Val-Kill which was Eleanor's retreat and hide-away from her hectic life as First Lady. The main building had been a furniture factory which closed in 1936. Eleanor and Franklin acquired the property and she converted the facilities into her retreat, office, and eventually, her home after Franklin died in 1945. Eleanor lived here until her death in 1962. Two lady friends, Nancy Cook and Marion Dickerman, also lived here with Eleanor. The cottage is preserved much as it was during the years Eleanor was a widow. Tours are available and there is a shuttle bus to and from the other Roosevelt historic sites. Address: 4097 Albany Post Rd., Hyde Park, NY 12538. Phone: 800-337-8484 (same as Franklin D. Roosevelt National Historic Site and Franklin D. Roosevelt Presidential Library and Museum). Website: www.nps.gov/elro.

KINGSTON is a county seat in the Hudson Valley about midway between New York City and Albany. It is just east of I-587 and on US-9W and SR-28. Kingston has three World War II memorials and all honor local citizens who served and/or died during WW II.

WORLD WAR II EAGLE MONUMENT: Location: Cornell Park and Wurts St.

WORLD WAR II GLOBE MEMORIAL: Location: Clifton and Highland Avenues

WORLD WAR II, WARD 4 MEMORIAL: Location: Delaware and Hasbrouck Avenues

The World War II Globe Memorial in Kingston, NY

NEW YORK CITY METROPOLITAN AREA: To many Europeans, the name "New York" was synonymous with "America." It was well known in Europe as America's largest city, largest seaport, home of the Statue of Liberty and the place where their countrymen went when they immigrated to America.

   During the war, there were numerous industrial plants in the area producing a very wide variety of items of war. There were also many military bases and military support facilities, and nearly every kind of war-related activity that went on in the rest of the country went on in New York.

New York City's harbor was a beehive of activity from the very beginning of the war in Europe when British and French merchant ships came to pick up war materials. Their warships also came to NYC for supplies and repairs.

Later, US and other Allied merchant ships flocked to New York to pick up Lend Lease goods and then returned with raw materials, wounded veterans and POWs. New York Bay became the primary gathering point on the East Coast for large trans-Atlantic convoys.

AMERICAN MERCHANT MARINE MUSEUM: This fine museum is on the grounds of the US Merchant Marine Academy located on the north shore of Long Island at Kings Point. Its mission is to inform visitors about the American Merchant Marine Service and also to tell the history of the Service and the history of the Academy. On display are ship models, nautical artifacts, paintings, uniforms, photos, trophies and much more. There are ample displays covering the WW II era.

Tours of the Academy can be arranged from the Museum and there is a very interesting gift shop.

Address: 300 Steamboat Rd., Kings Point, NY 11024. Phone and website: 516-726-6047; www.usmma.edu

BATTERY PARK: This magnificent 25-acre public park is at the southern end of Manhattan Island and has a magnificent view of the Statue of Liberty, New York Harbor, elegant gardens, pleasant walkways and several memorials, three of which are related to WW II.

American Merchant Marines Memorial: This thought-provoking memorial is on the west side of Battery Park and depicts two WW II merchant mariners stranded on a partially sunken piece of wreckage from their recently torpedoed merchant ship. This scene was taken from an actual photograph taken by the German submarine crew that sank their ship. The submarine did not rescue the two seamen and they eventually disappeared into the sea. A plaque on the Memorial reads "DEDICATED TO ALL MERCHANT MARINERS WHO HAVE SERVED AMERICA FROM THE REVOLUTIONARY WAR THROUGH THE PRESENT DAY."

The American Merchant Mariner Memorial at Battery Park in New York City

The East Coast Memorial is dedicated to the 4,609 men of the US armed Forces who lost their lives in US Atlantic waters during WW II. The memorial consists of a short staircase leading into a large open court which contains in its center a monument depicting a spread eagle laying a wreath upon the waters. On either side of the court are a total of eight stelae recording the names of those lost.

This monument is the centerpiece of the East Coast Memorial in Battery Park in New York City.

World War II Coast Guard Memorial: The inscription on this memorial reads "IN MEMORY OF THE MEN AND WOMEN OF THE UNITED STATES COAST GUARD WHO SERVED THEIR COUNTRY IN WORLD WAR II A.D. 1941-1945" The eight ft. bronze sculpture depicts two Coastguardsmen supporting a wounded comrade. The sculpture was created by Norman M. Thomas who was himself, a Coastguardsman during WWII.

BROOKLYN WORLD WAR II MEMORIAL: As everyone knows, Brooklyn is Brooklyn and not New York City. It is appropriate, then, that Brooklyn have its own WW II Memorial. Inscribed on this handsome stone memorial is the inscription "THIS MEMORIAL IS DEDICATED TO THE HEROIC MEN AND WOMEN OF THE BOROUGH BROOKLYN WHO FOUGHT FOR LIBERTY IN THE SECOND WORLD WAR 1941-1945 AND ESPECIALLY TO THOSE WHO SUFFERED AND DIED. MAY THEIR SACRAFICE INSPIRE FUTURE GENERATIONS AND LEAD TO UNIVERSAL PEACE."

The WW II Coast Guard Memorial in Battery Park New York City

Location: Brooklyn's Central Park

HARBOR DEFENSE MUSEUM OF NEW YORK CITY: This museum is in one of the original caponiers (1825-31) of Fort Hamilton which is one of the earliest coastal defense forts in the New York City area. The Museum chronicles the military history of the NYC area from the 17th Century to the present. There is special emphasis on coastal defenses with displays showing coast artillery, machine guns, mines, small arms, uniforms, maps, photographs, drawings and other military artifacts. WW II displays and artifacts can also be seen and tours of the Museum are available. Address: 230 Sheridan Loop, Fort Hamilton Military Community, Brooklyn, NY 11252-5701. Phone and website: 718-630-4349/4306 www.harbordefensemsueum.com

The Brooklyn World War II Memorial in the Borough of Brooklyn, New York City, NY

The World War II aircraft carrier, Interpid, in New York City

INTREPID SEA, AIR AND SPACE MUSEUM is a magnificent naval display located on the west side on Manhattan at Pier 86, 46th St. and 12th Av. The Museum has two warships, the WW II-and-postwar-era aircraft carrier USS *Intrepid*, and the postwar submarine *USS Growler*. Both ships are open to the public.

The *USS Intrepid* was built in 1943, saw service during the latter part of WW II and serviced the US Navy after the war for a total of 39 years. There are displays on the flight deck of the *USS Intrepid* and a collection of aircraft and missiles mostly from the post war era. The hangar deck is a large museum containing several Halls, each dedicated to a specific theme. The Intrepid Hall focuses on the aircraft carrier's activities during WW II when she saw action in the Pacific. Also there are many displays on the ship's WW II history and a video presentation entitled "Kamikaze Experience" which describes the day the carrier was hit by two Japanese suicide planes - the Kamikazes. Tours of the ship are available and the gift shop is a one-of-kind. Check it out. Address: Pier 86, West 46th St. New York, NY 10036. Museum phone: 877-957-7447 or 212-245-0072. Gift shop phone: 646-442-1693. Museum website: www.intrepidmuseum.org

NEW ROCHELLE WORLD WAR II MEMORIAL: New Rochelle is on the northern shore of Long Island Sound 15 miles NE of downtown Manhattan. The city has its own WW II memorial which consists of three stone monuments with plaques. On the plaques are the names of the citizens of New Rochelle who served in WW II. Location: On the lawn at City Hall

FRANKLIN D. ROOSEVELT FOUR FREEDOMS PARK: This is a new state park on the southern end of Roosevelt Island which lies in the East River and is accessible via the Queensboro Bridge. In Roosevelt's day, it was known as Welfare Island. The Park is triangular with riverfront walkways on both site, a large tree-lined grassy lawn in the center and a granite pier-like structure at its southern

point known as the "Room." The Room has three walls with its southern end open and leading to the sea that Roosevelt so loved. On the walls of the Room are inscribed passages from Roosevelt's famous 1941 speech to the US Congress when he defined the war aims of the Allied nations as the "Four Freedoms;" Freedom of Speech, Freedom of worship, Freedom from Fear and Freedom of Want. There is also a bust of President Roosevelt in the Park. Location: At the southern end of Roosevelt Island in the East River

Franklin D. Roosevelt Four Freedoms Park on Roosevelt Island in New York City

THE UNITED NATIONS HEADQUARTERS: The phrase "United Nations" was used throughout WW II and referred to the Allied nations and their military alliance rather than to the structured international organization that exists today. In those days, the League of Nations, an international organization, which had been established after WW I, still existed but was discredited and in shambles. It was foreseen by many that a new, and hopefully more successful, international organization could be created to replace it. Since the concept was promoted by the governments of most of the Allied nations, it was only natural that the name, "United Nations," should carry over to the new organization. The framework and structure of the "United Nations Organization" (UNO) was established during the war by a series of international conferences and summit meetings. In Oct. 1945, the UNO was officially born when the required number of member governments ratified its charter. On Dec. 10, 1945, the US Congress unanimously invited the UNO to establish its permanent home in the US and on Feb. 14, 1946 the UNO General Assembly, then meeting in London, accepted. A search for sites in the US then began. The site that was eventually accepted was an 18-acre area of land covering six square blocks on the east side of Manhattan between 42nd St., 48th St. and along the western shore of the East River. This area was occupied, at the time, by many old low-rise structures of varying degrees of value and importance. Millionaire John D. Rockefeller, Jr. gave the UNO $8.5 million to purchase the land and existing buildings. The land was purchased and cleared and in 1949 construction of the new UN buildings begun. Today, the UNO complex consists

The United Nations Headquarters in New York City

of several major buildings, the General Assembly Building, the Secretariat Building, the Library Building and the Conference Building. And, almost every nation on earth is a member of the UN and their facilities are open to the public.

There are historic exhibits in the General Assembly visitors' lobby, an extensive library, an archives collection, food services, a book store and a gift shop. Conducted tours of the UN buildings are available. Address: United Nations Organization, New York City NY 10017. Phone: General information 212-963-8687, Book Shop 800-553-3210, Gift Centre 877-286-4438. Web site: www.un.org

OSWEGO is a county seat on Lake Ontario at the mouth of the Oswego River 35 miles NW of Syracuse.

H. LEE WHITE MARINE MUSEUM: Here's something you won't see often, a WW II tug boat. This museum has two maritime harbor workhorses - a tub boat and a derrick boat. The tug boat, *LT-5,* was built in 1943, armed and saw extensive action during the Normandy invasion. In addition to pushing ships around, it shuttled men and supplies across the English Channel and, at times, fought off German aircraft. The boat is a National Historic Landmark and is the only remaining fully operational tug boat of its kind.

After the war, *LT-5* was sold to commercial interest, renamed *Nash,* and served for 30 years in the Great Lakes.

At various times of the year, rides are offered on *LT-5* and there is a small marine museum building on the site with many nautical artifacts - some of them from WW II. Address: End of West First St. Pier, Oswego, NY 13126. Phone and website: 315-341-0480; www.hleewhitemarinemuseum.com

OYSTER BAY AREA: This is a beautiful and historic area on the NE shore of Long Island. During the war, Oyster Bay was a small unincorporated community, but well-known as the home of the late President Theodore Roosevelt.

OLD ORCHARD MUSEUM: This was the home of Gen. Theodore Roosevelt, Jr. who was the assistant commander of the 1st Div. during the North African operations, and of the 4th Div. during the invasion of Normandy. Roosevelt had also been Governor-General of the Philippines. He saw considerable military action during the war but died suddenly in France on July 11, 1944 of a heart attack while on active duty.

The home was built in 1938 and contains many of the original furnishings and personal belongings of the General and his family. There are exhibits and an audiovisual program relating to the political and family life of the Roosevelt family. Address: 20 Sagamore Hill Rd., Oyster Bay, NY 11771. Phone and website: 516-922-4447; www.nps.gov/sahi

PLEASANTVILLE is a small community eight miles north of White Plains and on Saw Mill River Parkway, SR-117 and SR-141.

PLEASANTVILLE WORLD WAR II MEMORIAL: This large stone memorial is dedicated to those men of the local community who died in the war. An inscription above their names reads "TO THE GLORIOUS MEMORY OF OUR SONS WHO DIED FOR THEIR COUNTRY IN THE WORLD WAR 1941-1945. Location: In a small park on Memorial Dr./Grant St. between Bedford Rd. and Rebecca Ln.

PORT JARVIS is a small community on the NY/NJ state line on I-84, US-209, SR-97 and the Delaware River.

PORT JARVIS WW II MEMORIAL: This memorial consists of a large stone monument with a plaque and a flag pole above. It is dedicated to those of the local area who made the supreme sacrifice during WW II. Location: Pike St., Port Jarvis, NY12771

The WW II Memorial in Port Jarvis, NY

SARATOGA SPRINGS is a well-known resort area 40 miles north of Albany on I-87.

NEW YORK STATE MILITARY MUSEUM near downtown Saratoga Springs, preserves, interprets and disseminates the military history of the state of New York. The Museum has over 10,000 artifacts dating from the American Revolution to the present which include uniforms, weapons, artillery pieces and art. WW II is well-represented and the Museum highlights the 27th Army Division of both WW I and WW II and its well-known regiments, the 7th (Silk Stocking) Regiment, the 69th (Fighting Irish) Regiment and the 71st and 369th (Harlem Hell Fighters).

   There is a large collection of battle flags, a library, an archives collection, a research center and an extensive collection of oral histories of WW II. Address: 61 Lake Av., Saratoga Springs, 12866. Phone and website: 518-581-5100; http://.dmna.state.ny.us/historic/about.htm

STONY POINT is a small community south of Harriman State Park on the west bank of the Hudson River, US-9W and SR-210.

WORLD WAR II CARGO AND PASSENGER SHIPS MEMORIAL: When you arrive at this site, look out over the Hudson River and visualize 189 mothballed WW II ships anchored there. That's what this memorial commemorates. The ships were all veterans of WW II and were moored in this area from 1946 to 1971. Most of them were cargo and troop ships. During the years after WW II, they were slowly sold off or scrapped out. Location: Along US-9W in Stony Point

The WW II Cargo and Passenger Ships Memorial, Stoney Point, NY

VAILS GATE is a small community seven miles NE of West Point on I-87, SR-32, SR-94 and SR-300.

NATIONAL PURPLE HEART HALL OF HONOR: This attractive museum commemorated the extraordinary sacrifices of America's servicemen and servicewomen who were killed or wounded in combat. The mission of the Hall of Honor is to collect and preserve the stories of Purple Hear recipients from all branches of service and across the generations. Many WW II Purple Heart recipients are represented in the Hall of Honor. Address: 374 Tampa Hill Rd, Vails Gate, NY 12584. Phone and website: 845-561-1765 and 877-284-6667; www.thepurpleheart.com

The National Purple Heart Hall of Honor in Vails Gate, NY

WAPPINGER is a small community in the Hudson River Valley NE of and adjacent to Wappingers Falls on county Rd. 104.

The Wappinger War Memorial in Wappinger, NY

WAPPINGER WAR MEMORIAL: Look for the flag pole in Brexel Schlathaus Park. That's Wappinger's WW II memorial. It consists of a rectangular base with a large memorial stone in the center beneath the flag pole. Inscribed on the memorial stone is a passage called "The Cost of Freedom" which lists the American casualties of WW II: 292,131 killed in combat; 115,185 died in non-battle incidents; 670,846 wounded in combat; 78,987 missing in action. Location: Brexel Schlathaus Park on the corner of Myers Corners Rd. and All Angels Hill Rd

WATERTOWN is a county seat in NW New York south of the Thousand Islands area on I-81. To the NE of the city is the huge Fort Drum Military Reservation which, during WW II, was known as Camp Pine. The famous 10th Mountain Division trained here as did other Army units.

FORT DRUM MUSEUM: This inviting museum is on the grounds of Fort Drum Military Reservation with a mission to collect and preserve the material history of 10th Mountain Division and of Fort Drum from their inception to the present.
The 10th Mountain Division was formed during WW I but saw little action in that war. During WW II, however, it was reconstituted and served with great distinction in Italy.

The Museum is located in Fort Drum's Heritage Center building and has many artifacts and memorabilia on display. There is also an interesting gift shop. Address: Building 10502 South Riva Ridge Loop, Fort Drum, NY 13602. Directions: From I-84, take exit 48 and follow the signs to Fort Drum. Phone and website: 315-774-0391; http://www.drum.army.mil/AboutFortDrum/

The Fort Drum Museum in Watertown, NY

WEST POINT AREA: West Point is 44 miles north of NYC on the west bank of the Hudson River. It is famous throughout the world as the home of the United States Army's Military Academy.

US MILITARY ACADEMY MUSEUM: This excellent museum is on the grounds of the Academy and traces the history of the Academy and the US Army. It has one of the largest collections of military artifacts in the Western Hemisphere.

Of interest to WW II buffs are displays on the D-Day invasion of Europe, the Manhattan (atomic bomb) Project, Dwight D. Eisenhower, Omar Bradley and the original documents from the surrender of Nazi Germany in May 1945. There are also displays of military art and dioramas depicting famous battles and Army heroes. There is a fine gift shop with many unique and interesting items. Address: 2110 New South Rd., West Point, NY 10996. Phone and website: 845-938-3590; www.usma.edu/museum/

NORTH CAROLINA

North Carolina was, believe it or not, one of the major battlegrounds of WW II. The battlefield was the state's coastal waters. More Allied ships and more Axis submarines were sunk there than anywhere else in the Western Hemisphere. The battle reached its height during the first six months of 1942, and then continued intermittently thereafter until V-E Day in May 1945. Thousands of people lost their lives off the North Carolina coast and substantial damage was done to the merchant fleets of United States and her Allies.

The people of North Carolina, who were only minimally affected by the carnage taking place in their coastal waters, contributed in many ways to the war effort. First and foremost, their state was a large training ground for over two million GIs, Airmen, Sailors and Marines.

The construction of new military camps and the expansion of existing ones brought a much needed upsurge to the state's economy which had suffered badly during the Depression. North Carolina was also host to many enemy troops housed in the state's 17 main POW camps.

DIVEABLE WW II SHIP WRECKS IN NORTH CAROLINA COASTAL WATERS: Over 80 Allied ships were sunk in North Carolina's shallow coastal water during WW II. Many are accessible to sports divers and local inquiries should be made as to their locations and accessibility. Four German submarines, *U-85, U-352, U-576* and *U-701,* were sunk in these waters. The wreck of *U-576* has never been found but the other three have been located and are diveable.

U-85 **DIVE SITE:** On the early morning hours of April 14, 1942, the U-boat *U-85* was operating off Cape Hatteras within view of the Bodie Island Lighthouse when it was discovered by the US destroyer *Roper.* The *Roper* attacked and sank the German submarine with depth charges a few miles off Oregon Inlet. The wreck lies in less than 100 ft. of water. The hatch of the submarine has been recovered and is on display at the Cape Hatteras Lighthouse visitors center.

An Enigma Machine, Germany's top-secret encoding devise at the time, was removed and put on display at the Graveyard of the Atlantic Museum in Hatteras.

There were no survivors of the sinking but 29 bodies floating in life jackets were recovered. Some of the bodies were wearing civilian clothes and carrying wallets with US currency and US identification cards. Surely, they were spies that *U-85* intended to land somewhere on US soil. All 29 bodies were buried in the Hampton National Cemetery.

U-352 **DIVE SITE:** On May 9, 1942, this submarine was attacked and severely damaged by the Coast Guard cutter *Icaras.* The submarine surfaced and was scuttled by its crew. Twenty-three German seamen survived the sinking. The *U-352 rests* in 115 ft. of water 26 miles south of Morehead City and is frequently visited by sports divers.

U-701 **DIVE SITE:** On July 7, 1942, a US Marine Corps A-29 patrol bomber from US Marine Corps Air Station, Cherry Point attacked and sank the German submarine *U-701* 10 miles off the coast of the community of Avon.

The submarine was operating on the surface of the water and had, days earlier, planted magnetic mines at the mouth of Chesapeake Bay. Those mines sank several Allied ships.

The A-29 dropped three depth charges, two of which fatally damaged the submarine. Seven surviving crewmen, including the submarine's captain, were rescued two days later. The wreck of U-701 lies in 110 ft. of water.

ASHEVILLE is in the center of a popular tourist area in the western part of the state. In early 1942, the town's famous resort, the Grove Park Inn, was taken over by the Government and used for a very unique purpose.

GROVE PARK INN, about two miles north of downtown Asheville, was one of four luxury hotels leased by the US Government during the first months of the war at various locations throughout the US to house Axis diplomats and their families who needed to be housed temporarily and securely while they awaited exchange for American diplomats who had been serving in Axis countries.

The Greenbrier Hotel in West Virginia and The Homestead in Virginia, the first hotels leased, were acquired by the government in Dec. 1941 and soon filled. Grove Park Inn was then leased in Apr. 1942 and housed Italian, Bulgarian and Hungarian diplomats, their families, servants, pets and personal possessions. Axis diplomats from Mexico, Cuba and El Salvador were also brought here.

On June 11, 1942, the last of the diplomats left Grove Park Inn to begin their trip home. In Oct. 1942, the Navy took over the Inn and used it as a rest and rehabilitation facility for naval personnel.

Grove Park Inn housed mostly naval officers during this time.

In the spring of 1944, Manuel L. Quezon, President of the Philippines, and his entourage resided at the hotel for about a month. During that time, the hotel was the temporary headquarters of the Philippine Government-in-exile.

In July 1944, the Inn, along with three other resort hotels in Asheville, were leased by the Army and designated as a rest and redistribution center for returning combat veterans.

Grove Park Inn served the Army until Sept. 1945. It was then renovated at government expense, a condition stipulated in the original lease, and returned to civilian use. The hotel has information on the Axis diplomats and its other uses during the war and a portrait gallery showing many of the

famous people who have stayed at the hotel over the years. WW II personalities who stayed here include Franklin and Eleanor Roosevelt and Dwight D. Eisenhower. Address: 290 Macon Ave. Asheville, NC 28804. Phone and website: 800-438-5800; www.groveparkinn.com

BELMONT is a small community in western North Carolina on US-29 and 12 miles west of downtown Charlotte.

WORLD WAR II MEMORIAL: Topping this memorial is a sculpture of a crouching GI with a hand grenade in his hand which he appears ready to throw - a scene that was repeated hundreds of thousands of times during the war. The Memorial's base is a large stone monument inscribed "ERECTED IN HONOR OF ALL WHO SERVED IN WORLD WAR II." Location: Belmont Middle School, Belmont, NC

The World War II Memorial in Belmont, NC

CHARLOTTE is a major transportation hub in the south-central part of the state and one of the state's largest cities.

CAROLINAS AVIATION MUSEUM is located at the Charlotte-Douglas International Airport and traces the history of aviation in the Carolinas to the present day.

The Museum has over 60 vintage aircraft and missiles including about half dozen WW II aircraft. Some of the aircraft are in flying condition and there is a library, gift shop, educational program and the Museum has a monthly newsletter and offers storage. Address: 4672 First Flight Dr., Charlotte, NC 28208. Phone and website: 704-359-8442; www.carolinasaviation.org

CHINA BURMA INDIA MEMORIAL: Honored by this memorial are American air crews who flew American aircraft, loaded with war supplies, from India into Burma and China over the rugged Himalaya Mountains - "The Hump." For years they have been known as the "Hump Pilots." This memorial commemorates their efforts and the importance of their mission Location: Freedom Park, 1900 East Blvd., Charlotte, NC

The China Burma India Memorial in Charlotte, NC

DUNN is 22 miles NE of Fayetteville on I-95 and SR-421

THE GENERAL WILLIAM C. LEE AIRBORNE MUSEUM: This is the former home of Gen. Lee who became known as the "Father of the Airborne Infantry." Lee was given the assignment by President Franklin Roosevelt to organize and develop the Army's first airborne (parachute) units. His efforts led to the development of the Airborne Command which carried out numerous airborne assaults and other airborne operations during WW II. The Museum highlights the life of Gen. Lee and focuses on the early development of the Army's airborne units. Museum tours are available. Address: 209 W. Divine St., Dunn, NC 28334. Phone and website: 910-892-1947; http://generalleeairbornemuseum.org

The William C. Lee Airborne Museum in Dunn, NC

FAYETTEVILLE is a county seat in the south-central part of the state on I-95, US-301, US-401, SR-24 and SR-87. Nearby is a major Army facility, Fort Bragg. When the newly-developed airborne divisions were developed during WW II, Fort Bragg became one of their major training bases.

THE AIRBORNE & SPECIAL OPERATIONS MUSEUM: This excellent five-story, 23,000 Sq. ft. museum is located in downtown Fayetteville and relates the history of American airborne and special operations activities from their inception during WW II to the present. Special attention is given to the history and operations of Fort Bragg and there are considerable displays and information relating the US Army airborne operation in WW II. The Museum has hundreds of rare and significant artifacts many of which relate to airborne operations in North Africa, the Philippines and Normandy. There is an adjoining Memorial Garden, a 48-seat theater, an educational program, an excellent gift shop and the museum is available for ceremonies and social events. Address: 100 Bragg Blvd., Fayetteville, NC 28301. Phone and website: 910-643-2766; www.asomf.org

82ⁿᵈ AIRBORNE DIVISION MUSEUM: This museum is one of two museums on the grounds of Fort Bragg and is dedicated to those members of the 82nd Airborne Div. who have given their lives for their country. The Museum details the history of the 82nd from its days as an infantry division in WW I, an airborne division in WW II and to the present day. Displays include equipment used by parachute and glider troops, US and foreign uniforms, small arms, machine guns, artillery pieces, ordnance, field equipment and captured trophies of war. There is also an interesting gift shop with items you won't find elsewhere. Address: Bldg. C-6841, Fort Bragg, NC 28310. Museum phone and website: 910-432-3443/5307; http://82ndairbornedivisionmuseum.com; gift shop phone 910-436-1735

JOHN F. KENNEDY SPECIAL WARFARE MUSEUM: This is a second museum on the grounds of Fort Bragg and focuses on the history of the special forces of the US Army from the American Revolution to the present. Heavy concentration is on the Viet Nam era but WW II-related exhibits are significant and tell the story of the "Rangers," the OSS, "Merrill's Marauders" and other special units.

Among the very unique weapons in the Museum's collection is a glove pistol, an incendiary device designed to be dropped into a gas tank, an inexpensively-made gun called the "Woolworth Gun" designed for very close combat, one-shot guns designed to be concealed in the palm of the hand, sleeve daggers, silencers, mini-cameras and a leaflet bomb. There are also many captured enemy items on display and there is a very interesting gift shop with some varies unique items for sale. Address: Building D-2502, Ardennes and Marion Sts. Fort Bragg, NC 28307. Phone and website: 910-432-4272; http://www.soc.mil/swcs/museum/museum.html

JACKSONVILLE is a county seat in the SE part of the state 15 miles inland from the mouth of the New River and on US-17, US-258 and SR-24. South of the city is Camp Lejeune, one of the US Marine Corps' largest bases.

MUSEUM OF THE MARINE: This excellent new 40,000 Sq. Ft. museum is located in Jacksonville and its mission is to tell the story of those unique contributions made by Marines throughout the Carolinas. The Museum focuses on nearby Camp Lejuene which was built on the eve of WW II and, in the process, turned Jacksonville into a sudden boom town, and thereafter, home of one of the nation's most important military bases.

In the early 1940s, the Jacksonville site was selected for this major facility because the area had excellent beaches where Marines could be trained in the techniques of amphibious landings.

The exhibits in the Museum start with WW II and carry through to the present day. Emphasis on the Marine family is one of the major exhibits in the Museum and there is a Hall of Honor to recognize and reflect upon individual achievements and sacrifices of the Carolina Marines. The Museum has a library, educational program, offers tours and has an excellent Museum Store - check it out. Address: SR-24, Lejeune Memorial Gardens, Camp Roberts, Jacksonville, NC 28541. Phone and website: 910-937-0033; www.museumofthemarine.org

The Museum of the Marine in Jacksonville, NC

MANTEO is a very unusual place and had a very unusual experience during WW II. It is a county seat at the northern end of the North Carolina's Outer Banks on historic Roanoke Island and US-64.

Because of the intensive naval conflict that was under way off the North Carolina coast during the war, the American military leaders needed all of the help they could get in patrolling those dangerous off-shore water. One of the organizations they turned to was the Civil Air Patrol (CAP), a civilian organization comprised of pilots - both men and women. The CAP was formed in the 1930s to offer their services to the nation using their own personal aircraft and their aviation skills. Heretofore, the CAP has served the government mostly by patrolling American borders. Now, the government needed them to hunt for German submarines and stricken ships. A large number of CAP pilots and

planes were assembled at Manteo's local airport, Dare County Regional Airport, to offer their services. In the jargon of the day, their unit was known as Civil Air Patrol Coastal Patrol, Base 16.

CIVIL AIR PATROL MEMORIAL: This museum serves to honor those men and women who served in the local CAP. A beautiful memorial has been erected at Dare Airport which lists the names of those civilians who served. Included in the listing are the names of two individuals who gave their lives in the line of duty. Location: Dare County Regional Airport

The Civil Air Patrol Memorial at Mateo's Dare County Regional Airport

DARE COUNTY REGIONAL AIRPORT MUSEUM: At the west end of Mateo's terminal building is a small museum that records the history of the airport and has a considerable amount of information on the CAP when it operated here during the war. There are uniforms, model airplanes, photos and other artifacts. Address: 410 Airport Rd., Dare County Regional Airport, Mateo, NC. Website: www.museums.aero/museum/dare-county-regional-airport-museum

SHELBY is a county seat in western North Carolina on US-74, SR-18 and SR-150.

CLEVELAND COUNTY WORLD WAR II MEMORIAL: Those individuals from Cleveland County who served and died in WW II are honored and named on this memorial. There are 192 names. Location: Cleveland County Courthouse, Warren St., Shelby, NC

WILMINGTON, on the coast in south-coastal North Carolina, is a county seat with strong ties to the sea. It is at the end of I-40 and on I-140, US-17, US-74, US-76 and US-421.

***USS NORTH CAOLINA* BATTLESHIP MEMORIAL.** Here is one of the great warships of WW II. She is on display and at anchor on the west side of the Cape Fear River across from the Wilmington water front.

The Cleveland County World War II Memorial in Shelby, NC

This ship saw considerable action in the Pacific and fought in many of the critical battles there. Today, she is a memorial dedicated to the men and women who served aboard her and open to the public - all nine decks.

The Visitors' Center has detailed information about the ship, her history and many displays related to the ship. The ship is available for public and social events, tours are available, there is a snack bar, a picnic area, and educational program, a newsletter and a gift shop that you must not miss. Address: #1 Battleship Rd., Wilmington, NC 28401. Phone and website: 910-251-5797; www.battleshipnc.com

The business end of the battleship USS North Carolina, Wilmington, NC

NORTH DAKOTA

North Dakota was one of America's bread-basket states during WW II and produced large quantities of much-needed food for the war effort. Eighty percent of the state's economy was based on agriculture. During WW II, North Dakota's farmers broke one agricultural record after the other in producing food. The state produced wheat, oaks, corn, barley, rye, potatoes, sugar beets, flax, cattle, hogs, sheep and poultry.

North Dakota ranked last among the 48 states in manufacturing and the manufacturing that existed exist was devoted primarily to the processing of the state's agricultural products.

In 1941, the 3000-acre International Peace Park was opened on the North Dakota/Canadian border. At that time, the US was at peace, but Canada was at war.

During the war, the US Army and US Army Air Forces utilized North Dakota's flat land, clear skies and open spaces for several military needs.

FARGO is one of North Dakota's larger cities on the eastern border of the state on I-29 and I-94.

BONANZAVILLE USA, at the western edge of West Fargo, is a large reconstructed pioneer village and regional museum just off I-94. The Eagles Air Museum, one of the several parts of the facility, has an interesting collection of aircraft which include some WW II models.

Elsewhere in the facility is a WW II 60" search light, uniforms, ship models and a collection of captured Japanese weapons and artifacts.

In the antique auto collection is a 1936 Rolls-Royce which belonged to King George VI of England, Britain's wartime King. Address: 1351 West Main Av. West Fargo, ND 58078. Phone and website: 701-282-2822 and 800-700-5317; www.bonanzaville.org

FARGO AIR MUSEUM: This is an interesting air museum in three large hangars on the north side of Fargo at Hector International Airport with about 25 vintage aircraft including several WW II models. There are also WW II artifacts, posters, uniforms and memorabilia.

The Museum has a theater, a restoration facility, interactive children's' exhibits, a newsletter, offers tours, hosts regional events and has a well-stocked gift shop. Address: 1609 19th Av. North, Fargo, ND 58102. Phone and website: 701-293-8043; www.fargoairmuseum.org

The Fargo Air Museum in Fargo, ND

USS-ROBALO **SUBMARINE MEMORIAL:** After WW II, the US Submarine Veterans of WW II Organization assigned one each of the 52 submarines lost during the war to each state with the hopes that those states would construct a memorial to their assigned submarine. North Dakota complied and constructed this permanent tribute to their assigned submarine, the *Robalo.* She was lost on July 26, 1944 when she strayed into an enemy mine field off Palawan Island in the Philippeans.

On the front of the Memorial is a brief history of the submarine and inscribed on the back side of the Memorial are the names of the seamen who were lost. Nearby is a monument listing the names of the citizens of North Dakota who served aboard US submarines during the war. Location: Lindenwood Park on Roger Maris Dr., Fargo, ND

The USS Robalo Memorial in Fargo, ND

MINOT is a county seat in the NW part of the state on US-2, US-52 and US-83.

212

DAKOTA TERRITORY AIR MUSEUM: This excellent 10,000 Sq. ft. museum is located at the Minot International Airport and has over 30 vintage aircraft including several WW II era planes.

   On display are photographs, aviation literature, periodicals, aircraft-related equipment, memorabilia and flight gear. The Museum has a WW II wing, its own restoration facility, an educational program and, through the year, is host to air shows and other events. Don't pass up the gift shop. Address: 100 34th St. NE, Minot, ND 58702. Phone and website: 701-852-8500; www.dakotaterritoryairmuseum.com

The Dakota Territory Air Museum in Minot, ND

OHIO

   During World War II, Ohio was one of our great manufacturing states located in the American industrial heartland. The state had several large industrial areas centered around large cities in the northern, central and western parts of the state. Ohio eventually became fourth in the nation in the value of wartime industrial contracts. The state had many military installations, old and new, and six main POW camps with many branch camps.

BATAVIA is a county seat 30 miles east of Cincinnati on SR-32 and just off US-50.

TRI-STATE WARBIRD MUSEUM: This is a fine 20,000 Sq. ft. air museum on the grounds of the Clermont County Airport. The Museum specializes in the collection, restoration and display of WW II aircraft. Included in the collection is a flyable P-51D Mustang and a flyable B-25 Mitchell bomber. The Museum has WW II-related artifacts and memorabilia, its own professional restoration shop, a library, and a classroom and lecture facility. Address: 40121 Borman Dr., Batavia, OH 45103. Phone and website: 513-735-4500 and 513-646-9816; www.tri-statewarbirdmuseum.org

Map to the Tri-State Warbird Museum

CANTON is one of Ohio's larger cities and is a county seat 20 miles south of Akron on I-77, US-30 and US-62.

MAPS (Military Air Preservation Service) AIR MUSEUM is located at the Akron-Canton Airport on I-77 which is midway between the two cities. There are about 30 aircraft in the Museum's collection and WW II-era planes are well represented. Some of their aircraft are flyable and many of the planes are indoors. The Museum does aircraft restoration, has a number of interesting aviation artifacts, a newsletter, a fine gift shop and holds several social events throughout the year. Address: 2260 International Parkway, North Canton, OH 44720. Phone and website: 330-896-6332; www.mapsairmuseum.org

Bedford's World War II Memorial, Bedford, OH

CLEVELAND METROPOLITAN AREA: This large metropolitan area is in northern Ohio on the southern shore of Lake Erie. It is, and was during WW II, the state's most populated metropolitan area and its largest industrial center.

BEDFORD'S WORLD WAR II MEMORIAL: Bedford is a southern suburb of Cleveland on SR-14 and just off I-271. This attractive memorial consists of a large white marble stone that lists the names of the 40 local residents who gave their lives in WW II. Location: Bedford Commons which is the Bedford town square

USS COD (SS-224) **SUBMARINE MEMORIAL**: Here is a WW II submarine which is now a National Historic Site. It has been preserved in its WW II condition and is on display on Cleveland's lake front. The *Cod* is located at the western edge of Lakefront Airport and about one block east of the Rock & Roll Hall of Fame. The vessel is a veteran of seven wartime patrols during which she sank 12 Japanese ships.

   The vessel is unaltered since its days of service meaning that visitors must enter the vessel through its hatches by climbing down vertical ladders just as its crew did.

   During the Cold War, the *Cod* performed reconnaissance missions and was decommissioned in 1971.

   The vessel is a popular destination for school tours and has many visitors throughout the year.

   The *Cod* carried a wartime cameraman aboard and the films he shot are shown to visitors.

   There are several exhibits on shore including a Mark 14 WW II torpedo which was the standard weapon of American submarines during the war. Address: 1089 E. 9th St., Cleveland, OH 44114. Phone and website: 216-566-8770; www.usscod.org

COLUMBUS is the capitol of Ohio and located near its geographic center. During the war, there were several major military installations` in the area.

MOTTS MILITARY MUSEUM is a privately-owned military museum in Groveport, a SE suburb of Columbus, on SR-665. The Museum has a wide variety of military artifacts from America's various wars with a large collection of WW II artifacts. There are aircraft, vehicles, a rare Higgins Boat, weapons, uniforms, documents, personal stories, exhibits of well-known WW II personalities and more. Address: 5075 S. Hamilton Rd., Groveport, OH 43125. Phone and website: 614-836-1500; www.mottsmilitarymuseum.org

DAYTON is in the SW part of the state and is the center of another of Ohio's several major industrialized areas. Dayton was the home of the Wright Brothers and thanks to them and their early work with aircraft Dayton become the cradle of aviation. When WW II started, Dayton was a city very much involved with the airplane and it remains so today.

NATIONAL MUSEUM OF THE UNITED STATES AIR FORCE: This is a must-see museum. It is on the grounds of Wright-Patterson Air Force Base, is the oldest and largest air museum in the world. Here, under the guidance of the US Air Force, and in several large hangars, is accumulated one of the world's largest collection of military aircraft. Most of the aircraft are indoors.

On display are some 400 aircraft and the Museum owns many more aircraft which are in storage or on loan to other museums. The Museum also has some 10,000 artifacts and works of art on display and is home to the National Aviation Hall of Fame.

Many of the aircraft on display are one-of-kind models and others are very famous. The Museum endeavors to tell the story of aviation from its inception with the Wright Brothers of Dayton, Ohio to the present. Over 1.5 million visitors pass through the Museum each year. World War II models predominate in the collection and almost every well-known aircraft is represented. Among the most outstanding aircraft in the collection is the B-29 bomber, "Bock's Car," which delivered the second atomic bomb to Nagasaki, Japan. A replica of the Nagasaki bomb, "Fat Man," is on display as well as a replica of the Hiroshima bomb, "Little Boy."

The huge National Museum of the US Air force in Dayton, OH

Other WW II aircraft of importance at the Museum include a Messerschmitt Me-262A, the world's first operational jet fighter; a Bell P-59B Air comet, America's first jet fighter; various German and Japanese aircraft; President Roosevelt's personal plane, a C-54 named "the Sacred Cow;" President Eisenhower's personal plane and aircraft of several other post-war presidents.

The Museum has a research facility that maintains original prints, manuals and other technical data on historic aircraft. There is also a restoration facility, an IMAX theater, a cafe, and a large and very interesting gift shop.

On the grounds outside the Museum is a memorial park with memorials, statuary and plaques commemorating various military air units.

Nearby is a British-made Nissen Hut typical of the thousands of such huts that housed AAF personnel in Britain during WW II. The Nissen Hut also served as a model for the American-made Quonset Huts. And the "Missile Mall," in front of the Museum, displays several postwar rockets and missiles. Address: 1100 Spaatz St., Wright-Patterson Air Force Base, OH 45433. Phone and website: 937-255-3286; www.nationalairmuseum.af.mil

YOU AIN'T SEEN NOTHIN' YET UNTIL YOU'VE SEEN THIS MUSEUM!
(And it's free)

DELAWARE is a county seat 22 miles north of Columbus on US-23, US-42 and SR-37.

DELAWARE COUNTY WORLD WAR II MEMORIAL: This attractive stone memorial honors those men and women from Delaware County who gave their lives during WW II. Their names are inscribed on the Memorial. Location: Delaware County Courthouse lawn

LORAIN is a small lakefront community 30 miles west of downtown Cleveland on US-6 and SR-57 .

LORAIN WORLD WAR II MEMORIAL: Throughout the war, the Allied nations used the "V For Victory" phrase and symbol. Who can forget Winston Churchill giving his famous V For Victory sign. The citizens of Lorain have immortalized the symbol in their WW II Memorial. One arm of the V is inscribed with painted stars and stripes. Location: In Victory Park, 5th St. and W. Erie Av.

MARION is a county seat in west central Ohio on US-23, SR-4, SR-95 and SR-309.

MARION WORLD WAR II MEMORIAL: This is one of the larger WW II memorials in the nation. It consists of a series of circular black granite walls with a central column. Inscribed on the walls are the names of the citizens of Marion who served in WW II; Location: Marion Cemetery, 620 Delaware Av

The Delaware County World War II Memorial in Delaware, OH

MOHICAN MEMORIAL STATE FOREST: This is a state park in north central Ohio just south of Loudonville on SR-3.

OHIO MEMORIAL SHRINE TO THE WORLD WAR II DEAD: This impressive limestone building is located in a state park. Inside the Shrine is a large ledger containing the name of every son and daughter of Ohio who gave their lives in WW II.

The World War II Memorial in Marion, OH

ZANESVILLE is a county seat 58 miles east of downtown Columbus and on I-70, US-53 and SR-60

The Ohio Memorial Shrine to the World War II Dead in Mohican Memorial State Forest

216

VICTORY IN EUROPE MEMORIAL: This thought-provoking memorial consists of three sculptures of WW II GIs as they would have appeared in action in Europe during the war. They help each other, carry rifles, back packs and side arms.

  The Memorial was erected on May 8, 1995, the fiftieth anniversary of V-E Day, the Allied victory in Europe. A nearby plaque read "VICTORY IN EUROPE 1945-1995."

  A nearby commemorative memorial honors all World War II veterans from Muskingum County."
Location: In a small park, at 401 Main St., Zanesville, OH

The GI statues at the Victory In Europe Memorial in Zanesville, OH

OKLAHOMA

  Oklahoma was one of several states in the Union that was in desperate economic straits before the war, but emerged from the war in relatively healthy condition. During the 1930s, the production of, and prices of, the state's two main commodities, oil and food had been greatly depressed. The price of oil was depressed by an over-supply and food prices were depressed due to the general effects of the Great Depression, plus a series of disastrous droughts that turned western Oklahoma into a part of the famous "Dust Bowl."

  The state had some manufacturing, but it was mostly related to the oil and food industries such as refining, milling, meat packing and dairy products.

  In 1939, the beginning of the war in Europe helped stimulate a world-wide need for oil and food which, in turn, helped Oklahoma to some degree. With America's entry into the war, demands for oil and food surged and the state's oil interests and farmers responded eagerly.

The Federal Government added considerably to Oklahoma's new prosperity by building several large manufacturing plants and many military facilities in the state.

When peace came, Oklahoma had a robust and growing economy. The demands for oil and food continued in the postwar years and manufacturing became a permanent factor in the state's economy.

<u>ALVA</u> is a county seat in the north-central part of the state on US-64 and US-281.

ALVA POW CAMP was a main POW camp located on the outskirts of town. This was a main POW camp holding about 4500 POWs. During the summer of 1943, after the Americans realized that they had to separate ardent pro-Nazis and various troublemakers from more cooperative POWs in the various camps across the country, the Alva camp was selected to be one of those to receive those troublesome individuals. Once this was accomplished, the Camp was more heavily guarded than before and those POWs who were allowed to leave the camp for work were permitted to work only on jobs for the military where they could be carefully watched and wouldn't be a threat to civilians. The internal affairs of the Camp were controlled by the POWs themselves and, as might be expected, brought strict order to the Camp. As the war turned against Germany, the most fanatical of the POWs formed a suicide club based on the persistent, but erroneous, rumor that they would be sent to the Soviet Union after the war as slave laborers. Members of the club vowed that upon hearing of the collapse of Germany or the death of Adolph Hitler they would carry out a Japanese-style Banzai attack with whatever weapons they had and would attempt to kill as many Americans as possible before being killed themselves. Informants in the Camp warned the Americans of the club's existence and the club's leaders were very carefully watched, and at time, isolated. When V-E Day came nothing happened. After the war, the POWs were repatriated to Germany and the camp was closed.

The Oil Patch Warrior World war II Memorial in Ardmore, OK

<u>ARDMORE</u> is a county seat in the south-central Oklahoma near the Texas state line on I-75, US-70 and US-77.

OIL PATCH WARRIOR - WORLD WAR II MEMORIAL: This very unique WW II memorial honors the many oil field workers who produced America's oil which was of utmost importance America's war effort. It consists on a seven ft. bronze statue of a oil field worker carrying a large wrench. Location: Memorial Park, 410 W. Man St., Ardmore, OK

<u>BRISTOW</u> is a small community 38 miles SW of Tulsa on I-44 and SR-48.

VFW POST 3656: This VFW Post is located in Bristow's city park and has a number of stone memorials on it grounds commemorating various event in US military history. Three of the memorials relate to WW II; The Wake Island Memorial, The WW II Memorial and the *USS Gunboat Charleston (PG-51)* Memorial. This ship saw action during the invasion of Attu Island in Alaska. Location: City Park at the junction of County Rds. 2000 and 4300. Phone of the VFW Post: 918-367-3644

LAWTON is one of the state's larger cities on 70 miles SW of Oklahoma City on I-44 and US- 62/281. It has long been the home of one of the US Army's long-standing and very important military facilities, Fort Sill.

FORT SILL NATIONAL HISTORIC LANDMARK AND MUSEUM: This is the largest museum in the US Army. It consists of virtually the entire post and has two Army museums, the US Army Field Artillery Museum and The US Army Air Defense Artillery Museum. There are some 50 historic buildings on the Fort's

The war memorials at VFW Post 3565 in Bristow, OK

grounds, some of which date back to the days of the Fort's founding.

During WW II, the Fort had many temporary wooden buildings that continued to be used long after the war. But today, they are all gone. The buildings that are preserved did, of course, serve the US Army throughout the war.

Fort Sill was one of the US Army's primary training posts for field artillerymen and air defense artillerymen. Many of the field artillery pieces that were used here and in the nation's battles are on display at the Museums. Examples of, and information on, WW II artillery pieces, Army artillery units, their commanders and their activities are well displayed. Also on display are artillery shells, artillery support equipment, field equipment, uniforms, photos, historic documents, artifacts and memorabilia,

The Museum also has a library and the Post Trader's Store (gift shop) offers a wide variety of souvenirs to commemorate your visit. It's worth your time to check it out. Address: 372 Ganahi Rd., Fort Sill, OK 73503. Phone and website: 580-422-0201/0267/5123/0374; http://sill-www.army.mil/museum/

MOYERS is a small community eight miles north of Antlers on SR-2. Antlers is a county seat in SE Oklahoma on Indian Nation Turnpike, US-271 and SR-2.

AT6 MONUMENT: The AT6 was one of the US Army Air Forces' advanced two-seat training planes which was a mainstay in America's training program for future fighter pilots.

On February 20, 1943 a flight of 12 AT6s took off from Terrell, TX on a low level cross-county training flight to Manitoba, Canada. The planes were piloted by British cadets being trained in the USA.

As the planes flew into the Moyers area, they encountered an extremely heavy fog and the pilots became disoriented and the formation broke apart. Several of the planes turned back to Terrell and several others managed to land at an airfield in Miami, OK. Two planes, however, crashed into nearby mountains killing all four cadets.

The citizens of Moyers have commemorated the event by erecting a granite memorial in an area known as Kosoma on Big Mountain at one of the crash sites. The Memorial bears the names of the four cadets killed. Location: Ask locally for direction.

MUSKOGEE is a county seat 35 miles SE of Tulsa on The Muskogee Turnpike and US-69.

MUSKOGEE WAR MEMORIAL PARK & THE *USS BATFISH*: This park and museum complex are four miles NE of downtown Muskogee in the Port of Muskogee area on the Arkansas River. The Park is dedicated to Oklahomans of all the branches of the armed forces that have served this country in wartime.

The Park has a large museum housing military artifacts and displays from WW I to the present. On the grounds of the Museum, is the WW II submarine *Batfish* which had a distinguished career during the war and sank 14 Japanese vessels. It also served during the Korean and Viet Nam wars and eventually as a training submarine.

Also on the Museum grounds are 52 bronze plaques, one each for the 52 US submarines lost during WW II. What's more, there are large naval guns, torpedoes and military vehicles.

Inside the Museum are smaller artillery pieces, field equipment, small arms, aircraft and ship models, uniforms, documents, maps, photographs and more. Address: 3500 Batfish Rd., Muskogee, OK 74402. Phone and website: 918-682-6294; www.ussbatfish.com

The WW II submarine USS Batfish is on permanent display at Muskogee War Memorial Park.

OKLAHOMA CITY is the capitol of Oklahoma and is located near the geographic center of the state.

THE FORTY-FIFTH INFANTRY DIVISION MUSEUM: This is a fine state-operated museum in Oklahoma City dedicated to the 45th Infantry Div. which traditionally included the Oklahoma National Guard. The Museum is large, 27,000 Sq. ft., and is in a delightful 15 acre park. The Museum collects, preserves and exhibits object and equipment relevant to the history of Oklahoma's citizen soldiers. Displays range from the days of the American Revolution to the present with heavy emphasis on WW II including the Division's participation in the liberation of the Dachau Concentration Camp.

Of unique interest in the Museum is the Bill Mauldin Room which displays more than 200 original drawings by the famous WW II cartoonist. Mauldin was a member of the 45th Div. Another significant display is the Reaves Military Weapons Collection, one of the largest of its kind in the country.

There is a chapel and adjacent to the Museum is Thunderbird Military Park where vehicles, aircraft, artillery pieces and other equipment are on display. Museum tours are available and there is an excellent gift shop. Address: 2145 NE 36th St. Oklahoma, City, OK 73111. Phone and website: 405-424-5313; www.45thdivisionmuseum.com

The 45th Infantry Division Museum in Oklahoma City, OK

TUSKAHOMA is a small community in SE Oklahoma on US-271 in a 10,864 Sq. mi. area of the state known as the Choctaw Nation of Oklahoma.

WORLD WAR II MILITARY SERVICE MEMORIAL: This memorial reminds us that Native Americans (Indians) also served in the American armed forces during WW II. The Memorial consists of a long angular wall with the names of the individuals from the Choctaw Nation who served in the US armed forces during WW II. Location: On the grounds of the Choctaw Nation Capitol House in Tuskahoma, OK

The World War II Military Service Memorial in Tuskahoma, OK

OREGON

In Sept. 1939, when the war started in Europe, Oregon was remote from the war and was affected by it only in that the US military buildup had stimulated Oregon's economy and the draft had taken away some of her men for military service.

On December 7, 1941, that attitude changed overnight. Suddenly the US was at war with a well-armed and aggressive enemy that had boldly demonstrated its naval might at Hawaii, Oregon's nearest neighbor to the west. Many in Oregon believed that it was entirely possible that the naval force that had attacked Hawaii could sail on and attack the US West Coast. War jitters swept through the state and wild rumors spread (just as they had in California and Washington State) that enemy ships were lurking offshore, that there were secret Japanese-built airfields in the desert and that the local ethnic Japanese were in league with the Japanese Government acting as spies and planning sabotage and assassinations. These fears were amplified when, in mid-December, Japanese submarines appeared off the coast and attacked several American ships.

Actions were taken to strengthen Oregon's defenses and prepare her citizens for air raids and other types of attacks. Oregon's cities created civil defense organizations, practiced blackouts and prepared bomb shelters. When the order came to relocate the ethnic Japanese from the West Coast, Oregon's leaders and most of her citizens approved of it without question.

ASTORIA: This city is in the NW corner of the state at the mouth of the Columbia River. Since the Columbia River is such an important waterway, this area is one of the most militarily strategic parts of the state and has been protected by fortifications for many years on both the Oregon and Washington sides of the River. Those facilities were used during WW II.

COLUMBIA RIVER MARITIME MUSEUM is located on the south bank of the Columbia River just east of downtown Astoria. It houses the finest and most extensive maritime collection in the Northwest and preserves 200 years of river and naval history.

Exhibits related to WW II include the actual bridge of the destroyer *USS Knapp* which was launched in 1943 and served in both WW II and the Korean War. The bridge was donated to the Museum when the *Knapp* was scrapped in 1973.

The Museum's US Naval Gallery focuses on the WW II cruiser *USS Astoria*, which saw considerable action during the early days of the war but was sunk during the Battle of Savo Island, August 1942.

Other WW II displays include, a WW II torpedo, a large bronze propeller from a Landing Ship Tank (LST), twin 20 mm anti-aircraft guns, and considerable information about the US Coast Guard. The Museum also has a large research library and an inviting gift shop. Address: 1792 Marine Dr. (US-30), Astoria, OR 97103. Phone and website: 503-325-2323; www.crmm.org

FORT STEVENS MUSEUM: You would not have wanted to be at Fort Stevens during the night of June 21/22, 1942. Fort Stevens was one of the very few places in the continental US that was directly attacked during WW II by the enemy. In this case, the attacker was a Japanese submarine.

The grounds of Fort Stevens have been converted into a state park and this museum tells the history of the area with heavy emphasis on the Japanese attack.

On display are many artifacts relating to the Fort's long history and a generous number of WW II displays including fragments of the shells fired at the Fort by the Japanese submarine. The Museum offers tours of the park and the underground portions of Battery Mishler which was one of the Fort's main defense batteries during WW II. And the Museum has a very interesting gift shop.

If you are in an RV, you can camp on the very spot where the Japanese shells landed. Address: Fort Stevens State Park, Attn: Historic Area, Hammond, OR 97121. Phone and website: 503-861-1470; www.visitftstevens.com

The Shelling of Fort Stevens: At about midnight June 21/22, 1942, the Japanese submarine *I-25*, operating on the surface of the water, crept silently toward the Oregon shore with Fort Stevens beyond. The seas were calm, the weather clear and 72 degrees F. *I-25's* captain, Meiji Tagami, knew the area well. He and his submarine had been here during Dec. 1941 and patrolled the area for several days. He also knew exactly where he was because as he approached Fort Stevens he could navigate by three points of reference; the Cape Disappointment Lighthouse which was shining brightly, the light of the Coast Guard lightship *Relief* anchored at the mouth of the river and he could see the lights from the town of Gearhart to the south.

I-25 approached the shore through a small fleet of fishing vessels much to the surprise of the fishermen. The Japanese captain reasoned that where there were fishing boats there would be no US anti-submarine mines. Unknowingly, however, *I-25* approached Fort Stevens directly in front of, and within range of, the Fort's biggest guns. Tagami's mission was to fire his deck gun on Fort Stevens. A similar attack had been planned when he was here in Dec. 1941 but was called off at the last moment.

Tagami positioned *I-25* and, at the right moment, ordered his gun crew to commence firing. The crew began firing shells in rapid order in the general direction of the Fort. They had no specific target in view. The first shots alerted everyone on duty at the Fort and many civilians nearby. The flashes from *I-25's* gun could be seen clearly from shore. Unfortunately, Fort Stevens' defenses were not fully manned because it was a weekend and the Fort was in the midst of a chicken pox epidemic. Those on duty, however, quickly deduced that their attacker was a submarine and sounded the alarm. The Fort's base line stations quickly plotted the location of the sub and the AAF radar station at North Head also got a reading on the submarine's position. But the American guns remained silent. Not even the search lights went on. Somehow, incoming data to the Fort's command post erroneously indicated that the submarine was 500 to 1000 yards beyond the range of the Fort's guns. The Fort's commander therefore ordered that the guns not to fired nor the search lights turned on for fear that they would be seen by the attacker and immediately become targets.

After firing 17 shots, *I-25* quickly departed on the surface passing again through the fleet of fishing boats and the awe-struck fishermen. *I-25's* shells did very little damage. They destroyed a baseball diamond backstop and a tree. The worst damage came 16 months later when a nearby rural area had a sudden power failure. It was discovered then, that a fragment from one of *I-25's* shells had torn away the insulation from an overhead power line and the metal wire was slowly corroded through.

This monument on DeLaura Road commemorated the shelling of Fort Stevens, by the Japanese submarine I-25 on the night of June 21/22, 1942

223

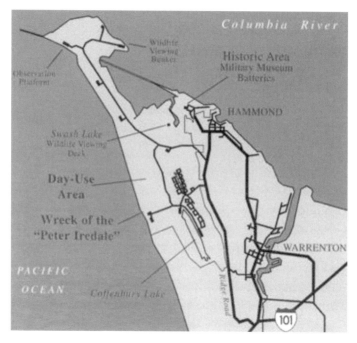

Fort Stevens Historic Area

The attack made national headlines, stimulated a whole host of rumors locally and brought sightseers and souvenir hunters from miles around. Over the next few weeks several hundred pounds of "genuine Jap shell fragments" were found and sold at healthy prices.

I-25 sailed northward and patrolled the waters off Canada and Alaska before returning to Japan on July 10.

BLY is a small lumbering community on SR-140 in the mountains 40 miles NE of Klamath Falls. It was near here that the Japanese achieved their greatest success from their bombing balloon campaign. One of their balloons killed a woman and five children. These were the only deaths recorded during the war due to the bombing balloons and the only deaths in the contiguous 48 states during the war due to direct enemy action.

MEMORIAL TO THE JAPANESE BOMBING BALLOON DEATHS ON GEARHART MOUNTAIN:
Beginning in late 1944, and carrying over to the spring of 1945, the Japanese carried out their bombing of North America by bomb-laden balloons. The balloons were carried across the Pacific by the upper air currents and were timed to descend upon reaching North America and begin dropping a series of incendiary bombs and one large concussion bomb. Their aim was to start forest fires wherever the bombs fell.

But the program was a failure because, during the winter months, the forests were damp and heavy with snow. By May 1945 the Japanese realized that the program had failed and ended the attacks. But, many downed balloons were scattered throughout the western part of the country and had not yet been discovered by the Americans.

On Saturday, May 5, 1945, the Reverend Archie Mitchell and his pregnant wife, Elsie, took his church's Sunday school class on a fishing trip into the forests on the slopes of Gearhart Mountain. The class consisted of five children. They traveled by car up a Forest Service road to reach a good fishing stream known to Rev. Mitchell. Mitchell stopped the car near a path which lead to the stream and let his wife and the children out of the car. Mrs. Mitchell and the children then proceeded to walk down the path while Mitchell backed the car down the road several yards to park it in a clearing. Nearby was a three-man Forest Service work crew working on a road grader that had become stuck. As Mitchell was walking back up the road towards the path he heard his wife call to him to come see what they had found. Seconds later there was a loud explosion followed almost immediately by a smaller explosion. Mitchell and the three workmen ran to the site to find Mrs. Mitchell badly injured her clothes on fire and four of the five children dead from the mysterious explosions. In the ground in the midst of the dead and injured was a smoking crater 12" deep by 15" wide x 36" long. Also lying about were strange-looking pieces of metal, fabrics and cords. Mitchell beat out the flames of his wife's clothing with his hands but within minutes she died. The fifth child also soon died.

Mitchell and the workmen, of course, sought help immediately and in the coming days the Army, Navy, FBI and County Sheriff investigated the incident and concluded that the devices that had exploded were the main 15 Kg high explosive anti-personnel bomb and one of the incendiary bombs of a downed Japanese bombing balloon. The consensus of opinion was that Mrs. Mitchell and the children were gathered around the devices when someone pulled or otherwise disturbed the bombs and they went off.

Federal authorities tried to keep the incident a secret, but word of the deaths spread quickly throughout southern Oregon and the story was picked up by several newspapers. The Federal authorities then did a complete about-face and decided to divulge to the American public the whole truth about the Japanese bombing balloons which, heretofore, had been successfully kept secret. The official opinion now was that the public should know of the downed Japanese balloons so that no more incidents such as this would happen. The Federal Government then began a program warning people that downed Japanese bombing balloons existed in large numbers throughout the western part of the US and if found should not be touched and the authorities notified at once. The program succeeded because balloons continued to be found and there were no more reports of injuries or death

**Memorial on Gearheart Mountain
Commemorates the deaths of 6 people
Killed by a Japanese bombing Balloon**

In June 1946, a second bombing balloon was found on Gearhart Mountain, but no one was injured.

In 1949, the Federal Government paid compensation to the families of those killed on Gearhart Mountain. The Reverend Mitchell was awarded $5000 and the family of each child $3000. By then, however, the Reverend Mitchell was in Viet Nam. In 1947, he had volunteered to do missionary work there. Mitchell was subsequently caught up in the Viet Nam War and disappeared. No further word was heard of him for several years. In 1973, when all military and civilian prisoners were released by the Viet Cong there was still no word of Rev. Mitchell.

In 1950, the Weyerhaeuser Corp. which owned the property upon which the incident occurred, erected a monument on the site and established a small park. The site is accessible today by car, but not during the winter months. Visitors should inquire locally for directions and road conditions.

For years after the incident, the citizens of Bly and the surrounding area harbored ill feeling against all people of Japanese heritage and they were not welcome in this part of Oregon.

McMINNVILLE is a county seat 15 miles NW of Salem on SR-18 and SR-99W. Here is one of the most fascinating museums in the country.

EVERGREEN AVIATION & SPACE MUSEUM: This is the home of Howard Hughes' famous "Spruce Goose" of WW II which was made in the Los Angeles, CA area during the war. This was the prototype of a large cargo plane made primarily of wood and intended to ferry military personnel and war materials great distances and across oceans. It flew just once, in a test flight, with Hughes at the controls, but never materialized into a production aircraft. It's a one-of-a-kind historical relic of WW II.

The Museum also has over 100 other aircraft including many WW II models. Many of the planes are flyable and there are numerous aircraft and WW II-related exhibits, displays and artifacts. Docent and group tours are available. There is a large firearms collection, the Oregon Aviation Hall of Fame, a large library and archive collection, an Imax Theater, two cafes, an educational program, a fascinating museum store and, for the kiddies - a waterpark. As might be expected, thousands of visitors pass through this museum each year and it is host to many social events and other activities. Address:

500 NE Captain Michael King Smith Way, McMinnville, OR 97128. Phone and website: 503-434-4185; www.evergreenmuseum.org

The Spruce Goose at the Evergreen Aviation and Space Museum in McMinnville, OR

PORTLAND was, as it is now, Oregon's largest city. Its wartime population was greatly swollen by the rapid influx of war workers who came to take jobs in the area's shipyards and defense plants. Many military personnel also came to Portland.   Portland was a very busy seaport during the war and was the principal port through which Lend Lease materials were shipped to the Soviet Union's main Pacific seaport, Vladivostok.

 In Dec. 1945, Portland was one of the ports used to deport those ethnic Japanese who had renounced their US citizenship during the war and were required, by law, to leave the US.

THE BOMBER COMPLEX: A preserved B-17G bomber mounted on pylons serves as the main attraction for the business of a former B-17 pilot, Art Lacey, of Milwaukee, OR (a southern suburb of Portland). Lacey's establishment, known as "The Bomber Complex," consists of a restaurant and several other related businesses. And there is an interesting gift shop with many unique items.

 On the walls of the Bomber Restaurant are World War II memorabilia and photographs explaining how the B-17G was brought to this location. Address: 13515 S.E. McLoughlin Blvd., Milwaukee, OR 97222. Phone and website: 503-659-9306; www.thebomber.com

OREGON MILITARY MUSEUM is located at Camp Whithycombe, the Oregon National Guard camp, near Clackamas, OR, a SE suburb of Portland. The Museum is the official military history repository of Oregon and endeavors to preserve the memory, sacrifices and devotion to duty of those Oregonians who served in all branches of the armed forces.

 The Museum traces the military history of Oregon from 1843 to the present. There is a very generous presentation of WW II-era equipment and displays including an amphibious DUWK (Duck), several WW II vehicles, a large gun collection and information on the 41st "Sunset" Infantry Division which served in the Philippines during the war.

 The Museum has an educational program, participates in military and community events and provides speakers. Address: Camp Whithycombe, Clackamas, OR 97015. Phone and website: 503-683-5359; www.ormilmuseum.org

TILLAMOOK is a county seat in the NW corner of the state, near the coast and 60 miles west of Portland on US-101 and SR-6.

TILLAMOOK AIR MUSEUM: This is a big museum - a really big - museum. It once held up to nine WW II blimps and was then known as Hangar B at the NAS (LTA), Tillamook, a US Navy blimp station. It can be seen easily from the highway and is one of the largest wooden structures in the world. Visitors can go into the hangar and experience its immense size.

 The Museum tells the story of the naval air station and the hangar from their inception during WW II to the present. The blimps are gone but on display are blimp engines, cabs, propellers and other blimp paraphernalia along with photographs, documents and a large collection of WW II memorabilia. The Museum has over 30 winged aircraft, many from WW II.

There is a WW II era cafe, The 40s/50s Cafe, and visitors can enjoy shopping in their nice gift shop. Address: 6030 Hangar Rd., Tillamook, OR 97141. Phone and website: 503-842-1130; www.tillamookair.com

Tillamook Air Museum, Tillamook, OR

PENNSYLVANIA

Pennsylvania's contribution to the war effort was many-fold. The state was a great manufacturing state, a food producer, rich in minerals - including oil - and was heavily populated - lots of service personnel. In the latter category an unusually large proportion of the state's population, 1/8 of the total, saw service in the armed forces. Of this number, 80,000 became war casualties and 20,000 gave their lives. Pennsylvanians won 35 Congressional Medals of Honor which was more than any other state.

As for war production, Pennsylvania ranked 7th among all the states in total war production, 4th in shipbuilding, 3rd in ordnance production and 1st in the number of expansions to existing industrial facilities to meet wartime needs.

When the US went to war, the state organized one of the largest civilian volunteer defense organizations in the nation, the Civilian Defense Corps. By the end of the war, some 1.6 million people had been mobilized by the Corps.

ANNVILLE is a small community 20 mile east of downtown Harrisburg on US-422 and SR-241. It is closely associated with Fort Indiantown Gap Military Reservation which is just north of town and the home of the Pennsylvania National Guard

PENNSYLVANIA NATIONAL GUARD MILITARY MUSEUM: When you walk into this museum you will be walking into WW II history. It's in a 1941 barracks building. The Museum relates the long history of the Pennsylvania National Guard including its service during WW II. There are several monuments on the Museum's grounds commemorating the Army divisions with which the Guard has been associated. They are the 28th Infantry Division, the 95th Infantry Division and the 3rd Armored Division. There is also a monument commemorating the Battle of the Bulge. The Museum has a library and an impressive bookstore. Address: Bldg. T-8-57, Fort Indiantown Gap Military Reservation, Annville, PA 17003. Phone and website: 717-861-8211; www.pngmilitarymuseum.org

The China-Burma-India Memorial in Carlisle,PA

<u>**CARLISLE**</u>: The town of Carlisle is a county seat 18 miles west of Harrisburg on I-76, I-81 and US-11. It is home to the old and famous US Army facility, Carlisle Barracks, which was used extensively during WW II and the home of the prestigious US Army War College.

CUMBERLAND COUNTY VETERANS MEMORIAL COURTYARD: In this Memorial Courtyard in downtown Carlisle is an attractive monument commemorating those individuals who served in the China-Burma-India (CBI) Theater during WW II. Also in the Courtyard are memorials to other US conflicts. Location: Across the street from the Cumberland County Courthouse

US ARMY HERITAGE AND EDUCATIONAL CENTER: This is a complex of several Army facilities, The Military Historical Institute, the Visitor and Education Center and the Army Heritage Museum. All are open to the public.

Army Heritage Museum: This fine museum is part of the US Army Heritage and Education Center complex and has extensive exhibits on the history of the US Army from the American Revolution to the present. WW II era exhibits in the Museum are extensive and present an overview of five Europeans campaigns during WW II; Normandy, Northern France, Rhineland, Battle of the Bulge and Central Europe.

   The Museum focuses on the experiences of the individual soldier from the rank of private to general. The life and career of WW II General Omar Bradley is highlighted with many photographs, artifacts and other information related to General Bradley.

   Other displays in the Museum include extensive displays of US Army equipment, arms, field equipment, captured enemy weapons and many other items. There is a research facility, an educational program, and a fine arts and photo gallery. Address: US Army Heritage and Education Center, 950 Soldier Dr., Carlisle, PA 17013-5021. Phone and website: 717-245-3419; www.carlisle.army.mil/ahec

<u>**DANVILLE**</u> is a county seat in east central Pennsylvania on the North Branch of the Susquehanna River and I-80 and US-11.

DANVILLE MEMORIAL PARK: This is Danville's main city park and, like many city parks, has a number of memorials dedicated to America's military conflicts. The Park has a very impressive WW II Memorial unlike any other in the Park. It is a stone gazebo which is used for park's social and other

The WWII Memorial in Memorial Park in Danville, PA

events. Mounted on the columns of the gazebo are plaques recording the names of Danville residents who gave their lives in WW II. Location: At the three-way intersection of Bloom St., Ferry St. and Church St.

ELDRED is a small community in north central Pennsylvania on SR-446 near the New York state line.

THE ELDRED WORLD WAR II MUSEUM is dedicated to the memory of the millions of men and women who fought in the war and those who provided the weapons of war. The city of Eldred has strong memories of WWII because a munitions plant was located here making bombs, mortar shells and fuses and employed 1500 local residents. Many exhibits in the Museum are related to the munitions plant. The Museum has a learning center, an interesting museum store and a library. Group tours are available. Address: 201 Main St., Eldred, PA 16731. Phone and website: 814-225-2220 and 866-686-9944; www.eldredwwiimuseum.org

ERIE is in the NW corner of the state on Lake Erie, I-79 and I-90. It is Pennsylvania's largest city on Lake Erie.

ERIE COUNTY WW II WAR MEMORIAL:
During WW II, Erie lost 727 men and women as war casualties. This fine memorial honors them and lists their names.

On the south side of the Memorial is a happier note. There is a pictorial history which features photos of many of the servicemen who returned safely after the war. Location: Erie Cemetery bounded by W. 18th St., Cherry St. and W. 26th St.

The Erie World War II Memorial in Erie, PA

ERIE WORLD WAR II MEMORIAL: This is a second WW II Memorial in Erie. It consists of a large black granite wall which, on one side, lists the names of the soldiers, sailors and airmen who died during WW II. In front to the Memorial is a large ground level compass. On the other side of the Memorial is a depiction of GI's in action silhouetted against the sky. Location: Between State St. and Glenwood Park Av., in Erie, PA

GETTYSBURG is one of the most famous small towns in the country because of the monumental and decisive battle that took place here during the Civil War. The town also has some significant WW II history and had a very distinguished resident.

EISENHOWER NATIONAL HISTORIC SITE: This was the last home of General, and later, President Dwight D. Eisenhower and his wife, Mamie. They lived here from 1950 until their deaths. The Eisenhower's purchased this working farm, which is adjacent to the Civil War battlefield, in 1950 while Ike was serving as president of Columbia University. They began modifying the main house almost immediately with Mamie supervising the details. The work progressed off and on over five years and upon completion Ike christened the house "Mamie's House."

The two farms on either side of the Eisenhower's farm were purchased by a friend, Alton Jones, to add to the Eisenhower's privacy. Ike and Jones went into business together raising purebred Angus cattle.

After becoming President, Ike visited the farm as much as he could and in 1955, while recuperating from his first heart attack, conducted the nation's business from here.

Many famous visitors came to the farm including Eisenhower's wartime compatriots Winston Churchill and Charles De Gaulle.

Upon completing his second presidential term in Jan. 1961, Ike and Mamie retired to the farm permanently. In 1967, the Eisenhower's donated the farm to the US Department of the Interior with the understanding that it would likely become a historic site after their deaths. Ike lived here until his death in 1969 and Mamie lived on in the house until her death in 1979.

The farm and buildings are open to the public and access is via shuttle buses from the National. Park Visitor Center at 1195 Baltimore Pike. The house

This was Dwight and Mamie Eisenhower's home in Gettysburg, PA from 1950 until their deaths. It was the only home they ever owned

is furnished much as it was when the Eisenhower's lived here in the 1960s and the out-buildings are much the same as when Mamie died. The house and outbuildings are open to the public and the farm has remained a working farm ever since Mamie's death. The Historic Site hosts special events, has a program for children and a very interesting book store. Address: Eisenhower National Historic Site, 1195 Baltimore Pike (Visitors Center), Gettysburg, PA 17325. Phone and website: 717-338-9114 Ext.4411; www.nps.gov/eise/

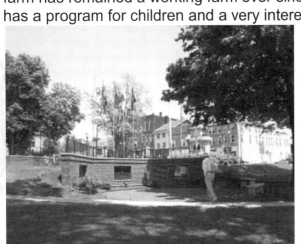

MERCER is a county seat in eastern Pennsylvania near the Ohio state line on I-79, I-80 and US-62.

MERCER COUNTY WW II MEMORIAL: This Memorial consists of an angular wall flag poles and memorial plaques. It is in downtown Mercer near the County Courthouse and commemorates all of the local veterans of WW II. Location: Near S. Diamond and Pitt Sts.

The WW II Memorial in Mercer, PA

NEWBURG is a small community 32 miles west of Carlisle on SR-641 and SR-696. (Caution: There is another Newburg in Pennsylvania near Allentown).

NEWBURG-HOPEWELL WORLD WAR II MEMORIAL: This fine stone memorial commemorates those individuals from Newburg-Hopewell Township that gave their lives during WW II. Their names are inscribed on the Memorial along with the tribute "THESE DIED THAT LIBERTY NOT PERISH." Location: In the center of Newburg on Main St. (SR-641)

The Newburg-Hopewell World War II Memorial in Newburg, PA

NEW TRIPOLI is a small community 17 miles NW of Allentown on SR-143 and SR-309.

The Lynn Township World War II Memorial in New Tripoli, PA

LYNN TOWNSHIP WORLD WAR II MEMORIAL: The Daughter of America Lodge erected this interesting WW II memorial which honors all of the Lynn Township residents who served in the US armed forces during WW II. It consists of two stone cairns and an inscribed center monument. There are 13 stars in the monument's plaque honoring the original 13 United States. Location: The Park at Ebenezer Union Church at 7293 Decatur St. (SR-143)

PHILADELPHIA AREA: Philadelphia was, as it is now, Pennsylvania's largest city. The Philadelphia metropolitan area was already heavily industrialized and during the war acquired 1/6 of the total defense contracts issued by the US government.

Philadelphia's harbor became very busy during the early stages of the war and was one of the main departure points for ships carrying Lend Lease goods to the Soviet Union.

All in all, Philadelphia prospered greatly during the war and much of that prosperity carried over into the postwar years.

PENN'S LANDING is a 37-acre park on the Philadelphia waterfront between Front St. to the west, the Delaware River to the east, Spring Garden St. to the north and Washington Av. to the south. It marks the spot where William Penn landed in 1682 to take possession of his very generous land grant from the King of England.

On display are several historic ships which are open to the public including the WW II submarine *Becuna*. This is a Balboa-class submarine, built in 1943, and saw considerable action in the Pacific with Halsey's 7th Fleet. The *Becuna* is credited with sinking 3.5 Japanese merchant ships. The submarine was known to its crew as "Becky."

In 1951, the *Becuna* was upgraded to a Guppy 1A type with sophisticated radar and torpedo equipment capable of carrying nuclear warheads. These improvements may be viewed by the public.

Also of interest to history buffs at Penn's Landing in the Spanish-American War-era cruiser, *USS Olympia* which served as Commodore Dewey's flag ship at the Battle of Manila. The *USS Olympia* also served in WW I.

The Museum has a library, and educational program and a must-see museum store. Address: Penn's Landing Site, 211 S. Columbus Blvd., Philadelphia, PA 19106. Phones and website: 215-413-8655; www.phillyseaport.org

PENNSYLVANIA RAILROAD COMPANY'S WORLD WAR II MEMORIAL: During WW II, 1,307 employees and former employees of the Pennsylvania Railroad Company gave their lives for their country. This striking memorial honors their memories and lists their names on bronze plaques. The Memorial depicts Michael the Archangel, carved in black granite, raising up a fallen soldier from the flames of war. Location: Inside the Main Concourse of the 30th St. Station in Philadelphia, PA

The Pennsylvania Railroad Company's
World War II Memorial
in Philadelphia, PA

UPPER MORELAND TOWNSHIP WW II MEMORIAL: This Memorial is in the community of Willow Grove, a northern suburb 18 miles north of downtown Philadelphia.

During the war, Willow Grove was home to a large naval installation, the US Naval Air Station, Willow Grove.

The Memorial is a circular concrete marker with golden discs honoring those who served in the US

The Upper Moreland Township WW II Memorial,
Willow Grove, PA

armed forces of WW II. Inscribed on the Memorial is the following: "ESTABLISHED AND MAINTAINED IN MEMORY OF THE MEN AND WOMEN FROM WILLOW GROVE WHO SERVED IN THE ARMED FORCES OF THE UNITED STATES OF AMERICA DURING THE SECOND WORLD WAR."

PITTSBURGH AREA, in western Pennsylvania had, before WW II, long been known as America's steel center and was the home of several of America's largest steel firms. Pittsburgh was a booming town before the war, and even more so when the war started, as the US built up its armed forces in the wake of developments in Europe and the Far East. By 1941, nearly all of Pittsburgh's major industries had converted to defense work and most of the steel mills were working at full capacity. By late 1945, the city's planners were beginning to get an upper hand on smoke and water pollution and traffic congestion problems that had plagued the city for some time. In that year, they began a major project to clear away an ugly slum and industrial area on the city's riverfront. What evolved was a large and beautiful park known as the Golden Triangle at the western tip-end of the city where the Allegheny and Monongahela Rivers merge to form the Ohio River. This project became one of the nation's models for urban renewal in the coming years.

CARNEGIE SCIENCE CENTER, near downtown Pittsburgh, is a museum displaying many aspects of science including a working foundry, industrial robots, lasers, cryogenics and electrical equipment. In front of the Center, anchored in the river, is the WW II submarine *USS Requin*. This submarine was completed in 1945 just as the war ended so it saw no military action. The *USS Requin*, however, served the US Navy until 1971.

The Center has a educational program and an interesting gift shop. Address: 1 Allegheny Av., Pittsburgh, PA 15212. Phone and website: 412-237-3400; www.carnegiesciencecenter.org

SOLDIERS AND SAILORS MEMORIAL HALL AND MUSEUM, located at 5th & Bigelow Sts. in Pittsburgh, honors Pennsylvania's veterans of all wars including WW II. On display are uniforms, weapons, photographs, documents, flags, medals and an exhibit on black military history. The history of WW II is adequately represented with displays and artifacts.

The facility has customized tours, one of which concentrates on WW II. Address: 4141 Fifth Av., Pittsburgh, PA 15213. Phone and website: 412-621-4253; www.soldiersandsailorshall.org

The Sewickeley World War II Memorial in Sewickeley, PA

SEWICKELEY WORLD WAR II MEMORIAL: Sewlickeley is a suburb of Pittsburgh eight miles NE of downtown Pittsburgh on the Ohio River and SR-65.

This memorial, consisting of a naval anchor, a flag pole and a bronze plaque, is in Sewickeley's Riverwalk Park and is dedicated to certain select naval services; the American Merchant Marines, US Navy Armed Guards and the US Navy Seabees. Engraved on the plaque is the image of a Liberty Ship and a text. Location: Riverwalk Park, Chadwick St., Sewickeley, PA

STATE COLLEGE is near the center of the state south of I-80, US-322 and SR-26, and is the home of Pennsylvania State University.

PENNSYLVANIA MILITARY MUSEUM is a 67-acre museum located on US-322 in Boalsburg, an eastern suburb of State College. It honors Pennsylvania's soldiers from the Revolutionary War to the present and emphasizes the role of the Army's 28th Infantry Division which the Pennsylvania National Guard became when mobilized during WW II.

The WW II era is well represented among the displays and consist of military vehicles, artillery pieces, small arms, uniforms, military equipment,personal documents, maps, paintings and drawings, dioramas, flags, medical equipment and other memorabilia. WW II tanks, half-tracks and personnel carriers are displayed in the museum and on the museum's grounds. Also on the Museum's grounds are two 14" guns from the battleship *Pennsylvania* which was at Pearl Harbor during the Japanese attack. The *Pennsylvania* survived that attack and served throughout most of WW II. But, she eventually gave her life for her country. The ship became a target ship during the atomic bombs tests at Kwajalein Island in the Pacific during July 1946. After that, she was studied for damage and residual radiation and eventually scuttled at sea in 1948.

The Museum has a nice bookstore and an ongoing educational program. Address: 602 Boalsburg Pike, Boalsburg, PA 16827. Phone and website: 814-466-6263 (Museum), 814-466-6401 (bookstore); http://pamilmuseum.org

WELLSBORO is a county seat in north-central Pennsylvania on US-6 and SR-287.

WELLSBORO WORLD WAR II MEMORIAL: This handsome WW II memorial consists of two engraved stone walls with a flag pole and smaller monuments mounted on a circular brick base. Sitting above a poem Speaking Stone is a unique sculpture of a tree by the artist David Bliss. A plaque at the base of the flag pole reads "TO HONOR VETERANS FROM THE ARMED FORCES FROM WELLSBORO AND THE AREA WHO SERVED THEIR COUNTRY IN WORLD WAR II FROM 1939 TO THE WARS END 1945." Location:Main St., Wellsboro, PA

The World War II Memorial in Wilkes-Barre, PA

WILKES-BARRE is a county seat and one of the state's larger cities located in NE Pennsylvania on I-81, US-11 and SR-309.

***USS WILKES-BARRE* MEMORIAL:** The Light Cruiser, *USS Wilkes-Barre* saw considerable action in the Pacific during the war and was decommissioned in 1947. But the citizens of Wilkes-Barre preserved her anchor. It now makes an appropriate memorial to the ship, its crew ad the city after which it was named. Location: In downtown Wilkes-Barre behind the Luzerne County Courthouse

The USS Wilkes-Barre Memorial in Wilkes-Barre, PA consists of the ship's anchor.

RHODE ISLAND

The 713,346 citizens of wartime Rhode Island, America's smallest state, proved to be an industrious lot during the war. They produced a wide variety of war materials and food for the nation and some 93,000 of their number served in the armed forces.

DIVEABLE WW II SHIP WRECKS IN RHODE ISLAND WATERS:

GERMAN SUBMARINE *U-853*: On May 5, 1945, Germany's new President, Admiral Karl Doenitz, who succeeded Adolph Hitler who had committed suicide, ordered all German submarines to cease attacks on Allied shipping. At that time, the German submarine *U-853* was operating in Rhode Island waters off Block Island. Being submerged, the submarine commander was unable to receive radio messages and did not know of Doenitz' order.

The next evening, May 6, while still submerged, *U-853* spotted, tracked and sank the US collier *Black Point* carrying a load of 7500 tons of soft coal. This would be the last American vessel sunk by a German submarine in the war.

US naval vessels and blimps were in the area and began an intensive search for the submarine. Using Sonar and other methods, US naval craft soon located the submarine and launched several attacks upon her and the submarine was sunk with all hands aboard.

Soon after the war ended, rumors circulated that the *U-853* had been carrying part of Germany's gold reserve, cash and other valuables. In the years that followed, several salvage attempts were made on the submarine but there was no indication of the reported treasures and the submarine was never raised. She lies 7.7 miles east of Black Island in 130 ft of water and is accessible to experienced sports divers.

DAVISVILLE is a small community 18 miles south of Providence between US-1, SR-4 and SR-403. During the war, it was the home of the Seabees and the famous Quonset Huts of WW II were built here in large numbers.

SEABEES MUSEUM AND MEMORIAL PARK: This is a five acre wooded park in which visitors walk from display to display which are in Quonset Huts. The major displays in the Park consist of a Fighting Seabee Statue and four variations of Quonset Huts built from 1942 to 1950.

One of the Huts contains historical memorabilia such as equipment, uniforms, insignias, and information on Seabee operations in foreign countries and another Hut is a barracks. Displayed at various locations in the Park are vintage construction and military equipment. There are walking trails, picnic tables and a very interesting Seabee Store. Address: 21 Iafrate Way (just NE of the intersection of US-1 and SR-403), Davisville, RI 02852. Phone and website: 401-294-7233; http://ww.seabeasmuseum.com

NEWPORT, on the southern coast of Rhode Island near the entrance to Narragansett Bay, was a resort community with many magnificent estates belonging to some of America's richest people. Newport was also a Navy town, with several important naval installations in the area including the US Naval War College.

US NAVAL WAR COLLEGE MUSEUM: This museum is located in Founders Hall (1820), a National Historic Site, on the grounds of the US Naval War College and traces the history of the War College and that of the Narragansett Bay area. In its broadest application, this encompasses theroies and concepts of sea power, international and maritime law, foreign policy formulation, diplomacy and naval operations. The Museum emphasizes the importance of professional implementation of strategic and tactical objectives.

On display are artifacts from the American Revolution to the present including a sizeable display on WW II. Tours are available and the Museum has a nice gift shop. Address: 686 Cushing Rd., Newport, RI 02841-1207. Phone and website: 401-841-4052/2101; www.ucnwc.edu/museum

PROVIDENCE is Rhode Island's capitol city and the largest city in the state.

PROVIDENCE WORLD WAR II MEMORIAL: This striking memorial consists of a large circular monument supported by eight columns. At the base of each column, etched deeply in stone, are

tributes to the major theaters of operation during WW II. Three of the columns commemorate the Pacific/Far East Campaign, two commemorate the European Theatre of Operations, and one each commemorates the Battle of the Atlantic, the Mediterranean Conflict and the Southeast Asia Campaign. Location: On S. Main St. (US-44) between Hopkins and Planet Sts. Providence, RI

WOONSOCKET is 13 miles north of Providence near the Massachusetts state line and is the state's second largest city.

The Providence World War II Memorial, Providence, RI

WORLD WAR II MEMORIAL STATE PARK: This 14 acre park is located near downtown Woonsocket on the Mill River and honors Rhode Island citizens who served in WW II. It has many of the amenities and recreation facilities of a traditions state park and is the site of many events in the summer and an annual Autumnfest in the fall. Location: On Social St., Woonsocket, RI

SOUTH CAROLINA

In the years before World War II, the state of South Carolina was beset with many problems. It was primarily a rural state with an economy that was dependent upon agriculture, some mining and some textile-making. South Carolina was a "Deep South" state, rigidly segregated and subject to occasional hurricanes. It had little power in Washington, DC and was of little interest to industrialists and the military.

In the late 1930s, with the Depression beginning to ease and with war clouds brewing in both Europe and the Far East, the fortunes of the state began to improve, albeit slowly. While other states were getting fat defense contracts to build ships, airplanes and tanks, South Carolina had to wait for the wartime prosperity to trickle down. While she waited, a hurricane roared through the state in Aug. 1940 causing considerable damage and killing more than three dozen people. In that year, though, one of the state's old friends, the US Army, established two large training camps in South Carolina that helped the economy considerably. One was at Columbia and other at Spartanburg.

In the summer of 1941, the US Army conducted large-scale maneuvers in northern South Carolina and southern North Carolina. This tore up some of the state's real estate, but brought in a lot of money. Some 400,000 men participated in the maneuvers which consisted of the "Blue Army" of North Carolina attacking the "Red Army" of South Carolina attempting to take the South Carolina town of Camden. The "Reds" had fewer men, but had two armored divisions. The "Blues" were able to knock out most of the Red Army's tanks and take Camden and win the contest. It was later said that these maneuvers were of great value to American forces in North Africa against the Rommel's Afrika Korps which was well equipped with tanks.

When the US went to war, the AAF built several new air fields in the state while the Navy, which had existing facilities in the Charleston and Beaufort areas, expanded its aviation holdings. During the war, the Army dotted the South Carolina landscape with some 20 Prisoner of War (POW) camps.

BEAUFORT is a county seat in the southern part of the state near the coast and on US-21 and SR-170. During WW II, there were two major military facilities in the area; Recruit Depot, Marine Barracks, Parris Island and the US Naval Air Station, Beaufort
.

PARRIS ISLAND MUSEUM: This interesting 8,000 Sq. ft. museum is located on the grounds of Marine Corps Recruit Depot, Parris Island and interprets the military and civilian history of Parris Island from the beginning of European occupation to the present. One of the Museum's main emphases is on the Spanish era and the Spanish settlement of Santa Elena. There is, of course, considerable information about the US Marine Corps, its training of recruits, care for Marine families and Marine veterans. The rich history of the Marine Corps is also explained in detail.

Displays include artifacts from WW II including uniforms, small arms, equipment, maps, photographs, artillery pieces and ship models. What's more, the Museum has a very interesting gift shop. Address: Bldg. 111, Marine Corps Recruit Depot, Parris Island, SC 29905. Phone and website: Museum phone 843-228-2951; Gift Shop phone 843-228-2166; http://parrisislandmuseum.com

CHARLESTON is one of South Carolina's larger cities and centrally located on South Carolina's coast at the end of I-26. It was a very busy seaport during the war. Many coastal and trans-oceanic convoys utilized the port and some formed up here. There were also several major US Army, US Army Air Forces and US Navy military facilities in the area.

THE CITADEL MUSEUM: This historical museum is on the grounds of the Citadel, one of the nation's oldest and most important military colleges. It traces the history of the school from it founding to the present. The Museum is near the Citadel's main gate.

There are some displays and exhibits on the school's role in WW II and considerable information on WW II General Mark Clark. Additional displays honors Citadel graduates who perished during WW II.

The Museum has an extensive archives collection, a library and museum tours are available. Address: 171 Moultrie St., Charleston, SC 29409. Phone and website: 843-953-6846; www.citadel.edu/museum

PATRIOTS POINT NAVAL & MARITIME MUSEUM: This excellent maritime museum is located across the Cooper River from downtown Charleston. Several historic ships are anchored here that participated in WW II. The largest of the ships is the aircraft carrier *Yorktown*, which saw considerable action in the Pacific and received 11 battle stars throughout the war.

In the 1950s, *Yorktown* was modified with an angled deck and served the Navy during the Vietnam War. It also participated in the recovery of the Apollo 8 astronauts and their capsule in 1968.

The ship was decommissioned in 1970 and later brought to this location. On the *Yorktown's* deck, and in the hangar deck, is a collection of aircraft that operated from the ship and some of them are of WW II vintage.

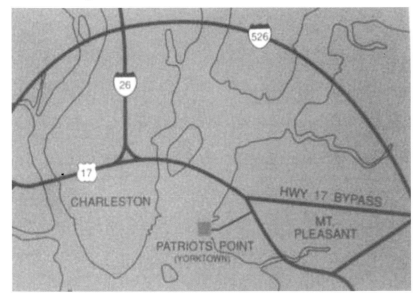

The destroyer *USS Laffey* is also on display at Patriot's Point. This was the second *USS Laffey* of WW II, the first having been sunk in November 1942 at the Battle of Guadalcanal. This *USS Laffey* was commissioned in early 1944, participated in the D-Day landings and later in the Pacific. On April 16, 1945, the ship was attacked by 22 Japanese bombers and Kamikaze aircraft off Okinawa. She was able to shoot down 11 of the planes but was hit by five Kamikazes, three bombs and two near misses. The ship survived and gained the title, "The ship that would not die." The *USS Laffey* was repaired and went on to support the atomic bomb tests at Bikini Atoll and served during the Korean War. She was decommissioned in 1975 after 31 years of service. The *USS Laffey* is the only surviving example of the Summer-class destroyer and is a National Historic Landmark.

The submarine *USS Clamagore*, a WW II-era submarine, is also on display at Patriot's Point but was commissioned too late to participate in that war. The submarine, however, did serve for 30 years during the Cold War.

Other exhibits at Patriot's Point include smaller craft, missiles, rockets and rocket launchers, artillery pieces, field equipment, ordnance items, naval mines, small arms, uniforms, ship models, maps and photographs.

Many activities are available at Patriot's Point including overnight camping, a cafe, an educational program and a souvenir-filled gift shop. Address: 40 Patriots Point Rd., Mt. Pleasant, SC 29464. Phones and website: Museum 866-831-1720, Gift Shop 843-881-5972; www.patriotspoint.org

COLUMBIA is the state capitol and is near the center of the state. During the war, there were several military installations in the area and today there are four important US Army museums at Fort Jackson which is east of the city.

FORT JACKSON:

Basic Combat Training Museum: Fort Jackson was established during WW I in 1917 as a basic training facility and has served the US Army in that capacity ever since.

This 7,500 Sq. ft. museum is dedicated to telling the story of how basic training in the US Army has developed since the Fort's founding to the present. There is a replica of a WW II GI barracks, US Army equipment, uniforms, photos, maps, unit newspapers and and an exhibit on a very necessary duty that every GI's experienced - KP duty.

There is a Medal of Honor Hall, a Korean Gallery, a Galley devoted to the activities of those father-figures of the US Army - the drill sergeants. There is a research library and on the grounds around the Museum are tanks, various Army vehicles and artillery pieces. Address: Building 4442, Jackson Blvd., Fort Jackson, SC 29207. Phone and website: 803-751-7419; www.jackson.army.mil

US Army Adjutant General Corps Museum and the US Army Finance Corps Museum: These two museums are located in the same building at Fort Jackson.

The US Army Adjutant General Corps Museum is dedicated to the history of the Army's Adjutant General's Corps from 1775 to the present. Displays include photos, documents, uniforms and equipment used by the Corps.

The AG Corps supervises and coordinates the Army's personnel and administrative systems. This includes the operation and maintenance of morale, welfare and recreation activities within the US Army, oversight of Army bands, postal operations and recreation activities. With regard to the latter, the movie star Bob Hope is honored here for his efforts in entertaining US troops during WW II. WW II era exhibits include some of the Army's first computers which were developed during WW II, typewriters, various pieces of WW II era office equipment and a 1941 Harley-Davidson motorcycle used by Army couriers.

Groups tours of the museum are available. Address: Bldg. 4392 Strom Thurmond Blvd., Fort Jackson, SC 29207. Phone: 803-751-1747. Website: see below

US Army Finance Corps Museum: This unique museum describes the duties and operation of the Army Finance Corps and tells how the troops are paid. It traces the long history of this branch of the US Army which is one of the oldest branches.

On display are photos, documents, ledgers, pay records, pay grades and other records of a financial nature. There are also displays of army script, both US and foreign. Address for both museums: 4392 Magruder Av., Fort Jackson, SC 29207. Phone: Adjutant General Army Corps Museum, 803-751-1747; Finance Corps Museum, 803-751-3771. Website: See below

US Army Chaplain Museum: This museum collects, preserves and displays artifacts related the the US Army Chaplain Corps from its beginning in 1775 to the present. There are photos, documents, uniforms and Army and religious equipment used by Army Chaplains of all faiths.

The largest of the several galleries in the Museum is the WW II Gallery.

Along with the artifacts and other historic items on display is information on the four chaplains, one of each faith, who perished on the troopship, *USS Dorchester,* which was sunk in February 1943. There is an interesting altar built by GIs in New Guinea made of artillery shell casings, parachute clothe, bicycle chains and other refuse of war.

The Museum also tells the story of the US Army chaplains who administered to the accused Nazi war criminals during their trials at Nuremberg after WW II.

The Museum has a research facility and tours are available. Address: 10100 Lee Rd., Fort Jackson, SC 29207. Phone: 803-751-8079/8827. Website for all five museums:www.jackson.army.mil.

MEMORIAL PARK: This is an enjoyable four-acre city park in Columbia with several military memorials. From the WW II era, there are memorials commemorating Pearl Harbor, the China-Burma-India theater, the Holocaust and the WW II cruiser *USS Columbia.* Location: Washington and Wayne Sts., Columbia, SC

The USS Columbia Memorial in Memorial Park, Columbia, SC

SOUTH CAROLINA MILITARY MUSEUM: This is South Carolina's National Guard Museum. As do most National Guard Museums, this museum traces the history of the National Guard over its more than 300 years of existence and its close association with units of the US Army.

On display are weapons, uniforms, photographs, documents and other artifacts. Highlighted in the Museum are the state's Congressional Medal of Honors recipients and the WW II era exhibits comprise a major part of the displays.

Outside the Museum are tanks, artillery pieces and other vehicles and weapons used by the Guard. Address: 1225 Bluff Rd. (behind the National Guard Armory), Columbia, SC 29201. Phone and website: 803-806-4440; www.scmilitarymuseum.net

WORLD WAR II MEMORIAL: The inscription on this memorial says it all. "IN MEMORY OF/THE BOYS OF/RICHLAND COUNTY/WHO MADE/THE SUPREME SACIFICE/IN WORLD WAR II/ERECTED/BY/THE CIVIC DEPARTMENT/OF THE/WOMEN'S CLUB OF COLUMBIA/DEDICATED APRIL 20, 1947." Those who dedicated the memorial almost certainly did not know that April 20 was Adolf Hitler's birthday. Location: On the median at the intersection of Devine, Saluda and Blossom Sts., Columbia, SC

*The World War II Memorial
in Columbia, SC*

GEORGETOWN is a county seat 55 miles NE of Charleston on US-71, US-701 and near the coast.

HOBCAW BARONY was the country estate of Bernard Baruch, a multimillionaire and one of the most influential men in the Roosevelt Administration. At the time of the war, the plantation house was over 220 years old and had 21 rooms.

During the month of May 1944, just prior to the Normandy Invasion, President Roosevelt came here for a quiet, unpublicized four-week vacation, the longest vacation he had had since becoming president in 1933. It was not only a vacation, but a rest cure. Roosevelt was experiencing the beginning stages of congestive heart failure and had been in poor health throughout most of the winter of 1943-44 suffering a bout of influenza and a more serious bout of bronchitis that required his hospitalization at Bethesda Hospital in Maryland in Apr. 1944. He recovered from the bronchitis, but the doctors advised him to quit smoking. He ignored their advice.

*President Roosevelt back at his desk after
his four-week vacation in South Carolina.
Within 11 months, he was dead*

At Hobcaw Barony he really did relax. He slept up to 12 hours a day, sunned himself, went fishing and crabbing in Winyah Bay, drove around the area and sat for hours on the porch. On one occasion, he went deep sea fishing 15 miles off the coast with Coast Guard boats and Navy blimps

240

on guard nearby.

When he returned to Washington, DC he was tanned, rested, thinner, looked better and told reporters that he felt good. But, he really was not in good health. Within 11 months he was dead at the age of 63.

Other WW II personalities that visited the Baruchs at Hobcaw were Winston Churchill and his daughter, Diana; Generals George C. Marshall, Omar Bradley and Mark Clark and Senator Robert A. Taft.

The Barony is on the National Register of Historic Places and guided tours are available. Address: 22 Hobcaw Rd., Georgetown, SC 29440. Phone and website: 843-546-4623; www.hobcawbarony.org

LYMAN is a small community west of Spartanburg on US-29, SR-357 and SR-292.

World War II Memorial in Lyman, SC

WORLD WAR II MEMORIAL: For a small community, Lyman has a very handsome WW II Memorial. The Memorial consists of a tall central column with a flag pole surrounded by smaller columns and a chain linking those columns. It was first elected to commemorate those from the local area who served in WW II but was updated to include those who served in Korea, Viet Nam and the Gulf War. Location: On Groce Rd. (SR-292) in Lyman,SC

McCLELLANVILLE is a small community on the central coast of South Carolina, US-17N, SR-45 and the Inland Waterway.

ST. JAMES SANTEE PARISH WW II MEMORIAL: This memorial was erected by the citizens of St. James Santee .Parish and is on the side of the road in a small park. The center column is flanked by two lower tables with the list of names of those from this area that served in WW II. The central figure is an eagle with wings held high and arrows clutched in its claws. The dates 1941-1945 are below the eagle. Location: S. Pickney St. in McClellanville, SC

The St. James Santee Parish WW II Memorial in McClellanville, SC

WALTERBORO is a county seat in the southern part of the state on I-95, US-17, SR-63 ans SR-64. During the war, the city had a US Army Air Forces training facility, Walterboro Army Airfield.

THE TUSKEGEE AIRMEN OF WORLD WAR II MEMORIAL: Here, in a city park, is this inspiring memorial to the famous Tuskegee Airmen who trained here during the war. The inscription on the Memorial reads "IN HONOR OF THE TUSKEGEE AIRMEN, THEIR INSTRUCTORS AND GROUND

SUPPORT PERSONNEL WHO PARTICIPATED IN TRAINING FOR COMBAT AT THE WALTERBORO ARMY AIRFIELD DURING THE SECOND WORLD WAR." Location: 537 Aviation Way, Walterboro, SC

WILLIAMSTON is a small community 18 miles south of Greenville on SR-20.

WORLD WAR II MEMORIAL: This is a large WW II memorial consisting of a large central panel with plaques, wings, flag poles and an entrance staircase. It is dedicated to the local area's veterans of WW II. Location: Williamston City Park

The Tuskegee Airmen of World War II Memorial in Walterboro, SC

The World War II Memorial in Williamston, SC

SOUTH DAKOTA

World War II proved to be a mixed blessing for South Dakota. Like the other high plains states, South Dakota was in bad economic condition when the war started because of having suffered through the double disasters of the Great Depression and the Dust Bowl. In 1940, South Dakota's population was only 642,961 with 75.4% of her people listed as "rural." When the war-induced industrial buildup began in the late 1930s it was of little benefit to South Dakota.

When war plants started up all over the country, South Dakota became one of the few states in the nation to lose population as people left the state to take high-paying defense jobs elsewhere.

In 1941, the mammoth artistic undertaking at Mount Rushmore in the Black Hills was completed and tourist began to flock to the state to see the faces of the four presidents carved into the mountainside. This bit of good fortune, however, was cut short by gas and tire rationing and the end of auto production. Because of the war and the downturn in tourism, the formal dedication of the Mt Rushmore Monument was postponed and then forgotten altogether until 50 years later. On July 4, 1991 President George H. W. Bush officiated at the belated formal dedication.

The formal dedication ceremony of the Mt. Rushmore Monument was postponed in 1941 due to war conditions. It was not carried out until 50 years later when President George H. W. Bush officiated at the formal ceremony on July 4, 1991

The WW II Veterans Memorial in Aurora, SD

AURORA is a small community 50 miles north of Sioux Falls just off I-29.

WW II VETERANS MEMORIAL: This memorial is in the center of Aurora in a small park. It is a multi-paneled structure and is inscribed "IN MEMORY OF THE MEN AND WOMEN OF THIS COMMUNITY WHO SERVED THEIR COUNTRY IN WORLD WAR II." Location: Main St., Aurora, SD

PIERRE is in the center of the state on US-14 and US-83 and is the state's capitol.

SOUTH DAKOTA NATIONAL GUARD MUSEUM is located near downtown Pierre and traces the history of the state's National Guard. Displays cover time periods from the state's territorial days to the present. The mission of the Museum is to acquire, preserve, protect and display military equipment, records, relics and memorabilia representing the state's military organizations. The museum's WW II display is sizable and there is historical information on both the South Dakota Army and Air National Guards. Museum tours are available. Address: 301 E. Dakota Ave., Pierre, SD 57501. Phone and website: 605-224-9991; http://mva.sd.gov/natl_guard_museum.html

The South Dakota WW II Memorial in Pierre, SD

WORLD WAR II MEMORIAL: This is a very unique memorial on the grounds of the state capitol building. It is built on a small man-made peninsula which extends into Capitol Lake and displays six larger-than-life bronze figures of WW II service personel representing the six branches of military service in which South Dakotans served during the war. The state capitol building is between Broadway Av. and Wells Av. in downtown Pierre.

RAPID CITY is in the SW part of the state on I-90 and is the home for Ellsworth Air Force Base.

SOUTH DAKOTA AIR & SPACE MUSEUM: This museum is adjacent to Ellsworth Air Force Base and relates the history of air and space activities in South Dakota and of Ellsworth AFB. Many artifacts and aircraft are on display including several WW II aircraft. One of the WW II aircraft on display is General Eisenhower's B-25 bomber which he used during the war.

The Museum has postwar missiles on display, The South Dakota Aviation Hall of Fame, its own

restoration facility and a nice gift shop. Tours of Ellsworth AFB are available from the Museum. Address: Rushmore Dr. (adjacent to the main gate of Ellsworth AFB) Box Elder, SD 57719. Phone and website: 605-385-5189; www.sdairandspacemuseum.com

This is General Eisenhower's personal aircraft, a B-25 bomber, which he used in Europe during the war.

SIOUX FALLS is the state's largest city and is in the SE corner of the state on I-29 and I-90.

BATTLESHIP *USS SOUTH DAKOTA* MEMORIAL is located a park in Sioux Falls and is dedicated to

the memory of the battleship *USS South Dakota* which saw lots of action during WW II and was one of the war's most decorated ships.

The ship is represented by a full-scale outline of its deck area by a low concrete wall. There are simulated gun turrets and a small forecastle which is a museum. In the museum, are artifacts from the ship, a scale model, uniforms, flags and other related items. The museum also has a small gift shop.

A plaque tells of the ship's WW II battles beginning in Oct. 1942 off Santa Cruz and ending with the Japanese surrender in Tokyo Bay. The actual ship was scrapped in 1962. Location: 12th St. and Kiwanis Av., Sioux Falls, SD 57104. Phone and website: 605-367-7060; www.siouxfallsparks.org/ContactUs/public_parks/Battleship_Memorial.aspx

The Battleship USS South Dakota Memorial in Sioux Falls, SD

STURGIS is a county seat in western part of South Dakota on I-90 and is home to Fort Meade, 4.5 miles east of town on SR-34 and SR-39. This was an old frontier fort established by the Army in 1878 and is still functioning today.

FORT MEADE CAVALRY MUSEUM: This museum is in one of the beautiful old brick buildings at Fort Meade. It interprets the history of the Fort from its beginning in 1878 to the present. Most of the displays are devoted to the early days of the Fort, but there are exhibits on the Fort's role during WW II and a handsome granite memorial on the Museum grounds devoted to the 4th Cavalry Group in the European Theater of Operations during WW II. Address: Box 164, Ft. Meade, SD 57741. Phone and website: 605-347-9822; www.fortmeademuseum.org

The Arlo L. Olson Memorial in Toronto, SD

<u>**TORONTO**</u> is a small community in eastern South Dakota near the Minnesota state line and just off I-29 and on SR-15 and SR-28.

ARLO L. OLSON MEMORIAL: Arlo L. Olson, a resident of Toronto, was awarded the Congressional Medal of Honor posthumously during WW II and the community has commemorated his memory with this memorial. The central monument in the Memorial is of polished granite and inscribed thereon is his official Medal of Honor Citation. Location: Toronto City Park just north of Main St., Toronto, SD

TENNESSEE

The state of Tennessee, like the other states in the Union, suffered the ill effects of the Great Depression so the surge of industrial and military activities in the late 1930s and early 1940s were a welcome stimulus to the economy. During the war, the state began to produce air planes, landing craft and, thanks to the cheap electricity and abundant water provided by the recently completed Tennessee Valley Authority (TVA), enriched uranium for the atomic bomb project.

<u>**BYRDSTOWN**</u> is a county seat in north-central Tennessee east of Dale Hollow Lake on SR-111, SR-295 and SR-325.

CORDELL HULL BIRTHPLACE MUSEUM, just off SR-325 and 1.5 miles west of SR-111, displays artifacts and memorabilia of Cordell Hull, Secretary of State from 1933 to 1944. Hull was born nearby in a log cabin and a replica of that cabin is on display at the Museum.
   On Dec. 7, 1941, it was Cordell Hull who received notice from the Japanese ambassador in Washington that Japan was about to declare war on the United States.
   Hull went on to serve as Secretary of State and a very able adviser to President Roosevelt for the greater part of the war.
   During the war, Hull was instrumental in the creation of the United Nations Organization and won a

Nobel Prize in 1945 in recognition of his efforts in that respect. The Nobel metal he received is on display in the Museum along with many other personal and political memorabilia. The Museum has a newsletter, is host to many local, and some national, activities and has a one-of-kind gift shop. Address: 1300 Cordell Hull Memorial Dr., Byrdstown, TN 38549. Phone and website: 931-864-3247; www.cordellhullmuseum.com

CHATTANOOGA is on the southern edge of the state on I-24, I-75, the Tennessee River and the Georgia state line.

NATIONAL MEDAL OF HONOR MUSEUM is located in downtown Chattanooga and honors those individuals who have, through the years, received the nation's highest award for valor, the Congressional Medal of Honor.

The placing of this museum in Chattanooga is most appropriate because the nation's first recipient of this award is buried in nearby Chattanooga National Cemetery.

All of the Medal of Honor winners of WW II are mentioned in the Museum along with their stories and citations.

The Museum has a large archives collection and an educational program. Address: Northgate Mall, SR-153 at Hixon Pike, Chattanooga, TN 37401. Phone and website: 423-877-2525; www.mohm.org

CROSSVILLE is a county seat in eastern Tennessee on I-40, US-70 and US-127. During the war, Crossville had a large prisoner of war camp in the area.

MILITARY MEMORIAL MUSEUM: This museum covers America's wars from the Civil War to the present but, because it had a large POW camp in the area during WW II, there is considerable information on that camp and its prisoners. There are photos of the camp during its operation, samples of camp equipment used by the guards and prisoners, uniforms, small arms, models of tanks and more. Address: 20 S. Main St., Crossville, TN 38555. Phone and website: 931-456-5520 and 931-788-1690; http://museum.homestead.com/Military.html

JASPER is a county seat is SE Tennessee on I-24, US-41, SR-28 and SR-150.

MARION COUNTY WW II MEMORIAL: Inscribed on this thoughtful memorial is the statement "DEDICATED TO THE MEMORY OF THE SONS OF MARION COUNTY, TENN. WHO GAVE THEIR LIVES IN WORLD WAR TWO 1941-1945." Their names are listed on the Memorial. Location: Courthouse lawn, Jasper, TN

The Marion County WW II Memorial in Jasper, TN

MEMPHIS is the state's largest city and is in the extreme SW corner of the state on the Mississippi River.

MEMPHIS WORLD WAR II MEMORIAL: This lasting tribute honors those veterans of Shelby Countywho gave their lives in WW II. The bronze plagues on the face of the Memorial bears 875

The Memphis World War II Memorial in Memphis, TN

names.Location: Veterans Plaza, Overton Park, Memphis, TN

NASHVILLE is near the center of the state and is the capitol of Tennessee. One of the city's most outstanding sites is the Bicentennial Capitol Mall State Park in downtown Nashville which commemorates important events in Tennessee history.

BICENTENIAL CAPITOL MALL STATE PARK: When Tennessee celebrated its 200th anniversary of statehood; this magnificent 19 acre state park was built in the shadow of the State Capitol Building. There is a visitors' center, an amphitheater, a carillon, a 1,400 ft. wall with granite pylons marking the important events in Tennessee's history, picnic pavilions and more.

At the north end of the Mall is a large and impressive WW II memorial consisting of a pattern of tall granite markers which give a brief history of the major events of the war including the attack on Pearl Harbor and the Battle of the Bulge. The center piece of the memorial is an 18,000 lb. black granite globe floating in 1/8 inch of water. The countries on the globe are as they were during the war. Also there is a small map of Tennessee with lines showing the mileage to different wartime theaters of operation. Visitors may stop at the globe and turn it by hand.

Elsewhere in the memorial are listed Tennessee's seven Congressional Medal of Honor recipients of the war and the names of the 5,731 Tennesseans who have lost their lives. Address: 600 James Robertson Pkwy., Nashville, TN 37243. Phone and website: 615-741-5280; http://.gov/environment/parks/Bicentennial/

The WW II Memorial in Nashville's Bicentennial Capitol Mall State Park

OAK RIDGE was a non-city during the war. It wasn't on the maps, most people never heard of it and it wasn't mentioned in the newspapers. But yet, it existed and was one of the most important communities in the nation.

When the scientists and engineers of the top-secret "Manhattan (Atomic bomb) Project" got underway in 1941 with the mission to build atomic bombs, it was clear that one or more huge and very specialized industrial complexes would be required to produce the ingredients needed for such weapons. From the scientific knowledge of the day, it was known that the extremely rare natural element uranium, a heavy metal, was the most likely element in which a fission reaction (the actual splitting of the uranium atoms) might be accomplished by mechanical means. By splitting atoms an exceptionally large amount of energy is released that would be capable of splitting adjacent atoms and thus causing an instantaneous chain reaction and a tremendous explosion from a relatively small amount of material.

The scientific data of the day also indicated that two different types of atomic bombs could be produced, one powered by enriched uranium and the other by a new man-made elements that could be produced from the uranium isotope U-238. This new man-made element was plutonium.

After an intensive search, the managers of the Manhattan Project selected the Bethel Valley in eastern Tennessee, 18 miles west of Knoxville, for the facility which would enrich uranium. Another site, for the production of plutonium, was selected in Washington state.

Once selected, the area in Tennessee soon became known to its developers as "Dog Patch" after the mythical hillbilly community in the popular comic strip of the day called "L'il Abner." Land was acquired and during Oct. 1942 the large industrial complex began to rise. Each major facility was located a considerable distance from the other and the overall complex was called Clinton Laboratories after the largest community in the area, Clinton, TN, population 1540. Utilities were brought in, roads and rail lines built and a new and sizable city built for the workers.

The enriched uranium was then sent to the "wizard's workshop" in Los Alamos, NM where the scientists and engineers used it to make an atomic bomb. The target date for deploying the bomb was late 1944 or early 1945.

When the Tennessee complex was completed and the processes got underway, it was renamed the Oak Ridge National Laboratories. By the end of 1943, usable amounts of enriched uranium were on their way to Los Alamos. By Sept. 1944, Oak Ridge was producing kilogram-lots of enriched uranium and by July 1945 the scientists at Los Alamos had 50 Kg of enriched uranium which was enough to proceed with the manufacture of several uranium-type atomic bombs.

Eventually, the US developed two types of atomic bombs and both types were eventually used. The Hiroshima bomb was a enriched uranium bomb and the Nagasaki bomb was a plutonium bomb.

At the end of the war, the importance of wartime contributions made at Oak Ridge, now a city of 75,000 people, were revealed to the public.

The American Museum of Science and Energy, Oak Ridge, TN

AMERICAN MUSEUM OF SCIENCE AND ENERGY: This is a large and excellent museum in Oak Ridge that has numerous exhibits on the wartime history of Oak Ridge and its on-going contribution to peaceful uses of atomic energy. The founding of Oak Ridge during WW II is told in a permanent exhibit entitled "The Oak Ridge Story." There are replicas of "Little Boy," the enriched uranium bomb dropped on Hiroshima, and "Fat Man," the plutonium bomb dropped on Nagasaki.

Other exhibits tell of the operations of the various facilities at Oak Ridge, the development of various energy sources through the ages and the fundamentals as to how energy is generated from atoms. The Museum also has an energy science lab and offers live demonstrations and lectures.

Visitors to the Museum may also gain access to the X-10 Graphite Reactor, the oldest atomic reactor in the world and the reactor which was crucial to the development of the atomic bombs.

The Museum has an educational program, hosts social events, and has a nice gift shop with items

Tennessee

that would be difficult to find elsewhere. Address: 300 S. Tulane, Oak Ridge, TN 37830. Phone and website: 865-576-3200; www.amse.org

SEVIERVILLE is a county seat on US-411, US-441 and SR-66 and is located in the famous Gatlinburg recreational area.

TENNESSEE MUSEUM OF AVIATION AND TENNESSEE AVIATION HALL OF FAME: This fine museum and hall of fame is located in a large hangar at the Gatlinburg-Pigeon Forge Airport two miles north of Sevierville on US-411. Within its 50,000 Sq. ft. space, it has a collection of some 20 vintage aircraft, most of which are flyable. Included in the collection are several WW II aircraft and a large collection of aircraft engines.

Among the aircraft memorabilia are photos, scale models and a 52 ft. long timeline display recording national, military and Tennessee aviation milestones.

The Museum has a restoration facility which visitors can view, an on-going educational program, a newsletter, hosts many social and aviation-oriented activities and, on special occasions, offers rides in the vintage aircraft. The Museum is also the official state repository and archive for Tennessee aviation history. And don't forget to take a foray into their interesting gift shop. Address: 135 Air Museum Way, Sevierville, TN 37862. Phone and website: 866-286-8738 and 865-908-0171; www.tnairmuseum.com

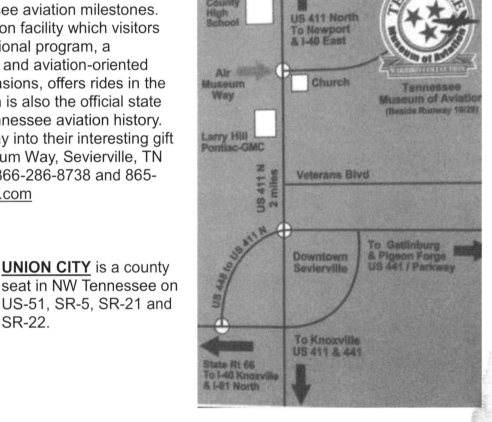

The World War II Memorial in Union City, TN

UNION CITY is a county seat in NW Tennessee on US-51, SR-5, SR-21 and SR-22.

UNION CITY WORLD WAR II MEMORIAL: This fine memorial shows the famous photo of the flag raising at Iwo Jima and gives the date of the raising, February 23, 1945. It is designed to honor the US Marines who served in WW II. Location: Courthouse lawn, Union City, TN

TEXAS

The state of Texas made a larger contribution to the war effort than did some of the Allied nations. This state, the largest state in the union at the time, provided a wide variety of weapons, ships, food and minerals, including one of the most precious wartime commodities - oil.

By 1940, the economy in some parts of Texas had improved from the depression days of the 1930s, but in other areas it was still struggling.

Aircraft manufacturers had discovered Texas' fine climate and central location and moved into Texas in significant numbers. In addition, the armed forces, in 1940 and 1941, began to build new military facilities in the state and enlarge existing ones.

During the summer of 1941, the Army carried out large-scale maneuvers in southeastern Texas that also extended into Louisiana and Mississippi.

As the war progressed, the state would have the dubious honor of seeing more of its young men and women enlist in the armed services than any other state. In addition to the many military installations in Texas, the state eventually had 120 POW camps, the most of any state.

Throughout WW II, Texas was used by all of the military services as a huge training ground for American service personnel and those of some of our Allies.

The Army Air Corps had long known that Texas had ideal flying weather and had established its headquarters and five of its major training airfields in the San Antonio area. During the war, it's successor, the Army Air Forces, and the air arm of the US Navy acquired many more airfields in the state and trained thousands of men and women in all phases of aviation.

By war's end, a total of 1.25 million service personnel had been trained in Texas.

Texas also had the third largest number of Congressional Medal of Honor winners in the nation with 26.

When the war ended, the economy of Texas was stable and growing. Texas had become the nation's third largest producer of aircraft after California and New York, and the aircraft industry had come to stay.

ABILENE/SWEETWATER AREA: Abilene is 140 miles west of Ft. Worth and Sweetwater is 40 miles west of Abilene. Both are on I-20.

12TH ARMORED DIVISION MEMORIAL MUSEUM: This interesting museum is near downtown Abilene and relates the history of the Army's 12th Armored Division which was created during WW II and trained at Camp Barkleley nine miles SW of Abilene. On display are vehicles, uniforms, military equipment, small arms, photos and more. The history of the 12th Armored Division during WW II is well documented in the displays.

The Museum offers educational programs, has a library, archives, reunion facilities and they're real friendly in the gift shop. Address: 1289 N. Second St., Abilene, TX 79601. Phone and website: 325-677-6515; www.12tharmoreddivision.com/museum.asp

THE WASP MUSEUM: W.A.S.P. - that stood for "Womens' Air Service Pilots," an organization which was created during WW II. This organization, composed of women pilots, served with the US armed forces during WW II in a very unique way. The ladies flew military aircraft to and from various destinations within the US to relieve male pilots for military duty. They trained at Avenger Field which is midway between Sweetwater and Roscoe, TX.

This is their museum. It is located in one of the pre-war hangars at Avenger Field and tells the stories of the WASPs; how and where they were formed, how they trained, how they lived and where they went in the 77 different aircraft which they flew.

On display are photos, murals, uniforms, aircraft models, posters and biographies of Jacqueline Cochran and Nancy Love who first formed the WASPs and their boss, General Harold "Hap" Arnold.

Also on display is a bronze statue of "Fifinella," the WASP mascot designed by Walt Disney Studios during the war.

The Museum has memorials, an educational program and a very interesting gift shop where one can find WASP-related souvenirs, books, apparel and other merchandise that can't be found elsewhere. Address: Avenger Field, Sweetwater, TX 79556. Phone and website: 325-235-0099; http://waspmuseum.org

The Jim Wells County World War II Memorial in Alice, TX

ALICE is a county seat in southern Texas on US-281 and SR-44.

JIM WELLS COUNTY WORLD WW II MEMORIAL: The men from Jim Wells county who gave their lives in WW II are honored by this fine stone memorial. Their names are listed on the memorial and many of them are of Spanish origin. Location: On the lawn of the County Courthouse in downtown Alice

AUSTIN, the state capitol, is 75 miles NE of San Antonio on I-35 and US-290.

TEXAS MILITARY FORCES MUSEUM: This large museum is located on the grounds of Camp Mabry, the home of the Texas Army National Guard, and traces the history of military forces and events relative to Texas history. Emphasized at the Museum is the history and activities of the Texas National Guard. The Museum traces Texas military history from early 1800s to the present and WW II displays comprise much of displays.

There are both outdoor and indoor exhibits with tanks lined up in rows, aircraft hanging from the ceiling, military vehicles, artillery pieces, uniforms, photos, posters and much more.

The Museum has an archives collection, a library, an art gallery, a Hall of Honor, information on Camp Mabry, WW II Summary Histories, dioramas, museum tours and a newsletter. And at certain times, one can dine and dance in the Museum at their many social events. Don't forget to stop at the gift shop. You will be glad you did. Address: 2200 W. 35th St., Camp Mabry, Austin, TX 78703-1222. Phone and website: 512-782-5659; www.texasmilitaryforcesmuseum.org

TEXAS WORLD WAR II MEMORIAL: Like most states, Texas has an official state WW II memorial. The Texas' World War II Memorial is in the large Capitol Square, a four block by four block campus in the center of Austin, which houses many of the state's governmental buildings. In this area, there are other monuments commemorating other American wars and historic events.

The WW II Memorial's plaque reads in part "THIS MEMORIAL HONORS THE 830,000 TEXANS WHO SERVED IN THE ARMED FORCES OF THE UNITED STATES DURING WORLD WAR II, THE MORE THAN 22,000 WHO GAVE THEIR LIVE AND THE MILLION WHO SUPPORTED THEIR

EFFORT FROM HOME..." Location: Capitol Square, Austin, TX

BONHAM is a county seat 60 miles NE of Dallas near the Oklahoma border on US-82, SR-56 and SR-78.

SAM RAYBURN HOUSE MUSEUM is located two miles west of town on SR-56. Here Sam Rayburn, who became one of the most influential politicians in the US during the war, grew to manhood with his eight brothers and sisters. Rayburn put himself through college, attained a law degree, went into politics, was elected to Congress and, in 1940, became Speaker of the House of Representative. Rayburn then held that office longer than any other man in US history to that date.

At the time, Rayburn was third in line for the presidency because the US Constitution specified that the man who held that office was next in line in the presidential succession after the President and Vice President.

The Texas WW II Memorial in Austin, TX

Rayburn became very close to President Roosevelt and was one of his strongest and most loyal supporters. When something absolutely had to be done in Congress, the top leaders in the Government went to Sam Rayburn. In this respect, he was one of the few political leaders in Washington that knew of the development of the atomic bomb because it was he who steered the $1.6 billion unnamed appropriation bill through Congress needed to finance the top secret "Manhattan Project."

All his life, Rayburn was a died-in-the-wool Southerner and kept of picture of Robert E. Lee in his office always facing south.

Rayburn's home is now a historic site and is open to the public. It is furnished with much of the original furniture and other items the family used. Rayburn returned to this house, which was the center of his family's 900 acre ranch, at every opportunity to be close to his family and friends. Several important people visited him here including his close friends Lyndon B. Johnson and Harry S Truman. Address: 890 W. SR-56, Bonham, TX 75418. Phone and website: 903-583-5558; visitsamrayburnhouse.com

Sam Rayburn's House in Bonham, TX. Rayburn was Speaker of the House of Representatives during WW II and served in that post longer than any other man to that date. During that time, he was third in line in the presidential succession.

SAM RAYBURN LIBRARY MUSEUM is on US-82 four blocks west of downtown Bonham. It preserves Rayburn's personal and official papers as well as his books, documents, records of his speeches and many other related items.

   The Library has a copy of the Congressional Record beginning with the first meeting of Congress in 1789 and exhibits that trace the life of Sam Rayburn from a farm boy to one of the most powerful men in American politics. A replica of Rayburn's Washington office is also on display in the Library. Address: 800 W. Sam Rayburn Dr., Bonham, TX 75418. Phone and website: 903-583-2455; www.bonhamchamber.com/

BROWNSVILLE/HARLINGEN AREA: This is a rich agricultural area at the southern tip of Texas on the Mexican border and near the mouth of the Rio Grande River. In the 1930s, the Brownsville area, because of its strategic location, had become an important air link with Latin America. It remained so during and after the war until long-range jet aircraft made its geographical location less important.

   Early in the war, a Civil Air Patrol unit was very active in Brownsville patrolling the Texas coastline, the US/Mexican border and offshore waters.

   No POW camps were located in this area because it was believed that the close proximity of Mexico would encourage escape attempts.

COMMEMORATIVE AIR FORCE MUSEUM: This unique museum collects displays and flies vintage aircraft many of which are of from WW II. It is located at Brownsville/South Padre Island International Airport and some of the planes are privately owned by members of the Commemorative Air Force Association.

   Other displays at the Museum include military vehicles, artillery pieces, small arms, field equipment, uniforms, dioramas, documents, photographs, paintings and drawings, flags, medals and more. There is also an inviting gift shop and you can visit the Barnstormer Lounge for a bit of refreshment. Address: 955 Minnesota Av., Brownsville, TX 78521. Phone and website: 956-541-8585; rgvwingcaf.com/

IWO JIMA WAR MEMORIAL is located on the south campus parade deck of the Marine Military Academy at the west end of Harlingen Industrial Air Park. The statue of the famous flag-raising at Iwo Jima on February 23, 1945 is the center piece of the memorial and was the original sculpture used as the model for the bronze memorial sculpture which was later placed at the entrance to Arlington National Cemetery in Virginia. This model was made of plaster but was then covered with fiberglass to preserve it. The figures are 32 ft. high, the flag-pole is 78 ft. long and the sculpture weighs 130 tons.

   Adjacent to the Memorial is a Museum and visitors center displaying many artifacts related to the battle of Iwo Jima and the histories of the men in the statue. There is also a very nice gift shop. Address: 320 Iwo Jima Blvd., Harlingen, TX 78550. Phone: 956-423-6006

COLLEGE STATION is a small community in east central Texas on SR-6 about 70 miles NW of Houston.

BRAZOS VALLEY VETERANS MEMORIAL: This is a large park in which visitors walk along pathways to various memorials commemorating all of America's major military conflicts. One starts at the Louis L. Adams Memorial Plaza which has a Wall of Honor and a bronze statue of a GI carrying

This is one of several impressive bronze statues at the Brazos Valley Veterans Memorial in College Station, TX. It shows a WW II GI carrying another wounded GI on his back.

another wounded GI on his back.   Further along the pathway, is the WW II Memorial which features a bronze statue of President George H. W. Bush in his WW II aviators uniform looking skyward. President Bush was, of course, a Texan.

As one walks along the pathways, there will be memorials to other conflicts including the 9/II disaster. Address: 3101 Harvey Rd. (SR-6), College Station, TX 77842. Phone and website: 979-450-3298; www.bvvm.org

MUSEUM OF THE AMERICAN GI: This is the Brent Mullins collection of military vehicles and is recognized as one of the finest privately held military vehicle collections in the world. Most of the vehicles are from WW II. There are tanks, tank destroyers, weapons carriers, Jeeps and armored cars. And there are several WW I vehicles and artillery pieces.

The Museum has a library and educational program and hosts social and military-related events. Address: 1303 Cherokee St., College Station, TX 77802. Phone and website: 979-777-2820 and 979-255-3675; www.magicstx.org

CORPUS CHRISTI is a major seaport in SE Texas on the Gulf of Mexico, I-37 and US-181. It has the deepest harbor in Texas and was an important seaport for the US Navy during the war.

USS LEXINGTON **MUSEUM ON THE BAY** is located on the Corpus Christi waterfront just across the ship channel from downtown Corpus Christi. Its centerpiece is the famous WW II aircraft carrier *Lexington.* This ship was commissioned in 1943 and saw a lot of action in the Pacific from Tarawa to Tokyo. Following WW II, the "Lady Lex" continued in operation and served the US Navy longer than

any other aircraft carrier in the history of the US Navy to date. In its last years of service, it was a training carrier for naval airmen and crewmen.

The ship was brought to Corpus Christi in January 1992 and opened to the public in October of that year. The *Lexington* has several WW II aircraft on display and, as a museum, focuses on education, US naval history, patriotism and entertainment. Tours of the ship are available and there is a free MEGA theater which shows a large format movie on the history of the ship. There is also a ship's store offering many interesting items related to Lady Lex and the US Navy in general.Address: 2914 N. Shoreland Blvd., Corpus Christi, TX 78402. Phone and website: 800-LADY-LEX (800-523-9539) and 361-888-4873; www.usslexington.com

The WW II aircraft carrier Lexington is on display and open to the public on the Corpus Christi waterfront.

DALLAS/FORT WORTH AREA: These two cities in NE Texas comprised the largest metropolitan area in the state. This was a major manufacturing area with factories that built Jeeps, aircraft and many other items of war.

NO. 1 BRITISH FLYING TRAINING SCHOOL MUSEUM: This unique museum is located at the Terrell Municipal Airport in Terrell, TX, on US-80, an eastern suburb of Dallas. During WW II, thousands of British airmen trained in the US at six civilian flight schools. The first and largest of these schools was here in Terrell.

  The Museum commemorates those historic events and the teachers and students who participated in the programs. On display are many artifacts related to the training activities: books, charts, maps, uniforms, log books, photos, memorabilia, personal items and more. The Museum is also host to fly-ins and social events. Address: 119 Silent Wings Blvd., Terrell, TX 75160. Phone and website: 972-524-1714; www.bftsmuseum.org

CAVANAUGH FLIGHT MUSEUM is located at Addison Airport in Addison, a northern suburb of Dallas. The mission of the Museum is to perpetuate America's aviation heritage and to preserve, maintain, restore and fly vintage aircraft. This is a large museum housed in four hangars and has a large collection of vintage aircraft including over 20 WW II warbirds. There are also aircraft from WW I, Korea and Viet Nam. Some of the aircraft are flyable and rides are offered at times.

  There is also a collection of military vehicles and civilian automobiles and many aircraft-related artifacts on display. The Museum has an impressive gift shop, a picnic area and a canteen. Address: 4572 Claire Chennault, Addison, TX 75001. Phone and website: 972-380-8800; www.cavanaughflightmuseum.com

DECATURE is a county seat 38 miles NW of Fort Worth on US-81, US-287 and US-380.

THE LOST BATTALION ROOM IN THE WISE COUNTY MUSEUM: This interesting museum room is maintained by the Lost Battalion Association and commemorated the men of the 2nd Battalion, 131st Field Artillery, a unit of the Texas National Guard. Some of the men were from this area in north Texas.

  The Battalion was aboard the cruiser *USS Houston* when it was sunk off the Dutch East Indies in March 1942. Some of the survivors of the Battalion swam ashore but were captured by the Japanese and endured 42 month of "hell" as prisoners of war. This museum honors those men and those who perished and commemorates their sacrifices. Their cruel and deprived treatment at the hands of the Japanese captors is explained in great detail in artifacts, photos, memorabilia and personal stories. The displays in the Museum Room also record the suffering of other American POWs during the war.

  The Wise County Museum, of course, has numerous displays of local interest and a fine gift shop. Address of the Museum: 1602 S. Trinity, Decatur, TX 76234. Phone and website: 940-627-5586; www.wisehistory.com/

DENISON is 65 miles north of Dallas on US-75 near the Oklahoma state line.

EISENHOWER BIRTHPLACE STATE HISTORIC SITE: General Dwight D. Eisenhower was born in Denison in 1890. His family lived here because his father worked for the local railroad. Six months after Dwight was born, the family moved to Abilene, Kansas. Dwight was the only one of the Eisenhower children to be born in Texas. In his younger days, he wasn't quite sure where in Texas he

This is the house in Denison, TX where Dwight D.Eisenhower was born in 1890. It is now a State Historic Site

had been born and when he entered West Point Military Academy he gave as his birthplace Tyler, TX.

Because Eisenhower was born in Denison and his military an political careers were so outstanding, his birthplace is classified as a State Historic Site.

The house has been restored and furnished to its 1890 appearance and is open to the public. Address: 609 S. Lamar Av., Denison, TX 75021. Phone and website: 903-465-8908; www.visiteisenhowerbirthplace.com/

EISENHOWER STATE PARK is a lake-front park five miles NE of Denison on US-75 and named in honor of Dwight D. Eisenhower. The Park offers camping, boating, picnicking, trails, swimming and other recreational activities. Address: 50 Park Rd. 20,Denison, TX

EL PASO is at the extreme western end of Texas on the Rio Grande River and the Mexican and New Mexico borders. The town was one of several western cities that experienced a rapid and permanent population growth during and after WW II.

Just north of town is Fort Bliss, one of the US Army's largest installations where many thousands of US servicemen trained during WW II.

On the early morning of July 16, 1945 some of the citizens of El Paso saw a sudden and strange flash of light in the northern sky. No one knew it at the time, but it was the flash from the world's first atomic bomb test at White Sands, NM 130 miles distant. At the time, they were told that a remote ammunition storage facility had exploded.

Just across the state line in New Mexico is the War Eagle Museum which has considerable information, artifacts and displays related to WW II. See the New Mexico listing for details.

FIRST ARMORED "OLD IRONSIDES" DIVISION & FORT BLISS MUSEUMS: These two museums are in the same building located on the grounds of Fort Bliss.

The First Armored Division Museum relates the history of that Army division from it's inception to the present. Over the years, the Division has been known as "Old Ironsides."

On display are tanks, military vehicles, uniforms, small arms, photos, documents and many other artifacts related the history of the Division.

The Fort Bliss Museum tells the origin and history of this old and historic US Army installation. Address: 1735 Marshall Rd., Fort Bliss, TX, 79916. Phone and website: 915-568-5412; www.bliss.army.mil/

US ARMY MUSEUM OF THE NONCOMMISSIONED OFFICER: This is another museum at Fort Bliss which, as the title indicates, traces the history of the Army's NCOs. The Museum features exhibits on the changing role of the Noncommissioned Officer in the US Army from 1775 to the present through displays of equipment and uniforms used by staff sergeants and other NCOs. Address: Bldg. 11331 Staff Sergeant Simms St., Biggs Army Airfield, Ft. Bliss, TX. Phone and website: 915-744-8646/8306; https://usasma.bliss.army.mil/

FORT WORTH (See Dallas/Fort Worth Area)

FREDERICKSBURG is a county seat 60 miles north of San Antonio on US-87 and US-290.

NATIONAL MUSEUM OF THE PACIFIC WAR: This is America's only museum devoted exclusively to the war in the Pacific. It also relates the personal history of Admiral Chester Nimitz who was born and raised in Fredericksburg.

   The Museum complex included the restored steamboat-styled Nimitz Hotel near downtown Fredericksburg which was built in 1852 by Nimitz' grandfather.

   Displays on the Museum's grounds are arranged in chronological order beginning with the days when Nimitz was a youth and ending with his death in 1966.

   A large part of the Museum is in another building, the George H. W. Bush Gallery. Bush was another Texan and President of the United States. This facility has its own gift shop, the George H. W. Bush Museum Store.

   On display in the Museum complex are many exhibits related to the major conflicts in the Pacific; Pearl Harbor, Guadalcanal, the Doolittle Raid (which includes a restored B-25 bomber of the type used in the raid), island hopping, the Philippines, Iwo Jima, the Japanese surrender and more. There are US and captured enemy weapons including a Japanese midget submarine.

   The Museum also has a Garden of Peace donated by the people of Japan, a picnic area and a large and interesting bookstore called the Admiral Nimitz Bookstore. Address of the Museum: 340 E. Main St., Fredericksburg, TX 78624. Address of The Admiral Nimitz Bookstore: 328 E. Main St., Fredericksburg, TX 78624. Address of the George H. W. Bush Gallery Museum Store: 311 E. Austin St., Fredericksburg, TX 78624. Phone and website of the Museum: 830-997-8600; www.nimitz-museum.org. Phone of the Admiral Nimitz Museum Bookstore; 830-997-8600 Ext. 208. Phone of the George H. W. Bush Gallery Museum Store; 830-997-8600 Ext. 252

The National Museum of the Pacific War in Fredericksburg, TX

GAINSVILLE is a county seat in north Texas on I-35 and just south of the Oklahoma state line. When you are driving south on I-35 and cross the Red River into Texas there is a Texas Welcome Center. This Center has a unique WW II memorial.

TEXAS WELCOME CENTER WW II MEMORIAL: This is a large memorial with a nine ft. bronze statue of a charging GI, carrying his M-1 rifle and ready for action. Surrounding this central figure are several stone monuments with plaques honoring the 847 men of the 103rd Infantry Division who gave their lives in WW II. The plaques give various statistics and historical information with regard to the Division and lists the names of the missing in action. Location: Texas Welcome Center, 4901 N. I-35, Gainesville, TX

The Texas Welcome Center WW II Memorial in Gainesville, TX

GALVESTON AREA: Galveston is a county seat on the Texas coast 30 miles SE of Houston and at the end of I-45. During WW II, it was one of Texas' most strategically located cities. From here, air patrols fanned out to cover and protect a large part of the Gulf of Mexico and Galveston Bay, which was the departure point of much of the state's oil that was shipped by sea. Large convoys formed up in Galveston Bay, loaded with oil and other vital war materials, and set sail for distant locations.

After the war, Galveston Bay became one of the larger mothball anchorages for the surplus ships of WW II.

GALVESTON WW II MEMORIAL: Inscribed on this tall stone memorial are the words "WORLD WAR II GALVESTON COUNTY WAR DEAD 1941-THESE GAVE ALL-1945." Their names are listed on the Memorial. Location: Broadway and 23rd St., Galveston, TX

*The Galveston WW II Memorial
in Galveston, TX*

LONE STAR FLIGHT MUSEUM is located at Galveston's International Airport at Scholes Field and specializes in the collecting of aircraft from the 1930s and 1940s. Military planes from WW II make up a large part of the collection. Most of the Museum's aircraft are flyable and rides for the public are offered.

The Museum is also the home of the Texas Aviation Hall of Fame, hosts social events and airshows, has an educational program and an excellent gift shop. Military vehicles are also on display. Address: 2002 Terminal Dr., Galveston, TX 77554. Phone and website: 409-740-7722/888-359-5736; www.lsfm.org

SEAWOLF **PARK** is located on the eastern shore of Pelican Island which is north of, and across the Port of Galveston Channel, from Galveston. The main facilities of the Park were once an immigrant quarantine station.

The Park bears the name *Seawolf* and serves as a permanent memorial to the WW II submarine, *Seawolf,* which was lost in action during WW II. In the Park is a three-story pavilion with historical displays, two WW II vessels, the submarine *Cavalla* and the destroyer escort *Stewart (DE-238).*

The WW II submarine, Cavalla, and the destroyer escort, Stewart, are on display at Seawolf Park in Galveston, TX

The *Cavalla* saw action in the Pacific and is credited with sinking one of Japan's largest aircraft carriers, the *Shokaku*. The submarine was decommissioned and arrived here at Galveston in 1971.

The *Stewart*, which was built in Houston, also saw action during the war in both the Atlantic and Pacific, and is one of the very few destroyer escorts to survive the war to become a memorial. Both ships are open to the public.

There is also a fishing pier and a fine gift shop which one should not pass up. Address: Seawolf

Parkway at 51st St., Galveston Island, Galveston, TX 77550. Phone and website: 409-797-5114; www.galveston.com/seawolfpark/

GATESVILLE is a county seat 38 miles west of Waco on US-84 and SR-36. Just to the south of town is the huge US Army facility, Fort Hood.

FIRST CAVALRY DIVISION MUSEUM: This is one of two cavalry museums associated with Fort Hood. This museum honors the men and women who served in the First Cavalry Division from its inception to the present. The 1st Cavalry Division has, for years, been located at Fort Hood.

The mission of the Museum is to collect, preserve, interpret, exhibit and educate military personnel and the general public on the composition of, and the history of, this famous US Army unit. Displays trace the entire history of the unit and there is considerable information about the unit's activities during WW II in the Pacific Theater of Operations.

One of the proudest moments in the Division's history was when it was given the honor of leading all American units into Tokyo in 1945 after Japan's surrender. The Division then served as one of the US occupation forces n Japan.

There is an extensive outdoor display to tanks, armored personnel carriers, artillery pieces and other vehicles used by the Division. WW II vehicles are a part of the display.

The Museum offers public programs, hosts social and military events, provides tours and has a very interesting gift shop. Address: 1st Cavalry Museum, Ft. Hood, TX 76545. Phone and website: 254-287-3626/254-286-5684; www.hood.army.mil/

3d CAVALRY MUSEUM: This is the second cavalry museum at Fort Hood and honors the men and women of the 3d Cavalry Regiment who served in this important Army unit throughout its long history. The Museum preserves, displays and explains many of the artifacts used by the 3d Cavalry. There is also a large memorabilia collection and considerable information about the unit's activities during WW II in the European Theater of Operations. The Museum has a research room, a children's exhibit and a gift shop that is well worth your time to visit. Address: Third Cavalry Museum, Fort Hood, TX 76545. Phone and website: 254-288-3590/254-287-8811; www.hood.army.mil

GREENVILLE is a county seat 40 miles NE of Dallas on I-30 and US-69.

AUDIE MURPHY/AMERICAN COTTON MUSEUM: The famous WW II hero and later, movie actor, Audie Murphy, grew up in Greenville. His father was a share cropper on a cotton farm.

The town's main museum, the American Cotton Museum, has honored their local son with a handsome memorial on the Museum grounds. It consists of a bronze statue of Murphy in action and serves as the centerpiece of a general memorial honoring all of the veterans who served in the US armed forces from Hunt County. Details of Murphy's heroic actions are etched into nearby stone monuments.

The Audie Murphy Memorial at the American Cotton Museum in Greenville, TX

The American Cotton Museum highlights the cotton industry in the Northern Texas Blacklands and the contribution of cotton and the industry to the people of Texas and the United States. Address: 600 Interstate 30 East, Greenville, TX 75403. Phone and website: 903-450-4502; www.cottonmuseum.com

HARLINGEN (See Brownsville/Harlingen Area)

HOUSTON AREA: This is a large metropolitan area in SE Texas near the Gulf of Mexico. It has long been a major seaport and much of the Texas oil used by the US military during WW II was shipped through this port.

The battleship Texas saw action in both WW I and WW II and is on display at San Jacinto State Historic Site near Houston, TX

BATTLESHIP *TEXAS* STATE HISTORIC SITE is located about 18 miles west of downtown Houston at San Jacinto Battleground State Historical Park. The *USS Texas* (BB-35) is the only battleship on display in the US that took part if both WW I and WW II. The ship was commissioned in 1914 and served the US Navy for 32 years.

During WW II, the *Texas* escorted convoys across the Atlantic, participated in the landings in North Africa, Normandy, Okinawa and Iwo Jima. The ship is now open to the public and is available for conferences, educational programs and overnight camping. Much of the ship's original equipment is still intact and there are displays of artifacts and other items associated with the ship. Address: 3523 Independence Parkway, La Porte, TX 77571. Phone and website: 281-479-2431; www.tpwd.state.tx.us

HOUSTON HEIGHTS WORLD WAR II BATTLEGROUND MEMORIAL: Houston Heights is a section of greater Houston and, during the war, many of its sons went to war. Some did not return. To commemorate those who served, the community has erected this beautiful circular memorial which lists their names. In the center of the Memorial is a flag pole and a pylon topped by a large stone globe. Location: 11th St and Heights Blvd.

The Houston Heights World War II Battleground Memorial. Located in Houston Heights, TX

NATIONAL UNITED STATES ARMED FORCES MUSEUM: In this museum visitors will see a wide variety of military vehicles and artifacts used by the various branches of the US armed forces. The Museum highlights many of the Army and Marine Corps Divisions and tells of their histories and exploits. Many of the units were activated during WWW II.

Information on the US Navy's Second, Third and Fifth Fleets is also detailed and museum tours are provided. Address: 8611 Wallisville Rd., Houston, TX 77029. Phone and website: 713-673-1234; www.nusafm.org

***USS HOUSTON* MEMORIAL:** The cruiser *Houston* was one of the first US naval casualties of WW II after the Pearl Harbor attack. The ship was sunk by Japanese action in late February 1942 in the Dutch East Indies and many of its crew members were taken prisoner by the Japanese and frequently maltreated during their captivity.

   The ship's bell was salvaged from the wreck and mounted atop the Memorial's tall granite monument which commemorates the ship and its crew. Location: Sam Houston Park, 1000 Bagby St. Houston, TX 77002

<u>KILLEEN</u> (See Waco/Temple/Killeen Area)

<u>LUBBOCK</u> is a county seat 105 miles south of Amarillo on I-27, US-62 and US-84. During the war, the city's local airport was taken over by the Army Air Forces to train glider pilots.

SILENT WINGS MUSEUM is located at the Lubbock International Airport north of Lubbock just off I-27. This unique museum is one of very few in that nation that highlights WW II gliders. Gliders were lightly built air frames without motors. They were loaded with men and/or equipment, towed to a location by a larger plane, let loose and landed on their own wherever they could find a suitable landing spot.

   The Museum has a restored Waco CG-4A glider which was the mainstay of the US Army's glider force as well as a C-47 transport plane that usually towed them into combat. There are also photos, airborne equipment, exhibits and artifacts related to gliders, a library, an archives collection and an educational program.

   The Museum has special events throughout the year and a fine museum store. When arriving at the International Airport, look for the tower with the silver "G-Wings" on it. That's the Silent Wings Museum. Address: 6202 N. I-27, Lubbock, TX 79403. Phone and website: 806-775-3049 (direct), 806-775-3796 (information); www.silentwingsmuseum.com

<u>McALLEN</u> is a county seat in the Rio Grande Valley of Texas close to the Mexican border on US-83 and US-281.

McALLEN VETERAN'S WAR MEMORIAL: Here is a very large and impressive war memorial honoring those individuals from the McAllen area, and all Americans, who served in the various American conflicts. The World War II Memorial section has many flag poles, beautiful landscaping, benches, walkways and eight granite walls used to inscribe names, facts, depictions, pictures, phrases, war facts and information on organizations and individuals tied to the WW II time period.
Wall 1 tells of the start of the war in Europe in September 1939 and the attack on Pearl Harbor.
Wall 2 tells of the fall of the Philippines, the early Pacific offensive and the Solomon Islands campaign.
Wall 3 describes the US campaign in North Africa and the invasion of Italy.
Wall 4 provides additional information on the actions in the South Pacific and describes the various island campaigns.
Wall 5 tells of US activities in the China-Burma-India (CBI) area and the D-Day invasion at Normandy.
Wall 6 gives accounts of actions in the South Pacific; Guam, Palau, the Philippines and the Battle of the Bulge in Europe.
Wall 7 describes the air war in Europe, the US crossing of the Rhine River, the death of Adolph Hitler,

261

the linkup of American and Soviet forces at the Elbe River and the German surrender. It goes on to relate the on-going conflict in the Pacific, the battles for Iwo Jima and Okinawa and the Japanese Kamikazes, the atomic bombs and Japan's surrender.

Wall 8 lists the casualties of the war for the various US branches of service, the Allies, the Axis nations and civilian casualties.

The Submariners of WW II Wall lists the American submarines involved in the war and those that were lost in action.

WAC, WAVE and Semper Fi Walls honor the American women who served in the war.

Mexican Expeditionary Air Force Escudron 201 Historic Wall: This is a very unique, one-of-a-kind memorial. During WW II, the Mexican Government sent a contingent of Mexican pilots to McAllen to be trained by the US Army Air Forces and serve with American forces in the Pacific. They flew P-47 fighter planes and were called the "Aztec Angels." They saw action in the Philippines and at Okinawa, flew over 1290 combat hours and lost seven of their number. This memorial honors those men and lists their names.

The Warrior Statue honors the American fighting spirit and has a dramatic statue of the GI throwing a hand grenade.

The location of the McAllen Veteran's War Memorial is at the intersection of Galveston Blvd. and S. 29th St. in McAllen.

The McAllen Veteran's War Memorial in McAllen, TX

The WAC, WAVE and Semper Fi Memorial in the McAllen Veteran's War Memorial in McAllen, TX.

<u>MIDLAND</u>: Midland is a county seat 250 miles east of El Paso on I-20.

COMMEMORATIVE AIR FORCE MUSEUM. This large and impressive museum is located at Midland International Airport and has a collection of over 30 vintage aircraft, several of which are of WW II vintage. The Museum focuses on the complete history of aviation during WW II with emphasis on the war in the Pacific, strategic bombing, D-Day and the atomic bomb. There are many artifacts and pieces of memorabilia from WW II, a research library, a large collection of original WW II nose art panels, an art gallery, a USO exhibit, the American Combat Airman Hall of Fame, military vehicles and a large and interesting gift shop. During the year, the Museum hosts public events and airshows. Address: 9600 Wright Dr., Midland, TX 79711. Phone and website: 432-563-1000; www.airpowermuseum.org

<u>ODESSA</u> is a county seat in west Texas on I-20 and US-385.

THE PRESIDENTIAL MUSEUM AND LEADERSHIP LIBRARY: This facility is on the campus of the University of Texas of the Permian Basin and is the only facility of its kind in the US. It is dedicated to those individuals who were US presidents or sought to be US presidents. There are many exhibits in the Museum and information on US election campaigning and the American political process.

Included in the exhibits is information on WW II personalities who had presidential aspirations: Franklin D. Roosevelt, Harry S Truman, John Nance Garner, Henry Wallace, Wendell Willkie, Charles NcNary (Willkie's VP running mate), Thomas Dewey, John Bricker (Dewey's VP running mate), Dwight Eisenhower, Richard Nixon, Douglas MacArthur, Robert Taft, Averill Harriman and Paul V. McNutt.

There are numerous displays of campaign materials, presidential artifacts, posters, newspaper clippings, inaugural addresses, First Lady dolls and much more. And in the gift shop one will find considerable information on the presidents and would-be presidents. Address: 4919 E. University Blvd., Odessa, TX 79762. Phone: 432-363-7737

PERRYTON is a county seat in the Texas panhandle on US-83 and SR-15 just south of the Oklahoma state line.

OCHILTREE COUNTY WORLD WAR II MEMORIAL: There are many names on this stone memorial, some with gold stars in front of them. These are the men from Ochiltree County who served in WW II and the gold stars indicate those who gave their lives. Location: Ochiltree County Courthouse lawn, 6th and Main Sts. in downtown Perryton

The Ochiltree County World War II Memorial in Perryton, TX

SAN ANTONIO is one of the state's larger cities and is in south-central Texas. Years before WW II, the Army had selected San Antonio to be the home of the Army's fledgling aviation service which, in its beginning, was under the control of the Army's Signal Corps. In 1917, two airfields were built in the San Antonio area to serve as an aviation cantonment of Fort Sam Houston, a long standing military post. They were Kelly and Brooks Fields.

The San Antonio area was chosen because of its good flying weather which was so important in those early days of flying. Here the Army Signal Corps trained its pilots, crewmen, maintenance men, administrators and other aviation personnel.

As the Army Air Corps gained its own identity and grew in military importance so did these facilities. New facilities were established elsewhere in the country, but they were almost always spin offs of the San Antonio airfields.

In 1928-30, a new and modern airfield, Randolph Field, was built in San Antonio confirming and solidifying the fact that San Antonio was the home of the Army Air Corps. Together, the three San Antonio airfields were referred to as the "West Point of the Air."

FORT SAM HOUSTON MUSEUM: This is one of two museum on the grounds of Fort Sam Houston which is three miles north of downtown Houston. The Museum traces the history of the Fort from its beginning to the present. There are exhibits on the US 5th Army and the 2nd Infantry Div., the birth of military aviation and the famous Americans who served here.

   The Museum has an extensive collection of POW artifacts from WW II, uniforms, military equipment, accouterments, arms, edged weapons, vehicles, flags and insignias. The Museum has a large library and an interesting museum store. Address: 1210 Stanley Rd., Fort Sam Houston, TX 78234. Phone and website: 210-221-0019. www.sanantoniocvb.com

US ARMY MEDICAL DEPARTMENT MUSEUM: The US Army Academy of Health Sciences is located at Fort Sam Houston and it is fitting that this museum, the second of two museums at Fort Sam Houston, is located here. This is the official museum of the Army's medical department and serves as an educational facility showing the history and development of the Army's medical department and military medical equipment. It also traces the history of the US Army's medical departments from 1775 to the present with ample displays and information on the Army's medical services during WW II. In addition, the Museum augments the training of the thousands of military and civilian students that attend the US Army Academy of Health Services at Fort Sam Houston each year.

   On display is medical equipment from the US and foreign countries, uniforms, vehicles, photos, works of art, films and more. There is an extensive archives collection, a library and a fine - don't pass it up - gift shop. Address: 2310 Stanley Rd., Building 1046,, Fort Sam Houston, San Antonio, TX 78234. Phone and website: 210-221-6358; http://ameddregiment.amedd.army,mil. Gift shop phone: 210-225-0015

SWEETWATER (See Abilene/Sweetwater Area)

TEMPLE is a county seat 38 miles south of Waco on I-35 and US-190. It is one of several townS closely associated with Fort Hood which is just west of town.

THE COMPANY I, 143rd INFANTRY REGIMENT, 36th INFANTRY DIVISION MEMORIAL: The 143rd Regiment of the US 36th Infantry Division was a unit of the Texas National Guard that saw considerable action in Europe during WW II. It fought at Anzio, Rome, the Ardennes and in Alsace.

   The unit gained considerable attention during the war for their exploits and were referred to as the "Texas T-Patchers" because of their distinctive shoulder patch which contains a large and bold letter "T."

   This memorial commemorates their efforts and bravery. Location: On the lawn of the Bell County Courthouse in downtown Temple

The Company I, 143rd Regiment, 36th Infantry Division Memorial in Temple, TX

UVALDE is a county seat 70 miles west of San Antonio on US-83 and US-90.

GARNER MEMORIAL MUSEUM is the former home of Vice President John Nance "Cactus Jack" Garner who was President Roosevelt's Vice President from 1933 to 1941. Garner was the local Congressman from the Uvalde area who rose to become Speaker of the House of Representatives and then Vice President for Roosevelt's first two terms. Garner actively supported Roosevelt's New Deal in the early years, but then turned against him. He sought the Democrat presidential nomination for himself in 1940, but was unsuccessful. He then actively campaigned against Roosevelt and his third term.

Garner eventually returned to Uvalde and lived out the remainder of his life in this house. He is buried in the town's cemetery.

The Museum has displays tracing the private and political life of Garner and has many of his personal artifacts. Address: 333 N. Park St., Uvalde, TX 78801. Phone: 830-278-5018

The Garner Memorial Museum in Uvalde, TX was the home of John Nance Garner, Vice President of the United States during the early part of WW II.

UTAH

Utah contributed to the successful conclusion of WW II in a variety of ways despite its relatively small wartime population of only 550,000 people. To solve the persistent labor shortage due to the small population, many women and imported laborers from Mexico worked on farms, in industry and in the mines. In 1952, Utah's mining industry added another commodity, uranium. The open pit uranium mine near Moab would become one of the nations largest.

In 1940-41, major military facilities were constructed in Utah at Ogden, Salt Lake City and Wendover which helped to stimulate the state's economy. In 1942, even more military facilities would be built in the state. Many of the military facilities in northern Utah were depots because it had long been recognized by the US military leaders that this area was strategically located for shipping supplies to seaports all along the US West Coast. Therefore, northern Utah became a storehouse and distribution point for war materials heading west.

BRIGHAM CITY is a county seat 20 miles north of Ogden on I-15/84.

The GI Statue in Brigham City, UT

GI STATUE: Standing atop the stone base of this impressive memorial is a bronze statue of an American GI of WW II. Plaques on the stone base list the names of citizens of Box Elder County who lost their lives during WW II. Location: On the grounds of the Box Elder County Courthouse, near the

265

intersection of Main and Forest Sts.

OGDEN, 25 miles north of Salt lake City on I-15/84, is a county seat and one of the state's larger cities. This was the city in the central Rocky Mountain area best situated to facilitate rail transportation to the West Coast. Ogden therefore became a prime location of military depots.

JOHN M. BROWNING FIREARMS MUSEUM is one of several museums located in the restored Ogden Union Station near downtown Ogden. It was from this station that much of the war materials stored in the Ogden area were shipped to the West Coast seaports.

  The Browning Museum honors the memory of John M. Browning, a gunsmith, who was instrumental in the development of several of the most widely used firearms of WW II. The Museum displays a wide selection of military and civilian firearms with some interesting models from WW II. Of particular interest, is a display of the prototypes and first production models of the Browning Automatic Rifle (BAR) which was used by almost every infantry squad in the US Army during WW II. There is also a 50 Cal. heavy-barrel machine gun that was used by all the services during WW II and a 37 mm cannon of the type used in the nose of P-39 fighter planes.

  There is a fine gift shop in the Union Station facility plus a railroad museum, and antique car museum and an art gallery. Address: Union Station, 25th & Wall Sts., Ogden, UT 84401. Phone and website: 801-393-9882; www.theunionstation.org/browningmuseum.html

HILL AEROSPACE MUSEUM: This impressive air museum is on the grounds of Hill Air Force Base and has a large collection of vintage aircraft and displays tracing the history of the base from its

construction during WW II to the present. Many of the aircraft are from WW II and are on display inside and outside the Museum. There are many other aircraft and aerospace displays inside the Museum as well as a restoration facility and a fine gift shop. WW II aircraft include a B-17, B-24, B-26, B-29, P-40, P-47, P-51 PT-17 and a German V-1 "Buzzbomb." Address: 7061 Wardleight Rd., Hill Air Force Base, UT 84056. Phone and website: 801-777-6868/6818; www.hill.af.mil/library/museum

HOOPER WORLD WAR II MEMORIAL: Hooper is an Ogden suburb, nine miles SW of downtown Ogden, and has a very interesting WW II memorial. It consists of two large WW II era artillery pieces and a stone memorial with a bronze plaque listing the names of those individuals from the local area who served in WW II. Location: In Hooper Park, 5600 S 6300 W, Hooper, UT

The Hooper WW II Memorial in Hooper, UT

RANDOLPH is a county seat in the NE corner of the Utah Panhandle on SR-16.

RICH COUNTY WORLD WAR II MEMORIAL: This attractive memorial consists of three stone panels with a statue of a WW II serviceman atop the center panel. Inscribed on the panels are the names of the local residents who served and died in WW II.

The Rich County World War II Memorial in Randolph, UT

Location: In front of the Rich County Courthouse at Church St. and Main

RIVERTON is a small community 13 miles south of downtown Salt Lake City just off I-15 and on SR-68.

US SUBMARINE VETERANS WORLD WAR II MEMORIAL: This handsome memorial is one of several memorials in Riverton's 30 acre Utah State Veterans Memorial Park which is adjacent to Camp W. G. Williams Military Reservation, home of Utah's Army National Guard.

  The Memorial consists of a WW II torpedo mounted on a base and housed in an open air pavilion which overlooking grave sites. There is a bronze plaque that pays special tribute to the crew of the submarine, *USS Harper,* which set a wartime record by sinking five Japanese destroyers in a period of five days. The *Harper* was later lost at sea. Location: 17111 Camp Williams Rd., Riverton, UT

The US Submarine Veterans World War II Memorial in Riverton, UT

SALT LAKE CITY is the capitol of Utah on I-15 and I-80. It is Utah's largest city and the home of historic Fort Douglas.

The Fort Douglas Military Museum is housed in one of the Fort's hundred-year-old buildings

FORT DOUGLAS MILITARY MUSEUM: This is a small museum on the grounds of Fort Douglas that offers displays and information on the history of the Fort. Included in the displays are military uniforms dating from 1853. There is The Fort Douglas Military Museum housed in one of the Fort's hundred-year-old buildings also a library and a nice gift shop. Displays on the WW II era are limited but interesting. Address: 32 Potter St., Fort Douglas, UT 84113. Phone and website: 801-581-1251; www.fortdouglas.org

TOOELE is a county seat 25 miles SW of Salt Lake City on SR-36 and SR-112.

TOOELE WORLD WAR II MEMORIAL: This is a simple but attractive stone memorial commemorating World War II. It is one of five similar memorials to American conflicts which are located nearby. Location: Veterans Memorial area in downtown Tooele

The Tooele World War II Memorial in Tooele, UT

VERNAL is a county seat in east central Utah near the Colorado state line and on US-40, US-191 and SR-121.

WORLD WAR II "THE WAR TO END ALL WARS" MEMORIAL: This memorial offers an optimistic note about ending all wars, shows a map of the world and two American WW II bombers. Etched into the stone base are the names of the 92 people from the Vernal area who served in the war. Unfortunately, WW II did not end all wars. Location: 147 E. Main St., Vernal, Utah

The World War II "The War to End All Wars" Memorial in Vernal, UT

WENDOVER is 110 miles west of Salt Lake City on I-80 and the Nevada border. It was just south of town, at Wendover Field, that the air crews who dropped the atomic bombs on Japan trained for those missions.

WENDOVER WELCOME CENTER: This welcome center is across the state line in West Wendover, Nevada near I-80 Exit #1 and has displays on Wendover Field and the 509th Composite Group that trained here and eventually dropped the atomic bombs on Japan. Also on display in the Welcome Center are uniforms, photos and memorabilia.

VERMONT

During WW II, Vermont had one of the smallest populations of all the states, yet, the 359,231 residents of the state made a meaningful contribution to the war effort. Vermont had a strong industrial base primarily in quality machine tools, foundry work and metal cutting tools. These much-needed products poured forth from Vermont's factories in great numbers during the war.

The state was the national leader in the production of asbestos and one of the top leaders in the production of granite, marble, slate, maple syrup and maple sugar. The two latter products became very sought-after commodities when sugar rationing was introduced throughout the nation.

In 1942, Vermonters gained the honor of leading the nation, per capita, in the collection of scrap metal and scrap rubber.

The World War II Memorial in Essex Junction, VT

BURLINGTON was Vermont's largest city during the war. It is a county seat on the NW edge of the state on I-89 and Lake Champlain.

ESSEX JUNCTION WORLD WAR II MEMORIAL: This is a large stone monument with plaques giving the names of those individuals from the Essex Junction area who served in WW II. Essex Junction is a suburb of Burlington seven miles east of downtown Burlington. The inscription on the Memorial reads "TO HONOR THOSE WHO BRAVELY SERVED. WE SHALL ALWAYS REMEMBER AND NEVER FORGET."

Location:Five Corners Junction, Essex Junction, VT

SAINT ALBANS is a county seat in NW Vermont on I-89, US-7 and near Lake Champlain. During the war, there was a popular boys' camp just west of town at Kill Kare State Park.

ST. ALBANS WORLD WAR II MEMORIAL: This interesting stone memorial commemorates those boys who attended the boys' camp at Kill Kare State Park and then served and died in the US armed forces during WW II. The inscription on the Memorial reads "IN MEMORY OF THE BOYS WHO GAVE THEIR LIVES IN WORLD WAR II-KAMP KILL KARE ALUMNI." The Camp closed in 1966. Location: Kill Kare State Park near St. Albans, VT

The St. Albans World War II Memorial at Kill Kare State Park near St. Albans, VT

VIRGINIA

The state of Virginia was a very busy place during World War II. The state's portion of Chesapeake Bay and Hampton Roads was a beehive of military activity, and the area around the District of Columbia was a beehive of military and political activity. Elsewhere in Virginia, soldiers, sailors, Marines, airmen and OSS agents were trained for war in large numbers, and along Virginia's coast submarine warfare was as hot as it was anywhere in the world.

The US Military had many facilities throughout the state and many more were added during the war.

DIVEABLE WW II SHIP WRECKS IN VIRGINIA COASTAL WATERS: A number of Allied ships were sunk in Virginia coastal waters during WW II. Some of the ships are in shallow waters and are accessible to sports divers. Divers should inquire locally regarding diving conditions and accessibility.

ALEXANDRIA (See Washington, DC Area)

ARLINGTON (See Washington, DC Area)

BEDFORD is a county seat in west-central Virginia on US-221/460, SR-43 and SR-122.

THE NATIONAL D-DAY MEMORIAL: This is a magnificent memorial devoted to the events of June 6, 1944 - the invasion of Normandy. It is located in Bedford because the citizens of Bedford have a very special connection to D-Day. Thirty-three men from Bedford were killed in the D-Day invasion - the highest per-capita loss of any town in the US.

The Memorial is located at the intersection of US-221 and US-460. Dramatic statuary depicts the agony and heroism that the American GIs underwent as they stormed ashore on this enemy breach. There is an invasion pool with GIs coming out of the water, a statue of a Ranger climbing a cliff at Normandy and an inverted rifle with its bayonet stuck in the ground and a helmet and dog tags resting on the top marking the temporary grave of a fallen GI. There is a victory arch, a victory plaza, a large amphitheater and five large granite blocks displaying the names of the five invasion beaches; Omaha, Utah, Gold, Sword and Juno.

Guided tours are offered. Also at the site, are the offices of the National D-Day Memorial Foundation and a fine Memorial Store. Address: 3 Overlord Cir. Bedford, VA 24523. Phone and website: 540-587-3619, 540-586-3329 and 866-219-6900; www.dday.org

Some of the dramatic statuary at the National D-Day Memorial in Bedford, VA

CHANTILLY (See Washington, DC Area)

DANVILLE is a county seat in south-central Virginia near the North Carolina border on US-29 and US-58.

AMERICAN ARMOURED FOUNDATION TANK MUSEUM: This is a large museum devoted to the collection and display of tanks, artillery pieces and other weapons of war. The Museum covers 89 acres of land, has 330,000 Sq. ft. of floor space and over 100 tanks and artillery pieces, many from the WW II era. There is a generous collection of small arms neatly organized in a Weapons Room and a Rifle Room. There are also thousands of artifacts such as uniforms, military field equipment, toys and more.

The Museum has a large library, a large and interesting gift shop, a facilities rental program, offers tours, has an educational program and hosts many events. Address: 3401 US Hwy. 29B, Danville, VA 24540. Phone and website: 434-836-5323; www.aaftankmuseum.com

HAMPTON/NEWPORT NEWS AREA: The cities of Hampton and Newport News are across the water of Chesapeake Bay from Norfolk and are on the strategic Hampton Roads waterway and the entrances to the James River, York River, Rappahannock River and Potomac River. The latter river leads to the nation's capitol.

THE CASEMENT MUSEUM: This museum is located within the walls of Fort Monroe, and old coastal defense facility. The Museum traces the long history of the Fort and the US Army's coastal artillery service. The Museum has very few displays directly related to WW II but does have extensive information on coastal artillery guns. Many of these antiquated guns were still functional and still in service during WW II.

After the war, most of the old guns were scrapped, including those at the Fort, but Fort Monroe remained an active US Arm facility. Address: 151 Bernard Rd., Fort Monroe, VA 23651. Phone and

MARINERS' MUSEUM is located on the western edge of Mariners' Museum Park in central Newport News. This is an excellent maritime museum with displays and information on ships and seafarers from ancient times to the present. There are displays on the US Navy during all of America's wars and a considerable amount of information on WW II. The Museum has a large and magnificent collection of ship models which include many WW II ships such as aircraft carriers, cruisers, troop ships, hospital ships and captured enemy ships.

There is an extensive display on how Liberty Ships were built, various marine artifacts, numerous paintings, photographs and hands-on exhibits.

The Museum's facilities can be rented for events, tours are available, there's a cafe, a park and lake, a library and archives and a fine and interesting gift shop. Address: 100 Marine Dr., Newport News, VA 23606. Phone and website: 757-596-2222; www.marinersmuseum.org/visitor-information

US ARMY TRANSPORTATION MUSEUM: This fine Army museum is on the grounds of Fort Eustis and relates the history of the Army's transportation services from their beginnings to the present. Many pieces of transportation equipment are on display from all of America's wars.

As for WW II, there are trucks, jeeps, aircraft, boats, trains, landing craft, DUKWs (DUCKs), early helicopters, horse-drawn wagons and several one-of-a-kind experimental vehicles. There is also an extensive collection of vehicle models from WW II and considerable information on WW II's famous

Liberty Ships. Address: 300 Washington Blvd., Fort Eustis, VA 23604. Phone and website: 757-878-1115; www.transchool.eustis.army.mil/Museum/Museum.html

VIRGINIA WAR MUSEUM is located in Huntington Park near the eastern terminus of the James River Bridge in Newport News. This museum has thousands of military artifacts displayed in several galleries and tells the stories of America's wars from 1775 to the present.

WW II is amply covered in the Museum with displays of weapons; American, Italian and Japanese uniforms, posters, the German Nazi Party, Dachau Concentration Camp, Prisoners of War, the Berlin Wall and information on this

The Jeep display at the US Army Transportation Museum at Fort Eustis, VA

area as a port of embarkation for troops going overseas.

Outside the Museum are vehicles, artillery pieces and a plaque commemorating the four Chaplains lost on the *SS Dorchester* off Greenland in 1943. The Museum is often host of historical, ceremonial and educational events. Address: 9285 Warwick Blvd. (US 60), Newport News, VA 23607. Phone and website: 757-247-8523; www.warmuseum.org

LEESBURG is a county seat, 32 miles NW of downtown Washington, DC on US-15, SR-7 and SR-267.

DODONA MANOR, THE GEORGE C. MARSHALL INTERNATIONAL CENTER; This was the private residents of General-of-the-Army George C. Marshall from 1941 to the time of his death in 1959. The Center honors the famous WW II General and has been restored to the time period during which he and his family lived here. The Center is situated on 3.88 acres and is in the center of Leesburg's historic district. The resident is open to the public and is a National Historic Landmark. Tours are available and the Center hosts exhibitions and public events throughout the year. Address: 217 Edwards Ferry Rd. Leesburg, VA 20176. Phone and website: 703-777-1880; www.georgecmarshall.org

Dodona Manor in Leesburg, VA

LEXINGTON is a county seat 30 miles NW of Staunton on I-64 and I-81. It is home to the famous Virginia Military Institute. One of the Institute's most famous graduates was General George C. Marshall of WW II fame.

THE MARSHALL MUSEUM AND RESEARCH LIBRARY: This is a large museum and research library just off the parade ground of VMI and was dedicated in 1964 by Presidents Lyndon Johnson and Dwight Eisenhower.

George Marshall rose to be one of the highest ranking officer in the US Army during WW II, was the instigator of the famous postwar Marshall Plan, President of the American Red Cross, Secretary of Defense, Secretary of State and a Nobel Peace Prize winner. Marshall's outstanding military and political career is outlined by displays and exhibits throughout the Museum. Many of Marshall's personal belongings, public papers and artifacts are on display. The Museum also has a fine gift shop and bookstore. Address: 1600 VMI Parade, Lexington, VA, 24450. Phone and website: 540-463-7103; www.marshallfoundation.org/

THE VMI MUSEUM: This is a second museum associated with the Virginia Military Institute. It traces the history of the school and many of the individuals who have been students here. On display are documents, uniforms, medals, student furniture, military equipment, photographs, paintings, drawings and other artifacts related to the school. Of interest to WW II buffs are letters from Presidents Roosevelt and Truman, personal artifacts of Generals Marshall and Patton and a number of displays on WW II. The Museum also has an interesting gift shop. Address: Jackson Memorial Hall, 415 Letcher Av.,Virginia Military Institute, Lexington, VA 24450. Phone and website: 540-464-7334; www.vmi.edu/

NEWPORT NEWS (See Hampton/Newport News/area)

NORFOLK/PORTSMOUTH/VIRGINIA BEACH AREA: To many people, before, during, and after WW II, the word "Norfolk" was synonymous with "Navy." The strategic location of Norfolk and the surrounding cities dictates that this is a place where the Navy should be. The Norfolk area is centrally located on the US Atlantic coast and guards the entrance to Chesapeake Bay and the various waterways that lead to some of America's most important cities including the nation's capitol.

Over the years, the Navy has acquired many facilities in the area and the Army and Coast Guard are also present.

The waters off Norfolk in Chesapeake Bay and Hampton Roads were deep and spacious so many large convoys were assembled here during the war and departed for distant locations. The first American convoy of the war left from here on Dec. 13, 1941 for Gibraltar.

HAMPTON ROADS NAVAL MUSEUM AND THE BATTLESHIP *USS WISCONSIN*: The Hampton Roads Naval Museum is located on the second floor of the Nauticus National Maritime Center, on the Norfolk waterfront and the *USS Wisconsin* is anchored in front of the Center. The Museum has exhibits on over 200 years of naval history in the Hampton Roads area. There are generous displays covering the WW II era.

The battleship *USS Wisconsin* (BB-64) was commissioned late in the war, April 1944, but saw considerable action in the Pacific. Also on display in the Museum are ship models, photographs and artifacts, many of which are related to WW II and the Battleship. Throughout the National Maritime Center are other exhibits with nautical themes. Address: One Waterside Dr., Suite 248, Norfolk, VA 23510. Phone and website: 757-664-1000; www.nauticus.org

THE MacARTHUR MEMORIAL is located in downtown Norfolk in MacArthur Square. This is a complex of four buildings which consist of the main memorial building (which was the former Norfolk City Hall), a theater, the Jean MacArthur Research Center (named in honor of the General's wife) and a large well stocked gift shop. The Memorial honors General Douglas MacArthur and traces his

military and private life. It also serves as his final resting place and that of his wife.

MacArthur was born into a prominent military family and never really had a home town. He adapted Norfolk as such because it was his mother's home town. The main building in the Memorial contains many of MacArthur's personal belongings such as his uniforms, corn cob pipes, medals, awards, gifts, papers and photographs.

In the gift shop building is the General's 1950 Chrysler Imperial limousine which he used in Tokyo for the many years he was commander of American occupation forces in Japan. Address: MacArthur Memorial, MacArthur Square, Norfolk, VA. 23510. Phone and website: 757-441-2965 (Memorial), 757-441-5389 (gift shop); www.macarthurmemorial.org

This is the statue of General Douglas at the entrance to the MacArthur Memorial in Norfolk, VA.

MILITARY AVIATION MUSEUM: This museum is home to one of the largest privately owned collections of WW I and WW II era military aircraft in the world. All of the aircraft on display are restored and many of them are flyable. In addition to US models, there are British, German, Japanese and several rare Soviet aircraft. Of special interest is a replica of the German Me-262, WW II's first and most famous military jet aircraft. Some of the Museum's aircraft can be rented.

There is a large collection of aviation-related ground equipment and many other items and artifacts on display.

273

The Museum hosts a variety of events throughout the year including air shows, flight demonstrations, military reenactments and social events. There are aircraft under restoration, and the Museum has an educational program, offers tours, has a library and has a very impressive gift shop. Address: 1341 Princess Anne Rd., Virginia Beach, VA 23457. Phone and website: 757-721-7767; www.militaryaviationmuseum.org

OLD COAST GUARD STATION is located on the ocean front in Virginia Beach at 24th St. This is one of the few remaining Coast Guard life-saving station out of hundreds that once dotted the US coastline for over 50 years. Most of them were still operative during WW II and for a short time thereafter. Such stations were manned around the clock by Coastgardsmen ready to take to sea in small boats in any kind of weather to aid stricken vessels off shore. This station was very active during WW II because of the many ships attacked along the Virginia coastlines. Throughout the war, hundreds of survivors were rescued by Coastguardsmen operating out of stations like this. The Stations also served, during the war, as places of residence for Coastguardsmen on beach patrols.

The Old Coast Guard Station in Virginia Beach is one of the few such stations remaining in the U.S.

During WW II, this station housed Coast Guard beach patrols and their horses.

The Station has been preserved much as it was during the latter days of its useful life. Inside the Station are extensive displays on WW II including information on the German mine laying operations at the mouth of Chesapeake Bay, the "Hooligan Navy," (civilian volunteers in private craft), the British trawlers (a reverse Lend-Lease program), beach patrols, aircraft, blimps, ships and German submarines. There is a very interesting gift shop and tours are available. Address: 2401 Atlantic Av. (24th and Boardwalk), Virginia Beach, VA 23451. Phone and website: 757-422-1587; www.oldcoastguardstation.com

PORTSMOUTH NAVAL SHIPYARD MUSEUM is near downtown Portsmouth at the foot of High St. and on the Southern Branch of the Elizabeth River. This fine museum relates the history of the US Naval Shipyard, Norfolk which is often referred to as the Portsmouth Naval Yard or the Norfolk Naval Yard.

The Museum has exhibits which trace the history of both the US Navy and the shipyard. There are many ship models, naval artifacts, photographs, paintings, documents, and a scale model of the shipyard as it appeared during WW II. And, there are many other displays in the Museum from the WW II era.

Another part of the Museum is the Lightship *Portsmouth* which was built in 1915 and served throughout WW II. The ship's quarters are fitted out realistically and there are many artifacts and memorabilia on display.

Don't pass up the Museum's interesting gift shop. Address: 2 High St., Portsmouth, VA 23705. Phone and website: 757-393-8591; www.portsmouthnavalshipyardmuseum.com

US SUBMARINE VETERANS MEMORIAL: The centerpiece of this memorial is a WW II Mark 14 torpedo mounted on pylons. In front of the torpedo is a small brick monument with a plaque which honors those men who served on submarines during WW II. Location: The Memorial can be reached from C St. west of 1st St. in the Post Office area in Norfolk

PETERSBURG is a county seat 20 miles south of Richmond on I-295. It is an historic Civil War site and home of Fort Lee, a major US Army installation.

US ARMY ORDNANCE MUSEUM: Here's a biggie - 300,000 Sq. ft. of heavy ordnance weapons and vehicles. The mission of the Museum is to collect, preserve and display historically important equipment pertinent to the history of the US Army Ordnance Corps. On display are many antique weapons from the 1800s and weapons and tanks from both WW I and WW II. From WW II, there are US, German, French, Japanese, Soviet and British tanks, and German, Japanese and Italian tank destroyers. Some of the tanks have had part of their armor removed so that visitors can view the inside.
    There are artillery weapons of many sizes, types and vintage. Outstanding among these weapons of WW II is a self-propelled 155mm gun, a Krupp K5 railroad gun and the US Army's postwar M65 Atomic Cannon. There are aerial bombs on display including a T12, the largest conventional bomb ever built at its time. Address: Fort Lee, VA 23801. Website: www.ordmusfound.org

US ARMY QUARTERMASTER MUSEUM: This is a large Army museum on the grounds of Fort Lee which traces the history of the Quartermaster Corps from its beginning in 1775 to the present. The Museum highlights the wide variety of services the QMC performs for the Army which include providing, food, clothing, transportation, petroleum products, aerial supplies and mortuary services. Items on display in the Museum include field kitchens, items of clothing, motorized and horse-drawn vehicles, flags, dog tags, chaplain's equipment, equipment for dogs and horses, maternity uniforms for women and general's uniforms. And the Museum has an impressive gift shop. Address: 1201 22nd St., Fort Lee, VA 23801. Phone and website: 804-734-4203; www.qmmuseum.lee.army.mil

US ARMY WOMEN'S MUSEUM: This is another museum on the grounds of Fort Lee dedicated to the women who served in all branches of the US military. It is the custodian and repository of artifacts and archival materials pertaining the women's roll in the US military. There are many artifacts such as uniforms, posters, photos and other items of interest on display, many of which are devoted to the WW II era. Special attention is given to women who lost their lives in the service of their country. The Museum has an educational program and offers tours. Address: 2100 A Av., Fort Lee, VA 23801. Phone and website: 804-734-4327, www.awm.lee.army.mil

PORTSMOUTH (See Norfolk/Portsmouth/Virginia Beach Area)

QUANTICO/TRIANGLE AREA: These two cities are about 30 miles south of Washington, DC on and near the Potomac River and just east of US-1 and I-95. Quantico is home for the giant US Marine Corps Base, Quantico which now surrounds the city and extends for about 30 miles to the NE.

NATIONAL MUSEUM OF THE MARINE CORPS: This large and modern museum is located adjacent to the US Marine Corps Base, Quantico. The Museum's soaring design evokes the image of the famous flag-raising at Iwo Jima during WW II and is the centerpiece of the 135 acre Marine Corps Heritage Center which also includes the Semper Fidelis Memorial Park, the Semper Fidelis Chapel, a parade ground, hiking trail and several other structures.

The Magnificent National Museum of the Marine Corps at Triangle, VA

Within the Museum's 120,000 Sq. ft. are several galleries with the WW II gallery being the largest of the war galleries. There are restored Marine Corps aircraft, vehicles, ground equipment, uniforms, weapons, flags, medals, works of art and many interactive exhibits. Most of the aircraft are pre-jet with a generous number of WW II aircraft on display.

The Museum has a theater, an educational program, restoration facilities and a large and well-stocked Museum store. Address: 18900 Jefferson Davis Highway, Triangle, VA 22172. Phone and website: 877-635-1775; www.usmcmuseum.com

RICHMOND is the capitol of Virginia. During the early part of the war, the Patent Office moved here from Washington, DC to make room for agencies more directly related to the war effort. Several important military installations were in the Richmond area.

VIRGINIA WAR MEMORIAL: This is the state of Virginia's primary war memorial. It is located a few blocks east of downtown Richmond on Belvedere St. (US-1) at the north end of the Robert E. Lee Bridge. This impressive memorial honors Virginians who died in all of America's wars with the WW II segment being adequate and impressive.

There is a visitors' center, a rose garden, an eternal flame, a reflecting pool and a Memorial store. Address: 621 S. Belvedere St., Richmond, VA 23220. Phone and website: 804-786-2060; www.vawarmemorial.org

VIRGINIA BEACH (See Norfolk/Portsmouth/Virginia Beach Area)

WASHINGTON, DC AREA: This is the area in Virginia that is directly across the Potomac River from Washington, DC. During the war, this area was a bustling part of the WW II activities that went on in the nation's capital and had several very important military installations including the Pentagon, the main headquarters of the US Armed Forces.

Alexandria was the largest city in the area and had a 1940 population of 33,500. Arlington, while it was well built up and had many residents, was not an incorporated city.

ARLINGTON NATIONAL CEMETERY is directly west of the Lincoln Memorial in DC with accessible via the Arlington Memorial Bridge which spans the Potomac between the District of Columbia and Arlington, VA.

Arlington National Cemetery is American's best-known and most prestigious national cemetery and many of America's most famous people are buried here. Federal laws regulates who may be buried at Arlington National Cemetery as well as other national cemetery around the nation.

The grounds of the Cemetery are beautiful and kept immaculately clean. Many ceremonies are conducted here, some on a daily basis, such as that at the Tomb of the Unknowns. Other ceremonies are held at the nearby Arlington Memorial Amphitheater.

Within the Cemetery, are many memorials and monuments. Some of those pertaining to WW II included the US Marine Corps Memorial (the huge statue of the raising of the flag on Iwo Jima at the entrance to the Cemetery), the American Defenders of Bataan and Corregidor Memorial, the Women in Military Service Memorial, the Netherlands Carillon and the SeaBee Memorial. And there are others. Many of the roads in the Cemetery are also named after WW II personalities.

Famous WW II personalities buried here include:

Gen. Creighton Abrams
Gen. Henry "Hap" Arnold
Gen. Anthony J. D. Biddle
Col. "Pappy" Boyington
Gen. Omar Bradley
Brigadier Evans F. Carlson of Carlson's Raiders and the creator of the "Gung Ho" slogan
Gen. Claire Chennault
Gen. Benjamin O. Davis
William J. "Wild Bill" Donovan, Director of the OSS
Adm. Frank J. Fletcher
James V. Forrestal, Secretary of the Navy 1944-47
William F. Friedman who broke the Japanese "Purple Code"
Adm. William F. "Bull" Halsey, Jr.
Gen. Lewis B. Hershey
Adm. Alan G. Kirk
William F. "Frank" Knox, Secretary of the Navy 1940-44
Gen. Walter Krueger
Adm. William D. Leahy
Lord Lothian, Philip H. Kerr, British Ambassador to US from Apr.1939 to Dec. 1941
Gen. George C. Marshall
Gen. Anthony C. McAuliffe
Adm. Marc A. Mitchner
Audie Murphy, Congressional Medal of Honor winner and movie actor
Adm. Forrest B. Royal
Gen. Walter C. Short
Gen. Walter Bedell Smith
Adm. Harold R. Stark
Gen. Maxwell Taylor
Gen. Hoyt Vandenberg
Gen. Jonathan Wainwright
Gen. Orde Wingate

Only persons visiting the graves of relatives and the physically handicapped are allowed to drive in the Cemetery. Other visitors must park in the parking lot off Memorial Dr. where a fee is charged. Tourmobiles leave the visitors center at regular intervals and offer a narrated tour of the Cemetery.   Phone and website: 703-607-8000; www.arlingtoncemetery.org

The famous Iwo Jima Memorial at the entrance to the Arlington National Cemetery

The Marine Corps Memorial at the entrance to the Cemetery is also known as the "Iwo Jima Statue" and is the largest cast bronze statue in the world. It depicts the famous flag-raising at Iwo Jima during WW II and is dedicated to all Marines who have given their lives for their country since 1775. The Memorial is located on Marshall Dr. just off of US-50. It is open 24 hours a day.

FOUR CHAPLAINS MEMORIAL: This unique memorial honors the four chaplains, one Catholic, two Protestant and one Jewish. Who were lost when their ship, the transport ship *Dorchester,* was torpedoed and sunk in the North Atlantic during February 1943. Theirs is one of the most inspiring stories of WW II. Location: In the James M. Goode suburb of Falls Church, VA

THE PENTAGON, in the SE part of Arlington, is known around the world as the headquarters of the armed forces of the United States and is the home of the US Department of Defense. This huge building was built during WW II due to the rapid expansion of the War Department (the prior name for the Defense Department) which simply ran out of space in its existing offices in Washington, DC.

The Pentagon was built on land that belonged to Fort Myer that was known as Fort Myer's South Area. At the time construction began, the land was being used by the Agriculture Department as a experimental farm.

Construction of the Pentagon began in Sept. 1941 and was supervised by Gen. Leslie Groves who would later head the "Manhattan (Atomic Bomb) Project." Construction proceeded around-the-clock and employed up to 13,000 construction workers. The accident rate was high and at times the construction crews got ahead of the architects.

To house the Pentagon's future workers, a small city was built south of the site called Fairlington. By May 1942, one section of the Pentagon was completed enough to receive the first War Department occupants and by early 1943, the building was completed. It contained 5,100,000 Sq. ft. of space, twice that of the Empire State Building in New York City, and was, at that time, the largest building in the world. Completion of the Pentagon concentrated the War Department's 24,000 employees in one facility where, before, that Department had been spread all over the District of Columbia in 17 different locations and several additional locations outside the District.

Parts of the Pentagon are open to the public and there are free one-hour guided tours which leave every 30 minutes from the visitors center. Tours are available by reservation only and it is recommended that tours be booked two weeks in advance. Address: Army Navy Dr. and Fern St. Arlington, VA 22202. Phone: 703-545-6700 and 571-372-0945. Website for tours: http://pentagon.afis.osd.mil./tour-selection.html

The Pentagon, the home of the US armed forces, in Arlington, VA

SMITHSONIAN MUSEUM NATIONAL AIR AND SPACE MUSEUM/STEVEN F. UDVAR-HAZY CENTER: This is a huge complex near the Washington Dulles International Airport that has over 150 vintage aircraft associated with the aviation history of the United States. There are a large number of WW II aircraft on display including the "Enola Gay," the B-29 bomber that dropped the second atomic bomb on Japan at the end of the war. Thousands of artifacts are on display including aircraft engines, flight simulators, experimental aircraft and much more.

Equally as large as the aircraft collection is the collection of space vehicles; spacecraft, rockets, satellites and other space-related items. The centerpiece of this collection is the Space Shuttle *Discovery.* For WW II buffs, there is a cutaway of a German V-2 rocket combustion chamber.

Towering above the Museum is the Donald D. Engen Observation Tower from which visitors can watch the air traffic at Washington Dulles Airport.

Another part of the Center is the Wall of Honor near the entrance of the Museum which honors thousands of individuals who have made significant contributions to America's aviation history.

The Museum has an IMAX Theater, food service and a fascinating gift shop. There is an educational program and guided tours are available.

The Museum owns more aircraft and space vehicles than can be displayed at the Udvar-Hazy Center so those are kept at another location, the Paul E. Garber Facility in Suitland, VA. Also, aircraft and space vehicle restorations are done there.

The US Air Force Memorial in Arlington, VA

The Garber Facility is not open to the public. Address of the Smithsonian National Air and Space Museum: 14390 Air and Space Museum Parkway, Chantilly, VA 20151. Phones and websites: 703-572-4118 and 202-633-1000; http://airandspace.si.edu/

US AIR FORCE MEMORIAL is located on a promontory in Arlington overlooking the Pentagon and adjacent to Arlington National Cemetery. It honors the service and sacrifices of the men and women of the US Air Force and its predecessor organizations. Most prominent in the Memorial are three spirals reaching skyward representative of flight and the flying spirit of the US Air Force. They represent the three core values of the Air Force - integrity first, service before self and excellence in all that is done.

Other elements of the Memorial include a Runway of Glory, a four-man bronze Honor Guard statue, a memorial park, a parade ground and two granite wall with the names of the fallen engraved thereon. There is also a Memorial store on the premises. Address: 1 Air Force Memorial Dr., Arlington, VA 22204. Phone and website: 703-979-0674; www.airforcememorial.org

WASHINGTON

World War II had a major impact on the state of Washington because of its strategic location and its industries. Being located in the northwestern corner of the United State, Washington was the gateway to Alaska and the North Pacific. Her magnificent Puget Sound area provided a strategic and excellent location for the military, especially the Navy, and her well-developed industries of shipbuilding and aircraft manufacturing were of utmost importance to the war effort.

When the Japanese attacked Hawaii in Dec. 1941, there was great fear that Washington cities might also be attacked. Wild rumors spread in the Puget Sound area that a Japanese attack was imminent. These rumors were false but, a few data after the Pearl Harbor attack, there were Japanese submarines operating off Washington's coast and several ships were attacked.

One of Washington's important new military facilities built during the war was the plutonium-producing Hanford Engineer Works at Richland which produced the plutonium used in the atomic bomb that devastated Nagasaki - and would have devastated other Japanese cities if the Japanese had not surrendered as they did.

BELLINGHAM is a county seat 80 miles north of Seattle and 28 miles south of the Canadian border on Rosario Strait and I-5.

HERITAGE FLIGHT MUSEUM: This museum is at the Bellingham International Airport which was expanded from a grass landing strip before WW II into what became the USAAF's Billingham Army Airfield, a training facility.
   The Museum has a collection of more than a dozen historic aircraft, several of which are of WW II vintage. They also have a Link Trainer and several military vehicles, an extensive photo gallery and a fine collection of memorabilia. There is an educational program and the Museum hosts air shows and social events throughout the year. Address: 4165 Mitchell Way, Bellingham International Airport, Bellingham, WA 98226. Phone and website: 360-733-4422; www.heritageflight.org

BREMERTON is the home of the huge Puget Sound Naval Shipyard and was, during WW II, the northern home port of the US Pacific Fleet. The town owes its existence to the shipyard, which was built first followed by the town that grew up around it.
   In the postwar years, Bremerton became home to one of the US Navy's largest mothballed fleets.

PUGET SOUND NAVY MUSEUM, in downtown Bremerton, preserves and interprets the history of the naval activities in the Pacific Northwest and of the US Navy in general. On display are many artifacts including ship models, uniforms, naval weapons, flags, photos, paintings and more. Other displays highlight the history of some of the US Navy's major warships of WW II. Today, the Museum is the home of the nuclear aircraft carrier, *USS John C. Stennis* which is on public display. The Museum has a research library and a well-stocked gift shop. Address: 251 1st St. Bremerton, WA 98337. Phone and website: 360-479-7447; http://www.history.navy.mil/

EVERETT is 30 miles south of Seattle on Possession Sound and I-5. During the war, its local airport, Paine Field, was taken over by the US Army Air Forces and used as an operational base - one of very few such bases in the territorial United States - to provide air protection for the Puget Sound Area of Washington. One of the main missions of the aircraft stationed at the Airfield was to intercept and shoot down incoming Japanese bombing balloons.

THE FLYING HERITAGE COLLECTION: This is a private collection of very unique and rare military aircraft from WW I, the 1930s and the 1940s. It was put together by collector, Paul G. Allen.
   The Collection is located in a large hangar on the SE corner of Paine Field in Everett. In the collection are US, British, German, Japanese, Soviet aircraft, a German tank destroyer, a Soviet battle tank, two versions of the German V-1 "Buzz bombs" and more. It is extremely rare to see such aircraft and vehicles in one collection. Address: Paine Field, 3407 109th St., Everett, WA 98204. Phone and website: 877-342-3404 (ticketing) and 206-342-4242 (office); www.flyingheritage.com

HANFORD ENGINEER WORKS (See Richland and the Hanford Engineer Works)

KEYPORT is an unincorporated community 12 miles north of Bremerton at the end of SR-308 on Port Orchard Inlet.

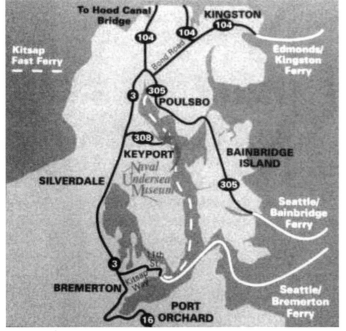

NAVAL UNDERSEA MUSEUM: This large museum, on the grounds of the Naval Torpedo Station, Keyport was established by the Secretary of the Navy to be a repository of documents, records and artifacts relating to the human and technical achievements of both military and civilian undersea history. It is the only facility of its kind in the country and has both indoor and outdoor displays. Many items on display are related to WW II. There is an extensive and permanent display of naval torpedoes, naval mines, displays on WW II and other historic military and non-military submarines, submarine technology, submersibles, diving apparatus and other items that have allowed mankind to venture under the seas.

The Museum has an educational program, a speakers' series and a very interesting and unique Museum store. Address: 1 Garnett Way, Keyport, WA 98345. Phone and website: 360-396-4148 (Museum), 360-697-1537 (Museum store); http://www.navalunderseamuseum.org

OLYMPIA is the capitol of the state of Washington and is at the southern end of Puget Sound on I-5 and US-101.

WASHINGTON STATE WORLD WAR II MEMORIAL: Like most states, Washington has a state WW II memorial. This unique memorial honors the more than 6,000 service men and women from the state of Washington who gave their lives during WW II. It was dedicated in 1999 and is located in downtown Olympia. Address: on the Washington State Capitol campus

The Washington State World War II Memorial in Olympia, WA

PORT TOWNSEND is a county seat on SR-20 on the western shore of Admiralty Inlet, a main entrance to Puget Sound.

COAST ARTILLERY MUSEUM: This museum is on the grounds of Fort Worden State Park which overlooks the entrance to Puget Sound. It's mission is to preserve and pass on to future generations the knowledge and lore of modern coast artillery and to honor the men who served in America's coastal defenses. The Museum covers over 50 years of coast artillery history with the activities of

WW II adequately recorded.

Inside the museum, are projectiles, displays on artillery plotting devices, a working model of a 12" disappearing gun and a 12" mortar. Fort Worden served as a coastal defense facility from the late 1800s until the end of WW II at which time it was converted into a state park. Museum address: 200 Battery Way, Port Townsend, WA 98368. Phone and website: 360-385-20373; http://pscoastartillerymuseum.org

RICHLAND AND THE HANFORD ENGINEER WORKS: Richland, in the SE corner of the state on the Columbia River, was an unincorporated farming community of 250 people when the war started. In 1943, the US Government began construction of what was called a super-secret war production plant. One of the first things to happen was the construction of a modest-sized temporary town called Hanford about 40 miles north of Richland, and further to the north of Hanford, work began on a complex of large buildings that were off-limits to everyone except those who were specifically allowed on the construction sites. As the large buildings rose on the horizon north of Hanford, workers began to pour in and take up residence in the temporary town. They had come from all over the country on the promise from Washington's Senator Warren Magnuson that if they accepted a job in this remote part of the country those job would be permanent after the war. This was a promise seldom given to war workers during the war years.

Within 15 months, the mystery plant, known only as the Hanford Engineer Works, was in operation producing a product that had no name and was never seen or heard or smelled. Only a handful of the employees knew what was going on. Nevertheless, the plant worked around the clock and there was plenty of overtime for the workers who, by early 1945, numbered some 20,000.

A thousand guards protected the plant's great secret and there were hundreds of soldiers stationed at nearby Camp Hanford to protect the plant from an enemy attack. The plant consumed millions of gallons of water from the Columbia River and large high-tension lines provided it with enormous amounts of electricity from the Columbia River's dams.

By the end of the war, the town of Richland had blossomed into a full-sized city of 51,000 people making it Washington's fourth largest city at the time.

On Aug. 6, 1945, the people of Richland were as startled as everyone else in the nation to learn that the Americans had a new super weapon called "the atomic bomb" and that that type of bomb had destroyed the city of Hiroshima in Japan. On Aug. 9, came word that a second atomic bomb had been used to destroy a second Japanese city, Nagasaki. With this, and the sudden end of the war in the Pacific, the secret of the atomic bombs was out and, for the first time, the people of Richland learned that their mysterious plant had played a very important role in the development of the 2nd bomb. The Hanford plant, from its inception, had converted natural uranium-238, into a new man-made element called "plutonium." This is a man-made fissionable material whose atoms can be split by mechanical means producing an atomic bomb. The material used in the Nagasaki bomb came from this facility.

B REACTOR: This was one of the main facilities at the Hanford Engineer Works that made plutonium. It has been declared a National Historic Site and has been preserved and is open to the public on a limited basis. To tour the B-Reactor, one must contact the B-Reactor Tour Headquarters at 2000 Logston Blvd., Richland, WA 99352. Phone and website: 509-373-2774 and 509-376-1647; www.b-reactor.org and http://manhattanprojectbreactor.hanford.bov

SEATTLE: Seattle, like every major city along the West Coast, became a boom town during WW II because it produced the things needed for war.

The Boeing Aircraft Company, one of the nation's major aircraft producers before the war, mushroomed into a gigantic operation with satellite plants not only in Washington, but in other parts of the country. In nearby Renton, WA, Boeing built one of the world's largest aircraft factories to produce B-29 bombers on an assembly line basis. A second plant was built in Wichita, KS. It was the B-29 that carried the conventional air war to Japan and eventually carried the two atomic bombs as well.

Seattle had several major shipyards which were greatly expanded to meet the nation's need for ships.

U.S COAST GUARD MUSEUM NORTHWEST: This is an interesting museum on Seattle's waterfront with exhibits covering the history of the Coast Guard from 1812 to the present day and highlights its activities in the US Northwest. On display are ship models, uniforms, lighthouse lenses, documents, flags, edged weapons, small arms, paintings, drawings, photographs and a wide variety of other Coast Guard nautical artifacts. Only a part of the permanent displays are devoted to WW II. Address: Pier 36, 1519 Alaskan Way South, Seattle, WA 98134. Phone and website: 206-217-6993; http://rexmwess.co/

THE MUSEUM OF FLIGHT: This is a huge museum located at King County International Airport (Boeing Field) with a display of over 200 aircraft, space vehicles and other machines of the air. There is a generous mix of commercial, military, experimental and special purpose aircraft and there are many US and foreign WW II aircraft models in the collection.

The mission of the Museum is to acquire, preserve and exhibit historically significant air and space artifacts which provide a foundation for scholarly research, the lifelong programs that inspires an interest in, and understanding of, science, technology and humanities.

The Museum has a Restoration Center, a library, the Dalhberg Research Center, a cafe and a fascinating - don't miss - Museum Store. Tours are offered and the Museum hosts many social events throughout the year. Address: 9404 East Marginal Way S, Seattle, WA 98108. Phone and website: 206-764-5720; www.museumofflight.org

TACOMA is at the southern end of Puget Sound on I-5 and was one of Washington's larger cities during the war. It is also home to Fort Lewis, one of the US Army's largest military installations which was a major training facility during WW II.

McChord Field, south of Tacoma, was a major training facility for the US Army Air Forces. In the postwar years, Fort Lewis and McChord Field were merged.

FORT LEWIS MILITARY MUSEUM: This is a large and interesting museum on the grounds of Joint Base Lewis-McChord near the intersection of I-5 and Main St. at exit 120. The Museum is housed in a beautiful old World War I building and has several galleries focusing on the history of the Army in the American Northwest from 1804. Special attention

The Fort Lewis Military Museum, located on the grounds of historic Fort Lewis, is housed in a beautiful old World War I building, and traces the history of the US Army in the Northwest from 1804

is given to the Army units that served at Fort Lewis over the years. WW II exhibits make up a significant part of the overall display.

On display are small arms, machine guns, field artillery, uniforms, patches, documents, maps, photographs, paintings, drawings, scale models and several dioramas.

Outside are amphibious landing craft, tracked vehicles, rockets and rocket launchers, missiles and anti-aircraft guns. The Museum offers tours and has a very nice gift store called The Cannon Gift Store. Address: Main St., Fort Lewis, WA 98498. Phone and website: 253-967-7206 (museum), 253-967-4184 (Gift Store); http://www.lewis.army.mil/dptms/museum.htm.

McCHORD AIR MUSEUM: This is a fine air museum on the grounds of Joint Base Lewis-McChord. It relates the history of the airmen and air units that served throughout the years, and were associated with, McChord Field (which later became McChord AFB during WW II and still later, Joint Base Lewis-McChord).

There are exhibits on Enlisted (Non-Commissioned officer) Pilots who, in the early years of military aviation piloted aircraft. There is also information on General Doolittle and his Tokyo Raiders, a gallery of aviation art, uniforms, scale models, flight equipment and much more.

Outside is a display of aircraft including several WW II models. The Museum has an ongoing educational program, a restoration facility, offers tours and has an interesting gift shop. Address: Building 517 "A" St.,
.McChord AFB, WA 98438. Phone and website: 253-982-2485/2419;
http://www.mcchordairmuseum.org

PIERCE COUNTY WW II HONORED MEMORIAL: This memorial is one of several in Tacoma's War Memorial Park. It consists of a tall black panel with the names of the residents of Pierce County who gave their lives during WW II. Location: War Memorial Park at the intersection of SR-16 and S. Jackson Av.

VANCOUVER is a county seat in southern Washington on the north shore of the Columbia River and I-5. It is also an inland seaport and is directly across the River from Portland OR.

The Pierce County WW II Honored Memorial in Tacoma, WA

THE GEORGE C. MARSHALL HOUSE: This is one of the stately old Queen Ann style houses along what was "Officers' Row" at Vancouver Barracks, one of the US Army's oldest and most historic facilities. Vancouver Barracks is gone, but several historic relics remain, including the house where General George C. Marshall and his family lived when Marshall was commander of Vancouver Barracks just before WW II. Before the Marshalls moved in, the house was occupied by a long list of distinguished military officers. In 1936, recently promoted General George C. Marshall, who was destined to become one of the most famous personalities of WW II, moved into the house with his family. Marshall had been sent to Vancouver Barracks as commander of the Army's 5th Brigade. It was his first major command. General Marshall lived here until 1938. He soon became the US Army's Chief of Staff during WW II, moved to Washington, DC and was promoted to a five-star general in 1944.

In 1947, he became Secretary of State, author of the famous Marshall Plan, Secretary of Defense in 1950-51 and Nobel Peace Prize winner in 1952.

The House is restored and decorated in period furnishings during Marshall's residency, and is open to the public. It is also available for public events and ceremonies. Address: 1301 Officers' Row, Vancouver, WA 98661. Phone and website: 888-693-3103 and 360-693-3103; http://usforting.com/

WALLA WALLA is a county seat in the SE corner of the state on US-12 and SR-125.

JONATHON M. WAINWRIGHT MEMORIAL: General Jonathon M. Wainwright replaced General Douglas MacArthur as commander of the Bataan and Corregdor defenders in the Philippines in early 1942 after MacArthur escaped to Australia. Wainwright was captured by the Japanese and spent the

rest of the war as a Japanese prisoner of war. He is remembered by the Jonathon M. Wainwright Memorial VA Medical Center in Walla Walla and on the grounds of the Medical Center is a larger-than-life statue of Wainwright serving as a memorial to him and his wartime ordeal. Location: 77 Wainwright Dr., Walla Walla, WA 99362

The Jonathon M. Wainwright Memorial in Walla Walla, WA

WEST VIRGINIA

The state of West Virginia had been hard hit economically by the Great Depression so the economic up-turn created by World War II was most welcome in the state. The state's primary mineral product, coal, was much in demand throughout the war to produce the electricity that powered the booming defense plants, ship yards, ordnance plants, military bases and crowded cities.

Since the state is very mountainous, it was not conducive to military flight training nor the training of large bodies of soldiers so very few military facilities were built in the state during the war. The state did have three major POW camps and several major ordnance and war production plants.

In the postwar years, Tokyo Rose and Axis Sally both came to West Virginia as a guest of the Federal Government to serve there prison time for aiding the enemy during the war. They resided in the Alderson Women's Federal Rrison near Lewisburg.

BECKLEY is a county seat in southern West Virginia on I-64 and I-77.

RALEIGH COUNTY WORLD WAR II MEMORIAL: This WW II memorial was dedicated to the honor of the area's veterans of WW II by the local Girl Scouts organization. The inscription on the stone memorial reads "IN GRATEFUL TRIBUTE TOWARD THE LIVING AND DEAD WHO THROUGH THEIR VALIANT EFFORTS AND BITTER SCRAFICE HAVE MADE AMERICA GREAT, IS THIS SHRINE DEDICATED By THE SENIOR GIRL SCOUTS OF RALEIGH COUNT. LET US HOLD IN HONORED MEMORY THOSE WHO SERVED THEIR COUNTRY IN WORLD WAR II." Location: On the grounds of the Raleigh County Courthouse, 215 Main St., Beckley, WV.

The Raleigh County World War II Memorial in Beckley, WV

CHARLESTON, in the SW section of the state on I-64, I-77 and I-79, is the state's capitol. In 1943, the nation's first large-scale synthetic rubber plant began operating here.

WEST VIRGINIA VETERANS MEMORIAL: This is West Virginia's state memorial honoring the more than 10,000 West Virginians who made the ultimate sacrifice in defending the nation in twentieth century conflicts. It is composed of four limestone monoliths surrounded by a reflecting pool, the interior walls are faced in polished granite etched with the names of those men and women who are honored by this memorial. Four statues are mounted on the memorial representing the four major twentieth century conflicts and the four major branches of military service. Location: In the State Capitol Complex in downtown Charleston

The West Virginia Veterans Memorial in Charleston, WV

The Monongalia County Commission World War II Memorial in Morgantown, WV

MORGANTOWN is a county seat in the north-central part of the state on I-68 and I-79.

MONONGALIA COUNTY COMMISSION WORLD WAR II MEMORIAL: This memorial, located in downtown Morgantown, consists of a red marble base with a bronze plaque honoring those citizens of Monongalia County who served in WW II. It is one of five such war memorials in Morgantown's War Veterans Memorial Plaza. Location: Chancery Row at High St., Morgantown, WV

ST. ALBANS is a small community 13 miles west of Charleston on US-60 and the Kanawha River.

YEAGER MEMORIAL: This is a memorial to Air Force General Charles E. Yeager, the first man to break the sound barrier (1947) in a jet aircraft. Yeager was born in nearby Myra and had a long and successful career as a fighter pilot in Europe during WW II. He became an "ace-in-a-day," a very rare honor, by shooting down five enemy aircraft in one day. He finished the war credited with 11.5 kills.

   After the war, he became a test pilot and was the first man to break the sound barrier, a feat that was later memorialized in a book by Tom Wolfe entitled "The Right Stuff." The book was eventually made into a movie. Memorial location: In a roadside park on Maccorkle Ave. SW (US-60) and the Kanawha River

WHITE SULPHUR SPRINGS is a popular health resort located in the SE part of the state on I-64.

THE GREENBRIER HOTEL is the largest and best known hotel in the White Sulphur Springs area with a reputation for elegant services, accommodations and prices to match.

   Soon after the attack on Pearl Harbor, the State Department leased the Hotel for the purpose of housing Axis diplomats and their families in a safe and comfortable facility until they could be exchanged for American diplomats in Axis nations. Several other luxury hotels were also acquired for the purpose in the eastern US.

   At first, a mix of Axis diplomats of different nationalities were sent here, but experience soon revealed that they were not all that compatible and had to be separated. The Greenbrier was thus selected to become an all-Japanese facility and the other Axis guests were sent elsewhere. For several months, therefore, the Greenbrier was a small Japanese community with women, children, pets, kids in school, Japanese cooks in the kitchen, Japanese taking traditional communal baths in the hot baths, playing tennis and an occasional baby being born - all under the watchful eyes of the FBI and the guards of the Immigration and Naturalization Service.

   Both Adm. Nomura, the former Ambassador to the US, and Japan's Special Envoy Saburo Kurusu resided here. These two men had been negotiating with Secretary of State Cordell Hull right up to the time of the Japanese attack on Pearl Harbor on Dec. 7, 1941. It was Nomura who handed Hull the document that was tantamount to Japan's declaration of war on the United States.

   By the spring of 1942, the diplomats and their families had all left the Hotel to be repatriated through neutral nations. In Sept. 1942, the Hotel was taken over by the Federal Government again for use as an Army general hospital. It was given the wartime name of Ashford General Hospital and treated war wounded. The Greenbrier's local air strip, two miles SW of town, was also taken over by the government and named Greenbrier Army Airfield and served the aviation needs of the hospital. The hotel-turned-hospital had 2025 beds and specialized in general medicine, neurology, neurosurgery and vascular surgery. Ashford also had a center for training military medical officers. The Hospital had one of West Virginia's main POW camp which held about 680 POWs who worked at the Hospital.

   By war's end, some 20,000 service personnel had been treated at Ashford. The Hotel remained a hospital until June 1946 at which time Ashford was closed and the Hotel returned to its former owners.

   In the late 1950s, a new wing was added to the Hotel, but it was considerably more than what it appeared. Beneath the new wing was constructed a very large, and very secret, bomb-proof bunker which was large enough to hold the entire Congress of the United States. The Federal Government had a plan at that time that in the event of an atomic attack, the Greenbrier Hotel would become the temporary home of Congress. The bunker is still there and is open to the public and tours are

provided. Phone: 855-453-4858

The Greenbrier Hotel in White Sulphur Springs, WV as it appeared in the 1940s

WISCONSIN

It is safe to say that nearly every member of the United States armed forces consumed at least two of Wisconsin's products during World War II - milk and cheese. Wisconsin was then, as it is now, America's Dairyland. For years, the state led the nation in the production of dairy products and the war years were no exception. Wisconsin was also a supplier of other important food items and a major manufacturing state.

In 1942, the state legislature made a unique contribution to the war effort by making military training compulsory in all state universities and set up a Council of Defense to direct the civil defense activity in the state.

By war's end, the state could counted 21 POW camps within its borders and a substantial number of new military facilities and manufacturing plants.

ARCADIA is a small community in the west central part of the state 38 miles north of La Crosse on SR-93, SR-95 and County Rd. J.

MEMORIAL PARK: For a small town, this community has a magnificent Memorial Park with statuary commemorating the veterans of America's wars. The WW II sculpture is a replica of the famous flag raising at Iwo Jima and is one of the most outstanding memorials in the Park. Location: County Rd. J and Garvey Rd., Arcadia, WI

The WW II sculpture in Memorial Park at Arcadia, WI

288

CAMP DOUGLAS is 50 miles east of La Crosse on I-90 and is the home to Camp Williams, the home of the Wisconsin Army National Guard.

WISCONSIN NATIONAL GUARD MEMORIAL LIBRARY AND MUSEUM: This facility is on the grounds of Camp Williams, the home of the Wisconsin Army National Guard. The Memorial Library has many interesting documents, diaries, scrapbooks, personal histories and films pertaining to the history of the Wisconsin National Guard. The Museum has artifacts and displays tracing the history of the Wisconsin National Guard from territorial days to the present. The WW II era is well represented.

   On the Museum ground and at other location throughout the Camp are several vintage military vehicles, artillery pieces and aircraft used by the Wisconsin Air National Guard.

   At Volk Field, the Camp's airfield is a WW II P-51 Mustang fighter mounted on pylons. Address: 101 Independence Dr., Camp Douglas, WI 54618-5001. Phone and website: 608-427-1280; www.wvmfoundation.com/

GREEN BAY is located at the SW end of Green Bay, an appendage to Lake Michigan. It is a county seat on I-43. US-41 and US-141.

General Eisenhower's WW II Command Train in Green Bay, WI

NATIONAL RAILROAD MUSEUM is located about two miles south of downtown Green Bay on the Fox River. This is a large railroad museum with about 70 railroad locomotives and cars dating from the 1880s.

   Of interest to WW II buffs is Gen. Dwight Eisenhower's command train which he used in England during WW II. The train consists of a London & North Eastern Railroad locomotive and several cars and is open to the public.

   Rides on some of the historic trains are available. Address: 2285 S. Broadway, Green Bay, WI 54304. Phone and website: 920-437-7623; www.nationalrrmuseum.org

HILLSBORO is a small community 65 miles NW of Madison on SR-33, SR-80 and SR-82.

ADMIRAL MARC MITSCHER MEMORIAL MARKER: Adm. Mitscher was born in Hillsboro and the citizens of that community have honored his memory with this fine Memorial Marker. Mitscher was the Captain of the aircraft carrier *USS Hornet* when that ship launched the bombers of General Doolittle's raiders who, early in the war, bombed Tokyo.

   Mitscher went on to serve with distinction in many other naval commands in the Pacific for the rest of the war. Location: Lake St. (SR-33/82) .1 miles west of Elm St.

The Admiral Marc Mitscher Memorial Marker in Hillsboro, WI

MADISON, in south-central Wisconsin, is the capitol of the state on I-39 and I-90/94.

WISCONSIN VETERANS MUSEUM: This is a fine state-run museum honoring Wisconsin's veterans of all of America's conflicts.

   The WW II section is extensive and has dioramas, vehicles, guns, uniforms, photos, artifacts, displays of specific WW II battles and more.

   The Museum has a research center, an educational program, a fine gift shop an hosts various social and historical activities throughout the year. Address: 30 W. Miffin St., Madison, WI 53703; Phone and website: 608-267-1799; www.wisvetmuseum.com

MANITOWOC is a county seat located on Lake Michigan 70 miles north of Milwaukee on I-43 and US-42. During the war, it was home to a large shipbuilding firm, the Manitowoc Shipbuilding Co. which secured a contract from the Navy to build submarines. It was very unusual for submarines to be built so far inland. The submarines were launched into Manitowoc River, tested in Lake Michigan and then sailed to Chicago. At Chicago they were gingerly towed over the many shallow places and under the many bridges that crossed the Sanitary Canal which connected to the upper reaches of the Illinois River. Each submarine was then placed in a floating dry dock and sailed down the Illinois River/Mississippi River route to the Gulf of Mexico.

   Manitowoc Shipbuilding Co. built and delivered 28 submarines this way during WW II and did it under-budget and ahead of schedule. The Manitowoc Shipbuilding Co. built other vessels for the Navy during the war including landing craft, patrol boats and crawler cranes.

WISCONSIN MARITIME MUSEUM, near downtown Manitowoc, depicts the history of shipbuilding on the Great Lakes and has on permanent display the WW II submarine, *Cobia.* The Museum has

60,000 ft. of floor space and offers considerable information on the construction of the WW II submarines by the Manitowoc Shipbuilding Co. And there are general exhibits on the activities of the US submarine force throughout WW II. There is a nice gift shop and tours of the Museum are available as well as overnight stays aboard the *Cobia.* Address: 75 Maritime Dr., Manitowoc, WI 54220. Phone and website: 866-724-2356 and 920-684-0218; http://wisconsinmaritime.org

The WW II submarine USS Cobia on display at the Wisconsin Maritime Museum in Manitowoc, WI

OSHKOSH is a county seat in the east-central part of the state on Lake Winnebago, US-41 and SR-21.

EAA (EXPERIMENTAL AIRCRAFT ASSOCIATION) AIRVENTURE MUSEUM. This is a large - really large - and well-known aviation center located at Oshkosh/Wittman Regional Airport, SE of Oshkosh near the junction of US-41 and SR-44. The Museum has over 250 aircraft and highlights experimental, sport, recreation and home-built aircraft but it also has many historic and vintage aircraft as well. WW II aircraft make up a relatively small percentage of the collection.

   Other displays include engines, cutaways, propellers, models and photos. The Museum is host to one of the largest annual fly-ins in the US, There is a fine library, a museum store, an educational program and the Museum hosts many social events throughout the year. Address: 3000 Poberezny Rd. Oshkosh, WI 54903. Phone and website: 920-426-4818; www.airventuremuseum.org

SUPERIOR is a county seat in the NW corner of the state on Lake Superior, I-35, I-535, US-2 and US-53.

RICHARD I. BONG VETERANS HISTORICAL CENTER. Richard I. Bong was America's top-scoring air ace of WW II with at least 40 kills and a recipient of the Congressional Medal of Honor. This center is devoted to his story and his memory. Bong was born in nearby Poplar, WI and died in a tragic air crash in January 1945. He was 25 years old.

   The Center's main attraction is a P-38 fighter plane of the type Bong flew in combat. There are other displays in the Center devoted to the Pacific war, Pearl Harbor and the home front. There is also a library and worth-your-while gift shop. Address: 305 Harbor View Pkwy., Superior, WI 54880. Phone and website: 715-392-7151 and 888-816-9944; www.bvhcenter.org

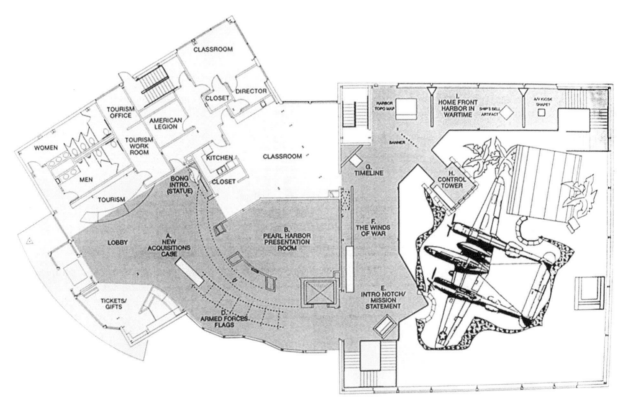

The Richard I. Bong Veterans Historical Center in Superior, WI

WYOMING

Wyoming was a pretty good place to be before, during and after World War II. Several decades before WW II, the state was one of the first to grant women the right to vote and from then on touted itself as the "Equal Rights" state.

In the 1930s, oil was discovered in the state, which stimulated the economy for the state's 250,742 residents, and in 1939 Wyoming led the nation in overall mineral production. Also in the 1930s, the Federal Government launched several major construction projects in the state, some of which included the construction of the Alcova, Kortes and Seminoe dams. These projects resulted in jobs, demands for local services, cheap electricity and long-term follow-up irrigation and electrification projects in many areas of the state.

During the war, the Federal Government built several military installations in the state including several POW camps and one of the relocation camp for ethnic Japanese.

In the 1950s, the state's economy was spurred along even further when large deposits of uranium were discovered in the state.

POWELL is in NW Wyoming 60 miles east of Yellowstone National Park on US-14 and SR-295. Just to the SW of town was one of the twelve relocation camps established during the war to house the ethnic Japanese who were evacuated from the US West Coast and Latin America. This was the Heart Mountain Relocation Camp.

The watch tower at the Heart Mountain Interpretive Learning Center in Powell, WY

HEART MOUNTAIN INTERPRETIVE LEARNING CENTER: This facility is both a learning center and a museum and is on the site of the former Heart Mountain Relocation Camp for ethnic Japanese. There were twelve relocation centers in the US during the war and all have memorials at their sites but most do not have a facility such as this. This 11,000 Sq. ft. Center is designed to resemble an original camp barracks in which the ethnic Japanese families lived and has permanent displays telling how the camps came about, where the people came from, how they lived and how they were treated. There is also a replica of a guard watch tower.

Some 14,000 individuals resided at this camp during the war and there is an introductory film that tells much of their story.

The Center has an educational program and a very interesting gift shop. Address: 1539 Road 19, Powell, WY 82435. (Location: about midway between Powell and Cody near the intersection of Road 19 and US-14 Alt). Phone and website: 307-754-8000; http://heartmountain.org

WHEATLAND is a county seat in the SE corner of the state on I-25.

STATUE OF LIBERTY/WW II MEMORIAL: What could be more fitting for a WW II memorial than the Statue of Liberty? This handsome memorial honors the citizens of Platte County, Wyoming who served in WW II. It consists of a large stone base with plaques giving the names of those who served and a statue of Liberty on the top of the base. Location: Downtown Wheatland at the Platte County Courthouse

The Statue of Liberty/WWII Memorial in Wheatland, WY

INDEX